Palgrave Studies in Economic History

Palgrave Studies in Economic History is designed to illuminate and enrich our understanding of economies and economic phenomena of the past. The series covers a vast range of topics including financial history, labour history, development economics, commercialisation, urbanisation, industrialisation, modernisation, globalisation, and changes in world economic orders.

More information about this series at
http://www.springer.com/series/14632

Simone Selva

Before the Neoliberal Turn

The Rise of Energy Finance and the Limits to US Foreign Economic Policy

palgrave
macmillan

Simone Selva
NYU
University of Naples – L'Orientale
Naples, Italy

Palgrave Studies in Economic History
ISBN 978-1-137-57442-8 ISBN 978-1-137-57443-5 (eBook)
DOI 10.1057/978-1-137-57443-5

Library of Congress Control Number: 2017948481

Printed on acid-free paper

This Palgrave Macmillan imprint is published by Springer Nature
The registered company is Macmillan Publishers Ltd.
The registered company address is: The Campus, 4 Crinan Street, London, N1 9XW, United Kingdom

The book is dedicated to my mother and father.

Preface

Following a three-decade period marked by either sluggish economic growth or slowdown all across the advanced industrial economies since the 1970s, the outbreak of the 2007–08 world financial crisis drew the attention of scholarships in international economic history, international economics and like-minded social sciences to reconsider the history of capitalist development since the 1970s on a worldwide scale. As a consequence of this shift in scholarly research, both historians of international relations and economic historians paid increasing attention to the world economic crisis of the 1970s. Unlike earlier works that appeared after the fall of the Berlin Wall and aimed to establish a linkage between the economic meltdown of the 1970s and transformations in the international economy, and the Westernization of the world economy since 1989, the outbreak of the Great Crash in the first decade of the new century led historical research and scholarship in international political economy to reconsider the history of capitalism since as early as the Great Slump of 1929. In evaluating the increased financial nature of twenty-first century capitalism, scholars narrowed down the scope of their research to the intertwining between development in the real economy, international monetary relations, and the financialization of economic activities; within this framework, most scholarship produced path-breaking new comparisons between the two most important economic crises of the twentieth century, in the 1930s and in the 1970s, and the Great Crash of 2007–08.

Within this framework, more than five years ago I began reasoning about the interconnectedness between the history of industrial development in the international economy since the 1970s and that of international finance. Before turning to reflect on the history of capitalism as the history of international financial integration and the fading away of Fordist mode of productions germane to the twentieth century, it was my understanding that a closer look at the origins of such watershed were worth researching. It was on the occasion of an issue of the Journal *900. Per una storia del tempo presente* that I co-edited with Elisabetta Bini, devoted to tackling the role of oil and international oil developments in the shaping of Western democracy throughout the twentieth century that I started focusing my attention on the interconnectedness between commodities and money in the challenging transformations that occurred from the postwar era to the new international financial and monetary environment set since the so-called Volcker revolution of 1979. This book hails from the idea that assuming the interrelation between the real economy and financial activities as a vital research perspective to better understand the economic world in which we live, the linkage between international oil developments and capital market transformations during the time frame in which either of them underwent historical changes, was an excellent research perspective. The role of international monetary relations in either regulating or deregulating such interconnectedness, that of the US currency as the key unit of account and means of payments throughout the course of those decades, as well as my specific interests and expertise in the history of US foreign economy policy, led me to frame such original research interest within the broader context of US foreign financial and monetary policies to manage and route the course of those path-breaking transformations in international oil markets, international monetary relations, and staggeringly new capital markets developments. The growing role played by the OPEC oil producing countries since around 1967 through to the outbreak of the second oil crisis of the 1970s in this story makes this monograph not only a study in international financial and monetary history, and in the history of international economic institutions such as the IBRD and the IMF, but also a chapter in the history of international relations and diplomacy between the United States and the OPEC oil producing countries, particularly Saudi Arabia, Iran and Kuwait.

As any multi-year research, this study is much indebted to a number of colleagues and academic institutions too vast to summarize here. To name a few, as my early reflections on the subject of this book began while co-editing the issue of a Journal, I learned from Luca Baldissara, the then director of the Journal *900*, how to develop my attitude to research the history of international economic relations without keeping it separate from categories and questions typical of contemporary historians. Much cutting edge reflections on how to shape a research project on the subject were carried out while in residence at the Center for European Studies at Harvard University, then directed by David Blackbourn, where I could get feedbacks by political economists such as Richard Rosecrance and Peter A. Hall.

This book would have never been published without the financial, institutional and personal support and encouragement from two European research institutions. I am much indebted on the one side to the German Historical Institute in Washington DC, then directed by Hartmut Berghoff and Uwe Spiekermann; by awarding me a year-long research fellowship, the GHI made possible extensive and detailed research across the United States federal and banking archives. During my stay at the GHI I also discussed preliminary results of my research there and elsewhere in Washington and across the US, with like-minded colleagues. I would like to mention the research seminar held at the GHI, David S. Painter, Melvyn P. Leffler, and Paul Pitman, among others, who guided me through the sticky routes and research issues that any researcher at US federal archives and Presidential libraries has to face up to. Many archivists directed me to research some repositories essential to this research: the archivists of the World Bank Group Archives, the International Monetary Fund Archives, and the Rockefeller Archive Center deserve a special mention. Upon my return to Europe, I had a chance to spend time researching, writing and disseminating the preliminary results of this work. Here comes the second institution I am hugely indebted to. At the University of Naples L'Orientale I could take advantage of full support and guidance from both Paolo Frascani and Giuseppe Moricola. Both of them encouraged me tirelessly and with enthusiasm during my journey to specialize in the history of international financial relations, and called my attention to the larger economic, social and political framework and implications in which research in twentieth-century international economic history deserved to be placed. This work would never have come to light without them. Since I repatriated to Europe, a number of colleagues and institutions hosted lectures and presentations based on research carried out in connection with this book: to name a few, George Depeyrot from the French National Center for Scientific Research, the EHESS in Paris, the Université Sorbonne, the European University Institute, the Financial University Under the Government of the Russian Federation, and the American University of Rome. During my visiting research professor appointment at the Centro de Estudios Històricos of El Colegio de México, Mexico City, I discussed my work with Sandra Kuntz Ficker, and was also able to benefit from feedback and insightful advice and comments on how the history of Latin American economies fits into my story from Carlos Marichal. I am much indebted to both of them. Likewise, during my stay in Mexico City I had the privilege of discussing my ongoing research and writing on the subject of petrodollars and the energy finance with Gustavo A. Del Angel. Moreover, insofar as this work delves into the interlocking between capital markets and the history of Latin American Least Developed economies, I was invited to attend conferences at the Universidad del Pacifico (Perù) and the Universidad de Chile.

Finally, at Palgrave I am grateful to Aimee Dibbens for giving me this opportunity to publish my book and to Thomas Coughlan for his editorial assistance, as well as to Karen Weller for her invaluable copy-editing work.

Naples, Italy Simone Selva

Contents

Abbreviations

ADB	Asian Development Bank
AT&T	Former American Telephone and Telegraph Company, now AT&T Corporation
BIS	Bank for International Settlements
C-20	Committee of Twenty
CEA	Council of Economic Advisers
CES	US Census Bureau's Center for Economic Studies
CFR	Council on Foreign Relations
CIA	Central Intelligence Agency
CIEC	Council for International Economic Cooperation
CPI	Consumer Price Index
DAC	Development Assistance Committee of the OECD
DDRS	Declassified Documents and Reference System: http://www.gale.com/us-declassified-documents-online/
DIB	Commerce Action Group on the Near East, US Department of Commerce
DM	Deutsche Mark
EEC	European Economic Community
EPC	Economic Policy Committee
ERP	European Recovery Program
Exim-Bank	Export-Import Bank of the United States
FCO	Foreign and Commonwealth Office
FNCB	First National City Bank, New York City

FOMC	US Federal Open Market Committee
FRB	Federal Reserve Board of the Federal Reserve System of the United States
FRBNYA	Federal Reserve Bank of New York Historical Archive, New York City
FRUS	Foreign Relations of the United States
G-10	Group of Ten
G8	Group of Eight
GATT	General Agreement on Tariffs and Trade
GDP	Gross Domestic Product
GNP	Gross National Product
GOK	Government of Kuwait
GPO	Government Printing Office, Washington DC
GZ	GiroZentrale
IBRD	International Bank for Reconstruction and Development
IDA	International Development Association
IET	Interest Equalization Tax
IFC	International Finance Corporation
IMDBI	Industrial and Mining Development Bank of Iran
IMF	International Monetary Fund
IMFA	International Monetary Fund Archives, Washington DC
IMI	Istituto Mobiliare Italiano
IRS	US Internal Revenue Service
ITT	International Telephone and Telegraph Company, now ITT Corporation
JCPL	Jimmy Carter Presidential Library and Museum, Atlanta, GA
JCPL, NLC	Archival documents from the Carter Presidential Library
JFKPL	John F. Kennedy Presidential Library and Museum, Boston, Mass.
LBJPL	Lyndon Baines Johnson Presidential Library, Austin, TX
LDCs	Non-oil producing least developed countries
LIBOR	London Interbank Offered Rate
LOC	Library of Congress, Manuscript Division, Washington DC
MEDAI	International Monetary Fund Archives, Middle Eastern Department Fonds
MHM	Missouri History Museum
NAC	US National Advisory Council on International Monetary and Financial Policies

NAM	US National Association of Manufacturers
NARA	National Archives and Records Administration, Archive II, College Park, MD
NATO	North Atlantic Treaty Organization
NBER	National Bureau of Economic Research
NSC	National Security Council
NSF	Kennedy Presidential Library and Museum, Boston, Mass., National Security Files
NSSM	National Security Study Memorandum
OAPEC	Organization of Arab Petroleum Exporting Countries
OAS	Organization of American States
OASIA	US Department of the Treasury, Office of the Assistant Secretary for International Affairs
OECD	Organization for Economic Cooperation and Development
OMD	International Monetary Fund Archives, Office of the Managing Director
OPEC	Organization of Petroleum Exporting Countries
P&B	Programming and Budgeting Department of the World Bank
RAC	Rockefeller Archive Center, Tarrytown, New York
RFA	Rockefeller Archive Center, Rockefeller Family Archive
SAMA	Saudi Arabian Monetary Authority
SCC	Special Coordinating Committee, Carter administration
SDRs	Special Drawing Rights of the IMF
TNA	The National Archives, Kew, Richmond, United Kingdom
UAE	United Arab Emirates
UN	United Nations
UNCTAD	United Nations Conference on Trade and Development
USSR	Union of Soviet Socialist Republics
VFCR	Voluntary Foreign Credit Restraint Program
WBGA	World Bank Group Archives, Washington DC

List of Figures

List of Tables

1

Introduction: The Reshaping of US Foreign Financial and Monetary Policies from the 1960s to the 1970s

The historiography of US foreign economic relations since the post-World War II era has largely focused on two historical turning points. Generations of scholars in this field have widely researched the role of the United States in the reconstruction of an orderly international economic system based on the strength of the value of the US dollar and its scarcity in the post-World War II international economy. Based on the earlier debates on the origins of the Cold War from wartime to the early postwar settlements, which pro-Western historians and leftward scholars wrangled over during the 1970s,[1] by far the deliberation on the postwar economic and monetary developments revolved around the reconstruction of Western European economies.

During the 1980s and early 1990s the bulk of this debate mostly focused on two theses. On the one side, a cohort of American historians and political economists made the argument that the European Recovery Program (ERP, also known as the "Marshall Plan") implemented to resurrect war-wrecked European economies had been vital and irreplaceable to set off the economic recovery and the ensuing upward growth.[2] On the other hand, a string of European scholarship contended that as early as the war effort and shortly thereafter, some European countries, first and

S. Selva, *Before the Neoliberal Turn*, Palgrave Studies in Economic History,
DOI 10.1057/978-1-137-57443-5_1

foremost Germany, had cultivated the macroeconomic seeds that lay at the origins of economic recovery and takeoff.[3]

Since 1989, this early wave of studies has paved the way to an increasing desire to explore the role of the United States in the international economic crisis of the 1970s.[4] With a few rare exceptions and some studies focused on specific topics such the history of US economic institutions and Bretton Woods' entities,[5] scant attention had been given to the period from the late 1950s, when for the first time the US balance of payments plummeted, to the centrifugal transformations that occurred in the 1970s. In light of this two-sided mainstream scholarship the prominent and continued international economic role of Washington in the postwar era was reduced to its unmistakable dominance in the late 1940s and 1950s, and to the unmanageable problems that the US administrations, most notably the Nixon and Ford presidencies, had to face up to since the White House chose to end the dollar convertibility into gold.

Within this scholarly framework, the history of Washington's foreign economic relations has mostly been portrayed in two ways. On one hand, it has been depicted as the history of the Marshall Plan and the international economic institutions that hailed from it the role of promoting domestic growth and international stability across the globe. On the other hand, it has been researched in light of the crushing consequences of the end of currency convertibility on Washington's relations with its partners and on the system of international relations. Against this backdrop, the history of the 1960s has largely been overlooked and treated as an age cut off from both the malaise of the 1970s, and the pace of international economic integration under US leadership that shaped the economic Cold War years of the 1950s. With a few exceptions, most of which focused on the process of international trade integration pushed forward during the 1960s,[6] the history of US international monetary and financial policy during that decade has so far been written by and large by authoritative monetary historians or international political economists engaged with general works and interpretations of the role of the US currency and institutions in the postwar international economic arena.[7] More recently, a strand of scholarship in the history of international relations pointed to the unmistakable topicality of US foreign financial and monetary policy in charting the trajectories of US foreign economic relations in the 1960s.[8]

The 1970s saw a particular focus on the history of the neoliberal era and its corollary, unleashed global integration, and marked the following three decades leading up to the Great Contraction of 2008.

The late 1960s to the 1970s was a period of transition for the advanced industrial economies. The long postwar compromise between capital and labor was based on a tradeoff between high level of labor productivity and moderate labor costs in return for substantial transfer of the tax burden from the poorer to the richer population within the framework of free movement of labor, capital and goods across nations.

The transition to the economic and capital deregulation germane to the 1970s set the groundwork for unfettered transnational capital movements and industrial hiving off, and was by and large the subject of remarkable studies and intellectual inquiries in economic sociology and other social sciences.[9] Collective studies on the origins of the 1970s collapse of the Keynesian compromise between capital and labor and the growing pressure on state finances and sovereign debt,[10] and works on the origins of contemporary deregulations in banking and credit policies, or on the meteoric ascendancy in political influence of American corporations and financial elites since that decade that appeared more recently,[11] confirm this intellectual grid. Much the same can be said for a recent flow of historical reconstructions in the history of international relations that investigated the role of international summitries and multilateral institutional arrangements in reshaping the international system in the economic meltdown and malaise of the 1970s.[12] This decade is invariably viewed as a kick-off to the neoliberal age, rather than the endpoint of a multi-decade historical period. The economic policies of the New Deal,[13] through to the expansionary policies promoted under the Carter administration, combined international market integration and demand management domestic economic policies, increased transnational flows in goods and capital, and internal expansionary policies, either in the United States or, much more vigorously, across the Western European economies.

Against this backdrop, by reckoning the continued central role of the US dollar and its unfettered weakening from the time the US balance of payments and the US economy plunged in the late 1950s through to its collapse in foreign exchange markets in the late 1970s, this book aims to provide a history of the US foreign economic policy through a detailed reconstruction of the initiatives in which the US federal and monetary authorities engaged to restore balance of payments equilibrium and to resurrect the value of the dollar in exchange markets from the late 1950s through to the end of the 1970s. This research places these efforts and trajectory in US foreign financial and monetary policy against the backdrop of a two-decade period marked by the end of cheap oil prices and by the meteoric rise of transnational private capital flows. These two dynamics provide the two-tier constraints that the Washington-based federal authorities and the monetary and banking elites of New York needed to come to terms within their twofold effort to reshuffle the dominance of the US dollar and to resurrect the US external balance. In the pursuit of this target the book focuses on a wide range of US foreign policymakers that includes not only the US government and the US monetary authorities, but also the largest US commercial banks; first and foremost the Chase Manhattan Bank, the flagship of the Rockefeller family, since the 1950s involved in both internationalizing the US economy, and in shaping a tangle of foreign financial and commercial bonds with some key oil producing OPEC (Organization of Petroleum Exporting Countries) member states of the Middle East. This inquiry into Washington's trajectories amid these two fundamental transformations that marked the international economy during the turn from the 1960s to the 1970s is conducted through a specific methodological approach that, so far, has rarely been adopted in historical scholarship focused on this time frame and subject. Unlike the vast majority of studies in both energy and oil history,[14] and research in international financial history on the globalization of financial markets during the Bretton Woods decades and thereafter,[15] this study establishes a linkage between the unbound ascendancy of private capital markets and financial capitalism on the world economic stage on the one side, and the ongoing importance of raw material and commodities in shaping international economic relations on the other. As anticipated in some studies this nexus is distinctive to the history of the twentieth century international economy.[16] The long postwar era of economic growth and increasing international economic integration that most advanced industrial economies enjoyed revolved around the unprecedented and unparalleled combination of fairly cheap commodity prices, and fixed although adjustable exchange rates. Fixed exchange rates and cheap oil prices were a fundamental contribution to the smooth and stable growth of material well-being and the financial markets that featured in the long postwar boom down into the 1960s. This book explores the ways in which rising oil prices and the soaring cost of money, triggered by the development of short-term unregulated capital markets, concurred to harness the attempts conducted by the United States in the 1960s and 1970s to remake a system of international trade with payments pegged to the US currency and revolving around the role of American finance as leading international lender.

Within the above-mentioned general framework, this inquiry into the US foreign financial and monetary policy aims at charting its changing trajectories throughout the 1960s and 1970s to its final demise in 1979. The then new president of the Federal Reserve System Paul A. Volcker's decision to undertake an unprecedented monetary tightening was a watershed in US monetary history. This was in striking contrast with domestic and foreign measures carried over during the previous two decades to revert the US balance of payments deficit and the increasing incapability of the American economy to finance international trade and payments.

In charting the history of US foreign economic policy since the teetering of Bretton Woods' stability in exchange rates and commodity prices this work aims to detect the historical dynamics that lay at the origins of such a path-breaking turn at the end of the 1970s.

The present reconstruction pays much attention to, and pinpoints a number of, continuities and discontinuities that featured in the US foreign monetary and balance of payments deficit financing policies during the two decades analyzed in the following chapters. From the late 1950s through the period of the Johnson administration a combined policy to resurrect the US current and capital account position proved to be increasingly unsuccessful owing to the crippling impact of ever-expanding dollar-denominated Eurocurrency markets on the strength of the dollar and on the balance of payments equilibrium. Throughout this early period, Washington based such strategy on the assumption that the causes of the malaise of the dollar and the US international payments position were linked to the external relations of the country. As a matter of fact, from the Kennedy administration to the Nixon era the US authorities traced the weakening of the US currency back to issues in foreign trade and to international monetary and commodity developments. At an early stage, under Kennedy and Johnson, Washington linked such continuing weakening of the US international payments position to American foreign trade policies, and US commitment to development policies, as well as overseas public expenditures. Later on, in trying to cope with a string of issues that ranged from the effects of the British pound devaluation on the dollar component of world money supply to the effects of the Suez Crisis in international oil markets through to the destabilizing effects of the decade-end gold crisis (all of which are investigated in Chap. 3), the Nixon administration pushed forward such outward-looking interpretation of the straining disturbances that afflicted the US international payments position and the strength of the US currency. Against this backdrop, after exploring in Chap. 2 a commitment by the Kennedy and Johnson administrations to improve the current account position through foreign military expenditure cuts and an increase in foreign military sales, Chap. 3 continues charting the American approach to the teetering of the US external balance by focusing on the foreign financial policies of the Nixon administration aimed at restoring equilibrium in the capital account position, and on its trade policies. By pinpointing the expansion in short-term highly liquid capital markets, with particular reference to developments in the Eurocurrency and Eurodollar markets, the course of the US balance of payments deficits, and the dollar's role in the international monetary system, all of which are specifically examined in Chaps. 3 and 4, the book makes the argument that the incapability of the US to reverse the outflow of dollars from the United States into short-term, inflation-sensitive, dollar-denominated Eurocurrency markets increased the dollar component of world money supply and caused a fundamental depreciation of the dollar. To put it another way, the structural transformations that marked the history of international finance throughout the 1960s, coupled with Washington's failure to govern that process, fundamentally concurred to the uptick in the cost of money for fixed capital investments and to the general inflationary spiral of the following decade through both the depreciation of the dollar and pressure on the exchange parity of Bretton Woods' currencies, and the impact of soaring cost of money on international trade and international trade financing. Neither Washington's measures to restrict capital outflows, nor the Federal Reserve System's monetary policy, as well as any effort to stabilize the interconvertibility between gold and dollar, proved to be successful in deterring and reverting such unfettered outflow of capital. Such a jungle of events that stemmed from the failure of Washington's policies laid the groundwork, (see Chaps. 3 and 4) for an uptick in oil and commodity prices in international markets that preceded and overlapped with Nixon's decision to suspend the dollar convertibility into gold. In charting this course of events, this research associates the very origins of the following domestic and international inflation with the unfettered expansion in cross-national flows of dollar-denominated private capital assets that neither Washington's measures to restore equilibrium on the capital account, nor the turn-of-the-decade debate on the reform of the international payments system and the useless search for alternative units of international accounts and reserves reverted. To summarize the arguments developed in Chaps. 2 and 3, over the course of the 1960s the US federal and monetary authorities failed in restoring equilibrium in either the capital or current account position. The combined 1967 devaluation of the British pound, the international gold crisis of the following year, and the Suez crisis added strains to the tottering US currency. From 1968 to 1973 this stream of multiple factors coupled the wobbling of fixed exchange rates and the declining strength of the dollar in international exchange markets with soaring international oil prices. By the early 1970s, when the oil producing countries negotiated an uptick in posted prices of oil and tax concessions, the weakening of the dollar triggered by such a variety of causes set in motion a rampant inflationary spiral in the cost of money for productive investments and international trade financing. Within this framework, a core argument of Chap. 3 is that the unfettered movements of dollar-denominated financial instruments from the United States to largely unregulated inflation-sensitive Eurocurrency markets was a decisive factor in determining this process. The growing gap between Eurodollar loan rates and the rates of short-term loans on most Western national capital markets accounts for this thesis. During the same time frame the United States pledged to restore balance of payments equilibrium not only through measures aimed at pinching the capital account position, but also by means of continued policies on the current account. In contrast to military and overseas public expenditures cuts implemented under the Kennedy administration, from the late 1960s through to the early 1970s, the United States expanded their commercial and financial bonds with the OPEC's oil producing countries that featured the largest domestic consumer markets. Based on earlier involvements in the financing of industrial development in countries such as Iran and Saudi Arabia, some leading American banks expanded their presence and operation in the Middle East to enhance the investments of American corporations in the region and the export of US manufacturing to those economies. The US foreign economic policymakers endorsed and promoted such twofold development, based on the assumption that it helped restore the US international payments position in two ways; increased presence and profits of US corporations in the region would turn into growing repatriation of profits to the United States, whereas the intermediation of American banking would stimulate US exports to the region, which might have a positive impact on the US balance of payments on current account. At the same time, increased purchases of American products by oil-rich nations reduced the dollar component of world money supply and lessened the risk of a foreign run on the US gold stock, which over the past decade had proved to be a development detrimental to the strength and stability of the US currency and the all system of world payments based on its full convertibility into gold.

The aforesaid development of Washington's financial and commercial relations with the OPEC oil producing countries of the Middle East to cope with the unfettered loss of international confidence in the dollar and a deteriorating US international payments position (whose early developments are analyzed in Chap. 3), initiated within the framework of rising prices of posted oil and increasing assertiveness by the oil producing member states of OPEC, was developed further after the outbreak of the first oil crisis. From the beginning of the decade through the creation of bilateral economic cooperation commissions established with some leading Middle Eastern partners, Washington continued to resort to some of the leading US commercial banks to promote US exports to these countries and to stimulate US investments and the positive entry to the US balance of payments that it represented, as well as direct OPEC investments in the US. However, since early 1974 this policy came at striking variance with the international financial implications of the first energy crisis; the huge financial assets that accrued to the OPEC countries as a result of the first quadrupling of oil prices, explored in Chap. 4, were largely—but not entirely—placed with the few largest US banks that at the time reflowed them in the Eurodollar and Eurocurrency markets. Therefore, the first energy crisis caused a further expansion in dollar-denominated short-term financial instruments a few months before the international recession of 1975 reduced the competitive position of the advanced industrial economies and plunged the business cycle into a downswing mode. Within this framework, the United States clearly linked the defense of the dollar and US balance of payments to a fight against the centrifugal effects of the energy crisis and the international recession on the global system of international trade and payments. The combined meteoric upsurge in oil prices, depreciating effects of growing OPEC's dollar holdings on the dollar, and the waning of limits to competitive devaluation to finance foreign exchange operations caused by the disbanding of fixed exchange rates, had potentially centrifugal effects on world trade and payments and extended to all nations and economies affected by the end of Bretton Woods and cheap energy. Accordingly, as Chap. 4 charts, the Ford administration, the International Monetary Fund (IMF) and the International Bank for Reconstruction and Development (IBRD) straddled to lock the OPEC countries' financial resources into a set of international financial arrangements. This would ease the US balance of payments from the pressure of bearing a large share of costs for development assistance and would help to cope with the implication of the international economic downswing on the current account deficit of the non-oil producing Least Developed Countries (LDCs), which had suffered the most from a staggering decline in the international demand for their commodities. Channeling the oil revenues of oil producers into existing and newly created multilateral arrangements under US leadership, aimed at lessening the financial burden of US development assistance to the LDCs, was in clear continuity with earlier US commitment in support for the external balance and purchasing power of non-oil producing LDCs in foreign markets that lay at the origins of US development policies in the 1960s. This strategy was coupled with a continued US policy (see Chap. 4) to shift the investment patterns of OPEC from short-term highly liquid placements to long-term financial assets, thought in Washington both to fight the depreciation of the dollar and to recast fixed capital investments to resurrect the business cycle amid the mid-decade recession. By pinpointing a series of hindrances that contributed to its unsuccessfulness, Chap. 4 highlights and explains the US incapability to implement such a recycling policy of the OPEC financial resources from 1974 to 1976: by that year OPEC created its own facility to provide the non-oil producing LDCs with financial assistance and went its own way in that direction. By the time Carter entered the White House such failure to link the financial ascendancy of the oil producing countries to the restructuring of the US foreign monetary and payments position overlapped with a sluggish domestic and international macroeconomic scenario.

A wave of scholarships on the Carter administration have argued that in the domestic and international economic policy arena the new presidency took a middle ground between interventionist demand policies and a market-oriented approach to let domestic credit and fixed capital formation reshuffle the business cycle.[17] Recently, and consistent with the general approach to the Carter administration, Daniel Sargent drew attention to the pace of President Carter's tax policy since it was first presented to the nation in January 1977, and to the contents of its final text, approved by Congress in May of that same year. He points to the tossing aside of some tax rebate measures announced in January and maintains that the law approved put into perspective the scale and scope of the new president's management of the business cycle. He suggests that the containment of the role of the federal state in managing the economy, suggested by some of the nations' leading economic policymakers, helps to better track Carter's weak position before Japan as well as any export-oriented advanced industrial economy at the London summit held in Spring 1977, when the implementation of expansionary policies across the western industrial economies was probably the most heated and disputed issue.[18]

By contrast, from the viewpoint of this inquiry into the US foreign financial and monetary policies to link the restructuring of a multilateral trade and payments system to the resurrection of the US dollar in foreign exchange markets, and the curbing of the US balance of payments deficit within the framework of long-standing trends in the international financial arena such as the development of recently booming short-term capital markets, this study situates Carter's stimulus policies in a different framework. Such stimulus policies took place in the context of both the course of Washington's monetary relations with the OPEC countries during the 1970s, and in a change of interpretation by the new presidency about the nature and origins of the dollar's depreciation. A comparison between the policies carried over from the Kennedy to the Ford administration, and the Carter presidency, highlights the extent to which Washington changed its approach. In this respect, this study makes the hypothesis that a striking discontinuity with past policies arose. As will be seen, from Kennedy to Ford, Washington associated the weakening of the dollar in foreign exchange markets with the tottering of US external equilibrium on current and capital accounts, and accordingly a number of measures were implemented to restore equilibrium in either position. What the US administrations changed from the early 1960s to the middle of the 1970s were the measures enacted to restore the US external equilibrium, over time focused either on current account or on capital account, or on the combining of both positions. Carter, the IMF, and as far as it was involved in the international financial investments of the OPEC countries, the IBRD, linked together the international capital supply based on the OPEC countries' oil revenues, a string of measures to achieve full capacity utilization across the manufacturing systems of the advanced industrial economies, and a policy shift in national fiscal and monetary policies deemed to stimulate domestic aggregate demand, to a rather different interpretation about the linkage between ever-growing transnational capital flows, the depreciation of the dollar in foreign exchange markets, and the general inflation of the decade. From the Kennedy administration through the middle of the 1970s, a clear linkage was established between the plummeting US balance of payments deficit and the surging in transnational capital flows and short-term Eurocurrency markets. In addition to a variety of factors having a bearing on the current account position that ranged from foreign trade to military assistance and outstanding debts owed to the US by the Western European allies, the US governments and Washington's monetary authorities pointed to the detrimental effects of capital flight on the dollar's strength and its role as unit of account. Accordingly, Washington straddled to reduce the dollar component in world money supply and the run on US gold stock through a number of international financial policies. In striking contrast with such interpretation, under Carter, the failure of measures to make the OPEC countries channel their oil revenues to the oil importing industrial nations and the non-oil producing LDCs through the Bretton Woods institutions and Western private capital markets (see Chap. 3), was combined with the idea that domestic inflation and domestic imbalances between capital supply and aggregate demand gripped onto the stunningly declining value of the dollar in international exchange markets. In other words, the Carter administration pointed to the internal imbalance between the supply side and the demand side to explain the unfinished teetering of the US currency and its effects on the stability of loan rates and commodity and consumer good prices. By the end of the decade a collapsing dollar jeopardized bilateral financial relations between Washington and the largest capital exporting OPEC countries at the center of this investigation, namely Saudi Arabia, Iran and to a lesser extent Kuwait. That is to say, during the Carter presidency, Washington linked the plummeting of the dollar in exchange markets to the overheating of domestic industrial economies based on aggregate demand outstripping a sluggish supply side, a capital supply for productive investments and fixed capital formation that fell back to the demand side, and the downward-sloping competitiveness of US manufacturing and credit tightness.

The combined continued deterioration of the dollar in exchange markets and its effects on the stability of US–OPEC financial relations, and unfettered current account deficit and inflation through 1978 in most Western countries, tracked the unsuccessfulness of this new strategy. The teetering of stable financial and economic bonds between Washington and the OPEC member states triggered the collapse of Carter administration's strategy aimed at striking the balance between capital supply and aggregate demand by increasingly favoring the inflow of OPEC's financial assets to fuel stimulus policies. Chapter 5 charts these developments with particular reference to the course of such stimulus policies and the progressive deterioration of stable relations between the United States, Iran, and Saudi Arabia to suggest that the seeds of the international economic disorders that followed the second oil crisis were well onset from 1978 to 1979. The last chapter points to the persistency of this US policy during that year in light of a continuous worsening of the international payments position of the US, some leading industrial nations and the non-oil LDCs. It was only after the repeated collapse in the value of the dollar in 1978, the effects of the Iranian revolution on both oil production levels and hoardings, and the waning possibility for Washington to advocate a moderate oil price policy and sustained production levels within OPEC (through active roles of the Shah and Saudi Arabia), that demand management policies based on combined shares of GNP invested on fixed capital formation and OPEC's equity and securities investments in the US, made way for a use of monetary policy to curb inflation and the US balance of payments deficit. This historical turn was epitomized by the unparalleled credit and monetary tightening decided upon by the new Chairman of the Federal Reserve Board Paul A. Volcker shortly after being appointed to the head of the US Federal Reserve System. The failure of policies grounded on expansionary measures to curb inflation and the decline of the dollar in international exchange markets also marked a striking shift in the financial assistance policies of the IMF. Such policy shift changed the concept of conditionality. Unlike the reasoning of a cohort of influential literature,[19] this work makes the argument that from the creation of the Fund to the middle of the 1970s the implementation of domestic monetary equilibrium and external stability were a prerequisite to attract private capital in the pursuit of domestic expansion and a high degree of economic openness and domestic growth in each IMF member state in balance of payments deficit. The creation of conditions seminal to attracting foreign investors was placed against the very aim of stimulating domestic growth and employment rates in its member countries. By contrast, since Volcker set out his stunning monetary stringency, such tradeoff between orderly domestic economic and fiscal policies and the allotment of financial assistance packages was part of a Fund's broader vision that placed economic stability and growth subject to monetary stability and creditworthiness in each member country.

Therefore, the ascendancy of monetarist thinking at the top of Washington's financial and monetary institutions tossed aside the view according to which it was possible to combine international financial and commercial integration, with stable economic growth across the industrial nations and any developing countries that took advantage from financial and monetary assistance from either the US governments or the institutions born out of the Bretton Woods conference.

Notes

1. Kolko and Kolko, 1972.
2. Maier, 1977.
3. Abelshauser, 1975, 1983; Milward 1984.
4. Spero, 1999; Gowan, 1999; Schulz and Schwartz, 2009; Ferguson, Maier, Manela and Sargent, 2010; Stein, 2010; Lifset, 2014; La Barca, 2013; Sargent, 2015; Bini, Garavini and Romero, 2016; Jacobs 2016.
5. Becker and McClenahan Jr., 2003; Bergsten, 1996; James, 1996; Sharma, 2017.
6. Evans, 1971; Hawley, 1987.
7. The political economy scholarship on the subject is too vast to summarize here. See for reference: Helleiner, 2015; Frieden, 2006; Eichengreen, 1996 and 2011. Monetary historians have traditionally approached the decades of the 1960s and 1970s through a century-long perspective: see for example Bordo and Wynne, 2016; Bordo, Humpage and Schwartz, 2015; Bordo and Orphanides, 2013.
8. Gavin and Lawrence, 2014.
9. Harvey 1992 and 2005; Arrighi, 1994; Duménil and Lévy, 2013; Baldwin, 2016.
10. Hall, 2013; Kotz, 2015; Buggeln, Daunton and Nützenadel, 2017.
11. Krippner, 2012; Baradaran, 2015; Altamura, 2017.
12. Romero-Mourlon Druol, 2014; Spohr-Reynolds, 2016.
13. by New Deal it is intended here the employment-targeting investment and public spending policies implemented in the US under the Presidency of F.D. Roosevelt.
14. This literature is too vast to summarize here: for a sample see Yergin, 1991; Vitalis, 2006; Parra, 2004.
15. See for instance Hawley, 1987; Battilossi and Cassis, 2002; Battilossi, 2010; Yago, 2013; Flores and Alvarez, 2014; Green, 2016.

16. Some scholarship anticipated to a certain degree this approach: see for instance Mitchell, 2011; Maier, 2006.
17. Hargrove, 1988; Fink and Graham, 1998; Biven, 2014.
18. Sargent 2015.
19. See for instance Rogers, 2012.

References

Abelshauser, Werner. 1975. *Wirtschaft in Westdeutschland 1945–1948. Rekonstruktion und Wachstumsbedingungen in der amerikanischen und britischen Zone*. Stuttgart: Anstalt.

———. 1983. *Wirtschaftsgeschichte des Bundesrepublik Deutschland 1945–1980*. Suhrkamp: Frankfurt am Main.

Altamura, Carlo Edoardo. 2017. *European Banks and the Rise of International Finance. The Post-Bretton Woods Era*. London: Routledge.

Arrighi, Giovanni. 1994. *The Long Twentieth Century. Money, Power, and the Origins of Our Time*. London: Verso.

Baldwin, Richard. 2016. *The Great Convergence. Information Technology and the New Globalization*. Cambridge, MA: Harvard University Press.

Baradaran, Mehrsha. 2015. *How the Other Half Banks. Exclusion, Exploitation, and the Threat to Democracy*. Cambridge, MA: Harvard University Press.

Battilossi, Stefano. 2010. The Eurodollar Revolution in Financial Technology: Deregulation, Innovation and Structural Change in Western Banking. In *Financial Markets and Organizational Technologies. System Architectures, Practices and Risks in the Era of Deregulation*, ed. Alexandros-Andreas Kyrtsis, 29–63. London: Palgrave.

Battilossi, Stefano, and Youssef Cassis. 2002. *European Banks and the American Challenge. Competition and Cooperation in International Banking Under Bretton Woods*. Oxford: Oxford University Press.

Becker, William H., and William M. McClenahan Jr. 2003. *The Market, the State and the Export-Import Bank of the United States 1934–2000*. New York: Cambridge University Press.

Bergsten, Fred. 1996. *Dilemmas of the Dollar. The Economics and Politics of United States International Monetary Policy*. London/New York: Sharpe-Council on Foreign Relations.

Bini, Elisabetta, Giuliano Garavini, and Federico Romero, eds. 2016. *Oil Shock. The 1973 Crisis and Its Economic Legacy*. London/New York: IB Tauris.

Biven, Carl W. 2014. *Jimmy Carter's Economy. Policy in an Age of Limits*. Chapel Hill: The University of North Carolina Press.

Bordo, Michael D., and Athanasios Orphanides, eds. 2013. *The Great Inflation. The Rebirth of Modern Central Banking*. London/Chicago: The University of Chicago Press.

Bordo, Michael D., and Mark Wynne, eds. 2016. *The Federal Reserve's Role in the Global Economy. An Historical Perspective*. New York: Cambridge University Press.

Bordo, Michael D., Owen F. Humpage, and Anna Schwartz, eds. 2015. *Strained Relations. US Foreign-Exchange Operations and Monetary Policy in the Twentieth Century*. Chicago/London: The University of Chicago Press.

Buggeln, Marc, Martin Daunton, and Alexander Nützenadel. 2017. *The Political Economy of Public Finance. Taxation, State Spending and Debt Since the 1970s*. Cambridge: Cambridge University Press.

Duménil, Gérard, and Dominique Lévy. 2013. *The Crisis of Neoliberalism*. Cambridge, MA: Harvard University Press.

Eichengreen, Barry. 1996. *Globalizing Capital. A History of the International Monetary System*. Princeton: Princeton University Press.

———. 2011. *Exorbitant Privilege. The Rise and Fall of the Dollar*. Oxford: Oxford University Press.

Evans, John W. 1971. *The Kennedy Round in American Trade Policy. The Twilights of the GATT*. Cambridge, MA: Harvard University Press.

Ferguson, Niall, Charles Maier, Erez Manela, and Daniel Sargent, eds. 2010. *The Shock of the Global. The 1970s in Perspective*. London/Cambridge, MA: Harvard University Press.

Fink, Gary M., and Hugh Davis Graham, eds. 1998. *The Carter Presidency. Policy Choices in the Post-New Deal Era*. Lawrence: University Press of Kansas.

Flores, Juan, and Sebastian Alvarez. 2014. Trade Finance and Latin America's Lost Decade. *Investigaciones de História Economica* 10 (2): 127–139.

Frieden, Jeffry. 2006. *Global Capitalism. Its Fall and Rise in the Twentieth Century*. New York: W.W. Norton.

Gavin, Francis J., and Mark Atwood Lawrence, eds. 2014. *Beyond the Cold War. Lyndon Johnson and the New Global Challenges of the 1960s*. New York: Oxford University Press.

Gowan, Peter. 1999. *The Global Gamble. Washington's Faustian Bid for World Dominance*. London/New York: Verso.

Green, Jeremy. 2016. Anglo-American Development, the Euromarkets, and the Deeper Origins of Neoliberal Deregulation. *Review of International Studies* 42 (3): 425–449.

Hall, Peter A. 2013. The Political Origins of Our Economic Discontents. Contemporary Adjustment Problems in Historical Perspective. In *Politics in the New Hard Times. The Great Recession in Comparative Perspective*, ed. Miles Kahler and David A. Lake, 129–149. Ithaca: Cornell University Press.

Hargrove, Erwin C. 1988. *Jimmy Carter as President. Leadership and the Politics of the Public Good*. Baton Rouge/London: Louisiana State University Press.

Harvey, David. 1992. *The Condition of Post-modernity. An Inquiry into the Origins of Our Time*. Oxford/Cambridge, MA: Blackwell.

———. 2005. *A Brief History of Neo-liberalism*. New York: Oxford University Press.

Hawley, James P. 1987/2016. *Dollars and Borders. US Government Attempts to Restrict Capital Flows 1960–1980*. New York: Routledge.

Helleiner, Eric. 2015. *States and the Reemergence of Global Finance. From Bretton Woods to the 1990s*. Ithaca/London: Cornell University Press.

Jacobs, Meg. 2016. *Panic at the Pump. The Energy Crisis and the Transformation of American Politics in the 1970s*. New York: Hill and Wang.

James, Harold. 1996. *International Monetary Cooperation Since Bretton Woods*. Oxford/New York: Oxford University Press.

Kolko, Gabriel, and Joyce Kolko. 1972. *The Limits of Power. The World and United States Foreign Policy 1945–1954*. New York: Harper and Row.

Kotz, David M. 2015. *The Rise and Fall of Neoliberal Capitalism*. Cambridge, MA: Harvard University Press.

Krippner, Greta R. 2012. *Capitalizing on Crisis. The Political Origins of the Rise of Finance*. Cambridge, MA: Harvard University Press.

La Barca, Giuseppe. 2013. *International Trade in the 1970s*. London: Bloomsbury.

Lifset, Robert, ed. 2014. *American Energy Policy in the 1970s*. Norman: University of Oklahoma Press.

Maier, Charles S. 1977. The Politics of Productivity. Foundations of American International Economic Policy After World War II. *International Organization* 31 (4): 607–633.

———. 2006. *Among Empires. American Ascendancy and Its Predecessors*. Cambridge, MA: Harvard University Press.

Milward, Alan. 1984. *The Reconstruction of Western Europe 1945–51*. London: Methuen.

Mitchell, Timothy. 2011. *Carbon Democracy*. London: Verso.

Parra, Francisco. 2004. *Oil Politics. A Modern History of Petroleum*. London: IB Tauris.

Rogers, Chris. 2012. *The IMF and European Economies. Crisis and Conditionality*. London: Palgrave.

Romero, Federico, and Emmanuel Mourlon Druol, eds. 2014. *International Summitry and Global Governance. The Rise of the G7 and the European Council 1974–1991*. New York: Routledge.

Sargent, Daniel. 2015. *A Superpower Transformed. The Remaking of American Foreign Relations in the 1970s*. New York: Oxford University Press.

Schulz, Matthias, and Thomas A. Schwartz, eds. 2009. *The Strained Alliance. US-European Relations from Nixon to Carter*. New York: Cambridge University Press.

Sharma, Patrick A. 2017. *Robert McNamara's Other War. The World Bank and International Development*. Philadelphia: University of Pennsylvania Press.

Spero, David. 1999. *The Hidden Hand of American Hegemony. Petrodollar Recycling and International Markets*. Ithaca/London: Cornell University Press.

Spohr, Kristina, and David Reynolds, eds. 2016. *Transcending the Cold War. Summits, Statecraft, and the Dissolution of Bipolarity 1970–1990*. Oxford: Oxford University Press.

Stein, Judith. 2010. *Pivotal Decade. How the United States Traded Factories for Finance in the 1970s*. New Haven: Yale University Press.

Vitalis, Robert. 2006. *America's Kingdom. Mythmaking on the Saudi Oil Frontier*. Stanford: Stanford University Press.

Yago, Kazuhiko. 2013. *The Financial History of the Bank for International Settlements*. London: Routledge.

Yergin, Daniel. 1991. *The Prize. The Epic Question for Oil, Money and Power*. New York: Simon & Schuster.

2

Capital Account, Foreign Trade and Development Assistance: US Foreign Economic Policy in the 1960s

2.1 The Historical Origins of a Seemingly Intractable Nexus Before the Oil Crises

Following the period from 1953 to 1957, the American economy showed unmistakable signs of economic slowdown, when it muddled through two recessions: the first recession occurred in 1957; the second one at the end of the decade. At this very dawn in the post-World War II history of American economic downturn, two distinctive features that marked the US macroeconomic history over the following decades were well under way. On the one side, any time the US economy slowed down, the balance of payments worsened; this interconnection sheds light on the longstanding nexus between domestic economic growth and external equilibrium. From the viewpoint of the present book, this linkage is of utmost interest in that it highlights the interlocking relation between trends in international payments of the advanced industrial economies and the way in which the competitive position of their manufacturing systems developed over time. The next chapters provide evidence to the attention paid by the American foreign economic policymakers to this correlation; US political and economic elites took it into account to

S. Selva, *Before the Neoliberal Turn*, Palgrave Studies in Economic History,
DOI 10.1057/978-1-137-57443-5_2

shape US foreign financial and monetary policies. Quite consistently, and particularly under the Carter administration, Washington linked the search for strengthening the value of the dollar and the competitive position of the American economy in foreign markets to recasting a sound equilibrium between capital supply and domestic aggregate demand. Recurrently, a sound economic growth was viewed as a precondition to bolster the competitive edge of the American economy and the wide international market integration revolving around it. This came about within the framework of a stable dollar in international exchange markets. Regarding the latter, if one briefly turns attention back to the period from the second half of the 1950s to the appointment of Kennedy to the White House, it is easy to identify a clear-cut monetary policy aimed at upholding confidence in the US dollar and countering economic downturns and recessions. Such monetary stance was based on tight monetary measures. Anytime it was carried over, the aim of monetary tightening was to ease pressure on the US balance of payments through monetary interventions on the capital account. This chapter explores the way in which—from the turn of the decade to the beginning of the 1960s—this outstanding policy was pushed forward; how, over the decade of the 1960s, it changed and became mixed up with foreign trade policies focused on resurrecting the balance of payments on current account. The chapter suggests that throughout the 1960s, and up to the outbreak of the first energy crisis, both the US government and Washington's monetary authorities changed their approach to restore the US international payments position. According to this reconstruction, during this period the United States made a policy shift and gave an increasing importance to resurrecting the balance of payments on current account through foreign trade. An inquiry into these developments is useful to explore the historical origins in the 1960s of the ways in which, during the following decade of the 1970s, Washington shaped the US balance of payments deficit financing policies. One of the centerpieces of this study is the argument that under the floating currency system of the 1970s, consistent with the previous decade, Washington mixed up measures to restore equilibrium on current account with policies focused on capital account. This policy mix was aimed at restoring equilibrium in the international trade and payments system. A core argument of this chapter is that the historical origins of such policies lay in the balance of payments deficit financing policies implemented during the fixed exchange rate system of Bretton Woods still under operation in the 1960s. In fact, since that decade US foreign economic policy makers have had to face up two seemingly intractable long-lasting issues: a depreciation of the US dollar and loss of confidence in it, and an increasingly strained US balance of payments equilibrium. This worsening US balance of payments and the depreciation of the US dollar stemmed from two developments vital to understand the weakness of the US currency throughout the following decade: first, capital flight and gold outflows from the US, both of which had grown since the end of the 1950s throughout the 1960s; second, it is worth mentioning the ensuing development of US dollar-denominated short-term capital markets across the Western financial centers outside the United States. Washington combined measures designed to resurrect the balance of payments on current account, credit restraint and a tight interest rates policy, in order to attract investors and prevent capital outflows. This chapter points to the interconnectedness between a worsening US balance of payments position, a downswing economic mode, and a jarring decline in the competitive position of US manufacturing on world trade markets. Both the US balance of payments and the competitive edge of US manufacturing declined way before the end of either cheap oil prices and commodity prices, or the increase in labor costs typical of the late 1960s. The chapter henceforth suggests that the interrelation between US domestic economic slowdown and downward-sloping competitiveness in foreign markets, the US dollar's depreciation and the rising US balance of payments deficit turned out way in advance of the tearing apart of fixed exchange rates in the first half of the 1970s.

To begin with, from 1953 to 1959 the US economy grew at the slow rate of 2.3 percent a year.[1] Throughout those same years, the United States experienced two major recessions: the first one occurring in 1957–1958, and the second one came about in 1960. From the end of the second quarter of 1957 to the end of the first quarter of 1958, seasonally adjusted US industrial production contracted by over two thirds and set the lowest level on record in January 1958, before slowly recovering through the beginning of the second quarter, when it jumped 20 percent over its July 1957 level.[2] Likewise, seasonally adjusted US unemployment rate figures registered an unparalleled and continued increase from November 1957 through the following winter, before leveling off over the course of spring and early summer of 1958. Afterwards, by August of that same year the unemployment rate decreased.[3] On the other hand, while quarterly data on non-seasonally adjusted Gross National Product (GNP) showed a substantial shortfall only from the third to the fourth quarter of 1957,[4] non-seasonally adjusted US personal income declined much less since the third quarter of 1957; by this time it registered two slight contractions in September and December. Thereafter, it leveled off through the second quarter of 1958, when it began to increase slightly.[5] Besides—quite remarkably—from June to November 1957 the index of US common stock prices based on 86 industries nosedived at an unprecedented rate. Thereafter, the index featured a number of ups and downs throughout the first quarter of 1958.[6] This sluggish recession overlapped with the beginning of the most grievous shortfall in the US balance of payments since the end of World War II. Moreover, by the time the US economy began suffering a slackening rate of growth, the US monetary authorities came to terms with another utterly intractable issue that plagued the stability of the US dollar in foreign exchange markets over the rest of the decade: the long-standing loss in US gold stocks that ruined both US reserves and Washington's strength in international exchange markets, explored in this chapter. These losses caused a decline in the US dollar equivalent price for bar gold on all major European gold markets that developed since as early as 1960. Such development hit the stability of the US dollar up to the eve of Nixon's decision to suspend the convertibility of the dollar into gold. During this year the dollar price of gold bars in London, Paris and Zurich, which was the benchmark to measure the value of the US dollar against gold, increased.[7] Therefore, on the eve of the election of John F. Kennedy to the White House all these trends were well under way.[8] By that time the worsening US balance of payments deficit was already a cumbersome issue: it negatively affected the shaping of the US foreign economic policy.[9] Since as early as these two recessions that occurred in the second half of the 1950s, a linkage can be established between this downswing economic mode, the outlook of US foreign trade and US industrial production, and the specific features of US monetary measures adopted in order to restore US balance of payments equilibrium. At the time the US adopted a set of monetary measures that included monetary tightening and a high interest rate policy. As a matter of fact, if one shifts attention away from macroeconomic figures and keeps an eye on data on US manufacturing, it is straightforward to see that in terms of industrial production, US manufacturing was on the ropes since as early as 1957. In aggregate, from 1956 to 1957 the corporate profits of US industries before taxes declined from a little over $26 million to around $24.5 million. In proportion, during the same period the corporate profits of the US manufacturing industry dropped much more, thus contributing substantially to the total decline in the corporate profits of US industry.[10] On the other hand, from 1959 to 1961 the added value of most US non-capital-intensive manufacturing sectors, such leather and leather products, primary and fabricated metal products or similar sectors underwent a staggering contraction. Remarkably, these low capital-intensive sectors depended the most on monetary policy and specifically on monetary intervention in foreign exchange markets.[11] Likewise, from 1958 to 1973 the number of production workers in the US manufacturing industry experienced a constant decline. During the same period production worker hours leveled off from 1958 to 1960 before coming through a sticky contraction in 1961.[12] As already mentioned, during those years the US stock markets declined; a linkage can be established between this downswing industrial mode of American industry, the shortfall in US stock indices, and a deterioration in the US balance of trade and payments. In particular, it is worth establishing a correlation between Washington's high interest rate policy and general credit stringency, a contraction of industrial production in US manufacturing, and the slackening in US stock markets. Most interpretations about the dynamics of labor productivity in the United States from the 1950s to the 1970s established a linkage between its ups and down and a number of macroeconomic trends like the quality of labor, the effects of government spending on economic growth, or changes in the capital–labor ratio.[13] In contrast, it is worth linking US productivity to monetary policy in order to pinpoint the impact of such decline in industrial productivity on the US external balance. As a matter of fact, straightforwardly the shortfall in the US international payments position hit the competitive position of American industry. At the same time, the combined decline in productivity and added value of US industry, and the rise in the cost of money caused by US monetary policy plummeted the US stock market into a sticky meltdown. Furthermore, the decline in productivity together with the increase in the rate of loans for investments reduced the rate of growth in loans and investments at commercial banks compared to the mid-1950s.[14] Consequently, investors scrambled to move away from the US equity market. This sequence of causal relations contributed to the subsequent outflow of private capital from the United States toward foreign financial centers that ran well into the first half of the 1960s. This sequence of developments are essential to make sense of the unsuccessfulness of a credit stringency strategy in order either to recover the productivity and competitive edge of US manufacturing, or to restore the US international payments position.

In fact, in the aim to better assess the US foreign monetary and financial policy it is crucial to stress the correlation between the impact of a weakening dollar in foreign exchange markets, and the dwindling competitive position of US industry in world trade markets. This crucial correlation was missed by most historical studies on the US international monetary policy implemented under Johnson and Nixon.[15] The relationship between these two issues helps to explain the impact of US trade deficit on US international payments imbalance and the role of monetary policy. In fact, unmistakably from 1958 to the middle of 1959, a worsening US trade position was the main cause of the deteriorating US balance of payments.[16] From 1958 onward, although receipts on exports of goods and services still outstripped payments on imports, the former ones leveled off, while payments scaled up.[17] By 1960, this trend became normalcy, thus charting a downward spiraling competitive position of US manufacturing and a worsening US balance of trade.[18] More importantly from the viewpoint of this study, this development came about within the framework of a tight monetary policy and a prolonged banking policy based on credit restraint by which Washington confronted the economic slowdowns of the late 1950s. Moreover, as detailed in the following paragraphs, this combined monetary tightening, plummeting competitive edge, and growing external disequilibrium overlapped with a sharp decline in US gold stocks and mounting capital outflows.

As mentioned above, from as early as the mid-1950s the US monetary authorities showed a constant and unstoppable inclination to monetary stringency. In short, this policy was implemented in three ways. In the first instance, during this period the Federal Reserve System tightened up the money supply. As a result, the growth rate of money supply was higher than that of GNP. From 1953 through 1959 when the American economy registered a sluggish 2.3 percent increase, the Federal Reserve expanded money supply by a little 1.8 percent a year.[19] Thereafter, from mid-1959 to the end of 1961, the money supply increased by a little over 1 percent, while GNP grew by over 10 percent.[20] Confronted with the 1957 economic downturn, the Federal Reserve Board (charged with coordinating the policies of regional Reserve Banks) and the Department of the Treasury were opposed to changing money market conditions and refused to ease pressures on bank reserves through open market operations. The open market operations were the Fed's instrument to raise the reserves of private banks by letting regional Reserve Banks purchase Treasury bonds and securities held by private investors. The American law required that regional Reserve Banks settle the purchasing of Treasury assets by issuing checks, and that a determined percentage of deposits held by private banks be turned into reserves. Due to these requirements, it was possible to increase the liquidity of banks and to ease the pressure of a tight money supply on the reserves of private banks. Likewise, this permitted private banks to issue credit without officially expanding the supply of money.[21] This was a way to expand credit without either easing money or reducing the reserve requirements of private banks. Therefore, foreign market operations were intended to strengthen the liquidity of banks and eschew any inflationary expansion of liquidity in support for currency in circulation. Throughout the second half of 1957, when the rate of growth of the American economy declined, the US monetary authorities engaged in a long-lasting dispute on monetary matters. The debate revolved around the issue of which policies were worth implementing to cope with the impending recession. Since the summer of 1957 the Federal Reserve Bank of New York and some regional Reserve Banks made a case for resorting to open market operations to prop up the business cycle. On the other hand, in September and October of that same year, when business activity and business loans declined, the Federal

Open Market Committee (FOMC) opposed such policy. On these occasions the FOMC upheld a traditional credit restraint approach to the slowdown in the business cycle and to the deteriorating US balance of payments under way.[22] Within the framework of this debate, during fall the Department of the Treasury undertook some financing operations; it firmly opposed any change in money markets conditions. Despite a sharp falloff in wholesale and consumer prices the Treasury opposed any reduction in the discount rate, viewed as a measure potentially harmful to its financing operations. Therefore, the Federal Reserve Bank of New York, the Department of the Treasury and the Board of Governors of the Federal Reserve System engaged in a lengthy quarrel over which action was most appropriate to sustain the business cycle without retrenching from monetary stringency. The New York Fed without question sponsored a clear turn to ease money: in fact, the Fed made a case for resorting to open market operations and for reducing the discount rate. On its part, the Department of the Treasury and the Board of Governors of the Federal Reserve System shared their orthodox monetary approach to the recession. Confronted with such sluggish economic juncture, finally the Federal Reserve Board approved a slight reduction in the discount rate that eased credit policy much less than requested by the Federal Reserve Bank of New York.[23] It is worth recalling this persisting credit restraint policy, as it is essential to understand Washington's reaction to the early internationalization of private capital markets from the turn of the decade through the 1960s. From the mid-1960s to the end of that decade the US monetary authorities and the US government pushed forward such credit restraint not so much by opposing any reduction in the discount rate, as by a string of other monetary, banking and fiscal policies. In the first instance, they repeatedly countered any decrease in reserve requirements of banks on foreign loans and banking operations. Secondly, they raised taxation on the foreign portfolio investments of US banks. Moreover, they pursued a continued, although unsuccessful, attempt to curb the flow of private capital from the United States to the European financial centers by raising interest rates on long-term financial assets. Finally, they urged US corporations to repatriate capitals.[24] As suggested in the following pages, preventing the outflow of capital from the US proved to be largely unsuccessful to restore equilibrium in the US balance of payments on capital account as short-term financial assets were the bulk of capital outflows from Wall Street throughout the period. The full-blown development of dollar-denominated short-term financial instruments outside the United States amid the two energy crises of the 1970s were grounded in these early developments in international capital markets and in these unsuccessful US monetary policies to handle such developments. This long-term transformation of international capital markets accounted for the progressive crisis and the final collapse of Bretton Woods' trade and financial system both during the 1960s, and amid the dismantling of fixed exchange rates. Likewise, the development of short-term capital markets and the outflow of capital from the US is essential to research the meteoric ascendancy of the Organization of Petroleum Exporting Countries (OPEC) on the world financial stage between the first and second oil crises of the 1970s in the context of floating currencies. As most of the literature has convincingly argued, and the International Monetary Fund (IMF) concurred with at the time, the attaining of full convertibility among the currency areas of Bretton Woods stimulated a steady increase in the transnational flow of private capital and lays at the very origins in the development of short-term capital markets.[25] This process grew so much over the first half of the 1960s and not simply as a result of US government overseas military spending and foreign economic assistance, tackled in the following paragraphs of this chapter. Likewise, the steady increase in foreign lending of US banks and in foreign investments of US-based corporations is not a satisfactory argument to account for the meteoric expansion of capital flows from the US financial markets to the Western European markets. Rather—and more importantly—to trace the historical origins of mounting short-term Eurocurrency markets during the 1970s fueled by the deposits of the OPEC countries, such early development of short-term financial instruments should be linked to a sharp loss in US gold reserves. This chapter highlights the latter issue in the following pages. However, it is worth being aware of the importance of the tight monetary policy adopted by both the Department of the Treasury and the Board of Governors of the Federal Reserve System in connection with a deteriorating US balance of payments on capital account, which by the beginning of the 1960s outpaced the current account deficit.[26] This was a heated issue that created problems and prompted debates by the new heads of US foreign monetary and financial policy. Since their appointments, President Kennedy and the Secretary of the Treasury Douglas Dillon had worked on devising foreign monetary and economic policy measures capable of both stimulating domestic investment and economic activity, and restoring balance of payments equilibrium on both capital and current account. Before embarking on a study of the Kennedy administration years, it is worth focusing a little more on the period immediately preceding it, to better catch how consistently the US authorities pursued such a credit restraint policy. In this respect, unmistakably, the year 1960 was a turning point. By this time a stiff domestic recession and a downward spiraling balance of payments overlapped, while the decline in US gold reserves was well under way. Therefore, since the beginning of the new decade the American economy suffered from both a combined series of dollar-denominated capital outflows and a stunning deterioration in US gold reserves. Both developments were clearly on track. All these factors contributed to weaken the US dollar in foreign exchange markets. Within this framework, the growth of dollar selling and buying orders registered during the following decade undermined both monetary conditions of the international trade and payments system, and the competitive position of US and British economies, the two leading units of accounts for international trade and payments, on world trade markets. This process came about—more importantly from the research perspective of this book—well in advance of the events that set off the dismantling of the fixed exchange rate system of Bretton Woods since around 1967 through Nixon's decision to suspend the dollar's convertibility into gold. Therefore, it is worth drawing attention to the US monetary and credit policy when tracing the continuities and pitfalls that marked the way in which US foreign monetary and financial policymakers approached a range of the most heated economic issues as wide as the US payments imbalances, the weakening of the US dollar, and domestic economic doldrums. As noted at the beginning of this chapter, the second economic downturn of the 1950s broke out at the very end of the decade. From December 1959 to December 1960, seasonally adjusted US industrial production was in constant decline,[27] while during the same period the employment rate registered a similar slowdown.[28] On the other hand, seasonally adjusted GNP in constant dollars declined through the first quarter of 1961.[29] The share of US manufacturing in GNP, which had constantly increased from 1947 through 1957,[30] plummeted stubbornly. According to the cumulated net diffusion index elaborated by the National Bureau for Economic Research (NBER), from the third quarter of 1959 to the second quarter of 1961 seasonally adjusted profits of US manufacturing corporations were down to about 20 percent,[31] while nominal GNP underwent a slight adjustment of about 1 percent before surging again from the second quarter of 1961.[32] The literature in economics that has focused on the two decades explored in this book established a linkage between economic growth, the expansion in monetary bases and capital inflow.[33] Compared to this literature, during the recession the US monetary authorities refrained from expanding the stock of money. They avoided monetary expansion in three basic ways. Headed by Governor Martin, the Federal Reserve Board showed its tireless reluctance both to increase bank reserves, and to decrease the reserve requirements that must be held by private banks. At the same time, the Federal Reserve Board showed a merciless insistence in sustaining high interest rates in order to favor the purchasing of US Treasury Debt certificates. All these tightening measures suggest a long-term US monetarist approach to resurrect the business cycle. Therefore, by comparing this recession with that of 1957–58 it is possible to identify a body of continuities on monetary policies and arrangements worth grappling with. Regarding the unfinished tightening of US interest rates, as early as March 1960 the Joint Economic Committee of the US Congress called upon Chairman Martin to reintroduce ceilings on long-term government bonds, viewed as a much-needed measure to prevent a further upswing in interest rates. Besides, the Committee urged Martin to expand the supply of money by using open market operations to increase the reserves of private member banks.[34] Throughout the first part of that year the Federal Reserve Board was opposed to expanding money supply. At the same time, in consistence with a position it had previously held, the Department of the Treasury was against a reduction in the discount rate in order to carry out its cash financing activities and to issue long-term bonds. Moreover, the Department of the Treasury firmly resisted any action that the US public opinion repeatedly advocated during that year, which was to let the Federal Reserve Board cut the cost of long-term investments. In particular, the Treasury opposed any initiative from the Federal Reserve System to purchase long-term government bonds and to sell short-term assets as a way to cut real long-term interest rates; the Federal Reserve System promoted this policy with the aim of easing credit for productive investments.[35] The argument of the Treasury was that instead of easing money, capital movements from long-term assets to short-term instruments were likely to decrease the supply of capital for productive investments and to prolong the economic downturn. The reason for this continued credit restraint policy was not only its consistency with the approach of US monetary authorities to curb the US balance of payments deficit. Indeed, in order to formulate an historical interpretation about such credit tightening, it is worth looking more closely at the US international payments disequilibrium. By 1960 the US balance of payments deficit clearly turned from a current account deficit to a capital account deficit. It is noteworthy to pinpoint this shift to interpret the persistency of credit tightening. As a matter of fact, during the two recent recessions of the second half of the 1950s, although monetary stringency neither helped curb the outflow of capital nor did it forestall the deteriorating competitive position of US manufacturing and the plummeting trade balance, the Treasury and the Federal Reserve System did not relax their traditional credit restraint policy. The shift in the balance of payments deficit from current account to capital account disequilibria came about quite rapidly and straightforwardly. From as early as 1959, the trade account balance showed a positive record: the excess of exports of US goods and services over imports run at a rate of about $3 billion a year, while outpayments run at $7 billion a year. Out of total outpayments—significantly—while military expenditures abroad led the current account component, categories typically falling under the balance of payments on capital account, such as US government foreign financial operations and capital investments, amounted to about $2 billion a year. Much more importantly, as early as 1959 the outflow of US private capital from Wall Street was reported to amount up to $2 billion a year.[36] Only one year later, by the fall of 1960, US trade surplus "had risen to a figure of around $5 billion,"[37] while the balance of payments on capital account registered a staggering and constant downswing. During the third quarter of 1960 the combined outflows of gold and the increase in foreign-owned dollar balances averaged about $500 million a month, as compared with a monthly average of $280 million a month during the second quarter of that year. Later on, over the course of the decade this gloomy picture was aggravated by the attitude of US corporations, in the framework of US credit stringency and enhanced control on capital outflow, to borrow in foreign markets.[38] Basically, as regards the very beginning of the decade, it is noteworthy to associate such continued and exceptionally tight monetary stringency with the aim of lessening private capital outflows with two developments. First, it is worth stressing the growing imbalance between interest rates in New York and the cost of borrowing in most Western European financial centers, first and foremost in London. This trend, which contributed to the decade-long gold outflow from the United States during the 1960s, is essential to catch the weakening of the US dollar in foreign exchange markets. Furthermore, it is vital to understand why the Bretton Woods' international trade and payments system deteriorated way before the meltdown of fixed exchange rates that developed from 1967 through the end of currency convertibility in the 1970s. In fact, this trend was well on track by 1960: as charted in the next two paragraphs, it ran throughout the decade and set off the history of short-term transnational capital flows that finally boomed since the first oil crisis onward. To make sense of that trend in financial markets, in August of 1960 the 3-month US Treasury bill rate was at 2.4 percent, steadily lagging behind the UK Treasury bill rate of 5.5 percent.[39] Since as early as 1960 this striking gap among interest rates across the Atlantic savagely rocked the US payments position on the capital account in two ways. Firstly, while borrowing was cheaper in New York than in London, investment banks and private investors showed a propensity to leave Wall Street[40]: this flow of American investors to London dried up the supply of capital and jeopardized economic recovery and the business cycle. Secondly, European and other major international corporations issued an increasing amount of securities on Wall Street. Both trends took place in the framework of long-standing postwar developments; on the one side since the mid-1950s the staggering rates of growth experienced in Europe led most European-based manufacturing industry to meet the increase in consumers' demand for goods by raising funds on the US capital markets. By and large these borrowings took the form of securities issued in New York, where the supply of capital was enough and interest rates were cheap. By 1960 the slowdown of business profits in Europe, which had further plummeted during the first half of the 1960s, reduced the capability of European manufacturing firms to self-finance their productive investments; this process contributed substantially to the development of Wall Street's security market.[41] On the other hand, the interest rates differential between Western Europe and the United States stoked the outflow of dollar-denominated private financial assets from the United States as part of a postwar trend. From 1950 to 1958 the total holdings of dollar-denominated assets by foreign commercial banks, non-banking enterprises and individuals increased by $500 million a year. As widely recognized at the time by a variety of high-ranking central bankers and monetary experts at the IMF and other international economic institutions, the attainment of full currency convertibility stimulated large-scale capital movements.[42] In light of strikingly different monetary conditions in Europe and the United States, from that year to the end of 1964 foreign residents increased their total holdings of dollar-denominated short-term financial instruments and long-term assets by $700 million.[43] By 1960 this two-pronged process of capital outflow was already under way. By that year both the total value of US direct investments abroad and the total amount of long-term and short-term US investments abroad had increased a little less than 50 percent from their 1955 levels.[44] This process came about regardless of the unfinished monetary stringency aimed at lessening the outflow of private capital from the United States. As such it sheds light on the unsuccessfulness of the explicit commitment to monetary stringency by the Department of the Treasury and the Federal Reserve Board aimed at grappling with both a dwarfing US international payments position and a domestic economic downswing. At the same time it is plain that fixed but adjustable exchange rates typical of this period favored the channeling of transnational capital flows into a variety of national capital markets and stimulated the Eurocurrency markets as exchange rate risks were kept to a minimum. Over the course of September 1960 the cost of money for private borrowing registered an upward trend due to the absence of tight ceilings on interest rates. Consider, for instance, the rates on short-term bills: as a result of soaring demand for loans by US manufacturers and as a consequence of the issuing of securities by corporations, from the second quarter to the beginning of the third quarter of 1960, rates on 3-month bills rose to over 2.5/8 percent, and rates on 6-month bills rose to around 2.7/8 percent.[45] Meanwhile, the aggregate US government deposits at regional Reserve Banks and at commercial banks, and demand deposits at private banks, lagged.[46] Along the way, from late April to the end of August 1960 seasonally adjusted money supply underwent a slight contraction.[47] Over the course of the year, the Federal Reserve Board was continuously opposed to use open market operations to expand bank reserves and to ease money, while the US Gross National Product contracted slightly.[48] On the other hand, the upward movement in high interest rates on long-term government bonds neither forestalled nor slowed down the impending process of private capital outflows. Therefore, continued monetary tightening failed in both countering the economic slowdown underway in the real economy, and in reverting the plummeting US balance of payments deficit.

Within the framework of this combined sluggish domestic business cycle, decline in domestic supply of capital, and the twofold outflow of capital through growing foreign financial investments and the development of borrowings to foreign residents through the US securities markets, it was only from September to October 1960 that the US monetary authorities showed a moderate tendency to undertake a set of expansionary policies. Clearly, the objective of such an action was to prop up the US business cycle and to cope with the ongoing deterioration of US outpayments. By October, US money supply showed the first substantial increase for some time. At the same time, the Federal Reserve System went for expanding credit to let private banks finance new securities offered by the Treasury: in the aggregate, from the third to the fourth quarter of 1960 the US monetary authorities increased money supply by 2 percent.[49] Moreover, consistently with this path-breaking new policy, from August to October of that same year the Board of Governors of the Federal Reserve System decreased the discount rate from 3.5 percent to 3 percent at all regional Reserve Banks. This move was aimed at reducing the cost of borrowing and at lowering the differentials between the discount rates and the markets rates of interest. In consistence with a growing call to ease money and to create credit to counter the downward economic juncture, from August to November 1960 the Federal Reserve System bought and sold a significant amount of Government securities. As a result, the US monetary authority increased its holding of government securities by about $1 million to encourage bank credit. Finally, from late November to December of that year, the Board of Governors reduced reserve requirements against net demand deposits at central reserve city banks by 1 percent, thus allowing banks to release funds for borrowing purposes.[50] However, during this period, in order to avoid excessive capital outflow, the United States refrained from cutting the discount rate, thus continuing support for long-term interest rates, which throughout the fall season had held fairly steady. Time deposits at commercial banks increased at a rate of over 1 percent a month, registering a total growth of over 6 percent in 1960.[51] At the same time, some high-ranking US monetary policymakers made a strong case for easing credit and at the end of 1960 the Federal Reserve System expanded its open market operations.[52] Therefore, what the Department of the Treasury and the Board of Governors implemented was a slow turn to undertake expansionary measures based on open market operations and a reduction in the reserve requirements on commercial banks. They did not cut the interest rates on long-term investments; with respect to the discount rate, as previously stressed, the US authorities limited their intervention to reduce the discount rate at regional Reserve Banks to squeeze the differentials between the discount rates and the market interest rates. Priority was therefore given to let the Treasury issue and place its long-term securities in order to successfully carry out its cash financing operations: this priority prevailed over a much-needed general interest to make private borrowings cheaper and stimulate investments. This string of measures had slight effects on the creation of liquidity and the business cycle. Over the course of the last quarter of 1960, for example, seasonally adjusted total deposits for all US commercial banks slightly increased over the preceding two quarters of the year.[53] Therefore, the turn-of-the-year outlook for both domestic economic activity and the balance of payments showed signs of weakness. This weakness occurred even though the US authorities went for expanding the stock of money without undertaking either a substantial decrease in the cost of money for borrowing or any structural reduction in the discount rate. At year-end, while long-term interest rates continued to soar, the US economy was clearly downward sloping: the unemployment rate was rising, while plant and equipment expenditure by US manufacturing firms had declined. The monetary policy so far pursued proved to be unfit to stem the recession and to resurrect the US international payments position. At the same time, as some Western European central banks went for cutting short-term interest rates, the US monetary authorities had one more chance to lessen the cost of money through a reduction in the discount rate. For instance, before the end of 1960 the British bank rate was reduced from 5.5 percent to 5 percent. At this time, several high-ranking US central bankers called on the Federal Reserve System both to release liquidity and to cut the discount rate; the Federal Reserve Bank of New York was in the forefront of pursuing this policy. Notwithstanding this and the unsuccessful attempts to counter the US domestic economic slowdowns and the weakening international payments position of the country through a high interest rates policy, on the eve of John Kennedy's election to the White House the Board of Governors of the Federal Reserve System and the Department of the Treasury did not substantially turn away from this long-standing policy.

2.2 American Economic Slowdown and the Failure of Foreign Financial Policy Under the Kennedy Administration

Based on the developments charted in the first paragraph, it is plausible to say that upon their appointment President Kennedy and the Secretary of the Treasury Dillon had to muddle through a jarring two-pronged domestic economic slowdown and continued strains on the balance of payments that neither a moderate expansionary policy nor the slight easing of monetary conditions undertaken in the fall of 1960 ameliorated substantially. In the first quarter of 1961 the combined decline in manufacturing productivity, the plummeting value of the US dollar in the international exchange markets and unfettered capital outflows from the United States confirmed the vital interconnectedness among all of these factors pointed out at the beginning of this chapter. Such interrelation between declining productivity and worsening balance of payments stability persisted through the long-lasting policy of high-interest rates and the measures of monetary stringency taken in 1960. In the aggregate, the shrinking rate of growth of the US economy from the last quarter of 1960 to the first quarter of 1961 exhibited this palpable downward mode: according to the Secretary of the Treasury, after reaching a peak of $506.4 billion, the seasonally adjusted GNP fell to $504.5 billion in the fourth quarter of 1960, falling again to $500.8 billion by March 1961.[54] More specifically, by the first quarter of 1961, total US industrial production fell by over 5 percent to the July 1960 level, while industrial production of most capital-intensive durables and non-durable consumer goods declined less than the average. This pattern sheds light on the negative and multiple effects of scarce expansionary policies and continued credit tightening on the technological upgrade and industrial productivity of capital-intensive chains. The persistence of monetary stringency stifled capital-intensive investments and the competitive edge of US manufacturing in international markets, an essential condition to stabilize the international payments position of the United States. More importantly, such a pattern points to the impact of limited foreign exchange rate adjustments on the least value added and labor-intensive non-durable producing industries that depended the most on monetary interventions in foreign exchange markets. This economic conjuncture suggests an enduring linkage under the Bretton Woods international monetary system; under the Bretton Woods era exchange rate policy was a pillar in shaping and sustaining the competitive edge of low-capital-intensive firms in foreign markets. For instance, as a result of prolonged tight discount rates, after declining slightly during the winter 1959, from March 1960 to March 1961, quarterly rates on business loans by US banks in 19 American cities stabilized at just under 5 percent.[55] Likewise, the US dollar exchange rates against the currencies of most leading instrumental goods-producing industrial economies or raw material-supplying developing countries did not show any substantial alteration. Certainly, the need to stimulate affordable imports in order to restore the competitive position of the US economy was pressing and widespread in the United States. Notwithstanding, if one looks at the official US exchange rates against vital trading partners in merchandise and machinery such as the Federal Republic of Germany and France, or an irreplaceable supplier of ore and raw material as South Africa, it is clear that the United States did not adopt any substantial exchange rate adjustment.[56] On the other hand, during roughly the same time frame, total industrial production of fabricated metal products and machineries fell by 7 to 5 percent, while the manufacturing of non-durables highly dependent upon foreign exchange rate adjustments contracted by 11 to 8 percent. By February of 1961, manufacturers' planned expenditures for new plants and equipments for the year 1961 amounted to $34.6 billion, a decline of 3 percent from 1960.[57] This outlook better highlights the inefficacies of moderate expansionary policies and easy credit conditions set off prior to January 1961, when Kennedy came to power. If one considers the downward-sloping US balance of payments deficit of the first quarter of the new year,[58] it is easy to point to the continued linkage between domestic economic downswing, declining productivity in industry, and the unfettered worsening of the international payments position that plagued the country during the two recessions of the late 1950s. Furthermore, such continued strains account for a much-heralded need to phase out the long-standing approach to the international payments imbalance of the country, based on restoring equilibrium on the capital account by means of monetary tightening and high interest rates. Such an approach to the US balance of payments deficit revolved around a concept of monetary stringency as a means of rupturing the interconnectedness between domestic slowdown and the decline of the US dollar in international exchange markets. The inefficacy of this perspective explains why, throughout the decade, the Kennedy and Johnson administrations turned to combine interventions in foreign exchange markets to promote the inflow of private capital and to deter the outflow of it, with a continued commitment to improving the US balance of payments on current account. Although they caught the distinctive feature of US foreign monetary and financial policies over the 1960s and the two-pronged policy aimed at tackling the US balance of payments deficit both on the current and on the capital accounts, most outstanding scholarships in international political economy overestimated the straining impact of the trade balance on the US balance of payments equilibrium. They henceforth focused attention on the

Kennedy administration's foreign trade policies to restore equilibrium in the balance of trade.[59] Much the same can be said for the wave of scholarship that approached the US foreign economic policy through the research perspective of US foreign military assistance and Washington's stance within the North Atlantic Treaty Organization (NATO).[60] Likewise, the long-established scholarly literature on the postwar trade liberalization policies stressed the reportedly pivotal importance that Washington placed on foreign trade to restore the US balance of payments.[61] On the other hand, most works by financial economists and historical economists on the development of short-term Eurocurrency and Eurodollar markets underestimated the linkage between such development in the financial markets and the broader US foreign monetary and financial policy. Such studies did not draw attention to the interconnectedness between US foreign policy and capital market developments. Indeed, the approval and implementation during the 1960s in Washington of a number of financial controls such as the so called Regulation Q, the Interest Equalization Tax (IET), and the Voluntary Foreign Credit Restraint Program (VFCR) did affect the strength of the United States in the international economy and Washington's foreign policy toward its trading and financial partners. In the following chapters this issue is explored through a case study of Washington's relations with the largest economies among the Middle Eastern oil producing nations.[62] In order to investigate such a mixing up of measures to restore the balance of payments on both the current and the capital accounts painstakingly pursued in Washington, it is vital to focus attention on US expenditure abroad and US foreign trade policy, as well as the effects of overseas capital investments. This approach helps catch the unfinished and ever-growing imbalance in US international payments, and its striking impact on the competitive position of US industry. The declining competitive edge of American industry preceded both the worsening of the US trade deficit, and the ending of stable monetary arrangements, as well as the collapse of fixed capital costs with the outbreak of the first energy crisis.

The Kennedy administration was at the forefront of this twofold policy; in particular, compared to the foreign economic policies of the second half of the 1950s, the newly appointed administration made significant efforts to improve the current account position.

Since he briefed the US Congress about the pivotal importance of foreign trade to US foreign economic relations as early as February 1961, President Kennedy showed the inclination of his administration to begin focusing attention on the current account position to restore equilibrium in the US balance of payments. At the same time the new administration and the Federal Reserve System turned their attention to capital account transactions by taking a series of measures to counteract the jarring gold and dollar outflows. These measures included an increase in short-term interest rates and borrowing from the IMF quota or the US gold tranche, as well as a US commitment to force surplus Western European allies to finance the US balance of trade.[63] Yet again, at the initiative of the Federal Reserve Bank of New York, the United States resorted to foreign exchange transactions in European currencies and to any feasible measure to absorb the gold glut that characterized the gold markets in Western Europe during the first half of the 1960s.[64] This American commitment to dry up the gold bubble was aimed at averting any further decline in the value of the US dollar in foreign exchange markets. This was a matter of concern in Washington as any substantial shift in the currency reserves of Western European central banks from US dollar holdings to gold reserves was likely to reduce the value of the American currency in exchange markets. Before turning to analyze the initiatives of the US governments to restore the balance of payments on current account—indeed, a line of action consistently pursued amid the economic downturn and external imbalances of the 1970s—it is worth tackling, in as much detail as possible, each of these measures and the persistence of the US balance of payments deficit on capital account. This helps to better understand the context of the late 1960s. By that time, the US ran into a staggering federal budget deficit that surged all along the decade. Turning to federal spending, since as early as 1963 US federal spending ran at a $3 billion annual increase.[65] At the same time, the end of postwar growth deprived the US governments and the institutions of Bretton Woods of fiscal policies and income policies necessary to prop up domestic growth and international competitiveness. In this context, the grim issue of transnational capital movements with the corollary of unstoppable dollar and gold outflows that hit the American economy throughout the 1960s were removed. In fact, at the very end of the decade, US gold losses and capital flight represented two unbearably cumbersome issues on the way to recasting a dollar-standard system of international trade and payments. Tracking this early story is all the more remarkable as it helps keep an eye on the long-lasting commitment by the Federal Reserve Bank of New York to manage the heated issue of transnational capital flows and its impact on the US international payments position. Similarly, such focus sheds light on the US monetary authority's engagement to strike a balance between short- and long-term capital assets in connection with the stock of money and the supply of liquidity necessary to nurture the supply side of the production chain. This last commitment by the New York Fed is important to pinpoint some continuities in the US foreign monetary and financial policy from the 1960s to the 1970s. In fact, from the first to the second oil crises, the New York Fed brought the issue of connecting capital market developments to capital supply for fixed investments to center stage in US monetary policy. By re-examining the 1960s, it is possible to unfold a string of continuities in US foreign monetary policies from the 1960s to the 1970s, and to investigate the way in which the Department of State and that of the Treasury wrangled over the debate on the reform of the international monetary system that arose from the shattering weakening of the US dollar in foreign exchange markets.

Shortly after coming to power, President Kennedy and Treasury Secretary Dillon set in motion a twofold policy aimed at improving the balance of payments on capital account and easing the cost of money on long-term investments without officially altering the discount rate. In the pursuit of this second target the Federal Reserve engaged in buying long-term bonds and securities to reduce the cost of borrowing on long-term investments and to stimulate the inflow of cheap money from abroad to finance productive investments and the business cycle. At the same time, such policy was thought to raise profits on short-term certificates and bonds to deter the outflow of capitals. At the time the outflow of short-term capital was mostly critical. It is easy to chart the policy—which took place within the framework of high interest rates on long-term borrowings contributing to the shrinkage in the US payments position on the capital account—by simply poring over data on Washington's international payments position. The new US government discussed both policies at the highest economic policymaking level since the beginning of

1961, when the US balance of payments showed a dip decline. If one breaks down the data on the US balance of payments during the first quarter of 1961, the persistency of this troubling issue is straightforward. Even without considering short-term liquid liabilities to foreign central banks and foreign commercial banks, US foreign military aid and transfer financed by it, in the aggregate the US balance of international payments was just a little over zero.[66] A focused attention to the outflow of capital is useful to make sense out of its impact on the overall international payments position of the United States. Throughout 1960 and 1961, excluding liquid dollar holdings held by foreigners, recorded US private short-term capital outflows less foreign short-term credits to the United States showed a deficit running roughly at $1440 million.[67] Before Kennedy gave a widely publicized and much-heralded official speech on the status and prospect for the US balance of payments before the US Congress on February 6, 1961,[68] within the Department of the Treasury several high-ranking officials made a strong case for a radical change in the US monetary policy. Treasury officials aimed to recast domestic aggregate output and demand. In so doing they argued that neither the tempered expansions in the supply of money for productive investments carried out during the fall of 1960 through open market operations, nor had a raise in bank reserves as well as the ease of reserve requirements at commercial banks been successful in striking the balance between domestic aggregate output and demand. Shortly after President Kennedy appointed him to the chairmanship of the Council of Economic Advisers in December 1960, Walter Heller, a well-known Keynesian economist who served on both the Kennedy and Johnson administrations, stressed absolutely the inescapability of resorting to monetary policy to stem the recession and trigger a smooth recovery. Compared to the policies so far conducted, Heller's position represented a clear-cut step forward. In his view, it was essential to finance larger expenditures for new business plants and equipments, public works and residential construction. Accordingly, he called President Kennedy to address the Congress about the importance of carrying out a two-pronged foreign financial policy. According to Heller, the new administration should focus its attention on reducing long-term interest rates to favor industrial investments, and on keeping the rates on short-term financial instruments quite competitive to make up for the outflows of long-term capital assets that a decline in yields on long-term loans would trigger. Indeed, throughout the 1960s keeping competitive the US short-term interest rates would also be essential to counteract the attractiveness to US investors of peaking interest rates in Western Europe and to curb the massive capital outflow that plagued the US capital market from the early 1960s to the 1970s. According to Heller, in the pursuit of this policy the Department of the Treasury had to require "that the Federal Reserve buy genuine long-term securities offsetting the effects of injecting money on the short-term rate by selling short or even by raising the discount rate."[69] On the eve of Kennedy's State of the Union address to the Congress, Dillon confirmed that the Federal Reserve showed its resilience in extending its operations to the longer-term markets.[70] By poring over data on the Federal Reserve's operations during the six weeks following the White House decision early in the year to undertake such a turn, the Federal Reserve bought over $600 million of maturities of over one year.[71] Apparently, therefore, the US moved to cure the unfinished problems that afflicted the US international payments position and to bolster US domestic business activity by tossing aside high interest rates and by easing the tight monetary policy that had dominated the US approach throughout the economic crises of the 1950s. At first glance, this path-breaking new policy looked genuine and consistently pursued. Undoubtedly, this approach to the intertwining between balance of payments problems and support for domestic aggregate output and employment through the easing of credit for investments was intended to reach a number of targets. In easing monetary stringency and cutting interest rates, the US aimed at both financing the supply of capital and stimulating domestic output, and at contrasting the current dip in short-term investments,[72] as well as at reducing the dependence of US industry on foreign lenders. A few months later, during an economic upswing, James Tobin, a well-renowned economist and a member of the Council of Economic Advisers, warned Under Secretary of the Treasury Fowler against choking off domestic business investment "by restrictive monetary policy in the hope of stretching it out, for this slows down the growth of final demand." In his view, such restrictions would have led to the destruction of the incentives to expand and modernize capacity. What he strongly suggested to the administration was to keep final demand growing at the rate the economy's productive capacity was currently running. He made a case for pursuing this policy, neither through an inflationary expansion in currency in circulation nor by foreign exchange rate adjustments, the latter being a measure that he considered disruptive of US international payments position. By contrast, he made a plea for undertaking expansionary fiscal measures to finance the budget deficit and to prop up the business cycle.[73] However, notwithstanding that this approach was widely shared by many US economic policymakers who worked on crafting the foreign financial and domestic economic policy of Kennedy's administration, from the beginning of 1961 through the first half of the 1960s a most troublesome issue came to center stage in Washington: the two-pronged process of dollar and gold outflow began running at an unprecedented pace, while at the same time developments in the gold markets outside the United States registered a meteoric rise. This two-pronged process increasingly contributed to hit the US international payments position and to weaken the dollar in foreign exchange markets. This process of dollar and gold outflows added to the outstanding stiff problems that were afflicting the external equilibrium of the United States. This set of multiple factors hurting the US balance of payments induced the highest ranking US economic policymakers to combine measures to restore equilibrium on the capital account so far examined in this chapter, with a string of policies aimed at improving the balance of payments on current account.

In fact, by the end of 1962 the US balance of payments deficits run roughly at $2 billion.[74] The outflow of liquidity and dollar-denominated financial assets contributed to trigger the outflow of gold, which in turn further undermined the fixed dollar value of gold, the value of the dollar in foreign exchange markets and monetary stability. The stability of the US currency was necessary for the smooth development of international trade and payments based on fixed but adjustable exchange rates. Three factors were dominant in triggering such a chain of unstoppable outflows that lay at the origins of the long-term deterioration in both the Bretton Woods fixed exchange rates, and the competitive position of US manufacturing firms way before the two energy crises of the 1970s.[75] In the first instance, as soon as the 1958 currency convertibility came fully into effect, most exchange controls were lifted. Within the framework of Europe's postwar economic recovery, in late 1958 most European countries moved to let foreign holders of financial assets denominated in the legal tender freely convert them into dollars or other currencies. The aim was to stimulate trade in goods and merchandise in international markets.[76] This decision triggered a steady and meteoric expansion of dollar denominated financial assets held by foreign residents outside the United States. In less than three calendar years, from December 1958 to September 1961, the estimated gold reserves and dollar holdings of Western European countries not including the UK increased from roughly a little over $17 million to a little over $23 million.[77] One year later, official and private short-term dollar assets held by foreign residents with banks in the United States were about $19.6 billion.[78] Secondly, as detailed below, US foreign military spending and the federal government's overseas expenditures became a cumbersome load on the current account deficit: as the Department of State stressed US overseas military expenditures financed dollar holdings by foreigners. US diplomats stressed that over the first half of the decade these dollar holdings were increasingly spent on purchasing gold in the US gold markets. While discussing bilateral negotiations on US military assistance to Italy, Under Secretary of State for Economic Affairs George Ball himself reasoned on this line: he established a connection between the worsening US balance of payments deficit from 1959 to 1961, the jarring loss in US gold stocks, and continued US military spending overseas.[79] Making matters worse, as broached in this chapter, throughout the Kennedy presidency and over the following years a sharp increase in nominal interest rate differentials between Wall Street and the Western European financial centers widened; this gap led investors to leave the US and plunged the US stock market into a downturn.[80] This growing gap in interest rates between Wall Street and Western Europe can be associated with the slowdown in growth rates all across the leading European economies compared with the economic upswing of the late 1950s. In this respect a timely analysis produced by the IMF in the fall of 1964, when the market attractiveness of short-term European capital markets to American investors and financiers specializing in short-term instruments was already palpable, is quite plausible. According to the IMF Research Division, throughout the post-

World War II era and up until 1956, over 70 percent of total European business enterprises' investments were self-financed. This high volume of self-finance in the private business sector stemmed from both the low propensity to distribute profits to shareholders, and the high rate of profit accumulation typical of the postwar European recovery and take off. The German and French private business sectors led the way: by 1962, 70 percent of their new fixed capital investments were self-financed, while among the leading Western European economies only Italy's private firms self-financed short of 50 percent of their total new investments.[81] Thereafter, this trend strikingly reverted to past levels: the rate of growth of self-financing first decreased and then slowed down. Owing to the widely known squeeze on profits in most Western European countries since about 1962, internally generated funds for expansions declined noticeably. This decline in profits prompted several European industrialists to look for external sources for funding their industrial investments.[82] As regards the outflow of private capitals attracted by West European interest rates, as early as the first half of the 1960s both high ranking US economic policymakers and the leading financial institutions called into question the idea that the US balance of payments crisis stemmed from a falloff in the competitive position of US manufacturers. Rather, they pointed to the capital leaving Wall Street as the most important issue, along with overseas military expenditures, as the cause of the worsening of Washington's external imbalance. Lastly, they established a linkage between the US international payments imbalance, the loss of confidence in the dollar, and the decline in industrial productivity.[83] At the same time, in the UK the influential and long-established National Institute for Economic and Social Research argued that in light of a downward British balance of payments and a declining British share of world trade the only way to revert such trends was to restore industrial productivity.[84] It is plausible to expand upon this argument to suggest that the effects of long-term and short-term capital outflows, ever-growing US overseas expenditures, and the losses in US gold stocks, on which it is time to focus attention, hit hard the competitiveness of US manufactures in so far as they all contributed to deteriorate the value of the dollar in foreign exchange markets. This chapter has already called attention to the plummeting added value of low capital-intensive US industry that depended the most on foreign monetary arrangements. If one scrolls down data and statistics about the balance of trade for the United States since shortly after the 1960 recession, further evidence to this interpretative path can be easily caught. At year-end 1961, for instance, the US trade surplus was accomplished more through a decrease in import than through an increase in export.[85] Likewise, by the second half of 1962, by and large the US trade surplus revolved around the US export of high added value merchandise to other industrial nations, while the development of US export of low capital-intensive consumer goods and instrumental goods to the Least Developed Countries (LDCs) showed a downswing mode.[86]

This variety of ways in which dollar-denominated financial assets left the United States continued recurrently to finance the buying of gold by foreign holders of dollar-denominated private and public assets. This process accelerated the decline in US gold stocks. In turn, it put under pressure the interconvertibility between the US dollar and gold, and made the defense of the dollar in foreign exchange markets and the stability of the system of fixed exchange rates set up at Bretton Woods even more difficult. As political economist Jeffry Frieden, among others, pointed out,[87] in the early 1960s, owing to the increasing weakness of the US currency and the loss of confidence in it, several foreign holders of dollar assets moved to purchase gold in the US and on the international gold markets to secure their investments for the future. In turn, this move accounts for the increase in the reserves' gold portion of most Western European countries, and for the corresponding decline in the dollar portion they held. Based on the data this trend becomes clear: in the aggregate, between 1952 and 1961 the proportion of gold to world total reserves declined from 67 percent to 63 percent. However, for all countries but the United States this proportion increased from 41 percent to 49 percent.[88] During the same period, the gold segment of total US reserves in billions of US dollars decreased from 69 to 44; in particular, they suffered from a stiff decline during the fourth quarter of 1960, when US gold holdings declined by $920 million.[89] By contrast, from 1952 to 1962, in most continental European countries and the United Kingdom the percentage of gold reserves to total reserves increased from 62 percent to 65 percent. In particular, Germany, Italy and the Netherlands led the way, while France, Switzerland and Belgium lagged behind.[90] In the following years, this tendency contributed further to the worsening value of the US dollar in international exchange markets.[91] Other and more general developments that took place in international gold markets from the very late 1950s through the early 1960s added further strain to the teetering interconvertibility between the US currency and gold. As a matter of fact, from the late 1950s to the first half of the 1960s an array of events led to a steady expansion in gold assets in international markets. In the first instance, since the turn of the decade the Soviet Union began to sell gold in international markets to finance its balance of payments. In particular, Moscow sold gold to finance imports and to repay some of the medium-term credits it obtained from Western countries since 1959. In the aggregate, during 1959 and 1960 the Soviet Union's total new production of gold run roughly at $1140 million, while Soviet sales of newly mined gold amounted to $255 million and $120 million in 1959 and 1960 respectively.[92] To be specific, as early as April 1959 the Soviet Union sold $50–75 million in just a two-day period: a string of large gold selling operations followed again in March 1961, while in several Western European countries this policy was pushed forward during the summer of that same year, when Moscow sold $100 million to finance the import of thousands of tons of flour from West Germany, with whom it was in negotiation.[93] Further gold selling took place in the London gold market, at the time the most important financial center in determining the gold value of the US dollar, in October 1962.[94] The impact that these massive selling operations by Moscow and the steady expansion of the international gold market had on the interconvertibility between dollar and gold and the stability of trade and payments was a matter of stiff debate in Washington. This debate highlights the pivotal importance of gold—and its perception in Washington—to the worsening US international payments position. For instance, in its economic intelligence reports and in its internal discussions about specific issues in US foreign economic policy, the Central Intelligence Agency (CIA) stressed that, "by introducing new gold into the system, the USSR helps its operation."[95] Moreover, according to the Office of Research and Reports of the CIA, the large Soviet gold sales of October 1962 took place in anticipation of usual foreign exchange requirements, as Soviet gold sales were generally inversely proportional to Soviet export of commodities. The CIA explained the exceptional gold sales of October by pointing out the additional pressures on the Soviet balance of payments that stemmed from "the need to repay some of the medium-term credits which the Soviet Union had obtained from Western countries since 1959."[96] Reasoning along these lines, some observers argued that pricing up the value of gold and straining the gold value of the dollar, far from hitting the international payments position of the United States, was a viable way to reduce the effects of Washington's commitment to provide the LDCs with development assistance. To be specific, a revaluation of gold in world commodity markets would reduce US foreign economic assistance to gold producing LDCs and help sustain the US balance of payments. In the columns of *The Statist*, for instance, John Heron proposed an increase in the value of gold in support of the buying power in foreign markets of LDCs like India, which were reported to have large private gold hoardings. According to his plan, a substantial rise in the price of gold could induce private holders to bring out gold hoards and to sell it in the domestic and international gold markets; the proceeds of these profits would be reinvested in Indian or other LDCs governments' bonds or in industrial securities and equities to finance industrial development. This stance was consistent with the traditional US policy of taking care of and nurturing the rising demand for loans to finance domestic industrialization and infrastructural modernization in some Latin American countries. Since as early as 1959, US diplomats and Congressmen called attention to the linkage between US foreign economic assistance—either via loans or exports—credit stability, and the competitive buying power of Latin American countries in foreign markets.[97] In turn, this way of funding the industrial modernization of some LDCs would "go some way towards reducing the burden that their needs impose upon America's balance of payments."[98] Irrespective of the approach to the gold issue that it pursued, such a line of reasoning demonstrates that in the United States as early as the 1960s several high ranking officials paid much attention to the interconnectedness between restoring the US international payments position and resurrecting the buying powers of the LDCs in foreign markets. The latter point was—as already pointed out in this reconstruction—a long-standing pillar of US foreign financial and monetary policies throughout the 1960s and the 1970s. As Chap. 4 highlights, during the decade of the 1970s restoring the buying power and the international payments position of the non-oil producing LDCs was a decisive factor in the decision taken by the US governments and American foreign financial policy policymakers to intensify diplomatic relations with some OPEC member countries and to draw on their booming financial wealth in order to resurrect the international trade and payments system. Therefore, in the framework of the economic slowdowns of the time, during both decades the United States strove to combine a much-heralded commitment to restore the US balance of payments and continued support for the buying power and terms of trade of the non-oil supplying LDCs. The US placed importance on the non-oil LDCs and provided them with their support as considered those countries a vital component of the international trade and payments system.

However, in contrast to this keenness to adjust the value of gold and to make the convertibility between dollar and gold adjustable, a variety of institutions and policymakers in Washington looked with great concern on the steep increase in the value of gold and the unfettered expansion of dollar-denominated instruments in total financial assets held by private and public holders in international markets, viewing this as harmful to the interconvertibility between the US dollar and gold. For instance, in pinpointing the process that led foreign central banks to increase their total gold reserves, the IMF research department warned against the effects of this process on total international reserves. When US residents pay dollars to a non-official foreign holder like a foreign private bank, a firm or an individual, these foreigners can either keep these dollars or transfer them to their central bank. In this latter case, international reserves are being created since those dollars are added to total world reserves. According to the IMF, "If these dollars are subsequently used to buy gold from the United States, the additional international liquidity is destroyed."[99] On its part, the CIA itself drew attention to the impact of large gold buying on European purchases of US consumer goods, merchandise and services; to put it another way, gold buying would reduce international liquidity and lessen European imports from the US consumer goods producing market.[100] Therefore, the US intelligence established a correlation between the increase in the value of gold and the decline in US export to the Western European markets. Certainly, the Kennedy administration showed a palpable concern about the impact of an ever-expanding international gold market on international trade and payments all the time it was in office. For instance, in the summer of

1962 the US Embassy in Switzerland pointed to the massive inflow of dollar assets in excess of the needs of the Swiss to finance the growing balance of payments deficit; according to some American diplomats in Zurich, the gold "outflow surely trigger loss of public confidence in dollars."[101] In its effort to list a string of arrangements to choke off the US balance of payments crisis, in early 1963 the US Long Range International Payments Committee made a case for covering the deficit during the two-year period 1963–64 by selling gold. However, it relentlessly stressed that, "the avoidance of an increasing rate of gold loss is vitally important to continued confidence in the dollar." Therefore, before this backdrop the Committee recklessly called on the administration to sell gold in order to finance the balance of payments, but sales should not increase US gold losses over $2 billion during 1963–64.[102] Certainly, the combined increasing tendency of foreign holders of dollars to buy gold instead of merchandise in the US markets already mentioned, and these US gold sales brought the interconvertibility between dollar and gold and the whole architecture of international exchanges in goods and capital under pressure. All along the first half of the decade this pattern accelerated in terms of both developments in the international gold market, and the portion of international liquidity denominated in US dollars. In fact, on the one side, by the early 1960s South Africa had led the way in increasing world gold production; by 1962 that country produced 70 percent of all gold produced in the free world. According to the IMF the increase in world gold mining certainly contributed to the expansion in monetary gold stock by $400 million. It is plausible to consider this process a decisive factor in accounting for the decline in the value of the dollar in international exchange markets.[103] Not least harmful to the system of international exchange in goods and capital of Bretton Woods, was the 1962 surge thereafter in interest rates all across the Western European financial centers, which pushed forward the outflow of short-term capital from the United States. This caused the expansion of Eurodollar and Eurocurrency markets throughout the second half of the 1960s. It is worth drawing attention to the linkage between the slowdown in the rate of domestic economic growth of most Western European economies by the early 1960s, and the high interest rate policy of European central banks. As early as March 1961 the Federal Republic of Germany and the Netherlands, soon followed by the Swiss monetary authorities, raised by official decree the value of their currencies by 5 percent.[104] As a result of this monetary policy by European central banks, by April 1963 nominal interest rates and industrial bond issues were almost 2 percent cheaper in the United States than in the United Kingdom, the Federal Republic of Germany and Belgium, and circa 1.5 percent cheaper than in Italy and France.[105]

Within this framework, monetary interventions aimed at counteracting the balance of payments deficit and expanding the stock of money required to resurrect domestic output and employment without expanding money supply exhibited their ineffectiveness. It is important to situate before this backdrop a string of systematic initiatives brought about during the presidency of John F. Kennedy and pushed forward under Johnson to pair the unfinished matter of redressing the balance of payments on capital account with a straightforward turn to monitor the trade balance and to restore equilibrium on current account. To put it another way, since the early 1960s, the strains on the US international payments position, and on the value of, and confidence in, the dollar in foreign exchange markets, as well as the increasing instability of international payments at large stemmed from a variety of causes. Such a string of factors induced the US authorities and the IMF to undertake a twofold approach that combined continued action on the US balance of payments on capital account and a tireless commitment to restore equilibrium on current account.

2.3 Foreign Military Policy, Exchange Market Operations, and US Commitment to Restore International Stability

The previous section pointed to the efforts by the Kennedy and Johnson administrations to combine measures to restore the balance of payments on current account and continued attention to stem private capital outflows and the development of short-term Eurocurrency markets. The Kennedy administration focused its attention on the current account, while the Johnson administration reconsidered the importance of curbing capital outflows. In so doing, Johnson spotlighted the strikingly contrasting approach of different American financial and diplomatic authorities to private financial markets from the 1960s to the 1970s. Contrasted with the 1970s, investigated in Chap. 4, the US administrations of the 1960s, and in particular the Johnson administration, considered the outflow of capital a threat to the US balance of payments and a hindrance to the American scramble for stabilizing the US currency and Washington's foreign economic relations. During his tenure in office Johnson curbed the outflow of capital, while after the first oil crisis of the 1970s the US monetary authorities entailed a positive correlation between the growth of dollar-denominated assets in world capital markets and the struggle to stabilize Washington's international payments position. As a matter of fact, during the 1970s the US authorities worked hard to reshuffle short-term capital markets and to make a shift in the international investment policies of oil producers and US banks charged with recycling their oil revenues in the most serviceable way to restore the US balance of payments. This is subject of specific investigation in Chap. 4.

As stated earlier, the Federal Reserve System strove to resurrect the dollar and the US international payments position by buying long-term financial instruments and by selling short-term assets in order at the same time to stimulate domestic output and to contrast short-term capital outflows. Among other measures promoted by the US monetary authority to strengthen the competitiveness of the American banking system it is noteworthy to recall "the repeal of the ceiling now imposed on the interest rate commercial banks may pay on time and saving deposits, to enable American banks to compete for funds"[106] As can be seen, notwithstanding these efforts by the US monetary authorities, continued gold outflows, the growing imbalance between gold and dollar in international markets, and the increase in the gold portion of reserves held by Western European nations, ravaged further the interconvertibility between gold and dollar and the US balance of payments deficit. After a mild and short-lived improvement in the value of the US dollar in foreign exchange markets,[107] traceable to an early activism by the newly elected Kennedy administration, by the late summer of 1962 the external equilibrium of the United States and the gold value of the dollar were once again on the ropes. During the first 3 months of 1962 the US balance of payments deficit run at a seasonally adjusted annual rate of nearly $2000 million (see Table 2.1).

Table 2.1 US balance of payments in US dollars/millions

Year	Balance on goods and services	Government grants and capital, net	Direct investments	Long-term portfolio
1955	2009	−2211	−823	−241
1956	3967	−2362	−1951	−603
1957	5729	−2574	−2442	−859
1958	2206	−2587	−1181	−1444
1959	134	−1986	−1372	−926
1960	3825	−2769	−1694	−850
1961	5143	−2777	−1475	−1006
1961–1st trimester	6484	−3316	−1828	−480
1961–2nd trimester	5272	188	−1076	−872
1961–3rd trimester	3856	−4052	−1716	−776
1961–4th trimester	4960	−3928	−1280	−1896
1962–1st trimester	4760	−3588	−920	−1588
1962–2nd trimester	5748	−3356	−1600	−1136
1962–3rd trimester	4148	−2008	−1200	−548

Year	Short-term portfolio	Foreign capital	Unrecorded transactions	Total
1955	−191	394	503	−1145
1956	−517	653	543	−935
1957	−276	487	1157	520
1958	−311	22	488	−3529
1959	−77	863	412	−3743
1960	−1338	335	−592	−3925
1961	−1472	606	−602	−2461
1961–1st trimester	−1928	792	−116	−1276
1961–2nd trimester	−1516	1096	−1464	704
1961–3rd trimester	−888	28	772	−3640
1961–4th trimester	−1516	508	−1600	−5632
1962–1st trimester	−1280	1160	424	−1968
1962–2nd trimester	404	464	−536	−904
1962–3rd trimester	−692	284	−1976	−2876

Source: Council of Economic Advisers. 1962. *Economic Indicators December 1962, Prepared for the Joint Economic Committee of the Council of Economic Advisers*. Washington, DC: GPO

At the time in Washington it was a widely shared view that from 1961 through the first half of 1962, a period during which the balance of payments bettered, debt prepayments to Washington by Western allies had contributed to such improvements substantially.[108] As was observed during a late August meeting of the Federal Open Market Committee, had the United States not received during July advance prepayments on outstanding debts from France and Italy for a total of up to $470 million, the balance of payments would have suffered from almost half a billion-dollar deficit.[109] Notwithstanding a slight improvement in the US international payments position during 1961, since this year the Kennedy administration called on its European partners to obtain advance prepayments on outstanding debts or loans. Not only did the worsening in the balance of payments lead the new administration to make a plea to its Western European allies to obtain such prepayments as a way to reduce disequilibrium on the capital account, but during the late 1950s economic slowdowns the Eisenhower administration and the US Congress, warned their Western European trading partners against buying gold in the United States and converting their outstanding dollar surpluses into gold.[110] In addition to such warnings, they made a case for a high interest rate policy to attract foreign lending and financial investors. In striking contrast to this course of action, the Kennedy administration deemed it necessary to devise ways other than raising interest rates to counter the balance of payments deficit on capital account. As stressed in this work with respect to the second half of the 1950s, the combining of monetary stringency and high nominal interest rates restored confidence in the dollar and resurrected the US payments position just slightly. At the same time this twofold policy depressed borrowing for fixed-capital investments, increased production costs, plunged the US domestic economy into meltdown and triggered a falloff in aggregate demand. To put it another way, monetary tightening revamped the US external balance but proved to be totally incompatible with sustained levels of domestic growth and hit the competitive edge of US manufacturing. In its search for alternatives to pair the stabilization of the US capital account position with the careful preservation of sustained and smoothly growing aggregate demand, the Kennedy administration proved to be knowledgeable about the recent ill-functioning of these measures of monetary policy. It is worth pointing to the effects of monetary and banking policy on the business cycle. In its report to President Kennedy of April 1963, the Long Range International Payments Committee suggested a variety of ways to curb the balance of payments deficit. Among other measures, it stressed the importance of freezing short-term US interest rates to restrain the outflow of funds without slowing down the US business cycle: "limiting as far as practicable the primary impact of reduced credit ease to short-term rates would minimize the adverse impact on the domestic economy. While additional balance of payments gains from higher long-term rates might be possible, they would be more costly for the domestic economy."[111] Quite tellingly, in discussing measures to counter the seemingly intractable and long-lasting US international payments imbalance, in 1963 the Secretary of the Treasury Dillon opposed President Kennedy's idea of raising the interest rates on long-term loans to stem capital outflows and to quickly recover the balance of payments. Throughout 1962 commercial and industrial loans leveled off and lagged behind the rate of increase in total US loans and investments[112]: this trend heralded the importance of easing long-term interest rates. Within this framework, during the fall of 1962 President Kennedy and the Chairman of the Board of Governors of the Federal Reserve System Martin wrangled over the possibility of cutting further the cost of money; on that occasion the White House looked with great concern on the outflow of investments and its adverse effects on the US balance of payments. Such concern prompted Kennedy to sponsor a rise in long-term interest rates,[113] while most policymakers viewed this measure as a threat to domestic growth. Much the same can be said for the hypothesis that appeared during the summer of 1962 of undertaking a systematic tax cut. It was not carried over because—among other reasons—it would have entailed a marked rise in long-term interest rates to compensate for the effects of tax cuts on the liquidity required to finance the US federal deficit.[114] Furthermore, soon thereafter Dillon firmly maintained that any rise in long-term interest rates, viewed by Kennedy as a way of attracting foreign financial investors and intermediaries to improve the US balance of payments on capital account, was likely to hamper growth and to hit hard the competitive position of US manufacturing firms. He was of the opinion that higher interest rates could eventually lessen aggregate demand and rise unemployment. In contrast to any idea of raising the cost of money for long-term lending, according to Dillon the only way to curb the balance of payments deficit and to decrease the budget deficit was the implementation of stimulus policies and a substantial expansion in aggregate demand.[115] Therefore, the search for a means of striking the balance between international payments stability and domestic economic growth paved the way for diverging views within the Kennedy administration: these diverging approaches led some of its highest ranking officials to split over it. Dillon's perspective is an important point as under the Carter administration, explored in Chap. 5, the very pillar of US economic policy measures to combine external balance and domestic growth levels would be a relentless pursuit by the new administration of demand side stimulus policies.

Certainly, at the time Dillon made a case for a turn in this direction, in Washington it was a widely accepted view to consider borrowing from capital-surplus European partners, and receiving early repayments on outstanding loans a suitable means of financing imports and outpayments. On the other hand, many US policymakers maintained that over the 1950s most Western European countries moved from deficit to surplus. According to them, such improvement in their balance of payments should prompt the US government to call on European partners to remove trade restrictions and to provide full support for the US buying power in foreign markets.[116] In addition to such an approach, based on payments and trade policies, the Kennedy administration placed importance on the monetary aspects that jeopardized the stability of US balance of payments and the dollar. In this framework, since the first half of 1961 the Kennedy administration offered its full support for a rise in the financial resources of major currencies other than the dollar and British pound available to the IMF. In making a case for raising the IMF quota of some Western European members of the Fund, Washington aimed at setting the conditions to meet the requests for drawing by the United States.[117] Clearly, such policy was thought to lessen the pressure that balance of payments deficit financing measures put on the two leading currencies of the international economic system. Washington could successfully conclude new arrangements to finance its drawing on the Fund in currencies other than the dollar and the pound in early 1962.[118] Meaningfully, at the time the US straddled to make other Fund's members use the IMF Special Drawing Rights in the pursuit of the same target; the US Executive Director in the Fund pressed for the use by other countries of convertible currencies other than the dollar or the British pound to avoid an increase in foreign dollar holdings caused by excessive drawings from the Fund.[119] Therefore, the share of dollar assets in world total supply, which would have been the subject of US debates and policies in the framework of the skyrocketing increase in dollar-denominated assets amid the two oil crises of the 1970s, was on the top of Washington's foreign financial policy already at this early stage. Along this line of action, the US government opted for resorting to the right that each IMF member country retained of converting a percentage of its quota into convertible foreign currencies. Clearly, this variety of measures was aimed at reducing the volume of financial transactions and exchanges in goods and commodities traded in the US dollar or British pound. Irrespective of these initiatives, certainly one of the most important measures adopted by the US was a firm call on the capital surplus of Western European countries to commit to early repayments of outstanding loans. This American pressure put on the European partners drove the US effort to increase Washington's holdings of convertible foreign currencies. As stressed in this chapter, this policy contributed to restore balance of payments equilibrium in 1962. Besides, as Secretary of the Treasury Dillon pointed out, as far as the accumulation of balance of payments surpluses by Western European allies increased dollar reserves in these countries, it created a potential gold demand on the United States.[120] In Washington it was a widely accepted view that any time the Japanese or the Europeans purchased gold from the United States, the gold reserves held by foreign central banks increased. As a result of such increase in gold reserves those foreign central banks reduced the dollar portion in their monetary reserves with negative impact on the value of the US dollar in exchange markets. Therefore, from 1962 to 1963 the US worked on concluding arrangements for early repayments with these European countries. These repayments were useful both to finance Washington's holding of foreign currencies required to finance foreign exchange transactions and foreign trade, and to reduce foreign run on US gold reserves in order to preserve the stability of the US currency in foreign exchange markets. From 1962 to 1963, in the aggregate the special foreign transactions of the federal government increased by roughly fivefold; they included early repayments from European trading partners, advances on military sales and the Treasury sales of medium-term, and nonmarketable securities.[121] In this respect, the US authorities focused attention on the Federal Republic of Germany and Italy, as on records Rome and Bonn were performing incomparably much better than any other Western partners in terms of balance of payments surplus. A number of agreements in the field were reached with these two partners with the aim of upholding the US capital account position. By the end of fiscal year 1963 early repayments on obligations owed to Washington by the Federal Republic and Italy totaled $389 million.[122] In addition to agreements on advance repayments of outstanding German obligations,[123] a series of German payments for use of cooperative logistics and payments for increased procurement of US equipment and services in the framework of the Atlantic Alliance's procurement policies were reached by the first quarter of 1962 and continued through the end of 1963.[124] The policy toward a strong reserve country such as Italy was much the same. As early as spring of 1962 the Department of State wished for an increase in US earnings from export to Italy, and from Italian tourism in the United States, suggesting diplomatic action to make Italy eliminate all remaining quota restrictions as well as any discrimination against American products; according to US diplomats the principle of liberal trade policies should be restored.[125] Later on that same year, the two countries reached agreements on a package of Italian purchases of US military hardware worth $100 million in orders to considerably offset the impact on the US balance of payments of the costs for NATO support in Italy.[126] Notwithstanding this string of traditional measures to better the US balance of payments, the bulk of Washington's policy toward Rome revolved around the early repayment of outstanding loans. The Department of State pointed to the importance of seeking "the prepayment of the indebtedness of Italian governmental and semi-governmental bodies to United States governmental agencies."[127] Prior to this move, Washington had resorted to Italy, Switzerland and some other surplus countries by borrowing from them as a means of financing its foreign exchange operations. Until as late as spring of 1961, in fact, Washington did not hold reserves of convertible foreign currencies and the balance of payments was in deficit.[128] It was only since March 1961 that the United States entered into foreign exchange transactions for monetary purposes. Following this pattern, the Federal Reserve Bank of New York was charged with this duty.[129] Therefore, if one tosses aside for a while the general objective of restoring equilibrium on the capital account, the very target of the American policy to have the European allies make advance repayments of outstanding debts and loans, as well as that of making them purchase American hardware or merchandise, was to finance the amount of convertible foreign currency reserves held in the United States. This was a condition essential to reduce the dollar portion of reserves held by foreign central banks, private financiers and banking intermediaries—a "must-do" turn to resurrect the dollar against all of the other leading currencies and gold. Therefore, the very objective that underpinned the Fed in having the repayments of outstanding loans and debts was sustaining the value of the dollar and letting down the exchange rate of overvalued currencies. It is worth saying in passing that this search for arrangements to finance the US balance of payments through early repayments of outstanding debts and loans by the Western European capital-surplus partners, and an increase in their purchases of military hardware, was consistently pursued throughout the decade and combined with foreign exchange rate adjustments. However, such policy focused on recasting the value of the US dollar did not connect the stabilization of foreign exchange rate to the bolstering of the internal economy and growth levels. In other words, at this early stage the US policies to strengthen the dollar were not viewed as a prerequisite to bolster domestic aggregate demand. In fact, Washington stimulated the export of military items and urged the repayments of debts to increase its holding of foreign exchange reserves, viewed as an essential step both to absorb dollars held at foreign central banks or financial institutions, and to stem a much-needed decline in the value of foreign currencies. This in order to stabilize the international exchange system established in 1944. These measures contributed to running counter to the outflow of gold from the US gold stock and to forestall the prolonged weakening of the US currency in foreign exchange markets. In turn, as the Department of State pointed out as early as 1962, resurrecting the value of the dollar was a prerequisite to deter unwarranted speculations and unwanted capital outflows.[130] Consistent with this policy of the early 1960s and within the framework of the seemingly intractable US balance of payments deficit that ravaged the US economy during the second half of the decade, in the late 1960s the Johnson administration reached agreements with the government of Rome and other capital-surplus countries to have advance repayments of some outstanding debts owed to Washington by the Italian government.[131] If one compares the cases of West Germany or Italy to France, it is worth stressing that bilateral monetary relations between Washington and Paris made an exception. In contrast with this policy of transatlantic cooperation on monetary and financial matters, since the early 1960s through 1968 France engaged in purchasing gold in the United States: this French attitude placed bilateral relations between Washington and Paris under the severest strain.[132] In the wave of the shaking gold crisis of the second half of the decade, the Office of Economic Research of the CIA charged De Gaulle with continually opposing the role of the dollar in international finance. According to the US economic intelligence, the French "called for an increase in the official price of gold and the use of gold as the only international reserve. Over recent years—did the CIA stress shortly after the 1967 devaluation of the British pound—the French have converted nearly all their official reserves from dollars into gold."[133] However, with the exception of the French case, as anticipated this American move in economic diplomacy to pressurize Washington's allies into early repayments was quite successful, as figures on German and Italian repayments suggest. At the end of 1967 the Department of State acknowledged unconditioned Italian activism "in standing firm with us to contain disorder in foreign exchange and gold markets following devaluation."[134] The balance of payments surplus Western European countries provided their support even as the United States engaged in large-scale foreign exchange operations conducted by the Federal Reserve and reshaped its foreign military assistance policy. It is now important to catch the way in which a policy to resurrect the balance of payments focused on the current account position as foreign military spending cuts and increase in foreign military sales, contributed to finance foreign exchange operations and to preserve the interconvertibility between dollar and gold. The rest of this section is devoted to shedding light on the demise of this policy within the framework of the budget deficit in the latter part of the decade. By that time, the US resorted to a more traditional action on the capital account to restore confidence in the dollar by way of curbing foreign portfolio investments and banking loans.

In fact, as early as 1961 the United States engaged in foreign exchange transactions for monetary purposes in forward and spot exchange markets to increase foreign exchange reserves. As anticipated, prior to March 1961 the United States did not hold any substantial amount of convertible foreign currencies[135]: from 1961 to 1962 most US foreign exchange operations were in Deutsche Marks (DM) and Swiss francs, while soon thereafter the Italian lira was involved in financing US foreign exchange transactions.[136] According to official estimates, forward exchange transactions were considerably larger than spot market operations: by the middle of 1961 forward transactions in DM and Swiss francs amounted to more than DM 1 billion and $150 million respectively.[137] The repayments of outstanding debts contributed to it manifestly: according to press reports, in 1961 the Department of the Treasury obtained about $160 million of Deutsche Marks from Germany as a result of the repayment of the German debt. On the other hand, in 1962 the repayment by Italy of some loans let Washington obtain up to the Italian lira equivalent of $75 million useful to carry out foreign exchange operations.[138] In addition, the Department of the Treasury borrowed the Swiss franc equivalent of $46 million from the Swiss government. Secretary of the Treasury Dillon himself called attention to this line of action: in his view it was a milestone essential to shape a US foreign financial policy aimed at protecting agreed upon exchange rates and the parity of the dollar against gold at $35 per ounce, considered a vital landmark to restore confidence in the dollar and to curb speculative runs on the US currency.[139] Therefore, quite straightforwardly, advance payments of outstanding debts and loans owed to Washington by the surplus countries were a way to acquire foreign currencies without buying them. This helps understand the role of debt repayments in propping up the US balance of payments and in drying up the volume of dollars in the world money supply. The latter measure was a pillar in the shaping of Washington's oil revenues recycling during the 1970s, as will be pinpointed in Chaps. 4 and 5. Under the guidance of Governor Martin, the Federal Reserve System conducted this new policy of foreign currency dealing in support for the value of the dollar in international exchange markets. Such acquisition of convertible foreign currencies created the finance for the purchasing of dollars through foreign exchange operations conducted by the Federal Reserve Bank of New York according to the aforementioned exchange rate adjustment mechanism. This initiative, aimed at increasing the assets on the balance of payments on the capital account, was soon paired with measures intended to lessen US liabilities to foreign financial institutions, as well as to reduce bonds and securities held by private holders. The passing of the so called Interest Equalization Tax, enacted in 1963, was aimed at deterring capital outflows through a tax on acquisition by Americans from foreigners of foreign debt and equity securities, both new and outstanding, maturing in three years or more.[140] This policy was consistently carried over under the new Johnson administration. From the time he took office, the new president made use of an amendment to the Tax Equalization Act to apply it to bank loans of one year or more. At the same time he called the US Congress to extend it for two years beyond the end of 1965, and to broaden its coverage to non-bank credit of one- to three-year maturity.[141] As Dillon himself pointed out, such measures to resurrect the balance of payments on capital account, combined with military exports and a reduction in overseas public expenditures, all concurred to lessen the US deficit. From fiscal year 1963 to fiscal year 1964 the US federal deficit declined from a rough figure of $2.8 billion to $800 million.[142] In the aggregate, since Johnson took office the outlook was for a slow but uninterrupted improvement in the US external balance: by the end of fiscal year 1964 the outflow of dollars abroad still exceeded dollar credit to the US from foreigners by $3 billion. Indeed, this was a "steady improvement over the $3.6 billion deficit in 1962 and the $3.3 billion deficit in 1963."[143]

Before this overall outlook for the US balance of payments, along with measures to finance foreign exchange operations for monetary purposes sketched in these pages, since 1962 the debate within the US administration and between Washington and its Western European partners, most notably the Federal Republic of Germany, on raising their financial contributions to the burden-sharing of NATO's military buildup and making them purchase supplies in the United States, was well underway. As a matter of fact, in addition to pressures on the government of Rome, Washington took on a hard diplomatic stance toward Bonn.[144] The most prominent literature on the subject has established a linkage between arrangements on NATO burden-sharing and the purpose of financing the US balance of payments deficit. This literature has stressed how cumbersome the issue of US overseas military spending and its financial contribution to the Atlantic Alliance was to the US balance of payments deficit throughout the 1960s.[145] It is worth pinpointing the interconnectedness between this American stance in foreign military policy and Washington's decision to implement measures to reduce the deficit on the current account to finance foreign market operations. Such a set of multiple initiatives focused on improving the balance of payments on current account can be considered as a complement to the policy aimed at restoring equilibrium on the capital account examined so far. Likewise, Washington engaged in a series of bilateral negotiations with most Western European allies to make them purchase equipment and hardware to help offset its balance of payments deficit. Bonn and Rome were not the only ones involved in this strand of economic diplomacy and trade bonds. Indeed, Washington also entered into negotiations to reach agreement with the French on purchases of US arms; quite tellingly these purchases were also aimed at deterring the development of French nuclear capability.[146] Furthermore, the US placed this policy toward the allies within the framework of a policy shift in Washington's foreign trade: such policy shift was intended at cutting US foreign military spending and increasing military sales overseas. Furthermore, the US straddled to increase civilian exports on foreign markets; this had implications on the US approach to the development of the military industrial complex in some member countries of NATO. Therefore, in the pursuit of restoring equilibrium on the capital account, such combined action to induce Washington's allies to early repayments of outstanding debts and loans, and measures to improve the terms of trade in the military field, was the way in which the US administrations strove to combine measures focused on the current account and actions on the capital account since the presidency of Kennedy thereafter. This twofold policy also helps catch the complex and challenging fashion in which these two lines of action intertwined each other to resurrect the system of international payments and trade erected at the conference of Bretton Woods under US leadership and pegged to a dollar standard monetary order.

As early as late 1961, according to the US authorities the combined overlapping between dollar and gold outflows, and the unsuccessfulness of monetary adjustments to stem capital outflows through measures in support of long-term investments and to stabilize short-term domestic US capital markets, made the long-lasting balance of payments deficit a seemingly intractable issue. They blamed on this variety of overlapping problems the US incapability of restoring balance of payments equilibrium and to withhold its leading international monetary position. Besides, according to US elites this jungle of multiple issues prevented the United States from stabilizing international trade in commodities and consumer goods, as well as payments. Clearly, the US monetary and federal authorities viewed these multiple issues as a hindrance to both the US external equilibrium and the international system of exchanges in capital and goods that revolved around it. Since 1961 the newly appointed Kennedy administration came under pressure to engage in a large program of trade liberalizations. The objective of these pressures was to increase the volume of US foreign sales and purchases of goods and merchandise as a means of financing US imports and dollar earnings; in this perspective, the United States should increase its sales and export to countries holding large amounts of dollars.[147] This approach, to a certain degree opposed by some US manufacturers, particularly firms based in former agricultural states such as Indiana,[148] reveals the interconnectedness between foreign trade and foreign exchange operations. The advocates of trade liberalization, the most outspoken of whom was probably Under Secretary of State for Economic Affairs George Ball, went for reducing trade barriers and rising US foreign purchases and sales. This in order to stimulate dollar-holding European trading partners to import American products and to finance the US dollar deficit.[149] The objective of the high-ranking US economic policymakers and diplomats was to trigger an increase in US dollar earnings or convertible foreign currencies, as well as to prevent the European Common Market from turning out to be a discriminatory trade area harmful to US exporters. More importantly, the aim was to provide support to the exporters of Latin American agricultural products and merchandise. This two-pronged policy based on continued attention to trade policy and concern for the future of non-oil producing LDCs, their terms of trade and buying power, marked the US foreign financial policy from the early 1960s to the malaise of the 1970s. Chapters 3 and 4 explore the importance that US foreign economic policymakers placed on making dollar-rich OPEC countries, the American banking system through which the oil producing countries invested the largest portion of oil revenues, as well as long-established economic assistance agencies such as the International Bank for Reconstruction and Development (IBRD) and regional development banks, finance foreign exchange operations and imports of the non-oil producing Latin American LDCs.[150] Therefore, this attention to the interconnectedness between trade liberalization, the US policy to resurrect its current account position, and the LDCs' buying power in foreign markets, is a clear line of continuity from the 1960s to the following decade. Likewise, as early as 1971 the Nixon administration focused on reaching agreements with the Common Market European partners on a set of measures to liberalize trade and capital investments on a bilateral basis between the US and the European Economic Community (EEC). At the time Washington worked on reaching such bilateral agreements before approaching any negotiations taking place in the General Agreement on Tariffs and Trade (GATT) to best navigate the US balance of payments deficit and to fix up Washington's dollar shortage.[151] Consistently, some ten years earlier, a cohort of the most high-ranking US foreign economic policymakers and their advisers relentlessly pressed for chasing after the same objective. Reference has just been made to the Kennedy administration's commitment to get trade arrangements with its European partners as a means of sustaining the value of the dollar through earning convertible foreign currencies to finance foreign markets operations for monetary purposes. As early as December 1961, among others, Seymour Edwin Harris, influential economic adviser to John F. Kennedy, made his case for such a policy.[152] On the other hand, a number of high-ranking US officials including Secretary of the Treasury Anderson, Harris himself and many other economic policymakers, established a linkage between the US trade and financial bonds with the economies of the EEC, and the destiny of the non-commodity producing LDCs, their terms of trade and purchasing power.[153] Paul Nitze himself reasoned on this line as early as 1959 to emphasize the reportedly vital role of the Department of State in pursuing such foreign economic policy agenda.[154] In the 1960s, for instance, the pursuit of a liberal trade policy was considered essential to foster the export of Latin American agricultural products to Western Europe and to deter any Soviet trading influence in the continent. Against this backdrop, since the early 1960s the Department of State made a strong case for getting the European partners involved in the development assistance programs carried over under the aegis of either the federal government, or the organizations of the United Nations (UN) and the IBRD. In the very early 1960s such pressure on the European countries took place in the framework of institutional arrangements such as the Development Assistance Group and, since 1962, the Development Assistance Committee (DAC) established within the Organization for Economic Cooperation and Development (OECD). The DAC was the most important forum of the OECD in which the principal donors of bilateral aid as well as the IBRD and the EEC were represented. Since the early 1960s, the United States worked on shaping a DAC common aid pledge to produce improved economic and social conditions in the LDCs; the long-term objective was to strengthen and to improve economic relations and commercial bonds with those countries.[155] As the US foreign economic policy moved from the 1960s into the 1970s this American stance, backed by the IMF,[156] focused on financing the purchasing power of non-oil producing LDCs. This policy was conducted both because Washington considered the LDCs essential to stabilize the international trade and payments system, and in order to fuel domestic development in the non-commodity-rich countries and their exports.[157] At that point, through a forum of creditor Western governments and institutions, as the DAC still played a role,[158] in addition to continued commitment by the IMF and the multilateral development banks to help restore equilibrium in the balance of payments, the IBRD led the way in shaping development assistance programs.[159] Likewise, as investigated in the next chapter, such institutional shift was accompanied by a turn from public financial contributions from Western governments and institutions to increase bond sales to the Western capital markets. Since the appointment of former Secretary of Defense Robert McNamara to the presidency of the IBRD, at the end of the decade the Washington-based Bretton Woods institution repeatedly resorted to the German, British, and United States capital markets to finance its development assistance programs. Later on McNamara turned to draw on the oil producing countries of OPEC to finance its bonds: such policy was favored by the United Kingdom and other Western European partners but irritated the US governments.[160] As of 1968 the IBRD had borrowed in the London market on three occasions,[161] while by fiscal year-end 1969 over half of the Bank's gross borrowing had been raised in the German and US private capital markets.[162] The next two chapters focus on the follow up to this story and the institutional arrangements that Washington set off amid the two oil crises of the 1970s.

Within the framework of this two-pronged foreign economic policy based on foreign market operations in support for the dollar and the US gold stock, and trade liberalization policies aimed at restoring equilibrium on the current account, the reshaping of US foreign military assistance both within the Atlantic Alliance and within the framework of bilateral relations with Western European countries together served the twofold purpose of improving the US terms of trade and stimulating the inflow of convertible foreign currencies. In the pursuit of this two-pronged target did the Kennedy and Johnson administrations move forward. Since 1962 through the following years the sequence of measures enacted to improve the capital account position made way for a much more coherent US commitment to improve the US balance of payments, the dollar's value in foreign exchange markets, and the steady gold drain through a comprehensive set of foreign trade measures, of which the reshaping of foreign military assistance was the cornerstone. A number of foreign military spending cuts and a steep increase in foreign military sales were likely to affect both the balance of payments on current account in the aggregate, and the financing of foreign market operations. The approval of the Trade Bill in 1962 provided the broad-based framework for such a turn. The groundbreaking idea laying at the origins of that trade bill was a widespread concern for the implications of unfettered liberalizations on the US balance of payments. The broad framework of such concern was widespread dollar saturation all across the Western European economies and their capital markets. In this context, most US policymakers established a linkage between reducing trade barriers toward the newly established European Common Market and the very objective of increasing US exports to improve the balance of payments and to increase the inflow of convertible foreign currencies.[163] In this context outspokenly aimed at making US foreign trade an instrument of Washington's target to reduce the nation's balance of payments deficit, within the Kennedy administration it was a widely shared view that US military spending on services and goods for troops stationed abroad should undergo severe cuts. At the same time, several policymakers and officials in the administration held the view that the US should increase sales of end items, instrumental goods and services to its political partners. At the outset there was a firm idea to replace American support for the creation of a local military industrial complex all across the European partners by providing an uninterrupted supply of end- items for the military buildup and security of Washington's trading partners. In this respect it is important to stress that foreign military spending on troops and military bases deployed across Europe had long been viewed in Washington as a preliminary step in the development of a local and self-sufficient military industrial complex in most beneficiary countries. The reverting of this path and the increase in military sales to West Germany made a detour from this established policy and signaled a path-breaking new policy aimed at propping up the US balance of payments and increasing US holding of convertible foreign currencies through military assistance to friendly Western nations. The first step in this direction was certainly the excising of political leverage on the Federal Republic of Germany to make the government of Bonn share the costs of US forces stationed in Germany. After a half a year-long set of bilateral negotiations, as early as October 1961 the Kennedy administration and the Germans reached an offset agreement: accordingly, in calendar years 1963 and 1964 West Germany committed to placing an amount of orders in the US that fully offset the foreign-exchange costs of US forces in the Federal Republic.[164]

Reasoning along these lines, Secretary of Defense Robert McNamara led the way. In late spring 1962 he pinned a memorandum about his department's contribution to ease the strains of defense expenditures on the US balance of payments in which he tackled the impact of foreign defense expenditures on the level of US gold reserves. In general, he stressed that any Department of Defense's foreign procurement should be critically reviewed to determine whether such procurement could not be made from US sources. In this policy paper he instructed the US armies to pay higher costs with no arbitrary limits in order to purchase military requirements and hardware in the United States. On the other hand, tellingly, he recalled that the Department he directed was committed "to persuade Allies to pay for the full support of their own forces, and to sell for cash or credit US equipment and supply."[165] That same summer in 1962, just a few weeks later, on the occasion of a military staff meeting, McNamara fixed the target of reducing the Department of Defense net adverse dollar balances entering the US balance of payments to $1 billion. In his view such spending cuts were unlikely to affect American military power abroad.[166] Before this overall target, the Secretary of Defense engaged in a number of study projects to reduce a variety of foreign military expenditures. They included overseas procurements of supplies and services for US military forces to construction programs, expenditures by US military personnel and their dependents abroad, as well use of foreign labor. This active commitment of McNamara to reduce the impact of foreign military spending on continued dollar outflow and US gold losses was implemented in close cooperation with Secretary of State Dean Rusk. Such initiative took place in the framework of the US government-wide struggle to lessen the balance of payments deficit by reducing foreign exchange expenditures and cutting off the liabilities in the current account position. This array of measures to cut defense expenditures was not a spot exercise as the following year they were reenacted once more.[167] Consistently, on its part as early as the summer of 1963 the Department of State laid down a comprehensive plan to close down 13 foreign posts and to reduce strength in 3 others, while other agencies had committed to cut their overseas expenditures. At the same time, however, as far as it entailed a steady increase in export of military end-items, components, instrumental goods and military services to US friendly nations, the initiative of McNamara and Rusk was seemingly aimed at improving the assets in the balance of payments on capital account. In some respects the Kennedy administration resorted to unsettled payments to finance foreign purchases of US weaponry. For instance, in 1963 the Department of Defense resorted to using a "blocked account" to finance military exports to the Federal Republic of Germany that amounted to a total of $230 million, a non-recurring one-shot means of financing German outpayments for military purposes.[168]

The US commitment to reduce foreign military expenditures and to increase foreign sales of military goods and services to Washington's allies as the linchpin for the American turn on redressing the terms of trade and on restoring the balance of payments equilibrium met a cohort of discontents within the Kennedy administration itself. Most of them viewed such a turn in the US foreign military assistance policy as a likely political and military disengagement from Europe and Asia with serious implications on the confidence of Western European allies in Washington's commitment to protect the Old Continent from Moscow. Walter Rostow, for instance, took it for granted that the reduction of US military troops caused by cutting overseas military expenditures would usher in troop withdrawals from Europe eventually leading "to the emergence of a nationalist Europe, with an independent nuclear force."[169]

Notwithstanding this string of criticism, the Kennedy administration turned away from policies focused on the capital account to measures on the current account within the framework of its support for full trade liberalization before its most important trading partners and the developing economies. From the early to the mid-1960s the US federal and monetary authorities began considering the restoration of US balance of payments deficit and the dollar's strength in foreign exchange markets a pivot in the search for equilibrium between domestic economic growth, the competitive position of US manufacturing, and the increasing integration of developed and developing economy into an open economy under US leadership.

Notes

1. Missouri History Museum, St. Louis, MO (henceforth MHM), William McChesney Martin Collection (henceforth Martin Collection), The Federal Reserve Board Years 1951–1970, series V, General Subseries A, 1951–1968: Federal Reserve Board Correspondence, b. 21, fold. 1, The Joint Economic Committee of the Congress of the United States to the Honorable William McChesney Martin (Chairman of the Board of Governors of the Federal Reserve System), March 12, 1960.

2. Data based on 24 industries by Moore, 1961, pp. 155 ff.
3. Bureau of Labor, 1967. Non-seasonally adjusted data suggested a very similar trend; see Department of Commerce, Bureau of the Census, 1959, monthly reports for the years since January 1956 onwards.
4. Department of Commerce, 1960.
5. Department of Commerce, Bureau of Economic Analysis, 1976.
6. Moore, 1961, p. 163; see also Standard and Poor's, 1978.
7. International Monetary Fund Archives, Washington, DC (henceforth IMFA), Executive Board Documents, Departmental Memoranda, 1960–Departmental Memoranda, IMF Office of the Treasurer, "Monthly Reports of Gold Prices in Various World Markets (IM/60/16)," May 12, 1960.
8. With respect to the outflow of gold from the United States in 1960 see, for instance, US Loses Gold Again. 1960. *The Financial Times,* August 2.
9. Federal Reserve Bank of St. Louis, 1961, pp. 2–9, passim.
10. Department of Commerce, Office of Business Economics, 1958, p. 203.
11. Department of Commerce, Bureau of the Census, 1975, Part 2, Chapter P: Manufactures, pp. 652 ff.
12. NBER, seasonally adjusted US Index of Production Worker Man hour in Manufacturing 01/1932-10/1962, in National Bureau of Economic Research, 2016.
13. Peden and Bradley, 1989; Wolff, Baumol, and McLennan 1985; Rasmussen and Iljoong, 1992.
14. Board of Governors of the Federal Reserve System, 1960a, p. 4, table 1.
15. See for instance Odell, 1982, Introduction and Chapter 3.
16. US Federal Open Market Committee (FOMC) Meeting, October 4, 1960, in Federal Open Market Committee Meeting Minutes, Transcripts, and Other Documents, retrievable at https://fraser.stlouisfed.org/title/677#!22828 (henceforth FOMC).
17. Department of Commerce, Bureau of the Census, 1975, p. 869.
18. Lederer, Pizer, Boddie and Lechter, 1961, pp. 15–23.
19. MHM, Martin Collection, The Federal Reserve Board Years 1951–1970, series V, General Subseries A, 1951–1968: Federal Reserve Board (henceforth FRB) Official Correspondence, b. 21, fold. 1, Congress of the United States, Joint Economic Committee to the Chairman of the Federal Reserve Board William McChesney Martin, March 12, 1960.

20. US Federal Open Market Committee (FOMC) Meeting, January 9, 1962, in FOMC.
21. MHM, Martin Collection, The Federal Reserve Board Years 1951–1970, series V, General Subseries A, 1951–1968, FRB Official Correspondence, b. 21, fold. 1, Congress of the United States, Joint Economic Committee to W. McChesney Martin (Federal Reserve Board, Chairman), March 12, 1960.
22. See a statement by FOMC Vice Chairman Hayes reported in the Committee's minutes: FOMC Meeting October 1, 1957, p. 9, in FOMC.
23. MHM, Martin Collection, The Federal Reserve Board Years 1951–1970, series V, General Subseries A, 1957–1960, FRB Official Memos attached reports, b. 21, fold. 3, Federal Reserve Bank of New York, "Memorandum on Problems Arising in Connection with the Discount Rate Reduction of November 14, 1957," December 2, 1957.
24. Lyndon Baines Johnson Presidential Library, Austin, TX (henceforth LBJPL), Papers of Henry Fowler, b. 52, Henry Fowler, Memorandum for the President, October 12, 1965; Bordo and Humpage, 2016, p. 112; Gibson, 1971, pp. 651–652; D'Arista, 2013, pp. 8–9.
25. Eichengreen, 1996, pp. 113–116; Kindleberger, 1965, p. 7; Frieden, 2006, chapter 15.
26. Department of Commerce, Bureau of the Census, 1975, Series U 1-25. Balance of International Payments 1790–1970, pp. 864 and 866.
27. Moore, 1961.
28. Department of Commerce, Bureau of the Census, 1959, series P-50.
29. Department of Commerce, Bureau of Economic Analysis, 1976; see also Department of Commerce, 1966.
30. Smits, Woltjer, and Ma, 2009.
31. Department of Commerce, Bureau of the Census, October 1964 and subsequent issues.
32. Gordon, 1986, Appendix B, Historic Data Tables.
33. See, for instance, Luan and Miller, 1979, pp. 88–89.
34. MHM, Martin Collection, The Federal Reserve Board Years 1951–1970, series V, General Subseries A, 1951–1968, FRB Official Correspondence, b. 21, fold. 1, US Congress Joint Economic Committee to W. McChesney Martin, March 12, 1960.
35. MHM, Martin Collection, The Federal Reserve Board Years 1951–1970, series V, General Subseries A, b. 21, fold. 3, US Treasury Paper, "Bills Only Policy," February 1960.

36. Statement by the Hon. Robert B. Anderson, Secretary of the Treasury and Governor of the Fund for the United States, at the Discussion of the Fund's annual Report at the 1959 Annual Meetings of the Boards of Governors of the IBRD and IMF, Washington, DC, September 29, 1959, in Central Intelligence Agency electronic reading room http://www.foia.cia.gov/search (henceforth CIA e-reading room).
37. Quotation from Governor Merger's statement at the FOMC Meeting of October 4, 1960, in FOMC.
38. Kramer, 1974, p. 73.
39. Board of Governors of the Federal Reserve System, Division of International Finance, British Commonwealth Section, 1960, p. 25.
40. Federal Reserve System, 1960, pp. 1–2.
41. IMFA, Executive Board Documents, Departmental Memoranda, 1964-Departmental Memoranda, IMF, European Department, "The Development of Capital Markets in Europe, prepared by D. Williams and approved by L.A. Whittome," October 15, 1964.
42. See, for instance, IMF, 1962b.
43. IMFA, Executive Board Documents, Departmental Memoranda, 1965, Departmental Memoranda, IMF, Research and Statistics Department, O. Altman, "International Liquidity and the Balance of Payments," September 15, 1965, pp. 3–4.
44. Department of Commerce, Bureau of the Census, 1975, Chapter U, International Transaction and Foreign Commerce, pp. 869–870.
45. FOMC Meeting Minutes, October 4, 1960, p. 8, in FOMC.
46. Council of Economic Advisers, 1960, p. 26.
47. Board of Governors of the Federal Reserve System, 1960a, table 9, p. 20.
48. FOMC Meeting Minutes, October 4, 1960, p. 4, in FOMC.
49. Gordon, 1986, Appendix B, Historic data Tables.
50. Federal Reserve System, 1961, pp. 4–5.
51. FOMC Meeting Minutes, October 4, 1960, in FOMC.
52. FOMC, Meeting Minutes, December 13, 1960, ibid.
53. Board of Governors of the Federal Reserve System, 1961.
54. Department of the Treasury, 1962, p. 7.
55. Board of Governors of the Federal Reserve System, 1960b, and Board of Governors of the Federal Reserve System, 1961.
56. Board of Governors of the Federal Reserve System, 1961, p. 383.
57. All these data and figures can be retrieved in Council of Economic Advisers, 1961, pp. 8, 14–15.

58. Council of Economic Advisers, 1963, p. 25.
59. See, for instance, Panitch and Gindin, 2012; Hawley, 2016, chapter 2.
60. Gavin, 2004.
61. Findlay and O'Rourke, 2007. For a different interpretation focused on the importance that Kennedy gave to the outflow of capital and the expansion of the Eurodollar market in accounting for the US balance of payments deficit see Prins, 2014.
62. Reasoning to a certain extent along the lines of this work is Swedberg, 1987, p. 324.
63. In this respect see the work conducted on the subject by the Long Range International Payments Committee: John F. Kennedy Presidential Library and Museum, Boston, Mass. (henceforth JFKPL), Papers of John F. Kennedy, Presidential Papers, National Security Files (henceforth NSF), folder "Principal Papers Prepared for the Cabinet Committee on Balance of Payments in connection with its Report to the President April 6, 1963," "Financial Measures for the U.S. Balance of Payments Deficit 1963–64," March 15, 1963, document attached to Robert V. Roosa, Memorandum to the Secretary "Report on Methods of Financing the Balance of Payments Deficits during 1963 and 1964," pp. 4–6.
64. U.S. Congress, 1963, pp. 27, 91, and 101; Federal Reserve Bank of New York, 1961b, p. 199. See Department of the Treasury, 1961.
65. This surge in budget deficit came all along the decade: see Federal Reserve Bank of New York Historical Archive, New York City (henceforth FRBNYA), Central Files, 765.43.2, Meetings of Secretary of Treasury with N.Y. Financial Men 1958–1981, "Meeting on March 12, 1963, of Secretary of the Treasury Dillon with representatives of New York banks and others indicated in the attached list, which also shows the representatives of the Federal Reserve Bank of New York in attendance," March 13, 1963.
66. IMF, 1962c, p. 116.
67. Department of the Treasury, 1963, Tables, Table 111 (US balance of payments by major components seasonally adjusted in millions of dollars) p. 835.
68. US Government, 1961, pp. 57–66.
69. JFKPL, papers of Walter Heller, W. Heller, "Monetary Policy and Debt Management."
70. JFKPL, papers of Douglas Dillon, b. 33, D. Dillon, Memorandum for the President, January 31, 1961.

71. JFKPL, papers of Walter Heller, b. 19, W. Heller, Memorandum for the President "The Impact of White House Conferences on Monetary Policy," April 13, 1961.
72. IMFA, Executive Board Documents, Departmental Memoranda, 1962—Departmental Memoranda, O. Altman (IMF International Research and Statistics Department), "Some Aspects of the Gold Problem," April 24, 1962.
73. JFKPL, Papers of John F. Kennedy, Presidential Papers, President's Office Files. Department and Agencies. Council of Economic Advisers (CEA), September 1961, James Tobin (Executive Office of the President, CEA), Memorandum for Under Secretary Fowler "Avoiding the Next Recession," September 6, 1961. Reasoning along these same lines was ibid., Arthur Okun, Memorandum for the Council "Must we have a 1963 Recession?" September 1, 1961.
74. Department of Commerce, 1963, pp. 17–20.
75. From the period 1957–60 to the period 1961–64 the value added in percentage of total manufacturing of the low capital-intensive industry that depended the most on foreign exchange adjustments declined from 1957 to 1960 and came further down from 1960 to 1964, whereas the highest capital intensive American sectors that traditionally depended the least on foreign monetary arrangements increased. See Department of Commerce, Bureau of the Census, 1966, Part III, table 5, p. 84.
76. Silberman, 1962, p. 3. For a detailed account of this turn see Department of the Treasury, 1960, pp. 52–53.
77. US Government, 1962, table B-80.
78. Department of the Treasury, 1963, p. 80.
79. JFKPL, Papers of John F. Kennedy, Presidential Papers, NSF, Country File: Italy General, 5/11/1962-5/20/1962, b. 120, George Ball, State-Defense-Treasury Message, May 11, 1962.
80. For a lively analysis about the linkage between real interest rates differentials and the decline in US stock market prices see FOMC Meeting Minutes, October 24, 1961, in FOMC.
81. Department of the Treasury, 1964b, p. 133.
82. IMFA, Executive Board Documents, Departmental Memoranda, 1964-Departmental Memoranda, David Williams-L.A. Whittome (IMF European Department), "The Development of Capital Markets in Europe," October 15, 1964, pp. 5–6.

83. IMFA, Executive Board Documents, Departmental Memoranda, 1963-Departmental Memoranda, p. 6; US Congress, 1963, pp. 49–60; ibid., O. Altman (IMF Research and Statistics Department), "Gold, the Dollar, and the Balance of Payments," February 18, 1963.
84. Big Rise in Gold Reserves Expected. Is Exporting really Fun? *The Times*, August 2, 1960.
85. in this respect see the statement of Treasury Secretary at the Meeting of the Board of Governors of the IMF, IBRD, IDA and IFC held in Vienna on September 22, 1961: Current Economic Developments "Move to Expand IMF Resources wins backing at Vienna Meeting," unclassified, September 26, 1961. In Office of the Historian, 1995, Document 190 https://history.state.gov/historicaldocuments/frus1961-63v09
86. FOMC Meeting Minutes, August 21, 1962, in FOMC.
87. Frieden, 2006, chapter 15.
88. IMFA, Executive Board Documents, Departmental Memoranda, 1962-Memoranda, O. Altman (IMF Research and Statistics Department), "Some Aspects of the Gold Problem," April 24, 1962, p. 2.
89. Board of Governors of the Federal Reserve System, 1962. As regards data on US gold reserves see also id., 1976, p. 900.
90. IMF, 1962a.
91. Board of Governors of the Federal Reserve System, 1976, table 15.23, pp. 1032–33.
92. For a review of these data see IMFA, Executive Board Documents, Departmental Memoranda, 1961-Departmental Memoranda, Peter Burman and A. P. Nose (IMF Research and Statistics Department), "Recent Changes in Official Gold Holdings," March 8, 1961; see also IMF, 1961.
93. CIA, "The President's Intelligence Checklist," September 21, 1963, in CIA e-reading room https://www.cia.gov/library/readingroom
94. CIA, Office of Research and Reports, Memorandum "Significance of Recent Soviet Gold Sales," December 12, 1962, in CIA e-reading room https://www.cia.gov/library/readingroom
95. Notes for Briefings on HIC Director's Senior Staff Meeting, "US Balance of Payments and International Gold Flows," June 10, 1963, in CIA e-reading room https://www.cia.gov/library/readingroom
96. CIA Office of Research and Reports, Memorandum "Significance of Recent Soviet Gold Sales," December 12, 1962; see also John A. McCone (Director of Central Intelligence) to Dean Rusk (Secretary of State), December 13, 1963, both in CIA e-reading room https://www.cia.gov/library/readingroom

97. Wolstan Crocker Brown (former monetary adviser to the Republican National Committee) to Charles Harley (Finance Committee Treasury Department), "International Trade and Credit Market," June 5, 1958, in CIA E-reading room https://www.cia.gov/library/readingroom
98. Heron, John. 1962. The Case for Raising the Gold Price. *The Statist*, February 2.
99. IMFA, Executive Board Documents, Departmental Memoranda, 1965-Departmental Memoranda, Oliver Altman (IMF Research and Statistics Department), "International Liquidity and the Balance of Payments," September 15, 1965.
100. Memorandum for the Record, "U.S. Balance of Payments Deficit and International Gold Flows," June 10, 1963 in CIA E-reading room https://www.cia.gov/library/readingroom
101. JFKPL, Papers of John F. Kennedy, Presidential Papers, NSF, Country File: Switzerland General 1962, The US Embassy in Zurich (Holt) to the Secretary of State, telegram, August 10, 1962.
102. JFKPL, Papers of John F. Kennedy. Presidential Papers, NSF, Principal Papers Prepared for the Cabinet Committee on Balance of Payments in Connection with its Report to the President April 6, 1963, "Financial Measures for the U.S. Balance of Payments Deficit 1963–64" (Summary Report from the Long Range International Payments Committee), March 15, 1963.
103. IMFA, Executive Board Documents, Departmental Memoranda, 1965-Departmental Memoranda, O. Altman (IMF Research and Statistics Department), Gold, the Dollar, and the Balance of Payments, February 18, 1963.
104. Silberman, 1962, p. 3.
105. Bank for International Settlements, 1963; *The Times*, April 16, 1963.
106. JFKPL, Papers of Walter Heller, Monetary Policy and Debt Management, January 25, 1961.
107. Board of Governors of the Federal Reserve System, 1976, table 15.24, pp. 1035–1047; see also Global Financial Data, 2011.
108. Department of the Treasury, 1963, p. 79.
     Major, 2014, p. 37.
109. FOMC Meeting Minutes, August 21, 1962, in FOMC. For a general appraisal about the positive impact of debt-prepayments on the US balance of payments see also Department of the Treasury, 1963, p. 79.
110. Major, 2014, p. 37.

111. JFKPL, Papers of John F. Kennedy, Presidential Papers, NSF, fold. Principal Papers Prepared for the Cabinet Committee on Balance of Payments in connection with its Report to the President April 6, 1965, Summary report from the Long Range International Payments Committee, "Financial Measures for the U.S. Balance of Payments Deficit 1963–1964," p. 6, March 15, 1963.
112. US Government, 1964, Table C-46-Bank loans and investments 1929–1963 in billions of dollars, p. 263.
113. MHM, The Federal Reserve Board Years 1951–1970, General, Series V, Subseries A, Federal Reserve Bank Official Memos and Attached Reports, b. 21, fold. 4, Memorandum on References to the Federal Reserve by President Kennedy before the Economic Club of New York, December 17, 1962.
114. FOMC Meeting Minutes, August 21, 1962, pp. 8 and 10, in FOMC.
115. FRBNYA, Central Files, 765.43.2, Meetings of Secretary of Treasury with NY bankers, "Meeting on March 12, 1963 of Secretary Dillon with representatives of New York banks and others indicated in the attached list, which also shows the representatives of the Federal Reserve Bank of New York in attendance."
116. See documentation in JFKPL, Papers of John F. Kennedy, Presidential Papers, NSF, Country File: Italy.
117. Letter from Secretary of the Treasury Dillon to the Belgian Finance Minister (Dequae), August 21, 1961; Department of State, Current Economic Developments, "Move to Expand IMF resources wins baking at Vienna Meetings," September 26, 1961. Both in Office of the Historian, 1995, Document 197 https://history.state.gov/historicaldocuments/frus1961-63v09
118. JFKPL, President's Office File, Treasury, Memorandum from Secretary of the Treasury Dillon to President Kennedy, "Fourth Quarterly Report on Balance of Payments," March 12, 1962.
119. Report from Secretary of the Treasury Dillon to President Kennedy "Report to the President on Balance of Payments," March 20, 1961. In Office of the Historian, 1995, document 3 https://history.state.gov/historicaldocuments/frus1961-63v09
120. Department of the Treasury, 1962, p. 82.
121. Elmer B. Staats Acting Director, Executive Office of the President (Bureau of the Budget), Memorandum for the President "International Transactions of the Federal Government, fiscal years 1962 to 1965," August 26, 1963, p. 1, in CIA e-reading room https://www.cia.gov/library/readingroom

122. Ibid., p. 8.
123. Memorandum from the Secretary of the Treasury Dillon to President Kennedy "Report on Measures to Improve the Balance of Payments," October 9, 1962. In Office of the Historian, 1995, document 18, https://history.state.gov/historicaldocuments/frus1961-63v09
124. JFKPL, Papers of John F. Kennedy, Presidential Papers, NSF, Country File: Italy general, 5/11/62-5/20/62, b. 120, The Department of State to the Amembassy Rome, Amembassy Bonn, Amembassy Paris, State-Defense-Treasury Message, May 11, 1962. Memorandum From Secretary of the Treasury Dillon to President Johnson "Report on the Balance of Payments," December 2, 1963, in Office of the Historian, 1995, document 39, https://history.state.gov/historicaldocuments/frus1961-63v09
125. JFKPL, Papers of John F. Kennedy, Presidential Papers, NSF, Country File: Italy, b. 120, Department of State, "Italy. Guidelines for Policy and Operations," May 1962.
126. JFKPL, Papers of John F. Kennedy, Presidential Papers, NSF, Country File: Italy, b. 120, The Amembassy in Rome to the Department of State, September 19, 1962. See also ibid., Rostow to Segni (President of the Italian Republic), undated (but October 1962). Final agreements on Italian purchases were signed later on in February 1963: ibid., The Amembassy in Rome (Reinhart) to the Secretary of State, February 12, 1963. See also NARA, RG59, Bureau of European Affairs, Country Director for Italy, Austria, and Switzerland, Records Relating to Italy 1943–1968, Lot File 67D319, b. 2, fol. finance.
127. JFKPL, Papers of John F. Kennedy, Presidential Papers, NSF, Country File: Italy, b. 120, Department of State, "Italy. Guidelines for Policy and Operations," May 1962, p. 18.
128. JFKPL, NSC, Western Europe country File: Italy, The US Embassy in Rome to the State Department telegram, May 16, 1962.
129. Bordo, Humpage, and Schwartz, 2015, pp. 336 ff.
130. JFKPL, Papers of John F. Kennedy, Presidential Papers, NSF, Country File: Italy.
131. See the relevant documentation in DDRS.
132. Schaufelbuehl, 2013, pp. 160–166.
133. CIA Directorate of Intelligence, Intelligence Memorandum, "French Action in the Recent Gold Crisis," March 20, 1968, pp. 1–2, in CIA e-reading room http://www.foia.cia.gov/search
134. Ed Fried to Walt Rostow, telegram, December 23, 1967, in DDRS.
135. Department of the Treasury, 1961.

136. Federal Reserve Bank of New York, 1961a, b. See also US Congress, 1963, pp. 27, 91, and 101.
137. Federal Reserve Bank of New York, 1962, p. 22; Banque Nationale Suisse, 1961, p. 6, http://www.snb.ch/fr/mmr/reference/annrep_1961_komplett/source/annrep_1961_komplett.fr.pdf
138. See documentation on this in DDRS.
139. See among other sources documenting this stance by the Secretary of the Treasury, Memorandum from Secretary of the Treasury Dillon to President Kennedy, 9 October 1962. In Office of the Historian, 1995, document 18, https://history.state.gov/historicaldocuments/frus1961-63v09
140. Department of the Treasury, 1964a, p. 52, and Department of the Treasury, 1964b, pp. 34–38.
141. L.B. Johnson to the Congress of the United States, February 10, 1965, in CIA e-reading room http://www.foia.cia.gov/search
142. Department of the Treasury, 1965, p. 47.
143. L. Johnson to the Congress of the United States, February 10, 1965, in CIA e-reading room http://www.foia.cia.gov/search
144. See for instance Memorandum of Conversation J.F. Kennedy-D. Rusk (Secretary of State)-Adenauer (Federal Republic Chancellor) Von Brentano (German Foreign Minister), Grewe (German Ambassador to Washington), Adenauer Visit "Balance of Payments Problem," April 13, 1961. In Office of the Historian, 1995, Document 44, https://history.state.gov/historicaldocuments/frus1961-63v09
145. Cromwell, 1992, chapter 3; Hawley, 2016; Thies, 2003; Zimmerman, 2002; Colman, 2010, pp. 94 ff.
146. National Security Council, Standing Group Meeting, March 9, 1962, Record of Actions, in CIA e-reading room http://www.foia.cia.gov/search
147. JFKPL, Papers of John F. Kennedy, Presidential Papers, NSF, Subjects: Trade, General: 1962, b. 309, S.E. Harris, Memorandum on Trade Policy, December 4, 1961.
148. Mellow, 2008, p. 57.
149. NARA, RG59, Central Files, 394.41/4.2861, Memorandum of Conversation G. Ball-Louis Scheyven (ambassador of Belgium)-Willy van Cauwenberg (commercial Attaché), "US Concern at the Rejection of the US Agricultural Package by the EEC Representatives at GATT XXIV: 6 Negotiations," April 28, 1961; JFKPL, Papers of John F. Kennedy, Presidential Papers, NSF, Subjects: Trade, General: 1962, b. 309, S.E. Harris, "Memorandum on Trade Policy," December 4,

1961. See also Princeton University Library, Mudd Manuscript Library, George Ball Papers, 1880–1994, b. 115.

150. The involvement of the OPEC surplus countries in financing either outstanding multilateral development assistance institutions as the IBRD and her bonds is explored further in the following chapters: see now LOC, Manuscript Division, Robert McNamara Papers, Part I, b. 29, fold 1 (International Development Bank, replenishment Fifth 1975), John H. Adler (Director P&B) to I.P.M. Gargill, "Preparations for IDA5" August 11, 1975; Robert McNamara to Jan P. Pronk, October 14, 1975; see also NARA, RG56, Office of the Assistant Secretary for International Affairs (henceforth OASIA), Subject Files of the Office of International Monetary Affairs 1968–1978, b. 6, fold. 2 (oil), IMF, "Statement by the Managing Director on Visit to Member Countries in North Africa and the Middle East at Executive Board Meeting 74/37, April 22, 1974," April 22, 1974; ibid., IMF, WP-3 Meeting, "Comments on the Economic Implications of the Oil Situation," April 18–19, 1974. Regarding bilateral assistance from OPEC members as Saudi Arabia and Iran, and multilateral programs negotiated among the OECD, IMF, NATO, the UN technical assistance agencies and OPEC see ibid., F. Lisle Widman (The Department of the Treasury, Office of the Assistant Secretary for the International Affairs) to Under Secretary Volcker, "Summary of Various Proposals to Assist Developing Countries to Deal with Oil-induced Development and Financial Problems," April 9, 1974.

151. NARA, RG56, OASIA, Office of the Deputy Assistant Secretary for International Monetary Affairs, Briefing Books 1971–1980, b. 1, fold. Atlantic Declaration Under Secretary Volcker May 1973, subfold. 2 (Sum 2/14/73 Flanigan Memo re Econ. Objectives Paper), Peter M. Flanigan, Memorandum for Jack Bennett and John Hennessey, "US-European Relations Economic Objectives," February 14, 1973.

152. JFKPL, Papers of John F. Kennedy, Presidential Papers, NSF, Subjects: Trade, General: 1962, b. 309, S.E.H. Harris, Memorandum on Trade Policy, December 4, 1961.

153. "Statement by Robert B. Anderson, Secretary of the Treasury and Governor of the Fund for the United States, at the Discussion of the Fund's Annual Report," September 29, 1959, in CIA e-reading room http://www.foia.cia.gov/search. P. Nitze, Memorandum on US Balance of Payments, November 24, 1959, in CIA e-reading room http://www.foia.cia.gov/search

154. P. Nitze, Memorandum on US Balance of Payments, November 24, 1959, in CIA e-reading room http://www.foia.cia.gov/search
155. See, for instance, JFKPL, Papers of John F. Kennedy, Presidential Papers, NSF, Country File: Italy, b. 120, Dean Rusk to the Amembassy in Rome, Amembassy in Paris, April 26, 1962.
156. NARA, RG56, OASIA, Subject Files of the Deputy Assistant Secretary for Developing Nations Finance 1976–1977, b. 3, fold. Boards, Committees, Organizations Panels, Working Groups, subfold. DA 9-6, Department of the Treasury, Office of Development Policy, International Financial Matters PRM 8, "Strategy for Relations between Developed and Developing Nations," March 8, 1977.
157. See a speech by the Executive Director of the IMF at the joint annual Meeting of the Board of Governors of the IMF-IBRD-IFC-IDA held in Washington DC on September 30, 1974: LOC, Manuscript Division, Robert McNamara Papers, Part 1, b. 28, fold. 8 (inflation 1974), statement by H.J. Witteveen in Presenting the Twenty-Ninth Annual Report of the Executive Directors to the Board of Governors of the Fund.
158. WBGA, Records of the Office of the President, Records of President Robert S. McNamara, Contacts with Member Countries: United Kingdom, General Correspondence 02, D.H. Rickett, Memorandum for the Record "The United Kingdom," October 4, 1971.
159. NARA, RG56, National Advisory Council on International Monetary and Financial Policies (henceforth NAC), NAC Alternates Minutes and Agenda, NAC Principal Minutes and Agenda, NAC Steering Committee Minutes, Nac Semi Annual Debt Review 1971–1975, b. 1, fold. NAC Alternates-Minutes, Meeting N. 75-1 through Meeting N. 75-8, January 16, 1975–December 3, 1975, National Advisory Council Alternates Meeting Minutes, Meeting 75-1, January 16, 1975, Review of IBRD/IDA Program and Financial Policies; WBGA, Records of General Vice Presidents and Managing Directors, Records of Sir Denis Rickett, Oil and Energy, Memos and Reports 1973 through 1974, Volume 3, Sir Denis Rickett (IBRD Vice President), "The Provision of Additional Resources to Developing Countries and the Respective Role of the Fund and the Bank," undated.
160. WBGA, Records of the Office of the President, Records of President Robert S. McNamara, Contacts with Member Countries: United Kingdom, General Correspondence 03, John Morrian to Robert McNamara, Office Memorandum, "R. McNamara interview with

Douglas Ramsey, Economic Development and Raw Material Correspondent of the Economist," July 28, 1975; ibid., "Meeting with Chancellor of the Exchequer, October 1, 1974 (present: McNamara, Denis W. Healey, Derek Mitchell, Richardson, Wass, Rawlinson, France, Cargill)," October 2, 1974.

161. WBGA, Records of the Office of the President, Records of President Robert S. McNamara, Contacts with Member Countries: United Kingdom, General Correspondence 02, W.M. Van Saagevelt to Mr. D. Love, "Memorandum on the Bank Group's Relationship with the United Kingdom," August 11, 1967.
162. See respectively WBGA, Records of the Office of the President, Records of President Robert S. McNamara, Contacts with Member Countries: United Kingdom, General Correspondence 01 (1968–1969), Summary Memo of conversation D.S. Rickett-R. McNamara-The Governor of the Bank of England, "Annual Meeting 1968—United Kingdom," October 9, 1968; and ibid., D.S. Rickett (IBRD Vice President), "Annual Meeting 1969. Meetings with Governors of Part I Countries. United Kingdom," September 24, 1969.
163. JFKPL, Papers of John F. Kennedy, Presidential Papers, NSF, Subject Trade General 1962 Trade Bill, 1962, b. 309, Seymour E. Harris, Memorandum on Trade Policy, December 4, 1961.
164. Memorandum for the President "Report on Measures to Improve the Balance of Payments," 1963, in DDRS.
165. JFKPL, Papers of John F. Kennedy, Presidential Papers, NSF, fold. Reduction of Forces, R. McNamara, Principles for Department of Defense Actions to Improve the Balance of Payments, June 26, 1962.
166. Ibid., R. McNamara, Memorandum for the Secretaries of the Military Departments, the Director of Defense Research and Engineering, The Joint Chiefs of Staff, The Assistant Secretaries of Defense, The General Counsel, "Revised Project List-List of Projects and Actions for Reducing Defense Expenditures Entering the International Balance of Payments," July 10, 1962.
167. JFKPL, Papers of John F. Kennedy, Presidential Papers, NSF, fold. Reduction of Forces, D. Rusk to all American Diplomatic Posts, telegram, July 19, 1962; David Klein (Department of State), "Coordination with Defense on Balance of Payments," September 9, 1963; ibid., U. Alexis Johnson (Department of State) to the Secretary of State, "Coordination with Defense on Balance of Payments Actions," September 6, 1963.

168. The Deputy Assistant Secretary of the Treasury Memorandum to the Cabinet Committee on Balance of Payments and to The Director of the Bureau of the Budget, McGeorge Bundy, White House, August 31, 1963; Elmer B. Staats (Head, General Accounting Office), Memorandum for the President "International Transactions of the Federal Government Fiscal Years 1962 to 1965," August 26, 1963, both in CIA e-reading room https://www.cia.gov/library/readingroom/search/site
169. JFKPL, Papers of John F. Kennedy, Presidential Papers, NSF, fold. Reduction of Forces, W. Rostow to the Secretary of the Treasury, May 18, 1963.

References

Bank for International Settlements. 1963. *Capital Markets Development*. Basel: Bank for International Settlements.

Banque Nationale Suisse. 1961. *Cinquante-Quatrième Rapport de la Banque Nationale Suisse*. http://www.snb.ch/fr/mmr/reference/annrep_1961_komplett/source/annrep_1961_komplett.fr.pdf

Big Rise in Gold Reserves Expected. Is Exporting really Fun? 1960. *The Times*, August 2.

Board of Governors of the Federal Reserve System. 1960a. *Banking and Monetary Developments,* November (12): 1–3.

———. 1960b. *Federal Reserve and Statistical Releases*, September 19.

———. 1961. *Federal Reserve Bulletin* 47 (3).

———. 1962. *Federal Reserve Bulletin* 48 (9).

———. 1976. *Banking and Monetary Statistics 1941–1970*. Washington, DC: GPO.

Board of Governors of the Federal Reserve System, Division of International Finance, British Commonwealth Section. 1960. *Capital Market Developments in the United States and Canada Including Monthly Review of Financial Developments in the United Kingdom*, September 6. Washington, DC: GPO.

Bordo, Michael, and Owen F. Humpage. 2016. Federal Reserve Policy and Bretton Woods. In *The Federal Reserve's Role in the Global Economy. A Historical Perspective*, ed. Michael Bordo and Mark A. Wynne, 89–121. New York: Cambridge University Press.

Bordo, Michael, Owen F. Humpage, and Anna J. Schwartz. 2015. *Strained Relations. US Foreign Exchange Operations and Monetary Policy in the Twentieth*

Century. Chicago: The University of Chicago Press-National Bureau of Economic Research.

Bureau of Labor. 1967. *Employment and Earnings and Monthly Reports on the Labor Force* 13 (9).

Colman, Jonathan. 2010. *The Foreign Policy of Lyndon B. Johnson. The United States and the World 1963–1969*. Edinburgh: The University of Edinburgh Press.

Council of Economic Advisers. 1960. *Economic Indicators, Prepared for the Joint Economic Committee by the Council of Economic Advisers*. Washington, DC: GPO.

———. 1961. Economic Indicators. *March 1961. Prepared for the Joint Economic Committee by the Council of Economic Advisers*, 87th Congress, 1st Session. Washington, DC: GPO.

———. 1963. Economic Indicators. *May 1963. Prepared for the Joint Economic Committee by the Council of Economic Advisers*. Washington, DC: GPO.

Cromwell, William C. 1992. *The United States and the European Pillar. The Strained Alliance*. New York: Palgrave Macmillan.

D'Arista, Jane. 2013. State of the Art. The US Central Bank at 100. *International. Journal of Political Economy* 42 (3): 5–23.

Department of Commerce. 1960. *Supplement to the Survey of Current Business*, August.

———. 1963. *Survey of Current Business* 43 (1).

———. 1966. *Supplement to Survey of Current Business*, August.

Department of Commerce, Bureau of Economic Analysis. 1976. *The National Income and Product Accounts of the United States 1929–1974, Statistical Tables. A Supplement to the Survey of Current Business*. Washington, DC: GPO.

Department of Commerce, Bureau of the Census. 1959. *Current Population Reports, Labor Force*, Series P-50, Monthly Reports. Washington, DC: GPO.

———. 1964. *Business Cycle Developments*, October 1964 and subsequent issues. *Survey of Current Business*, various years.

———. 1966. *Long-Term Economic Growth 1860–1965. A Statistical Compendium*. Washington, DC: GPO.

———. 1975. *Historical Statistics of the United States, Colonial Times to 1970, Part 2, Bicentennial Edition*. Washington, DC: GPO.

Department of Commerce, Office of Business Economics. 1958. *US Income and Output. A Supplement to the Survey of Current Business, Statistical Section. Tables, VI. Income and Employment by Industry*. Washington, DC: US Department of Commerce.

Department of the Treasury. 1960. *Annual Report of the Secretary of the Treasury on the State of the Finances for the Fiscal Year ended June 30, 1959*. Washington, DC: GPO.

———. 1961. *Treasury Bulletin* 12.

———. 1962. *Annual Report of the Secretary of the Treasury on the State of the Finances for the Fiscal Year Ended June 30, 1961*. Washington, DC: GPO.

———. 1963. *Annual Report of the Secretary of the Treasury on the States of the Finances for the Fiscal Year Ended June 30, 1962*. Washington, DC: GPO.

———. 1964a. *Annual Report of the Secretary of the Treasury on the State of the Finances for the Fiscal Year Ended June 30, 1963*. Washington, DC: GPO.

———. 1964b. *A Description and Analysis of Certain European Capital Markets. Materials Prepared for the Joint Economic Committee, Congress of the United States*. Paper No. 3. Washington, DC: GPO.

———. 1965. *Annual Report of the Secretary of the Treasury on the State of the Finances for the Fiscal Year Ended June 30, 1964*. Washington, DC: GPO.

Eichengreen, Barry. 1996. *Globalizing Capital. A History of the International Monetary System*. Princeton: Princeton University Press.

Federal Reserve Bank of New York. 1961a. *Monthly Review* 41 (12).

———. 1961b. *Monthly Review* 43 (12).

———. 1962. *Monthly Review* 42(2).

Federal Reserve Bank of St. Louis. 1961. The United States Balance of Payments 1946–1960. *Federal Reserve Bank of St. Louis Monthly Review* 43 (3): 2–9.

Federal Reserve System. 1961. *Annual Report of the Board of Governors of the Federal Reserve System. Covering Operations for the Year 1960*. Washington, DC: GPO.

Findlay, Ronald, and Kevin O'Rourke. 2007. *Power and Plenty. Trade, War and the World Economy in the Second Millennium*. Princeton: Princeton University Press.

Frieden, Jeffry. 2006. *Global Capitalism. Its Fall and Rise in the Twentieth Century*. New York: W.W. Norton and Company.

Gavin, Francis. 2004. *Gold, Dollars, and Power. The Politics of International Monetary Relations 1958–1971*. Chapel Hill/London: The University of North Carolina Press.

Gibson, William E. 1971. Eurodollars and US Monetary Policy. *Journal of Money, Credit and Banking* 3 (3): 651–652.

Gindin, Sam, and Leo Panitch. 2012. *The Making of Global Capitalism. The Political Economy of American Empire*. London: Verso.

Global Financial Data. 2011. https://www.globalfinancialdata.com/

Gordon, Robert J. 1986. In *The American Business Cycle: Continuity and Change*, ed. Robert J. Gordon. Chicago/London: The University of Chicago Press.

Hawley, James P. 2016. *Dollars and Borders. US Governments Attempts to Restrict Capital Flows 1960–1980*. London: Routledge. (or. ed. 1987).
Heron, John. 1962. The Case for Raising the Gold Price. *The Statist,* February 2.
IMF. 1961. *International Financial Statistics* 14 (3).
———. 1962a. *International Financial Statistics* 15 (4).
———. 1962b. *Annual Report 1962*. Washington, DC: IMF.
———. 1962c. *Annual Report of the Executive Directors for the Fiscal Year Ended April 30, 1962*. Washington, DC: IMF.
———. *Annual Report on Exchange and Trade Restrictions*, various years.
Kindleberger, Charles. 1965. Balance of Payments Deficits and the International Market for Liquidity, Department of Economics, Princeton University. *Essays in International Finance* 46: 3–30.
Kramer, Gerald. 1974. Borrowing on the International Capital Markets. *Columbia Journal of World Business* 9 (1): 73–77.
Lederer, Walther, Samuel Pizer, John B. Boddie, and Max Lechter. 1961. Recent Developments in International Trade and Investments. *Survey of Current Business* 12: 15–23.
Luan, David C., and Norman C. Miller. 1979. A Monetary Approach to International Capital Flows Applied to the United State: Note. *Journal of Money, Credit and Banking* 11 (1): 87–90.
Major, Aaron. 2014. *Architects of Austerity. International Finance and the Politics of Growth*. Stanford: Stanford University Press.
Mellow, Nicole. 2008. *The State of Disunion. Regional Sources of Modern American Partisanship*. Baltimore: The Johns Hopkins University Press.
Moore, Geoffrey H. 1961. *Business Cycle Indicators*. Vol. 2. Princeton: Princeton University Press for NBER.
National Bureau of Economic Research. 2016. *NBER Macrohistory: VIII. Income and Employment*. Cambridge, MA: National Bureau of Economic Research. http://www.nber.org/databases/macrohistory/contents/chapter08.html
Odell, John S. 1982. *US International Monetary Policy. Markets, Power, and Ideas as Sources of Change*. Princeton: Princeton University Press.
Office of the Historian. 1995. In *Foreign Relations of the United States (FRUS), 1961–1963, Volume IX, Foreign Economic Policy*, ed. Evans Gerakas, David S. Patterson, William F. Sanford, and Carolyn Yee. Washington, DC: GPO.
Peden, Edgar A., and Michael D. Bradley. 1989. Government Size, Productivity, and Economic Growth: The Post-war Experience. *Public Choice* 61 (3): 229–245.

Prins, Nomi. 2014. *All the Presidents' Bankers. The Hidden Alliances that Drive American Power*. New York: Nation Books.

Rasmussen, David W., and Kim Iljoong. 1992. The Growth of US Labor Productivity 1950–1989. *Applied Economics* 24: 285–289.

Schaufelbuehl, Janik Marina. 2013. Gold as a Diplomatic Tool: How Threat of Gold Purchases Worked as Leverage in International Monetary Relations 1960–1968. In *The Global Gold Market and the International Monetary System from the Late 19th Century to the Present. Actors, Networks, Power*. London: Palgrave.

Silberman, Lee H. 1962. Dollar's Defense. US Steps Up Trading in Foreign Exchange to Stabilize Currency. *The Wall Street Journal,* March 1.

Smits, Jan-Pieter, Woltjer Pieter, and Debin Ma. 2009. *A Dataset on Comparative Historical National Accounts ca. 1870–1950: A Time Series Perspective.* Groningen Growth and Development Center Memorandum GD-107. Groningen: University of Groningen. http://www.ggdc.nl/publications/memorandum/gd107.pdf

Standard and Poor's. 1978. *Standard and Poor's Statistics: Security Price Index Record.* New York: Standard's and Poor's Corp.

Swedberg, Richard. 1987. The Impact of an Exogenous Event: The Oil Shocks, the Private Banks and the Origins of the Debt Crisis. *International Social Science Journal* 113: 323–335.

The Times. 1963. April 16.

Thies, Wallace J. 2003. *Friendly Rivals. Bargaining and Burden-Shifting in Nato.* London/New York: Sharpe.

U.S. Loses Gold Again. 1960. *The Financial Times,* August 2.

US Congress. 1963. *Outlook for United States Balance of Payments. Hearings Before the US Joint Economic Committee. Sub-Committee on International Exchange and Payments,* Eighty-Seventh Congress, Second Session, December 12–14, 1962. Washington, DC: GPO.

US Government. 1961. *Public Papers of the Presidents of the United States, John F. Kennedy, Volume 1.* Washington, DC: GPO.

———. 1962. *Economic Report of the President Transmitted to the Congress January 1962 Together with the Annual Report of the Council of Economic Advisers.* Washington, DC: GPO.

———. 1964. *Economic Report of the President Transmitted to the Congress January 1964 Together with the Annual Report of the Council of Economic Advisers.* Washington, DC: GPO.

Wolff, Edward N., William Baumol, and Kenneth J. McLennan. 1985. *Productivity Growth and US Competitiveness*. New York: Oxford University Press.

Zimmerman, Hubert. 2002. *Money and Security. Troops, Monetary Policy and West Germany's Relations with the United States and Britain 1950–1971*. Cambridge: Cambridge University Press.

3

Oil, Private Capital Markets, Inflation: The Tottering of the International Payments System 1968–1973

3.1 A Defining Year for the US Balance of Payments: Exchange Rate Instability and Oil Price Hikes in 1967

Chapter 2 focused on pinpointing the failure of the two-pronged US foreign economic policy conducted throughout the 1960s. That policy was aimed at raising the inflow of convertible foreign currencies through early repayments of outstanding loans or debts, and the export of military goods and services, while cutting overseas public spending. At the same time, it was designed to support the US balance of payments on capital account. The latter objective was pursued by promoting foreign investments in the US and by increasing control over capital flights from the country. The objective of curbing capital flows was to stem the outflow of dollars and the decline of the American currency in foreign exchange markets, as well as to improve the US terms of trade. As highlighted in Chap. 2, the Kennedy administration's foreign military assistance programs were clearly aimed at restoring the balance of trade, while the Johnson administration insisted much more on getting early repayments of outstanding debts and loans from its Western partners,

S. Selva, *Before the Neoliberal Turn*, Palgrave Studies in Economic History,
DOI 10.1057/978-1-137-57443-5_3

as well as on implementing measures to curb the outflow of capital from the United States. Either way, Washington's measures clearly failed the very target of easing pressure on the US balance of payments and restoring international confidence in the US dollar. Consider first the impact of the new foreign military assistance programs on the US external balance and the dollar through its impact on the competitive position of US manufacturing. Within this framework, it is noteworthy to draw attention back to the interaction between the US balance of payments deficit and the economic decline of American industry in foreign markets during the major economic recessions that gripped the US economy in the late 1950s, analyzed in Chap. 2. The decade-long US foreign economic policy implemented during the 1950s failed to resurrect the industrial productivity and competitive edge of US manufacturing on world markets. From the time the Kennedy administration engaged in combining a number of measures to restore the balance of payments deficit on capital account, together with the creation of a set of trade liberalizations up to the worldwide gold crisis in the late 1950s, the total cost of material of US manufacturing industry skyrocketed: from 1961 to 1970 it increased by roughly 50 percent, while since the demise of the convertibility of the US dollar into gold from 1971 to 1973 it hiked up by over 100 percent. Similarly, consider the total cost of electricity and fuel for industrial use: during the same time period it increased at a constant annual rate before flaring up in 1975, when the quadrupling of oil prices added to the unfavorable exchange rate conditions triggered by the weakening of the dollar and the substantial loss of confidence in it at international level.[1] Against the backdrop of Bretton Woods' fixed but adjustable foreign exchange rate policy, such uptick in the price of strategic material or instrumental goods for industrial use throws light on the unlikelihood of recasting the US balance of payments on current account through a reshuffling of foreign military assistance. Likewise, the case of low capital-intensive US manufacturing firms and the dynamics of that sector's share in international trade adds further evidence to this interpretation. In fact these firms, that traditionally depended the most on foreign exchange rates and monetary conditions, were likely to suffer the most from unfavorable exchange rate conditions. It is telling that the soaring US balance of payments deficit registered at decade-end[2] coincided with a decline in the American export of labor-intensive merchandise and low capital-intensive consumer goods to the oil producing countries of the Middle East. Notwithstanding the policies enacted over the decade to restore equilibrium on the US balance of payments on both current and capital accounts, a plummeting balance of payments deficit and a weakened dollar led the low capital-intensive sectors to lose ground to West European surplus economies and the Japanese economy: the Middle Eastern countries' imports from Western Europe and Japan outpaced that from the United States. In 1972, not only was the downturn of US exports to that area attributable to higher freight costs and production costs, but also to the decline of the dollar in foreign exchange markets.[3] With a still-fixed gold value of the dollar and a fixed exchange rate system, this decline in US exports provides further evidence to the failure of the balance of payments deficit financing policies carried over by the Kennedy and Johnson administrations. Neither Kennedy's foreign military and loan repayment policies, nor Johnson's foreign financial policies to stem capital outflows slowed down the weakening US international payments position.

In order to better understand such failure, in addition to the declining competitive edge of American exporters, it is all the more worth drawing attention to the size and persistence of private capital outflows, the losses in US gold stocks, and the level of convertibility between dollar and gold. This is the second research trajectory to chart the failure of the policies conducted during the 1960s. In fact, these indicators help us to better understand to what extent, by the second half of the decade, the stability of the dollar-pegged international trade and payments system, and the official price of gold were already under the severest strain. In this respect it is worth keeping 1967 as the benchmark year. By and large, so far the historical and economic literature has offered two prominent interpretations about the period stretching from the devaluation of the British pound to the collapse of Bretton Woods fixed exchange rate system and the subsequent international energy crisis of 1973. On the one side, a widely accepted and prominent historical view portrays the time from the end of postwar reconstruction through the first oil crisis as a continuous period of international economic stability and integration that revolved around the undisputed dominance of the US currency: such literature points to the role of the US dollar as the ultimate means of payment and international unit of account.[4] Many of these studies consider the postwar era as a continuous period based on the premises of ever-rising levels of world oil and energy production and consumption; such an international oil regime—they stress—broke down only with the twofold devaluation of the dollar and the outbreak of the first oil crisis. This interpretation viewed the first oil shock as the starting point for Western dependence on supply from the oil producing country members of the Organization of Petroleum Exporting Countries (OPEC).[5] According to this scholarship, a linkage can be established between declining industrial productivity, and the profitability and soaring oil prices in wealthy advanced industrial economies.[6] All these works defer the slipping away of the postwar economic system and the end of growth levels associated with it to the period following 1973. US labor productivity declined only as recently as 1976/1977[7]: based on this trend, this scholarship makes the argument that prior to 1973 none of the industrial economies tossed aside the rules of Bretton Woods, nor did they alter the steady flow in capital and goods across nations. The Western nations stuck to it, however, notwithstanding the increasing instability that featured fixed exchange rates and jeopardized the rate of some leading currencies in foreign exchange markets during the late 1960s.[8] On the other hand, due to path-breaking transformations that shook up the international commodity markets and the international monetary system since 1973 thereafter, many reconstructions considered the very late 1960s as the groundwork for the outbreak of oil price hikes, considering that period a stepping-stone in the rising assertiveness of OPEC on the world economic stage. According to this literature, the Suez crisis and the mounting turmoil in the Middle East epitomized by the outbreak of the Arab–Israeli conflict, briefly sketched in this chapter, helped set off the conditions for the end of cheap posted prices of oil and for a growing assertiveness of the Mediterranean and Middle Eastern oil producers, which in the beginning of the 1960s had been united in the OPEC. According to these studies the oil price policies of OPEC can be considered as a major cause for the skyrocketing inflation that rocked the advanced industrial economies in the 1970s.[9] Reasoning on this line, even this second strand of scholarship suggests that the oil producing countries increased their leverage power toward

Washington only after the demise of the dollar's convertibility and the outbreak of the first oil crisis. On the other hand, this literature has viewed the floating currency system as the hallmark for the dollar's declining role in the international economy. In contrast, in this chapter the focus is on combining the decline in the competitive edge of the American industry that depended the most on exchange rates, with events in international monetary relations that anticipated the crisis of Bretton Woods. The aim is to unfold the interrelation between the declining competitive edge of US manufacturing, international monetary developments, and the failure of US policies implemented during the 1960s to resurrect the American balance of payments. As a matter of fact, by the end of the decade the OPEC oil producers ventured both on pushing forward a more aggressive foreign oil policy, and also on reaching trade agreements with the Soviet Union and Iran for the import of military weapons and merchandise.[10] Likewise, by 1967 the rules of international monetary cooperation established at Bretton Woods had largely been tossed aside in many countries. A number of events signaled this development; to summarize the most important ones, it is worth mentioning the 1967 devaluation of the British pound,[11] the devaluation of the French franc in 1969 and the revaluation of the Deutsch Mark that the German government undertook in that same year in order to squeeze the German external surplus and to avoid the international transmission of inflation to the German economy.[12] Besides, the striking structural imbalance in the US balance of payments, whose 1968 surplus revolved in its entirety on the temporary massive capital inflow from Europe,[13] was mismatched by a sluggish trade deficit. All of these factors are usually regarded as early landmark monetary events that laid the groundwork for the collapse of the Bretton Woods fixed-exchange rate system a few years later.[14] In order to track the failure of American policies to resurrect the dollar and the balance of payments under the Kennedy and Johnson administrations which, as discussed in the previous chapter, were conducted through either foreign trade and military policies, or measures to deter capital outflow and force the return of outstanding lending, attention paid so far to the decline in the competitive position of low capital-intensive US manufacturing should be combined with a close focus on a number of international monetary developments of the late 1960s. To be specific, it is worthwhile to focus attention on the stunning decline in US gold reserves, the unfettered outflow of capital, and the early weakening of the dollar's convertibility into gold.

Therefore, from this research perspective, the interpretations of the period from around 1967 to the outbreak of the first oil price hike so far depicted are disputable.

In fact, in contrast to these prominent interpretations, based on a shift of attention in the years prior to 1967 and on a close focus on the unresolved problems grappled with in Chap. 2, it is plausible to draw a well-founded assessment. The seemingly irreconcilable weakening in the US international payments position throughout the 1960s, notwithstanding Washington's attempts to forestall it, suggests that the seeds of international economic disarray and instability that churned away in the international financial system in the following decade were well established as early as 1967. In this regard, through the perspective of international monetary and oil developments that took place within the framework of the US foreign economic policy, this chapter moves away from the idea that 1973 was as much a historical as an uneven cleavage, suggesting that the year 1973 precipitated a variety of international monetary, financial and oil developments, well underway over the past few years. Since 1967, the combined effects of exchange rate adjustments wider than the range of adjustments agreed upon at Bretton Woods, and the increase in the posted price of crude oil, accelerated the crumbling of the economic system laid down some thirty years earlier.[15] Regarding the issue of exchange rate instability, according to the US Department of the Treasury, in 1967 the devaluation of the British pound caused a loss in global reserves that accelerated international monetary arrangements to create a new reserve unit. In 1968, the creation within the IMF of the Special Drawing Rights (SDRs), conceived as a new international reserve unit to supplement dollar-denominated international liquidity,[16] was thought to reduce dependence of the international system on gold for market purposes. Furthermore, the SDRs were supposed to ease off the pressure that the international run on the US gold reserves put on the dollar.[17] This turning point could have a string of centrifugal effects on the Bretton Woods system. In the first instance, a continuous run on gold could increase the unregulated transnational flow of capitals already well underway during the decade; according to the Washington-based economic policymakers such development would revolve around the weakness of the British currency. According to the US economic intelligence, had the devaluation of the British pound been followed by speculative attacks on the British currency, this might have induced most countries of the sterling bloc that held their official reserves in London to start pulling those reserves out of the United Kingdom.[18] Therefore, in the monetary field the devaluation of the British currency severely undermined the stability of dollar's convertibility into gold and set off an unstable international monetary environment well before the crumbling of fixed exchange rates that occurred in the new decade. However, the most crushing effects of this critical deterioration of Bretton Woods' exchange rate stability happened on the supply side. Consider again the British case: the combined 1967 British devaluation and the so-called oil surcharge posed by British Petroleum on the selling price of oil within the United Kingdom, and to the rest of the British pound area since the end of 1967, had remarkable effects on the competitive position of the British economy for years to come.[19] After the first increase in the posted price of oil, as early as 1967, free market crude petroleum prices were hiked up in 1971.[20] During the negotiations on crude exports from the Persian region and the Arabian Gulf that led to the Teheran agreements of February 1971 between some oil producing countries and Western oil companies,[21] the British government showed a tangible concern based, not merely on the possibility of further oil prices hikes, but also on the likely overlapping of higher posted prices by OPEC and the negative impact of unfavorable exchange rates on the real price of imported commodities, caused by the weakened position of the British pound in international exchange markets. According to some of the British government's estimates, this overlapping might result in a total increase of the British oil bill amounting to as much as £150 million.[22] Such well-documented British concern signals the interrelation between the tottering of the fixed exchange rate system since 1967 and declining supply side conditions generated by soaring costs for oil import in the UK and the Western economies in general. Such a trend led the British political system to markedly reshape London's national energy policy, since then reshuffled on the basis of a long-term bet on nuclear policy, a general commitment to make arrangements to revamp coal mining in the short run, and a struggle to develop the North Sea gas fields.[23] Much the same can be said for other oil-importing Western European countries. For instance, this was the case in Italy, where the government had implemented nuclear power projects since the balance of payments crises of the early 1960s. In light of the rising assertiveness of OPEC and its capability to exert influence on the Western oil companies, the governments of Rome unsuccessfully straddled to broaden Italy's nuclear power programs.[24] Likewise, the Federal Republic of Germany engaged in pursuing an energy diversification policy; in particular, as early as the second half of the decade the German chemical corporations went down the way of resuming coal conversion technology and developing nuclear power producing plants to offset the impact of increasing oil prices and unstable exchange rates, which were particularly adverse to importers prior to the revaluation of the Deutsch Mark.[25] On its part, in 1967 the US mapped the newly minable coalfields of Virginia, West Virginia and the Appalachian region. In so doing, Washington showed its willingness to make new coal productions available to its oil-importing partner members of the Organization for Economic Cooperation and Development (OECD); within the OECD, the US Assistant Secretary of the Interior for Mineral Resources Cordell Moore made an offer to Western European countries to increase coal production for export to them. He went so far as to invite the OECD partners "to invest in American coal properties and production facilities" to develop sources under direct control of European concerns and governments.[26] However, notwithstanding this string of initiatives to implement policies of energy diversification, by 1967 the international energy system faltered substantially. A number of dynamics in international energy and financial markets best signaled such instability: it is worth recalling the combined decline in the strength of the dollar in foreign markets, the process of unfettered transnational capital flows underway, and a downward competitive position of US manufacturing, as well as the weakening in the US balance of payments. Such overlapping among all these monetary and financial developments help chart the tottering of the international system much more straightforwardly than any of the critical conditions on the supply side mentioned above. By 1967 a grim outlook on the international position of the United States was combined with the overheating of the domestic economy.

Upon his arrival at the White House, president-elect Nixon had to face a domestic growth rate running at 6 percent and a surge in inflation of 5 percent.[27] On the other hand, as stressed in Chap. 2, looking back at the period from the late 1950s to around 1967–1968 is essential to understand the historical origins and to make sense of the foreign financial, monetary and trade policies typical of the United States in the 1970s as the combined attention to the US balance of payments deficits and continued American concern for the international payments position of non-oil-exporting Least Developed Countries (LDCs). The US foreign economic policymakers established a linkage between restoring equilibrium in international trade and payments, and avoiding the falling apart of non-oil producing LDCs, way before the international economic malaise of the 1970s. In this respect, a turn-of-the-decade speech delivered by US Under Secretary of State Elliot Richardson before the OECD Ministerial meeting in February 1969 is eye-opening. He pointed to the much-heralded expansion of world trade on a multilateral and non-discriminatory basis as the broader framework essential to maintain financial stability in the advanced industrial economies and to achieve sound economic expansion all across the developing countries: "If we are to promote a better structure of international payments and to maintain optimum levels of economic growth, existing obstacles to trade must be reduced and tariff discrimination must be eliminated."[28] Consistently with this approach, from around 1967 to the eve of the first oil crisis, the Washington political elites and the financial elites based in New York and other US financial centers paid continual attention to the US development policies to the non-oil producing countries. In light of the continued importance placed by the US elites on development assistance, this period was consistent with past development assistance programs based on foreign expenditures or assistance programs based on US export, foreign direct investments, and international lending fueled by US banking. Likewise, the remedies devised to resurrect the US international payments position pushed forward foreign trade measures that had been carried over earlier in the decade. In consistence with the Kennedy administration, Nixon resorted to policies of trade liberalization to target the balance of payments deficit, and went for curbing ever-growing cross-national private capital flows as a crucial move in the defense of the dollar and the stability of the system.

Among the other measures adopted by the new administration it is worth recalling foreign investment disincentives, efforts to stem the outflow of dollars, and restrictions on foreign lending.[29]

Therefore, by the time the Suez Crisis broke out with its implications on international trade in weapons and commodities, and the fixed exchange rate system began crumbling, all major issues and options with which US foreign monetary and financial policy would be grappling with in the following decade had all come boiling to the surface. It is noteworthy to list them as a sum-up to this section. In the first instance the seemingly intractable balance of payments problems have not been fixed, while their impact on the stability of the US dollar and gold placed further under strain the US dollar as the reserve currency of the international monetary system and as the unit of international account. Secondly, by that time Washington viewed trade liberalization and the removal of foreign exchange controls by European partners as a linchpin of utmost importance to finance foreign market operations for monetary purposes. Foreign market operations were considered essential to counteract the outflow of dollars and to prop up the US dollar in foreign exchange markets. Based on this reconstruction the topicality of this linkage is straightforward between foreign trade policy and US foreign monetary policy in the 1970s: such perspective helps reappraise a recently held view of the 1970s as a period marked by a general Western retrenchment from trade openness.[30] Thirdly, by 1967 it was a long-established policy to connect the recasting of US balance of payments and international confidence in the dollar with continued American commitment to prevent the non-oil-supplying LDCs from leaving the international payments system. Such mighty course was considered the blueprint for retrenching into protectionist policies and devaluation as a means of financing much-needed US imports. Lastly, as pinpointed in the last two paragraphs of this chapter with respect to the path-breaking approach to the turn-of-the-decade unfettered developments of the Eurodollar market, from roughly 1967 onward curbing the growing share of dollar-denominated short-term private capital assets in international capital markets in defense of the dollar was a target already on the top of the agenda of American political elites and international financial institutions. Yet again, it is worth recalling that in the 1970s this policy turned into a defense of the value of OPEC profits and the financial assets they held in the United States and Western Europe. In particular, a multilateral debate on the tax treatment and protection of OPEC investments in the industrial countries took place within the multilateral Council for International Economic Cooperation (CIEC), a supranational entity that united industrial economies and oil producers up until 1977, and within the Group of Eight (G8).[31] Within this framework, one of the arguments held in this and the next chapters is that the weakening of the dollar and the incapability to devise a worthy substitute for gold as a means of payments for monetary purposes put pressure on the dollar and eventually led to a rise in the loan rates on the Eurodollar market. In turn, this pattern undermined US nationally-issued financial assets, including taxable government bonds issued by governments to finance the public debt and corporate bonds traded in the private markets, which surged as a reaction to the upswing in Eurodollar rates. Furthermore, such upsurge in the cost of money on the Eurodollar market pushed up the cost of commodity prices on world markets (see Fig. 3.1). Such trend in interest rates marked the three years prior to the first oil crisis.

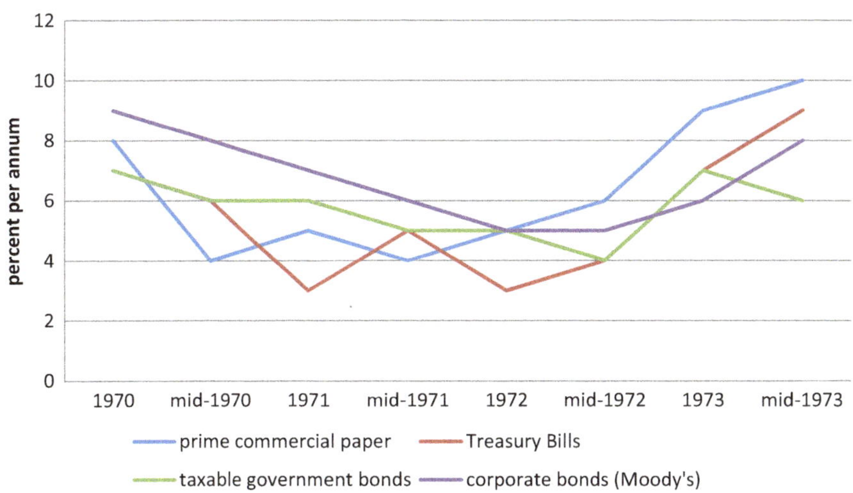

Fig. 3.1 Bond yields and interest rates (Sources: Board of Governors of the Federal Reserve System; Moody's Investors Service; Standard and Poor's Corporation; Council of Economic Advisers, *Economic Indicators*, December 1974, p. 33)

As anticipated by Robert Mundell in his theoretical fine-tuning, the origins and early steps of these developments all occurred way before the 1973 oil embargo and the subsequent fourfold increase in oil prices. To put it another way, the early depreciation of the US dollar and the crisis of Bretton Woods' stability over the five-year period that proceeded its disbanding and the oil price shock had effects on international trade and capital markets developments. Such combined upward movement in commodity and consumer goods prices, and the remarkable increase in short-term financial assets, over this period suggest that in addition to the oil crisis a variety of other causes laid at the origins of the decade's inflation. Similarly, such patterns in international commodity and capital markets prompt the argument that the overheating of the international economy began much earlier than the outbreak of the 1973 oil crisis.[32]

3.2 An Irreversible Path: The Ongoing US Failure to Improve the Current Account Position in the Late 1960s

Even with the two oil crises of the following decade, by the time the US Under Secretary of State gave his speech at the OECD Ministerial Meeting, it was already straightforward to what extent the weakened international payments position of the United States had a gloomy impact on the domestic economy. In early 1969 the country's Gross National Product (GNP) rose by more than 6 percent in the first half of the year and by slightly less than 6 percent over the rest of that year. At the same time, the cost of living run at an average of 5 percent throughout the second half of 1968, while an uptick was reported in the seasonally adjusted unemployment rate from 3.3 percent in the last quarter of 1968 to 4 percent in December 1969.[33] The impact of these inflationary strains and the overheating of the economy on the external equilibrium of the United States added to the sharp deterioration in the balance of payments outlook that all the main indicators considered in this study do suggest. The very bulk of this chapter revolves around US foreign military sales, cuts in US military expenditures overseas, the inflow of convertible foreign currencies and the losses in US gold reserves. Likewise, the chapter charts data on the deterioration and ever-worsening current account deficit and the declining competitiveness of US industry. The combined deterioration of all these indicators and the overheating of the US economy set the stage for the ensuing falloff in the share of US manufacturing in world markets. A rough analysis of these data helps to better understand the failure of American policies to recast the US international payments position through the replacing of initiatives to curb the capital account deficit with policies aimed at improving the country's foreign trade balance. Such policy was aimed at the same time at improving the terms of trade and at reducing the outflows of dollars by acquiring convertible foreign currencies. In the first instance, it is worth assessing whether or not the most important policy instrument used by the Kennedy and Johnson administrations to import convertible foreign currencies, foreign military sales and commercial bonds, worked out. Reported data on US foreign military sales from 1962 to 1967 track a mild increase from 1963 through 1965. Thereafter, as reported in Table 3.1, this supposedly vital asset to acquire dollars in foreign exchange markets slackened off until the first quarter of 1967, when the US involvement in overseas military operations escalated and prompted a steep rise in US foreign military sales that continued through the second trimester of that same year.

Table 3.1 US balance of payments/year (merchandise, income on investments, military sales)

			Income on investments		
Year	Total	Merchandise	Private	Government	Military sales
1962	30.350	20.604	3.948	471	656
1963	32.426	22.071	4.131	498	657
1964	37.099	25.297	4.929	460	747
1965	39.147	26.244	5.376	512	844
1966	43.039	29.168	5.360	595	847
1966-1st trimester	42.044	28.812	5.264	612	836
1966-2nd trimester	42.472	28.724	5.528	612	888
1966-3rd trimester	43.652	29.528	5.776	572	824
1966-4th trimester	43.988	29.608	6.832	584	840
1967-1st trimester	45.444	30.704	5.692	620	1.356
1967-2nd trimester	45.448	30.868	5.544	644	1.344

Source: Council of Economic Advisers, *Economic Indicators*, December 1967. Washington, DC, GPO, 1967, p. 24

On the other hand, by browsing official data on planned foreign military spending cuts, which both US governments and Defense Secretary McNamara pledged to in the early 1960s, it is possible to reveal that they failed in reducing the liabilities on the current account balance. As a matter of fact, after slightly declining by roughly 4 percent from 1962 to 1963, by the middle of the decade Washington's foreign military expenditures leveled off before experiencing a substantial increase in the first quarter of 1967 as a result of the growing US military commitment in East Asia.[34] After peaking in the second half of 1967, the following year the US military expenditure overseas increased much more slowly than in 1967, amounting to $4.6 billion.[35] As regards the US export of military end items, spare parts and services, if one considers the monthly index of new machinery order for export, from the first quarter of 1962 to the first quarter of 1969, such category of export underwent modest and scattered increases.[36] Other measures that the US administrations had deployed prior to the late 1960s to finance foreign exchange operations for monetary purposes included early repayments of outstanding debts by surplus European countries and the promotion of foreign direct and portfolio investments in the US; they all contributed little to finance foreign market operations and the US balance of payments deficit. In the fall of 1968, shortly before stepping down from office, US President Lyndon Johnson took two initiatives to have his Western European partners finance American operations in foreign exchange markets for monetary purposes. The Secretary of the Treasury Henry Fowler and Under Secretary Deming put pressure on Italy both to make the Italian government stick to its commitment to compensate the United States for military expenditures in Italy by a corresponding amount of Italian military purchases in the United States, and to induce Rome to purchase non-liquid securities through the Bank of Italy.[37] Therefore, the US administrations consistently engaged in a stream of measures to tackle both the American trade balance and the capital account position. Notwithstanding these measures, the balances on the US liquidity basis showed signs of deterioration: out of a total liquidity deficit that from 1966 to 1967 soared from over $1300 million to over $3500 million, seasonally adjusted annual rates of net foreign capital flows to the United States increased from 1966 to 1967. However, during the first three quarters of

1967 the inflow of net foreign capital slightly progressed before slackening off at the end of the year.[38] Besides, during the third quarter of 1967 repayments on US Government credits were about $50 million less than in the second quarter, while receipts of advance payments from foreign countries dropped from $415 million in the second quarter to $110 million in the third.[39] This downward trend in foreign capital flows into the United States during 1967 is attributable to a tangle of causes. In the first instance, certainly it is worth mentioning easier monetary conditions in the United States during 1967 as compared to 1966; as Washington undertook an easy monetary policy, this both prompted the US banks to lend money abroad, and caused a decline in foreign capital investments in the US financial market.[40] Secondly, as the Kennedy administration was aware,[41] agreements on early repayments of outstanding loans and debts were nothing short of temporary and limited measures, which the United States could not count on in the long-term. Concerning the failure to attract new investments by foreign central banks and private investors, two points help to better understand the slow development of foreign investments in the United States. As regards investments and deposits by foreign governments in the US, the 1967 Arab–Israeli conflict in the Middle East reversed any previous positive trend; since the outbreak of the conflict the central banks of Egypt, Iraq, Algeria, and Sudan suddenly drew down their balances at the Federal Reserve Bank of New York to a nominal or zero amount. These countries ordered to pay out their funds to Paris banks (Iraq), to Russian and Swiss banks (Egypt), and to Switzerland (Algeria). Although their deposits at the New York Federal Reserve consisted of limited amounts as compared to the total capital account balance, the implication of hostilities in the Middle East did matter to such course of international investments.[42] Thirdly, and more importantly, patterns of short-term capital flows accounted for the failure to increase US holdings of convertible foreign currencies. As long as the outflows of short-term capital from the United States contributed to total US balance of payments deficit, the monetary policies of European central banks on short-term investments jeopardized Washington's efforts to attract foreign investments to the United States. As anticipated, the long-lasting run on gold and the speculative attacks on the dollar triggered an increase in the rate of short-term Eurodollar loans: the more the loss of confidence in the dollar developed and the US monetary authorities proved to be unable to uphold the official price of gold at $35 per ounce, the more the US currency came under strain. Against this backdrop American investment banks and brokerage houses pulled low powered dollars out of the US to finance high-powered reserves and financial assets in London and other European financial markets. This investment pattern triggered a steady rise in the loan rates in the Eurodollar market as demand for Eurocurrency loans flared up. The interconnectedness between Eurodollar and Eurocurrency markets, the changing US foreign financial and monetary policies from the 1960s to the 1970s, and the origins of the international inflation of the 1970s, will be explored in more detail later. What is worth pointing out first is the overlap between private capital flows from the US to Europe and the mild and declining contribution of US military exports and overseas sales to improve the US current account position. Second, it is worth stressing the reaction of the central banks of countries home to the Eurocurrency markets during 1967. In the aim to discourage short-term investments, some European monetary authorities decided to do anything possible to eliminate incentives to put funds in the Eurodollar market. For instance, in early 1967 the German authorities altered the reserve requirements for their banks in the pursuit of this objective. As the Department of State noted, this measure was likely to gradually reduce not only investments in the Eurodollar market, but also foreign lending by commercial banks.[43] Over the course of the decade some world-class German banks contributed much to the volume of foreign portfolio investments in the US and purchased dollar-denominated bonds issued by international financial institutions such as the International Bank for Reconstruction and Development (IBRD); GiroZentrale (GZ) and Deutsch Bank, for instance, bought a significant portions of World Bank-issued bonds and securities and pledged to make public and private placements in the German markets.[44] The involvement of German banks in financing the IBRD development programs was a means of easing the burden of the IBRD development assistance programs on the US balance of payments. In this context it is easy to understand the linkage between the policies of European central banks to contain the development of the Eurocurrency markets and the sluggish recovery of the capital account component in the US balance of payments during that year. The policies pursued by Western European central banks to reduce returns on investments in the Eurocurrency markets across Europe led to raised interest rates and general investment conditions that made the European bond and securities markets attractive to investors, and as such, attractive investment outlets alternative to the IBRD.[45] The reverse occurred in the United States in 1969 and in Germany in 1970, when tight monetary conditions led several American and German banks and corporations to borrow from the Eurodollar market, thus contributing much to the demand for Eurodollar loans and Eurodollar financial instruments.[46] In the context of tightening monetary conditions, the increase in Eurodollar loan rates and the bountiful development of very short-term financial instruments induced several American investment banks to plead with the US Department of the Treasury to extend outstanding issues instead of issuing new Treasury offerings in the maturity area of intermediate notes.[47] In addition, it is noteworthy to mention the effects of the devaluation of the British pound on British investments in the United States: prior to the devaluation of its currency, the Bank of England increased the discount rate and doubled the reserve requirements for the British banks. These measures were aimed at attracting capital to the United Kingdom and discouraging British banking from overseas investments, including investments in the United States.[48] Thereafter, the devaluation of the British pound in November 1967 induced the United Kingdom to liquidate its portfolio of US corporate securities with adverse effects on the US liquidity balance.[49] Therefore, the devaluation of the British pound added to the effects of Western European monetary policies designed to discourage investments in the Eurocurrency markets. Moreover, it contributed to increase pressure on the US balance of payments on capital account. On the other hand, a close focus on monthly data on the US gold reserves since the beginning of the decade through the rattling international gold and payments crisis of 1967 suggests that by that year Bretton Woods' monetary and financial foundations were already faltering to a great extent. For instance, the combined devaluation of the British pound and the international gold crisis that broke out in 1967 were major causes for the sharp deterioration in the US gold

Table 3.2 US gold stocks in millions of dollars

Year-month	US gold stocks in millions of dollars
1967	11.982
1968-January	11.984
1968-February	11.883
1968-March	10.484
1968-April	10.484
1968-May	10.384
1968-June	10.367
1968-July	10.367
1968-August	10.367
1968-September	10.367
1968-October	10.367
1968-November	10.367
1968-December	10.367

Source: Federal Reserve System, *Annual Report of the Board of Governors of the Federal Reserve System*, 1968, Table 16, pp. 384–385

stock (Table 3.2): over the course of calendar year 1968 the US monetary gold stock in millions of dollars declined by roughly over 12 percent compared to its 1967 average.

In addition to the use of dollars by foreign holders to make a run on gold, among other reasons that plausibly accounted for such losses it is important to mention the widely known policies that were conducted by France in the international gold markets. As stressed in Chap. 2, according to US economic intelligence sources, since the beginning of the 1960s Paris ran counter to the role of the dollar in international finance, promoted the use of gold as the only international reserve, and instigated other Western countries to convert large amount of their dollar holdings into gold. The Central Intelligence Agency (CIA) held the view that before the gold crisis of November 1967 the French both converted nearly all their dollar reserves into gold and reduced their cooperation with the other financial powers by withdrawing from the London gold pool.[50] Furthermore, Paris contributed to the weakening of the gold parity of the US dollar by questioning agreements on, and adoption of, US proposals for increasing world reserves through the creation of a new international reserve asset to be established under the auspices of the International Monetary Fund (IMF). Although the CIA recognized that after the gold crisis of 1967 the French adopted a milder position toward the dollar,[51] the international monetary policy of Paris is worth mentioning in order to formulate a comprehensive explanation of the continuing losses in US gold stocks. Similarly, such French foreign economic diplomacy is useful in order to account for the problems Washington met with in trying to uphold the convertibility of the dollar into gold, notwithstanding the decade-long American policies to revert the outflows of dollar. Likewise, it is worth mentioning that by the fall of 1967 a surge in the non-monetary demand for gold was recorded[52]: in one year industrial demand for gold had increased by $50 million, amounting to a total of more than the current gold production, excluding the USSR production. Furthermore, by late 1967 a steady rise in traditional gold hoarding was reported, mostly in Asia and the Middle East.[53] Lastly, two other reasons help explain the run on US gold: the increased gold demand caused by political turmoil in the Middle East, and the USSR's decision to freeze its gold selling in 1966 and 1967, which in turn reduced international supply of gold.[54] For sure, the scale and scope of US dollar losses, and the impact on the composition of foreign central banks' reserves in dollar and gold, reached a peak in spring 1968 as a result of the ongoing gold crisis. The Johnson administration defined such pace of loss "untenable," and pointed to a string of measures in support for the international monetary system and the official dollar value of gold. They included, in addition to collective commitment to contrast foreign speculators and hoarders, the institution of agreed standards with respect to the gold and dollar components in the reserves of all major financial countries of the world.[55] The ways in which the US and its Western European partners reacted to the gold crisis and took up measures to prevent a gold revaluation will now be investigated. It is worth noting that the US Department of the Treasury established a crucial linkage between the preservation of the interconvertibility between dollar and gold and the restructuring of US reserves, and the capability to make the world monetary system sustain high levels of employment and growth.[56] Meaningfully, the CIA fully shared this view: in late December 1967 an intelligence memorandum pointed to the interconnectedness between exchange rate instability stemming from the devaluation of the British pound, and economic growth and aggregate demand in the Western industrial economies.[57] This linkage between stability in foreign exchange markets and international payments on the one side, and the pace of economic growth across the industrial nations on the other, would be a critical point in the restructuring of the system of international trade and payments between the two energy crises of the following decade. In particular, this was much the case of the Carter administration's foreign financial policy toward OPEC and Carter's foreign economic policy toward the European Economic Community (EEC); this important point is investigated in Chap. 5.

3.3 The Gold Crisis, the Suez Crisis, the British Pound Crisis, and the Origins of the 1970s Inflation: Unfettered Pressures on the Dollar

The gold crisis of 1967, with its effects on exchange markets, the dollar, and the interest rates of short-term financial instruments such as the Eurodollar market, deepened a trend well underway by that time. At the same time, it added to the pressure put on foreign exchange markets and international payments by the oil price increases that stemmed from the disruption of the normal pattern of supplies caused by the Arab–Israeli war and, in particular, by the closure of the Suez Canal that same year.[58] In fact, notwithstanding the scale and rapidity of the gold crisis during the second half of the decade, the long-standing decline in US gold stock sheds further light on the decade-long American incapability to contain the outflow of gold and to preserve the interconvertibility between gold and dollar. In order to better assess this, it is worth recalling that in the period from the last quarter of 1961 to the end of 1967 reported monthly data on the US monetary gold stock show a pace of slight but constant decline that culminated in a substantial diminution at the end of the decade.[59] Therefore, when the gold crisis broke out, the US gold stock had long been suffering a decline and the weakening of the dollar's fixed value against the gold was well underway. In addition, in order to account for the failure of American policies based on the combining of capital account measures and current account policies pushed forward over the preceding few years, it is definitely telling to pinpoint the ratio of US foreign exchange rate to the acquisition of convertible foreign currencies in the United States. With respect to the decline of the dollar in exchange markets, it is possible to capture it both by charting the dollar's value against the British pound, and by measuring its value against all other major currencies. As regards the exchange rate between dollar and pound, before the devaluation of the British pound London led New York in interest arbitrage. For instance, from the beginning of 1966 to devaluation, both rate differential with forward exchange cover and rate differential with three-month forward rate, as well as three-month Treasury bill rates, were largely in favor of London over New York. Consider now the spot exchange markets: after performing a puzzling downward trend from mid-1964 to the end of 1966, since then both the Dutch guilder, and the Belgian and French francs regained their footing and led the US dollar through the end of 1967. Much the same can be said for the Italian lira, while during the same time frame both the German mark and the Swiss franc fluctuated significantly. Notwithstanding these fluctuations, throughout the period they all led the US dollar per unit value.[60] Therefore, the closer it was to the British pound devaluation and the rupture of fixed-but-adjustable exchange rates, the more it plummeted the value of the US dollar in terms of all major currencies, compared to the beginning of the decade. Quite remarkably, during the same time span the US foreign financial and trade policies described in Chap. 2 failed in their attempt to increase foreign exchange reserves. Based on a breakdown of international reserves held by advanced industrial economies over the postwar decades, the United States was the only industrial nation that experienced a continuing decline. From 1949 to 1966 US international reserves uninterruptedly declined from over $26 million to little short of $15 million, while both surplus Western European countries and Japan, as well as countries suffering from a sticky balance of payments deficit, performed either a constant rise (Japan, France, Austria, Italy, the Netherlands, Spain) or a substantial increase mixed with sudden falloffs (Germany), as well as ups and down (United Kingdom).[61] A detailed look at aggregate data by each country's holdings of convertible foreign currencies unmistakably suggest that the United States total holdings, including holdings by the Department of the Treasury and the Federal Reserve System, increased remarkably during the period from 1962 to 1966. However, holdings of convertible foreign currencies peaked only from the last quarter of 1967 through the end of 1968. More importantly, such increases did not help offset the outstanding run on gold. From 1962 to 1967—years that were clearly dominated by the unstoppable US endeavors to increase holdings of convertible foreign currencies through foreign military sales, and achieve early repayments of outstanding loans or similar measures—the total US gold stock declined uninterruptedly before collapsing in 1968 in the context of the international gold crisis briefly examined here.[62] Considering that by the middle of the decade the US government repeatedly pledged support to the IMF, this negative trend clearly sheds light on the limited effectiveness of American policies to resurrect the dollar in foreign exchange markets through the policies on the current and capital accounts conducted over the preceding few years. Since as early as 1962 the Long Range International Payments Committee suggested the possibility of US drawing on the IMF to finance part of the prospective US balance of payments deficit. Among other measures, such hypothesis suggested drawing on part of the roughly $4 billion of medium-term credit available from the Fund.[63] In June 1965, $259 million was subscribed to the Fund in respect of the US quota increase, which became effective in February 1966. Considering that in accordance with Fund policies the United States had the right to draw foreign equivalent to its reserve position in the Fund virtually automatically if needed, such quota increases were supposed to help expand US holdings of foreign currencies, and to increase US dollar and gold reserves. The effectiveness and decisiveness of direct financial assistance from the IMF to the United States gold reserves were overestimated: indeed, they were believed to help counteract the run on US gold stock much more than the official figures indicate. For instance, although the IMF engaged in a string of emergency measures, the US gold stock declined; beginning in the last quarter of 1965, the Washington-based institution deposited a tranche of gold to mitigate the impact on the US gold stock of purchases by foreign countries for gold subscriptions on increased IMF quotas. Moreover, in Spring 1968, following the closure of the London gold market at the height of the international gold crisis analyzed in the following pages, in preparing a round of interim negotiations with the other Gold Pool member countries to make arrangements before the activation of the IMF Special Drawing Rights (SDRs),[64] the Fund currency at the time being conceived to make up for any loss in global reserves triggered by the devaluation of sterling, Washington was ready to draw on the IMF. Such drawing was aimed to offset and absorb expected moderate increases in dollar holdings by non-gold pool member countries.[65] All taken into account, through the end of 1968 gold sold by the IMF to the United States amounted to $1 billion, with potentially positive effects on either the stability of US gold reserves, or US holdings of convertible foreign currencies to increase dollar reserves and keep apace the official dollar value of gold.[66] Notwithstanding these measures by the IMF and the Washington's eagerness to go this way, the run on US gold stock continued. Under these circumstances, certainly the policies of trade liberalization promoted and enacted by the United States failed in reversing such deteriorating US external balance and gold reserves. The governments of Washington failed to achieve high levels of military sales or substantial foreign military spending cuts, while a variety of factors contributing to shape the international gold markets, which included French policies, increased demand for gold for industrial uses, and production cuts from irreplaceable suppliers such as the USSR, jeopardized further the stabilization of US gold stocks, US dollar holdings and the value of the American currency against the currencies of most capital-surplus countries. Notwithstanding, during 1968 the US was able to improve its holdings of convertible foreign currencies: at year-end, US international reserve assets had increased by $1.25 billion. This improvement let Washington increase US gold holdings, which resulted primarily from purchases from France during the first half of the year and from Germany at end of the year.[67] Notwithstanding all these gains, on aggregate US gold stock declined and the seemingly unachievable reduction of dollar assets held by foreign central banks and private foreign banking did not occur. This trend contributed to push forward the depreciation of the dollar. Therefore, the combined seemingly intractable international gold issue, the effects of the closure of the Suez Canal, and the inefficacy of the US balance of deficit financing policies in recasting the current account position, all account for the gloomy external balance of the United States and the pressure put on the dollar as early as 1968.

By drawing attention to the hypotheses that circulated in Washington when the world-scale gold crisis hurt the US gold stock it is easy to find further confirmation that American foreign exchange and financial policies were unsuccessful in stabilizing the international payments position of the United States. To highlight how by that time the convertible foreign currencies that flew to the US were short of total US means of payments required to purchase dollars in foreign markets and to forestall US gold losses it is worth mentioning a proposal by Gardner Ackley. Ackley, a macroeconomist who served under President Kennedy and contributed to the shaping of the foreign economic policy of Washington, did not step down from his position upon the coming to power of Lyndon Johnson. Ackley, chairman of the US Council of Economic Advisers under Johnson, suggested that the United States transfer all its gold to the IMF in return for claims on the Fund to let the United States manage the exchange rate of the dollar against other strong currencies by purchasing foreign currencies through the IMF.[68] This proposal was formulated a few times before some capital-surplus advanced industrial economies pressed for activating the IMF's Special Drawing Rights to ease the run on the dollar and reduce pressure for an increase in the price of gold. In this respect, among other events, a path-breaking case in point was Italy, which during the first eight months of 1969 suffered a dollar outflow worth up to $800 million and was, among other countries, a prominent advocate for the activation of the SDRs.[69] Within this framework, Ackley's proposal was widely regarded as a harmful step toward the demonetization of gold. It is quite significant in that it sheds light on the need to procure a volume of convertible foreign currencies larger than the amount the US could acquire through early repayments of outstanding debts and loans or through a steady increase in the volume of military and civilian merchandise sold to capital-surplus Western European countries.[70] Furthermore, the prospect for currency floating and exchange rate realignments, for which the devaluation of the British pound paved the way, made matters worse: it added further pressure on the dollar, weakened its value in exchange markets and made US foreign exchange market operations harder to achieve.[71] According to a paper prepared in early 1968 by the US Department of the Treasury, a shaky currency realignment was likely to induce both private dollar holders in Europe, and dollar holders in non-industrial countries, as well as some Americans, to flee the dollar in favor of strong European currencies such as the Swiss franc "with a resulting dollar accumulation in foreign official hands."[72] In other words, the prospect for a depreciation of the US dollar stemming from a currency realignment would trigger massive dollar sales that would translate into further pressure on the US currency. Therefore, the deterioration of exchange rate stability made matters worse in that American failure to acquire dollar assets through foreign currency operations made way for dollar selling operations in international financial centers by both foreign central banks and private dollar holders. This wave of selling operations posed further threat to the value of and confidence in the US dollar. In this respect, based on data available on exchange rates of major currencies against the US dollar from the early 1960s through the overheating of the US dollar's convertibility into gold around 1968, it is easy to identify a correlation between the impending gold crisis and the depreciation of the US dollar. This was particularly the case, with the exception of the British pound against the American currency, in the three-month forward exchange rates of major currencies against the dollar from 1967 to 1969.[73] Naturally, any time American dollar holders sold their dollar holdings, this process also contributed to the outflow of dollars from the United States. Therefore, the closer to the end of the decade, the more the inefficacies of the US balance of payments policies on current and capital accounts overlapped with the deterioration of the fixed exchange rate in putting pressure on the dollar and its full and stable convertibility into gold. This interconnection helps explain the multiple causes that undermined the stability and confidence in the US dollar and the Bretton Woods system at large. Such causes set the stage for the dollar's depreciation and the increase in commodity and consumer good prices in international markets way before the 1973 oil price hikes. Owing to the incapability of the United States since the early 1960s to finance foreign exchange market operations through the acquisition of convertible foreign currencies, this combined loss of gold and capital outflows not only hit the dollar, it also had a wealth-crushing impact on the capital supply for fixed capital investments in the United States. In the second half of 1966 an extraordinary credit pressure brought the US capital markets to a credit bursting point, forcing numerous American banks to take in substantial amounts of Eurodollar deposits to meet domestic credit needs. This credit shortage, clearly linked to the nearly decade-long capital outflow from the US, led European branches of American banks and European banking institutions to transfer $2.3 billion in Eurodollar funds to the US. This massive flow triggered an upswing in the loan rates of short-term deposits; for example, the three-month deposit rate rose from 5.25 percent in January 1966 to over 7 percent in late November of that same year.[74] This development in short-term interest rates in foreign financial centers accounts for the causal relation that linked the inefficacy of US foreign financial policy to lessen the outflow of dollars through a rise in convertible foreign currencies, to the depreciation of the dollar in foreign exchange markets that increased the cost of borrowing and laid the seeds for the international inflation that ensued a few years later. To put it another way, the failure to reverse the outflow of dollars through the acquisition of convertible foreign currencies led both to the weakening of the dollar in foreign markets and the rate rise on short-term highly liquid financial instruments at the time required to meet domestic credit needs. The interconnectedness between the deterioration of the dollar in foreign exchange markets, the credit crunch in domestic capital markets, and the growth of unregulated short-term financial instruments, at the time epitomized by the expansion of Eurodollars, surged once more (as will be seen in Chap. 4), shortly after the first oil price hike of late 1973. Based on this reconstruction, it is plausible to argue that the beginning of exchange rate instability since 1967 interacted with the failure of American monetary and financial policies to reduce the outflow of dollars through foreign currency dealings. These two factors interacted in a challenging fashion that contributed to depreciate the US currency and most dollar-denominated financial assets held by international economic institutions, central banks and private banking. In turn, such depreciation of the American currency led investors to leave regulated dollar-denominated financial instruments and caused a surge in interest-sensitive short-term dollar assets such as the Eurodollar market. This process was combined with the outflow of capital from the United States. A comparison between developments in short-term interest rates in Western financial centers and the London Eurodollar market is striking; for instance, as early as the period from the beginning of 1966 to the end of 1967, based on a comparison between three-month Treasury bill rates in the UK, US, Japan and Canada, and the three-month deposit rate for Switzerland to

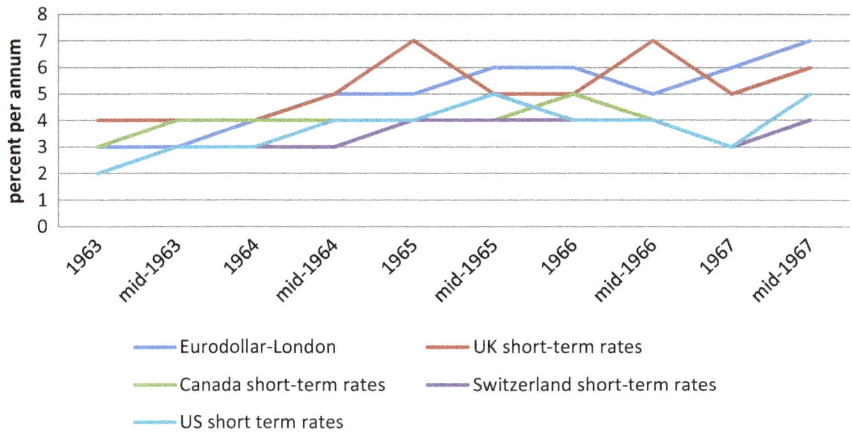

Fig. 3.2 Short-term interest rates (Source: Board of Governors of the Federal Reserve System, Division of International Finance, *Capital Market Developments Abroad*, 1967)

the three-month rate for US dollar deposits in London, the Eurodollar rate kept continuously ahead of other short-term rates and surged during the second half of 1967 (Fig. 3.2).

The case of the expanding Japanese debt during the 1968 worldwide gold crisis is an exemplary case in point of this surge in short-term interest rates: in March 1968 the increase in Eurodollar loan rates had a crushing effect on the $1.4 billion of Japanese balance in borrowed Eurodollars.[75] In other words, the failure of American foreign financial policies to resurrect the balance of payments on the current and capital accounts in order to prop up the dollar and stabilize international payments, coupled with the deterioration of fixed exchange rates, plunged the dollar and hiked up short-term interest rates. This process brought to center stage the most crucial issues at stake in the stabilization of the international trade and payments system between the two energy crises of the 1970s and the ensuing development of short-term Eurocurrency markets: (i) the meteoric rise in Eurodollar assets outside the United States and other Eurocurrency deposits,[76] and the declining buying power of most dollar holdings held by governments and private holders in world financial markets; and

(ii) the steady decline in their earnings on goods and commodities traded in US dollars. According to a study by the authoritative US National Bureau of Economic Research, borrowing by American banks from foreign branches and European banks trading in Eurocurrency deposits jumped from $1.2 billion in 1964 to a high of $14.5 billion in 1969.[77] Within this framework, quite similarly to what happened to the OPEC countries in the 1970s, the ensuing dollar's depreciation reduced the market value of dollar assets either in the equity markets or in the capital markets, and diminished the purchasing power of dollar-holders in foreign markets. This explains why, from the first half of the 1960s to the end of the decade, the dollar value of the oil producing countries' investments in the Eurodollar market skyrocketed way before the spectacular rise they experienced since the first oil price shock of 1973.[78] This meant that the development of the Eurocurrency markets reduced the value of investments in dollar-denominated equity and capital markets and lessened the competitive position of those countries that made much business from international exchanges paid for in US dollars. There is an exemplary case of the American family of financiers that, due to the family's role at the highest US foreign economic policy level under the Ford administration, the Rockefeller family, whose business interests in both international finance and oil was twice as affected by pressure on dollar and run on gold. This is more extensively examined in the following chapters.

Both the international lending activities of the Rockefellers, carried out by the Chase Manhattan Bank, and their business in the international commodity markets, controlled by the Standard Oil Group, were denominated in dollars. Although the history of the family's business was tightly bound to the dollar and the US currency area, the weakening of the dollar and the sharp deterioration in the US balance of payments led the family to plan a diversification of its investments way before the dollar plummeted and the system of fixed exchange rates collapsed. In the spring of 1967, the trust fund in which a substantial amount of shares of the family-controlled oil company, Mobil Oil Corporation, were placed, planned to diversify the holding of the Corporation's stock and to commence a diversification program into other equity investments: this move was clearly aimed to diversify into a basket of currencies.[79] Plainly, the objective of such currency diversification was to lessen the risk stemming from a one-currency investment policy. Thereafter, the sticky effects of the weakening of the dollar on the purchasing power of any company and country that did business with the dollar currency area, or traded in the US dollar, came to an end shortly after the disbanding of fixed exchange rates in 1971. At that time, quite remarkably, the oil companies operating in the Gulf and the Minister of Finance of Iran made arrangements to establish a "committee of experts" to meet at OPEC in Vienna to determine the actual impact of shifts in exchange rates caused by the flotation of the US dollar on the purchasing power of the proceeds of the oil exports of OPEC countries.[80] Therefore, well in advance of the 1971 monetary events, by the time the Arab–Israeli crisis broke out, signs of international monetary collapse as structural instability in exchange rates began casting a grim shadow on world oil and other commodities markets and led to turbulent times. By the time tensions in the Middle East between Arabs and Israelis resulted in the June 1967 conflict, the monetary and financial foundations of the system of exchange in goods and capital under US leadership were already severely undermined. At the same time, developments in the capital markets and seemingly intractable deteriorating exchange market conditions plummeted them into further instability. The historical literature has established a linkage between the closure of the Suez Canal, which followed the beginning of Israel's assaults on an Egyptian airfield on June 5, 1967, and the subsequent upswing in crude petroleum prices.[81] Certainly this linkage did exist, although the impact of the stunning increase in oil crude prices on the dollar's strength, the US balance of payments and the competitive edge of Western goods and capital in international markets took place on the heels of those developments in international capital markets just described. In fact, after the outbreak of the war, the OECD oil-importing countries felt the pinch of a shortfall in oil export from the Arab countries; oil production cuts and, more importantly, the closure of the Suez Canal and lack of tankers to carry the oil accounted for this steady decline in oil export. After the resumption of oil production and export by Saudi Arabia and Kuwait over the course of the month of June, key Middle Eastern oil producers as Iran, Kuwait and Saudi Arabia were still producing below pre-crisis levels because there were not enough tankers to carry the oil.[82] Certainly, by the end of July 1967 the cost of purchasing tankers had significantly increased, and the shipping rates had doubled for some tankers carrying oil, with Western European countries such as Italy and France mostly affected by the closure.[83] The impact of rising shipping costs and soaring costs for purchasing tankers led the OECD Council to charge the International Industry Advisory Group, an advisory group gathering a number of representatives from the oil companies, "with managing the use of tankers to obtain maximum supply to Europe." For sure, such shortfall in production and shipping problems had direct impact on the sharp rise in prices, leading the United States in July to plan an increase in its production to make possible a substantial rise in export to Europe.[84] Over the course of fall 1967, the effects of the Arab–Israeli war on world oil supply and prices afflicted West European imports and prompted a rising assertiveness by some OPEC member states. In September, notwithstanding the Khartoum Conference of Arab states removed the ban on oil supplies destined for the UK, the USA and the Federal Republic of Germany, supplies to Europe and prices continued to have adverse effects on European importers. In those circumstances, according to British Minister of Power, supply to Europe could only be "increased by the opening of the 'Tapline' from Saudi Arabia to Syria or the resumption of export from Nigeria."[85] Therefore, predictably, as far as it triggered a rise in crude petroleum prices, the war had a much more adverse effect on international payments and the buying power of Western European oil-importing countries than on the United States. In turn, these adverse effects put pressure on the current account component of the Western European countries' balance of payments. However, the Arab–Israeli conflict affected also on the US balance of payments on capital account in so far as it reduced the profits of American oil companies and firms operating in the Arab countries. According to a study of the Department of State prepared in the fall of that same year, about 65 percent of the oil produced in the Arab countries was from United States investments there. These investments returned an annual profit of about $1.5 billion to the American oil industry and made a net contribution of over $1 billion per annum to the US balance of payments. According to the Department of State, although this loss in profits would have no more than a temporary economic effect, "the loss of $1 billion annual credit to the US balance of payments would be a matter of very great concern to the US government." At the same time the likely adverse development represented by the nationalization of Western oil companies in the Arab world was estimated in Washington to trigger a further upswing in the US balance of payments deficit by $1 billion per year less receipts for compensation.[86] Just three years later, according to a 1971 estimate from the National Security Council, the increases in oil revenues demanded by the OPEC meeting held in Caracas in December 1970 might cost the oil producing Western companies to the order of $2 billion annually.[87] Therefore, from the viewpoint of the US government, the Arab–Israeli war added to the rupture of international payments that was already underway, not so much because of the oil price increases, but to the decline in the flow of net financial assets to the US capital markets. Furthermore, it put pressure on the US current account balance in so far as Washington halted foreign military sales and prohibited private US manufacturers from selling weapons and military components to radical Arab countries like Algeria, with which diplomatic relations broke down following the outbreak of the conflict.[88] The impact of the June 1967 war on Washington's exchange earnings usually accruing to the US current account from the sales of American arms to the Mediterranean and Middle Eastern countries represented a significant effect of the Arab–Israeli conflict on the US balance of payments; the Johnson administration was well aware of it quite shortly after the outbreak of the conflict.[89] Reasoning on this line, as early as June 1967 the Arms Control Group of the Department of State called attention to the moderate Arab states—namely Morocco, Tunisia, Libya, Lebanon, Jordan, and, above all, Saudi Arabia. The Group stressed that preserving diplomatic relations with these countries was essential not only to protect and to promote US corporations' oil investments in the region, but also to prop up the flows of military assistance, export of weapons and shipping of commodities from both the US Department of Defense and US firms. Therefore, the tangle of business relations with these countries should be shielded from the trade-crushing effects of war not only to uphold the US balance of payments on capital account as it was affected by alterations in drilling activities of American companies in those countries and the decline in the repatriation of profits to the US. Indeed, the war also affected the US current account position in so far as American–Arab trade relations were a way to carry over Washington's strategy to resurrect the dollar in international exchange markets through foreign exchange earnings based among other measures on military export.[90]

Notwithstanding this impact of the Suez Crisis on the rise in prices and its contribution to the plummeting US balance of payments deficit, the unfinished deterioration of the dollar in foreign exchange markets and the irreversible crisis of the British pound put definite strains on this bad-looking situation. These strains account for the worsening buying powers of Western countries and declining real profit margins by oil companies and oil producing countries. Within this framework the devaluation of the British pound in November 1967, with its tangle of consequences on world monetary reserves and the ensuing increase in the run on US gold stock and speculative attacks on the dollar, made matters worse. Since the middle of the decade the United Kingdom had sterling liabilities to foreigners of over $11 billion. This downward balance of payments outlook stemmed from the effect of rising domestic demand outstripping imports. From the fall of 1964 to the spring of 1965 the British government made an attempt to tackle its balance of payments deficit through a tight fiscal policy coupled with monetary stringency with the aim of curbing the overburdening pressure of domestic demand on imports.[91] Notwithstanding this stream of measures carried over in 1966 and 1967 through tight monetary policy, credit restrictions on exporters, and a harsh standstill on wages to reduce demand for imports, what looked like a long-standing disequilibrium led to the fall 1967 devaluation of the British pound. In a matter of few months, this had a staggering impact on British buying power in foreign markets and depreciated the cost of domestic borrowing: as soon as fall of 1968 a symptomatic rise in British export and a reduction in bank rates to 7 percent was recorded.[92] The reverse of these immediate positive effects of the British pound devaluation occurred in the international monetary system. The devaluation of the British currency further eroded confidence in the world's reserve currency; during the winter following London's decision to devalue its currency, a record-setting capital flight into gold was recorded.[93] At the same time the run on US gold stock deepened; shortly after the devaluation taken up in London, following a five-month period of stability, from November 1967 to the end of the year total US gold reserves plummeted by roughly 8 percent,[94] while from November to April 1968 the dollar exchange rate adjustment against most European currencies recorded a slight slippage.[95] Based on this sequence of events the combined effect of the gold crisis and the devaluation of the British pound on the strength of the US dollar in foreign markets and its full convertibility into gold is evident. As a matter of fact, by the time London unilaterally tossed aside the rules of Bretton Woods, the pressure on the convertibility between dollar and gold and international confidence in the dollar, which was undermined in the first half of the decade, had come under further strain. The functioning of the gold pool club founded in 1961 had been disbanded; in 1966 gold sales to private hoarders and industrial users began to outpace purchases from new production and diminishing gold sales of newly mined gold.[96] This excess in outpayments over gold earning by the gold pool members jeopardized the settlement mechanism of the gold pool, whose member countries began to lose increasing amounts of gold to the free markets. Understandably, this development could put a potentially enormous pressure on the dollar and lead to increase the price of gold in the free markets. The effects of the run on gold on the value of the US dollar in foreign markets had an adverse effect on the US currency, not only on exchange rate adjustments but also on arbitrage on Treasury bills: during the first part of 1968 the spread in favor of London on Treasury bill rates recorded a moderate but continued increase.[97] On the other hand, on the domestic economy the weakening of the dollar in foreign exchange markets led the Federal Reserve System to raise the discount rate throughout the year in order "to strengthen the international position of the dollar and to combat domestic inflationary pressures" stemming from such slipping position against other currencies.[98] Furthermore, as US Under Secretary of State George Ball had predicted as early as the summer of 1965, the devaluation of the British pound had potentially crushing effects on the US federal budget and overseas military expenditures. In his view a devaluation was likely to force the British to cut back their defense commitments around the world, leaving the US "more than ever to be the policeman of the world" and to assume permanently additional overseas commitments.[99] Consequently, on the eve of devaluation of the British pound, as a result of a combined weakening dollar in foreign exchange markets and rising US overseas military spending, from the third to the fourth quarter of 1967 on a seasonally adjusted liquidity basis the US balance of payments deficit soared from $522 billion to $802 billion.[100] On the other hand, the rattling pressure of the ensuing gold crisis on the official price of gold at $35 per ounce triggered a profit squeeze for all oil transactions, usually traded in US dollars. It is worth recalling that such effects of the mounting gold crisis on the dollar's value and the international payments system surged even as, in 1968, the political motives underpinning the 1967 war and the small increase in oil posted prices were being institutionalized. As a study on OPEC presented within the Survey Discussion Group of the US Council on Foreign Relations nailed it a few years later, the creation of the Organization of Arab Petroleum Exporting Countries (OAPEC), founded that same year by Kuwait, Saudi Arabia, and Libya, and later on joined by other leading Arab oil producers as Iraq, palpably showed the political objective of the oil price increases, thought to force Israel to withdraw from the Arab territories it occupied during the June 1967 war.[101] In glossing over the specifics of this political target that underpinned the oil price increases, it is noteworthy to observe that it added to the then wobbling stability of gold's official price and the pressure on the dollar. Following the nearly decade-long tendency of Western central banks to buy gold in the US and to sell it in the London gold market, the devaluation of the British pound, which left the US as the world's sole reserve currency, sparked a reduction in world currency reserves and increased gold buying in international markets, thus accelerating the weakening of the dollar in foreign exchange markets.[102]

As stressed in this chapter, it had occurred earlier in the decade that gold buying in the US had increased the gold component of Western European central banks' reserves and reduced reserves in dollars, with depreciating effects on the US currency. From November 1967 this process deepened, as long as the devaluation of the British pound put up international demand for gold. For instance, from November to March 1968, the reserves in gold held at the US Department of the Treasury declined by nearly 30 percent.[103] At the same time, the devaluation of the British pound triggered both a reduction in world reserves and a substantial shift in reserves in many areas of the world; for instance, six months after devaluation the Middle Eastern countries had moved out of sterling and into gold. This shift, combined with a decline in the proportion of international reserves held in the form of sterling from roughly 42 percent to 38 percent of total global reserves from November 1967 to the following spring, put added pressure on the dollar.[104] During that winter, the US government and the Federal Reserve System, led by Chairman Martin, called their gold pool partners to refrain from converting hard currency reserves into gold and from promoting an increase in the official price of gold. Although the Governors of the European Central Banks reaffirmed President Johnson's statement about US commitment to the $35 per ounce, over the course of the fall and winter the losses in US gold reserves accelerated and market support for the official price of gold faded away.[105] Consequently, during the winter gold buying by international speculators brought to a height international demand for gold, thus taking to bursting point the excess in demand over total newly mined gold and gold sales by the Soviet Union underway since 1966. The effects of such developments on the dollar's strength affected exchange rate adjustments, Treasury bill rates and open market rates, forcing the Federal Reserve to raise discount rates and to tighten monetary policy. But it also impacted the international position of the US dollar; for example, across Western Europe international confidence in the dollar collapsed so much so that in many sectors such as, for example, the leisure industry in Spain, some exchanges and hotels were reportedly refusing dollar instruments, while some European central banks, notably the Bundesbank in Germany, engaged in massive dollar buying as an emergency measure to counteract the collapse of the dollar and the likely increase in the official price of gold.[106] After selling $6 billion during the six months preceding the March 1968 reorganization of the international monetary and payments system, upon request of Washington the gold pool terminated its gold tranche allocation mechanism.[107] The supply of gold with the aim of limiting the appreciation of gold continued to be carried on: in March the Bank of England, in the forefront in this effort, offered some of its African gold held in reserves on the Paris market.[108] Despite this, a new reserve policy was much needed to avert the rupture of interconvertibility between gold and dollar, the depreciation of US currency and its inflationary effects on both world commodity prices traded in US dollars and dollar-denominated international financial assets, and in particular the short-term international money market. In order to restore order in foreign exchange markets by the end of the year it was quite a widely shared view in Washington that there was a need to move away from a gold-based international monetary system.[109] In straddling to uphold the official price of gold, since winter of that same year the White House, the Federal Reserve System and the Council of Economic Advisers pointed to the activation of SDRs as the most plausible way to finance reserves of the Fund's member countries.[110] Technically, the SDR was a new fiduciary international reserve asset established in the books of the IMF. Its creation, mustered by the US government and agreed upon at the Annual Meeting of the IMF held in Rio de Janeiro in September 1967, was aimed at establishing a new reserve asset to meet increased international demand for reserves, and at easing pressure on the dollar, which, according to the US monetary authorities, was doomed to mount after the devaluation of the British pound. In fact, the SDRs were proposed as a successor to the Bretton Woods reserve currencies, particularly dollars held by national monetary authorities, and as a successor to gold as the ultimate official reserve asset into which currencies should be convertible.[111] Although for many years in the past the IMF had already been generating reserve assets in the form of gold tranche drawing rights and liquid loan claims to assist countries in payments difficulty, the SDRs were "the first reserve asset to be supplied on the basis of a deliberate assessment of the global need for reserves and reserve growth."[112] Besides, in so far as it was deemed to replace the dollar as the unit of international account the SDRs were thought to reduce the run on it, to tame the growing share of dollar-denominated assets in the international capital markets and to lessen the depreciating effect of this process on the dollar. In mid-March 1968, president Johnson wrote German Chancellor Kiesinger: "We can act together through the central banks to contain the speculative movements of funds that will almost surely occur in the next few weeks. Above all, we can act promptly to ratify and implement a plan for Special Drawing Rights as a means of replacing the reserves destroyed by speculation since devaluation, and of meeting our needs for growth in reserves."[113] Before the SDRs became fully operative, the US monetary and diplomatic authorities pressed their Western monetary partners to implement a number of interim measures. Before the creation of SDRs, the Federal

Reserve System, the Department of the Treasury and the Congress made a variety of arrangements to uphold the official price of gold and to stress the willingness of the United States to correct the expanding balance of payments deficit and the wobbling value of the dollar in exchange markets. During the winter, among other measures discussed and implemented in Washington to avert an increase in the official price of gold considered harmful to the dollar and to international transactions, it is worth recalling the removal of gold cover on banks' lending, advocated, among others, by the chairman of the Federal Reserve System Martin.[114] In March 1968, the US requested its gold pool partners with large gold reserves not to convert dollar into gold during the interim period prior to the activation of SDRs.[115] On his part, Secretary of State Dean Rusk went so far as to request European partners not to shift reserves from one currency to another.[116] Owing to persistent gold selling and speculative attacks on the dollar that led some central banks across the globe to suspend foreign exchange transactions in dollars and induced some nationwide banks like Banco de Chile to attempt a shift from dollars into German marks in New York,[117] at the request of the Nixon administration in March the Bank of England temporarily closed the London gold market.[118] At the same time, after lengthy debates among the highest monetary authorities within the Johnson administration, Washington proposed to its gold pool partners the separation between monetary gold from commodity gold, by prohibiting central banks from selling gold from monetary stocks to the private market when the price there was above the monetary price. During the 1960s much of the run on gold had stemmed from purchases by central banks in the United States at the official price of $35 per ounce and gold selling into the free market, first and foremost in the London gold market, where the price of gold averaged $38 or $39.[119] This practice by central banks contributed to putting the stability of exchange rates under strong pressure and to eventually depreciate the value of the dollar, as well as to inflate the international money markets and the world commodity markets that were part of the US dollar area. The onset of the two-tier gold system,[120] established by the central bankers of the gold pool gathered on the third weekend of March 1968 at the request of Washington, was intended as an interim measure prior to the activation of SDRs, scheduled by the end of that year. According to these agreements the price of monetary gold exchanged among central banks, and between the banks and the gold producers, would be kept fixed at the Bretton Woods official dollar price of $35 per ounce, while in the free market the price of gold could fluctuate. Therefore, following such agreements central banks could neither buy nor sell gold in the free markets. Likewise, all central banks that agreed on these rules were bound not to sell to central banks not pledged to this commitment.[121] However, the new monetary arrangements set up with some urgency in the United States in the spring of 1968 to counteract the blowing away of international monetary stability could do little to halt this trend and restore stability in both financial markets and international commodity markets. From 1968 through the eve of the system's collapse in 1973, the market price of gold was substantially above its nominal official value, turning the two-tier system into an "unsatisfactory and [a] destabilizing factor in the system," borrowing from a study dropped on the desk of Federal Reserve System Chairman Arthur Burns in late 1972.[122] Shortly after his appointment as US Secretary of the Treasury, William Simon showed his willingness toward an early removal of the legal ban on ownership of gold by private US citizens, and considered suggesting that President Nixon issue an executive order permitting Americans to buy, sell, and hold gold.[123] This position marked a turn in the US government's policy to establish newly created alternative units of account as a way to stabilize the interconvertibility between gold and dollar. The failure of this further attempt to uphold the value of the dollar in the international exchange market in order to preserve stability in international trade and payments was combined with turn-of-the-decade federal and congressional measures to counteract liabilities on the capital account position.[124] The failure of such attempt stemmed from both the inadequacy of the measures taken in March 1968, and a string of issues examined in this section crucial to navigate the continuing deterioration of the US balance of payments, the unfettered depreciation of the dollar, and the mounting difficulties that undermined and weakened the international payments system through to the eve of the 1973 turn in the oil supply and price policy of OPEC. In this respect, it is worth mentioning, first, the unsuccessfulness of any measure taken to replace gold as the reserve unit of international account through the implementation of

SDRs. Second, it is useful to highlight the failure of multiple measures set off to absorb the share of dollar-denominated assets in international liquidity through a shift in the currency unit for transactions in the international money and credit markets. Third, it is worth recalling the failure of the Nixon administration's policies to push forward banking and credit policies aimed at preventing capital outflows and to restore equilibrium in the capital account. With respect to the role of the Eurodollar market during both the period from the end of dollar convertibility into gold in 1971 to the outbreak of the first oil price hikes and thereafter, it is essential to account for the failure of this credit control policy and the turn that American monetary authorities undertook thereafter with respect to inflation-sensitive short-term Eurocurrency markets.

3.4 Mounting Interaction Between Instability in Exchange Markets and International Oil Developments 1968–1973

The activation of SDRs entailed an allocation plan stretched over a three-year period: the equivalent of $3.5 billion of SDRs were distributed at the beginning of 1970, while $3 billion each were distributed at the beginning of 1971 and 1972.[125] Notwithstanding this allocation increased international monetary confidence, in many respects the SDRs proved to be an unsatisfactory monetary arrangement to reform the international monetary system and to ease pressure on the US dollar. The activation of SDRs contributed little to contain the weakening of the dollar and the deterioration of the system of international trade and payments, which during the time frame from the attempts to reform it in 1968 to the eve of the first oil crisis was being brought under further pressure by the increasingly assertive foreign energy policy of oil producing countries like Libya and international organizations like OPEC. Developments in international oil markets of the time are worth exploring to better grasp the overlapping of multiple causes that plunged the system of international payments into an irreversible collapse on the eve of the first oil crisis. They are also useful to continue charting the causal relation between unsuccessful US measures to stabilize exchange markets, capital market developments, and the string of inflationary strains that undermined trade and payments when the fixed exchange rate system was still operative. To put it another way, here the argument is made that turn-of-the-decade international oil developments added to the issues that undermined the smooth functioning of international trade and payments and the US policies to anchor it to a strong US currency. At the dawn of the 1970s some prominent oil-supplying Mediterranean countries like Libya and worldwide organizations like OPEC, which operated on the international energy scenario, engaged in a set of negotiating arrangements on concessions with multinational corporations operating on their soils. Following the upswing in oil posted prices, freight costs, and production shortages that stemmed from the June 1967 war described above, in 1970 rising oil prices and developments in the international oil markets interacted with ever-mounting pressure on the dollar and the US balance of payments in a complex fashion, with potential centrifugal effects on the purchasing power of dollar-pegged currency areas and their stability in foreign exchange markets. From mid-1970 to early 1971 the combined closing of the Trans-Arabian Pipeline and production cuts decided in Libya made room for a sharp increase in the demand for shipping Middle East oil to Europe via the Cape of Good Hope; this turn drove up freight rates worldwide. Moreover, as oil demand was surging, Libya successfully negotiated with Western oil companies substantial increases in the posted prices of crude oil exported from Libyan and East Mediterranean ports, as well as a raise in tax rates.[126] Soon after, in the early fall of 1970, both of these measures were adopted by Persian Gulf oil producing countries and also Venezuela.[127] On the other hand, in February 1971 the governments of six oil-supplying countries (Iran, Iraq, Saudi Arabia, Kuwait, Abu Dhabi, and Qatar) and Western oil companies reached agreements in Teheran that resulted in a major increase in oil posted prices and consolidated tax rates.[128] This process, by 1973 compounded by exceptionally bad weather and harvest conditions in nearly all of the world's food producing countries,[129] reinforced the inflationary effects on commodities traded in the US dollar and on private financial assets denominated in US dollars that the continued weakening of the American currency in foreign exchange markets and the ensuing remarkable growth of short-term Eurocurrency markets in the Western European financial centers, had caused. With respect to the causal relation between these turn-of-the-decade increases in oil prices and inflation, in the United States the Federal Reserve Bank of New York estimated that the 1973 quadrupling of imported oil prices amounted to about 2 percent of the United States GDP. Even Paul Volcker, who once made the argument that a higher import price in one commodity had a potential deflationary impact equal to a tightening of domestic fiscal pressure in so far as it reduced domestic private spending and increased savings, admitted that although posted price increase "does not account for all our inflation [...], it has clearly contributed to the recent rate of price increase."[130] It is worth pointing to the role and contribution of oil price hikes to the depreciation of the dollar and continued capital outflows from the United States, which from 1970 to 1972 triggered a steady increase in the outflow from the United States of both long-term private capital and non-liquid short-term private capital (see Table 3.3).

In this respect the rise in demand for Eurodollar loans and the rising borrowings from other inflation-sensitive and largely unregulated capital markets, such as the Eurobond market, by oil-importing countries, was remarkable.

This rising demand for inflation-sensitive investments was pursued during the period following the first oil price hike of 1973 in order to resurrect the balance of payments deficit on current account caused by the quadrupling of the oil posted price. The oil price and consolidated tax rates on which OAPEC member countries and Western oil companies reached agreements from 1969 through 1972, and above all the 1973 fourfold oil price hikes, increased borrowings for the purpose of financing balance of payments deficits in the Eurodollar and Eurobond markets. This steady increase accounts for the rise in the Eurodollar loan

Table 3.3 US capital movements

	In US$ millions, seasonally adjusted		
Credits/debits	1970	1971	1972
Long-term private capital flows, net	−1.429	−4.401	−152
Non-liquid short-term private capital flows	−482	−2.347	−1.637

Source: Board of Governors of the Federal Reserve System, *Federal Reserve Bulletin*, January 1974

rates and mounting pressure on the discount rates of borrowing countries. Even after the December 1971 realignments of exchange rates, money market conditions in the United States looked worse than in the Eurodollar market and major European money markets; for instance, by early 1972 three-month deposits and US Treasury bills fell consistently behind three-month deposits in both the Eurodollar market and the German and British money markets.[131] According to a 1979 statement by Anthony M. Solomon, at the time Under Secretary of the Treasury for Monetary Affairs, prior to the quadrupling of oil prices of 1973 the current account deficit of all countries in a deficit position taken together averaged at about $15 billion annually. Solomon stressed that this deficit triggered an expansion in demand for international credit met by private banking, multilateral institutions and governments, which from 1974 through the end of the decade had a meteoric rise.[132] This fact—let alone the technicalities of the debate about the development of the Eurocurrency markets in the European financial centers—did contribute to growth in US money supply and is briefly charted in the next chapter.[133] In order to better understand the linkage between increases in commodity prices and the upswing in the cost of money caused by increased demand for lending to stabilize the international payments position of the industrial and LDCs countries most affected by the oil price hikes, the meteoric expansion of the Eurobond markets in the three years following the 1973 oil price increases is an eye-catching case in point. Unlike the foreign bond markets, the Eurocurrency markets have traditionally been relatively free from controls. According to the IMF, during the period from 1973 to 1975, marked by mounting balance of payments difficulties in most LDCs and oil-scarce industrial nations, the most severely affected developing countries placed bonds both in foreign currency markets and in the Eurobond markets. According to other studies, the non-oil producing LDCs began borrowing from the Eurocurrency markets as early as from 1971/1972.[134] In contrast to this tendency, after 1975 borrowers turned their attention to the least regulated and untapped money markets. From 1976 to 1977, when the international payments position of the non-oil producing LDCs shrank even further, almost three quarters of such bonds were placed in the Eurocurrency markets; at the end of 1978 this pattern had accelerated markedly, with a shift toward raising funds in Eurocurrency credits.[135] Owing to the largely unregulated interest rate policy of such markets, this pattern increasingly brought the upswing in LDCs' foreign borrowing for deficit financing purposes to stimulate rising interest rates and inflationary upswings in capital markets that contributed to the depreciation of the dollar in exchange markets. If one leaves aside the LDCs and pinpoint the case of the advanced industrial economies, it is worth drawing attention to the United States: in the beginning of 1971 the Export–Import Bank of the United States made a $1 billion, 3-month offer in the unregulated Eurodollar market to finance the US balance of payments deficit.[136] Moreover, in addition to the depreciating effect on international commodities traded in the dollar and on capital assets denominated in the American currency, the combination of increases in oil posted prices and unfettered short-term capital outflows from Wall Street had a harsh impact on both the current and the capital account components of the US balance of payments in so far as it expanded liabilities in the current account and reduced assets in the capital account. Therefore, short-term capital market developments and international oil developments interwove each other in a complex way that contributed to further hurt the US balance of payments deficit.

In order to chart the extent to which international oil developments and capital market developments pushed forward this process, it is worth taking a detour at this point. It was just one year prior to Libya's decision to put up oil posted prices that the US domestic financial market felt the pinch of growing Eurodollar loan rates and began viewing the resurrection in the value of the dollar in foreign exchange markets. This book has repeatedly drawn attention to a measure, vital to avert capital outflows and prevent investors from moving low-powered money from New York into high-powered reserves in London and other European-based Eurocurrency markets, as a seemingly intractable issue.[137] In the late spring of 1968, the effect of a depreciating dollar on private capital markets, coupled with the effect of the devaluation of the British pound on world reserves and declining confidence in the dollar, caused US investment banks to borrow from the London-based Eurodollar market to face up to domestic liquidity shortage in order to finance public issues and bonds, as well as fixed capital investments in the United States. At that time this reflowing of funds caused by the weakening of the dollar in international exchange markets came through a heavy volume of banks' holdings to the United States through the London branches of US banks.[138] Thereafter, in March 1969 this longstanding weakening of the dollar in exchange markets made American investment institutions based in New York suffer sizeable actual and book losses on their bond portfolios, while underwriters took severe losses on a number of bond offerings.[139] Furthermore, at this early stage in the history of the financial ascendancy of oil producing countries on the world financial stage, the weakening value of the dollar in exchange markets adversely affected not so much dollar-denominated financial assets held by OPEC countries abroad, still not so huge in scale as they became since 1974. Rather, it adversely affected their oil profits; this was an outcome rather different from that of the second half of the 1970s, when, as explored in Chap. 4, the unfettered tottering of the US dollar in exchange markets jeopardized both the purchasing power of the OPEC oil producing countries and the real value of their foreign financial and equity investments. At the end of the 1960s, in order to ease the strains of the plummeting dollar's strength in foreign exchange markets and substantial alterations in the exchange rates of leading currencies as pound sterling, franc and the German mark on the value of international transactions in goods, the OPEC called on the advanced industrial economies for making arrangements to bolster the profits of its member countries. Shortly after Nixon's decision to terminate the interconvertibility between dollar and gold, several meetings—focused on the impact of the new international monetary scenario—were held between the oil companies operating in the Gulf and the Minister of Finance of a leading oil producing country, such as Iran. On those occasions, it was agreed to set up a committee of experts from both parties to meet in Vienna to try to calculate the actual effects on various OPEC countries of the changes in exchange rates that followed the flotation of the US dollar.[140] Thereafter, the Geneva agreements signed between OPEC and oil companies in compensation for the international realignments of currencies of December 1971, established a parity index designed to compensate for major realignments in average exchange rates of nine industrial countries with the US dollar. Around one year later, following the January 1972 increases in the posted price of oil in North Africa and the Middle East and the successive increases in the posted price of crude oil by about 6 percent on 6 April 1973 that followed the devaluation of the US dollar, at the request of the OPEC countries a new index of eleven industrial countries' currencies was created to give OPEC's member countries full compensation for the devaluation of the US dollar that resulted in an increase of about 12 percent over posted prices of 1 January 1973.[141]

Based on this intertwining between oil prices and exchange market developments, it is therefore straightforward to point to this combining of increases in the posted prices of crude oil and the effects of a long-lasting dollar depreciation in foreign exchange markets with the disorderly exchange market conditions described in this study. This interaction not only resulted in a steady increase in the price of oil traded in the US dollar, but also pushed up the prices of a variety of other commodities from 1970 to 1972, and even more after the devaluation of the US dollar in February 1973. This process affected the non-oil producing LDCs the most. For instance, exogenous increases in the price of wheat and food, in general attributable to significant alteration in fixed exchange rates, increasing capital flows and cross-national interest rates differentials to stabilize private capital markets and sustain fixed capital investments, increased the import bill of many LDCs steadily. According to a study of the IBRD, the import bill of cereals for 40 LDCs increased at an average of $3 billion from 1970 to 1972 and escalated to over $8 billion in 1973.[142] Promptly, the LDCs countries caught the intertwining between the early decade alteration in exchange rates and floating rates since 1973, and the oil price increases, in shaping their balance of payments deficit. At the 1971 Lima meeting of the so-called Group of 77, the developing nations drew attention to the implications of alteration in exchange rates and currency realignments on the value of their reserves; on that occasion they made the argument that their reserves suffered because of fluctuations in the value of currencies used as reserves, and appealed to the United States for help in offsetting their current account imbalances stemming from such a steadily rising import bill. Reasoning along these lines, they specifically called on the United States for exempting them from the 10 percent import surcharge.[143] However, as the next chapter details, the government of Washington and the international financial institutions born out of the Bretton Woods conference devised a strategy to rebound the LDCs' imbalances; such strategy was aimed at targeting liabilities from current account transactions, not at propping up the assets on their current account position. In fact, as early as 1974, the highest ranking officials of the IBRD made a rough estimate of the amount of financial resources needed by developing countries in addition to the currently available financial resources channeled through multilateral organizations in order to keep up their development efforts. According to the World Bank, in order to sustain their investment plans and to undertake specific investment programs necessary to adjust their economies to higher energy prices, all developing countries required about $10 billion per year over the following three years for immediate balance of payments assistance, and around $4.5 to 5.5 billion per year in intermediate-term lending.[144] The next chapter explores the involvement of private American commercial banks, the OPEC, and the commitment of multilateral organizations to channel a substantial portion of the OPEC's oil revenues in this way within the framework of the US foreign economic policy of the decade. At this point in this reconstruction it is essential to stress that the financial resources required to fuel the adjustment process in non-oil producing LDCs contributed to the upswing mode in the Eurobond and Eurocurrency markets that had been brought about by the Western oil importing countries. Prior to the beginning of floating exchange rates on which the next chapter focuses, most LDCs attempted to make balance of payments adjustments to hold domestic consumption and pre-oil price rise levels, with resulting jumps in government budget deficits, trade and current account deficit, and inflation[145]: instead of searching for exchange rate adjustments and expanding money supply to fuel fixed capital formation, they borrowed heavily from the Eurocurrency markets. By 1974 such balance of payments deficit financing strategy triggered cost-push effects on these markets, with premium charged for rolling over or additional credit extension, rising bond yields in secondary markets, striking differentials appearing on new bond issues, and failing efforts to syndicate Euro-credits.[146]

Therefore, both the oil-importing advanced industrial nations and the non-oil producing LDCs borrowed from the Eurocurrency markets to offset the impact of higher oil prices, or in the case of the US of capital outflows, on the current account component of their balance of payments deficit before the 1973 fourfold oil price increase and production cuts, thus fostering upward movements in short-term lending. This dynamic further strengthens the idea at the center of this chapter's argument by which increases not only in consumer goods but also in the cost of money in private capital markets soared well in advance of the oil price hikes of 1973. In the eyes of US monetary authorities the early 1970s international oil developments did not affect solely the cost of borrowing in money markets and commodity prices. In its exercise of reappraising current and recent capital market developments, the Federal Reserve Bank of New York noted that heavy borrowing from foreign branches of US resident banks that held Eurocurrency deposits might increase US banks' lending to foreign oil consumers through their foreign branches by providing additional resources to their Eurocurrency holdings. As charted in Chap. 4, such Eurocurrency holdings expanded as a result of the recycling in the international capital markets of the oil revenues that accrued to the OPEC countries since 1974. This foreign lending by US banks was viewed with palpable concern within the Federal Reserve Bank of New York in so far as it could lead US private capital to flee domestic capital markets, with resulting downward impact on US interest rates.[147] Therefore, before the 1973 oil price increases, as far as they were affected by the rising posted price of oil, and consolidated taxes that occurred from the very late 1960s through to the very beginning of the new decade, capital market developments contributed to the outflow of dollars from the US capital markets through the development of Eurodollar markets and increased foreign lending by US banks. This jumble of movements contributed to depreciating the dollar and to worsen the US balance of payments on current account and long-term capital, the so-called basic balance (see Chap. 4, Table 4.2).

Therefore, the inefficacy of SDRs and any other attempt to reform the international monetary system can be referred to and accounts only in part and to a very limited extent for the failure to stabilize on a non-inflationary basis the international flows in goods and capital and to prop up the dollar in exchange markets. However, it is worth mentioning the shortcomings in SDRs and the two-tier gold system established in March 1968. First, from 1969 through to the termination of the two-tier system the separation between monetary gold and gold for commercial purposes brought under severe strain international reserves. In 1972, it was the General Manager of the Bank for International Settlements (BIS) Rene Larre who suggested that the disparity between the market price and official price of gold had resulted in a freezing of gold and gold-guaranteed assets held at central banks' reserves; based on data published in the *International Financial Statistics* of the IMF of October 1973, gold and gold guaranteed assets (SDR and IMF reserve position) totaled nearly $35 million or 37 percent of total reserve assets. According to Larre, "the freezing-up of them leaves many central banks vulnerable to the event of adverse balance of payments developments. This situation is likely to make governments and central banks reluctant to defend their parities in the face of external deficit, even though the deficits could prove to be temporary if the parities were defended. Such an attitude would not only mean a weakening of the presumption of fixed rates but also make more difficult for the dollar to regain a firm position."[148] Such assets were a large proportion of total reserves; besides, by the mid-summer of 1972, the price gap between the official price and the free market price of gold was up 25 percent. This ongoing discrepancy caused concerns among the US policymakers; the Department of the Treasury exhibited its fear for the two-tier system's implication on the inadequacy of reserve assets to protect from adverse balance of payments deficit, while at the same time envisioning either a demonetization of gold or an increase in the official price of gold in US dollars.[149] In addition to this sticky issue proper to the functioning of SDRs as a unit of international account, it is worth recalling that the SDRs came into being very late and some top ranking American economic policy makers were skeptical about the consequences of such change on the system of international payments and warned against the issue of dollar inconvertibility. In general, prior to 1973 American monetary authorities considered the implementation of SDRs a vital step to foster the dollar and stabilize international monetary relations. Since the establishment of SDRs, on many occasions the US Department of the Treasury formulated plans regarding the issuance of Special Drawing Rights Certificates to the Federal Reserve System to run counter the depreciation of the dollar.[150] Besides, in light of the international debate about monetary reform after the suspension of dollar convertibility into gold, within the US Department of the Treasury in early

1972 it was still quite a shared view that the SDRs as the principal reserve asset could serve the purpose of creating an appropriate volume of liquidity creation that would ease international pressure on the dollar. The American business community itself favored the implementation of SDRs; during the trilateral business talks held in Monte Carlo in the late spring of 1973, where business people from Japan, the EEC and the United States gathered to discuss international economic and monetary problems, representatives from the American business community took the lead in supporting floating exchange rates and in opposing controls on capital movements. At the same time they favored the substitutions of SDRs for national currencies or gold as reserve assets.[151] However, notwithstanding this large consensus on the functioning of SDRs to ease pressure on the dollar and reduce dependence on gold and gold supply, in making such a bet on the SDRs as a reserve unit the Nixon administration showed a palpable concern for the likely implications of the dollar's inconvertibility on other currencies. The US Under Secretary of State for Economic Affairs made a case for implementing the SDRs as a reserve unit; at the same time he made a case for pushing forward negotiations on international monetary reform "to head off a growing consideration of the possible need by other countries to use exchange controls, multiple exchange practices and other controls as an alternative to accumulating further inconvertible dollars." Moreover, as the growth of SDRs could be rationally planned and its value maintained constant, that would help restore stability in capital markets and ease short-term capital flows.[152] Therefore, during this period the US focus on implementing the SDRs should be interpreted as a way to sustain the value of the dollar alternative to Washington's long-lasting policies to prop up the value of the US currency by curbing the expansion of dollar-denominated assets in world capital markets or by implementing measures to freeze the quantity of gold reserve assets held at Western central banks. Although US monetary and financial authorities placed such importance on SDRs, it was only in early 1973 that the United States denominated the par value of the dollar in SDRs and Germany did the same with the central rate for the Deutsche Mark, thus curbing the effects on international trade and payments of speculations in gold stemming from the recurrent exchange crises of the past few years. In particular, such chain of crises and speculations occurred during the British pound crisis of June 1972 and in correspondence to the second devaluation of the dollar on 12 February 1973, when the dollar price of gold in the private market reached $90 an ounce.[153] The two-tier gold market system was finally terminated in November 1973,[154] when the devaluation of the US dollar and the harsh decision of the Arab oil producing countries to cut supply and increase posted prices caused it to become outdated. By this time it was clear that not only the failure of US balance of payments deficit financing strategies on either the current or capital accounts, but also the most important attempts to reform the international monetary system, failed to avoid the depreciation of the dollar and its inflationary impact on both the money and commodity markets. The negotiations to reform the international monetary system, convincingly sponsored by the US Department of the Treasury and begun under the Committee of Twenty of the IMF, being expected to reach final agreements by mid-1974, slid away as a result of the oil price hikes of the fall of 1973. Although authoritative studies produced in the US Department of the Treasury described it as an excuse for the Committee of Twenty "to admit agreement on a new set of rules for fixing exchange rates and reserves policies was a long way off,"[155] for sure, international oil developments added to the termination of the two-tier gold system and to the ill-functioning and delay in implementing SDRs. Likewise, international oil developments contributed to depreciating the dollar and the destabilization of foreign exchange markets. This tangle of multiple issues brought the dollar under further strain and stretched to the extreme American incapability to resurrect the balance of payments showed by American policymakers since long before the Nixon era. Certainly, there is a seamless continuity in the history of US foreign economic policy throughout the two decades worth noting. Although traditional measures on the current and capital account position implemented since as early as the Kennedy administration were integrated with measures to stabilize the dollar convertibility into gold and to prop up the US currency through open support for the introduction of the SDRs, the combined meteoric rise of Eurodollar and other short-term capital markets and international oil developments prolonged the agony of the US balance of payments and that of the US currency. As anticipated, this long-standing weakening of the dollar jeopardized first the stability of international capital flows with growing Euromoney markets and, in turn, the cost of borrowing for governments' deficit financing purposes, for tapping the balance of payments deficit of oil-importing nations caused by the oil bill, and the loan rates for private credit. By 1970 the long-standing Federal Reserve policy to halt short-term private capital outflows by means of altering the discount rate that was consistently pursued throughout the 1960s made way for the implementation of capital controls and a set of stringent banking policies; within this framework it is worth placing the decline in both short-term financial instruments and long-term bonds registered in Wall Street in early 1970. In other words, easier money conditions did not stem from substantial improvements on the capital account but from a US policy shift from monetary measures to banking policies.[156] Along with an increasingly assertive price and concessions policy by the OPEC countries, it is worth situating within this framework of growing costs of borrowing the inflationary strains that churned both the international oil and commodity markets and the American bonds and securities markets both before and following the 1973 production cuts and increases in crude oil prices. The loss of confidence in the US dollar and the growing instability in foreign exchange markets began to adversely affect the value and size of US private capital markets even as it contributed to increase oil prices: as early as late 1968, the inflationary strain that crushed the international oil markets began churning Wall Street as well. In December of that same year—according to a report presented by the First Boston Corporation to the World Bank—many investors were backing away from bonds and investing a significant amount of their funds in equities or in temporary holdings of short-term indebtedness as a result of the current 4 percent erosion of the dollar due to inflationary pressures.[157] Therefore, the centrifugal effects of declining exchange rate stability and increasing instability in cross country interest rate differentials added significant uncertainty to the political developments underway in the Middle East and to the increasingly assertive oil policy of OPEC. In light of this book's reconstruction, the combined unsuccessful US attempts to forestall the gold-pegged monetary system through monetary reforms and longstanding abortive American policies to bolster the dollar through balance of payments deficit financing policies on either the current or capital accounts, triggered capital outflows, a growth in short-term Eurocurrency markets and markedly expanding interest rate differentials across the Atlantic Sea that put up the cost of borrowings in Europe. Therefore, unlike Mundell's interpretation, which identifies with massive private capital flows from long-term financial assets to short-term securities, and from the United States to the West European financial centers the origins of the inflationary strains on both the capital and commodity markets germane to the 1970s, this study points to a much more intricate tangle of causes.[158]

3.5 Missing the Link Between Eurocurrency Markets, Oil Prices, and Inflation: The Financial Policies of the Nixon Administration

Within this framework, the newly appointed Nixon administration began managing its foreign oil policy by failing to realize the extent to which international monetary developments affected it. As noted in the previous section, from the devaluation of the British pound to the gold crisis of spring 1968, it became straightforward that a speculative run on gold, massive dollar selling and untapped dollar outflows due to the failure of US gold policies accounted for the overheating of exchange rates and the decline of the dollar in international exchange markets. Likewise, such a path of developments threatened the whole system of international trade and payments nurturing the expansion of unwise highly liquid Eurocurrency and Eurodollar money markets. Over the course of 1973 these developments were taken to the extreme in the context of Nixon's decision to suspend convertibility of the dollar into gold. As a result of that, the net outflow of dollars on official reserves transactions was halted, as any tendency toward the outflow of dollars triggered the rate of floating foreign currencies to rise.[159] These developments explain why, notwithstanding the dawn of the new decade was relatively free from hectic speculative activity and the realignments of exchange rates agreed upon at the Smithsonian meeting in December 1971 were supposed to prop up the US balance of payments and the dollar in exchange markets, from

1969 to 1972 the US balance of payments recorded a staggering downswing. From 1969 to the very beginning of 1972, driven by the exodus of US private capitals fleeing the country,[160] the outflow of liquid private capital doubled, while non-liquid short-term private capital outflows grew eightfold, with the balance on current account and long-term capital—the so-called basic balance—registering by 1972 a deficit somewhat greater than the deficit of $9.3 billion recorded in 1971.[161] As anticipated, this dwindling US balance of payments recorded from 1972 to 1973 occurred notwithstanding the realignments of exchange rates agreed upon at the Smithsonian meeting of December 1971. In light of a much-heralded need to reform the system of international monetary relations to adapt it to the structural changes that occurred in the world economy, as the economies of Europe and Japan advanced rapidly and became strong competitors to the United States, and after several months of negotiations, agreements were reached at the Smithsonian Institution in Washington on 18 December 1971 on a new pattern of exchange rates among the major nations. As part of this realignment, the United States agreed to reduce the par value of the dollar by 7.9 percent. Other countries changed the value of their currencies in proportion to the devaluation of the dollar; these measures resulted in an average realignment between the dollar and the currencies of other industrial countries (excluding the Canadian currency, which continued to float) by 12 percent.[162] In addition to such realignment, Japan and the European community reduced certain trade barriers to improve access of US products to their markets and agreed to initiate a comprehensive round of trade negotiations in 1973. The next paragraph and Chap. 4 explores to what extent US foreign trade policy stood up for the US policy on the current account to restore equilibrium in the international trade and payments system both in the 1960s, as charted in Chap. 2, and during and shortly after the quadrupling of oil posted prices, when Washington turned to it to avert the non-oil producing LDCs from slipping away from the system of international trade.[163] Notwithstanding these realignments, the combined transnational capital flows and growing interest rate differentials, international oil developments and failing monetary reform to replace the dollar with a new unit of international account, further hit the US balance of payments deficit as described above. The search for compensation for major exchange rate realignments by the OPEC oil producing countries from 1971 suggests this clear-cut correlation between the mid-term impact of the 1968 gold crisis on the stability of the US dollar, the long-standing deterioration in international exchange markets, and the worsening US balance of payments on capital account, which was tempered only in 1972 by the combined exchange rate realignments and by the tightening of the US money market. Such combination brought about a temporary reversal in the flows of interest-sensitive funds; as a matter of fact these factors caused an improvement in both short-term capital movements and long-term capital flows.[164] This unchecked deterioration in the US international payments position accounted for the dwarfing in US foreign exchange earnings and the hard-to-overcome intricacy of foreign market operations much more than developments on the current account, the surge in international oil prices and the effective functioning of or shortcomings in US trade liberalization policies aimed at sustaining the value of the US dollar by improving the current account balance.[165] Likewise, it painstakingly accounts for the likely impact of the dollar's depreciation on the profits of oil producing countries and their call on the Western economies for making exchange rate adjustments compensate for it. As already recalled, the tottering of the dollar and its impact on the oil producing countries' financial wealth and purchasing power was another continuous issue from the 1960s to the late 1970s. At this time, the impact of a weakened dollar on the oil producing countries' profits was offset by the expansion in their oil supply and export to the rest of the world, as well as by the new concession arrangements negotiated at the beginning of the new decade. From 1970 to 1973 oil-importing countries paid about $13 billion to oil exporters and in 1973, the bill had risen to about $46 billion.[166] As early as March 1968, amid the sticky international gold crisis, in light of Washington's call on all countries around the world for not buying gold, most Arab and non-Arab oil producing members of OPEC exhibited their intention to cooperate with the United States to avoid any further run on gold and speculative attack on the dollar. For instance, the deputy governor of Libya held the view that running counter to gold buying and hoardings was also a priority to his government in so far as the largest portion of his country's foreign exchange earnings were in dollars.[167] On the other hand, the US Embassy in Teheran noted the reluctance of Iranian commercial banks to buy pounds and, more importantly from the viewpoint of this study, the anxiety of the Iranian government to get pending oil payments before pressure on the US dollar could result in a reduction in oil revenues and receipts.[168] These public statements of intents confirm the impact of international gold and monetary developments on international commodity markets and international oil payments, as well as the impact of wobbling fixed exchange rates on the oil producing countries' foreign exchange earnings—at the time by and large denominated in US dollar—at this early stage in their repositioning in international capital markets and in the international economic system of the 1970s. Among the OPEC countries these concerns blew up since the Nixon administration declared the inconvertibility of the dollar and set off the floating of the American currency. Shortly before agreements were reached to realign currencies in December 1971, that same fall OPEC—through the chief of its economics department—made an inquiry with officials of the IMF to get a rough estimate about the possible adverse impact of recent international monetary developments on the purchasing power of the proceeds of the oil export of OPEC countries.[169] In contrast to this archival evidence, based on the research conducted for this study it was not possible to track a record of any concern within OPEC about the impact of a declining value of the dollar and mounting pressure on its convertibility into gold on the investments of the OPEC countries on the international equity markets and their portfolio investments prior to the 1973 fourfold increase in oil prices. In the spring of 1974, after the quadrupling of oil posted prices and its effects on the stability of prices and cost of money, according to a US economic intelligence report, it was highly unlikely that an Arab search for more aggressive portfolio management or alterations in interest rate differentials would induce them but to very limited shifts between currencies in response to exchange market developments. Reflecting their outlook, the US intelligence pointed to the tangible risk of eroding the value of existing unconverted assets.[170] Thereafter, from 1975, owing to the decline in the value of the dollar in foreign exchange markets occurred between October 1974 and February 1975,[171] within OPEC a growing number of member countries, most notably Algeria and Kuwait, suggested that

OPEC did not use the dollar to price oil. As an alternative, these countries made a strong case for fixing oil prices in terms of some basket of currencies. In the spring of 1975 a number of OPEC countries' central banks no longer fixed official buying and selling rates for their currencies against the US dollar; they decided to determine the exchange value of their currencies on the basis of a composite of other currencies, which in some cases was the same used to determine the value of the IMF's SDRs; in others it differed.[172] This string of concerns within OPEC varies significantly from a pressing need to protect the investments of the oil producing countries in the equity markets of the advanced industrial economies or to shield their exposure in the non-oil producing LDCs where they held a substantial portion of those countries' external debt. Such last concern came to center stage in their foreign investment policies from 1976 through the second oil shock.

Shortly after coming to power, Richard Nixon and his administration underestimated this cumbersome impact of international monetary and financial developments on international oil markets and prices. In this respect, it is noteworthy both to pinpoint the theoretical debate on the nature of the early inflation of the 1970s that churned the US economy, and to remind the reader which legislative measures were taken to counter the development of inflation-sensitive short-term capital markets. In either case, the Nixon administration correctly established a linkage between the meteoric expansion of the Euro-money markets and overheating macroeconomic conditions. However, it never linked price patterns for international commodities to the impact of mounting inflation-sensitive short-term unregulated financial markets on the dollar and on the stability in exchange markets. From 1971 to 1972, changes in transnational capital flows and the persistence through 1969 of dollar outflows from the United States called the US Department of the Treasury and the Federal Reserve System to reflect on the phenomenon. The Fed's Chairman Arthur Burns, for instance, paid utmost attention to the development of highly liquid, short-term transnational capital flows, but focused his attention on the demand–pull nature of the 1971 domestic and international inflation. In fact, he fiercely and relentlessly criticized the attitude of most European central banks to place funds in the Eurocurrency markets as this triggered an expansion in the stock of money on the supply side. In his view this shift of funds had a potentially expansionary effect in so far as it reduced the quantity of money bound to reserve requirements. According to Burns, such deposits in the Eurodollar market had added to the explosive growth in monetary reserves in Europe, flooded European economies with unwanted liquidity, expanded money supply and contributed to the increase of inflationary pressures.[173] In the summer of 1971 the Board of Governors of the Federal Reserve that he himself chaired approved a report by the Standing Committee on the Eurocurrency markets that deplored the placing of official funds in the Eurocurrency markets; according to the report, as such placements "do not give rise to an initial contraction of domestic liquidity in the depositing country," they were likely to have undesirable expansionary effects.[174] On the other hand, although he placed much importance with the uneven development of short-term transnational capital movements, Burns convincingly depicted the early decade's upward price levels as the combined effect of demand–pull inflation worth managing with appropriate fiscal and monetary policies with cost–push inflation mostly attributable to upward labor costs.[175] In his analysis he tossed aside the upward movement in international commodity prices; at the same time, he did not link the meteoric rise of short-term Eurocurrency markets to the deteriorating value of the dollar in international exchange markets or to the rising posted price of oil on international markets and the world-based inflation already happening. Therefore, in his reflections Burns linked capital markets developments to inflation, but he did not catch its implications on exchange markets and through it on commodity prices.[176]

A close focus on the measures taken under the Nixon administration highlights the extent to which the White House and the Congress went down this road. At the end of their mandate, consistent with laws approved in the 1960s, the Johnson administration implemented a set of measures to discourage foreign lending and restrict capital outflows to target the balance of payments deficit on capital account; in particular, during the last year he spent in office, Lyndon Johnson raised both interest rates and taxes: from November 1967 to November 1968 the discount rate at the Federal Reserve Bank of New York was raised from 4 to 5.25, while during the same time frame the price of long-term Treasury bonds increased from 70.00 to 72.20.[177] Along with passing some measures congruent with Johnson, the Nixon administration undertook two fundamental lines of action. In the first instance it engaged in trying to achieve the reform of the international monetary system and the introduction of the IMF's new reserve to ease pressure on the dollar. In the pursuit of this objective, on the one side the new administration promoted any workable way to absorb the scale of dollar-denominated financial assets and transactions in international capital markets in addition to its world-based diplomatic action toward monetary and trade partners to reduce the purchases of gold charted in Chap. 1. This study has pointed to Washington's prompt support for the activation and implementation of SDRs. In this respect, the activation of SDRs was part of Washington's strategy to defend the par value of the dollar and its strength in international exchange markets. Indeed, in addition to the issues that jeopardized the functioning of SDRs referred to, since their implementation the issue of balance of payments deficit financing was a worldwide problem that gripped many central banks across the globe. This prompted several national monetary authorities to sell their quota of SDRs in exchange for hard currencies to finance foreign market operations. By 1973, in so far as the dollar was still the dominant currency for reserve and payments, this triggered a concentration of SDRs assets in the United States and partially accounts for the early decade's outflow of dollars from the country. This process helps explain the early 1970s' increase of dollar assets in international reserves, which were still growing in 1970.[178] On the other hand, the Nixon administration conducted a battle to restore equilibrium on the capital account as the other cornerstone in its policy to avoid the depreciation of the US dollar in exchange markets without linking it to the implication of these monetary developments on oil and other commodities market.[179] The bulk of this strategy was the combined reduction in US overseas and foreign assistance and further decrease in the dollar component of international capital markets. This was the case of the bond and security markets of international economic institutions backed by the White House and the US Congress. In this respect it is eye-opening to make reference to the borrowing policies of the IBRD since the appointment of former US Secretary of Defense Robert McNamara to the presidency of the Washington-based institution in 1968. A few months after his appointment to the head of the IBRD, some of the

World Bank's high-ranking officials met representatives from the largest US banks to discuss their participation in financing the new president's ambitious plans to expand the World Bank's lending operation to finance developments policies across the globe. If one lets alone some arguments by these bankers about the very low lending rate that the World Bank offered to the American banking system, the very issue that stemmed from these conversations was the currency denomination of the Bank's bonds and securities offered on the market; Bank of America's representatives and officials of Brown Brothers Harriman, for instance, called attention to the implications of the US balance of payments deficit on the bankability of bonds issued by the IBRD and denominated in US dollars.[180] One year later, while leading US financial institutions such as Morgan Stanley stressed "the need for the Bank to renew and broaden its contacts in the investment community in the US; and for McNamara to become better known to that community,"[181] the Bank had issued a substantial portfolio of bonds to currency markets other than the dollar. In particular, from late summer 1968 to late summer 1969 the Bank pursued a diversification policy through offering both public and private issues in the German markets and in the Swiss capital market.[182] By the beginning of 1974, when the oil-induced balance of payments disequilibria began afflicting the non-oil LDCs, in the pursuit of its development assistant programs to halt this jungle of centrifugal effects on international payments, the World Bank had already borrowed \$388 million in Kuwaiti dinars, \$129 million in Libyan dinars, \$25 million in Lebanese pounds, and was negotiating a bond issue denominated in Venezuelan bolivares in the amount of about \$25 million. Though most American authorities suggested that the Bank convert these bonds into SDRs to protect borrowers from exchange rate risks, this policy of currency diversification clearly demonstrates the World Bank's policy to reduce the dollar component in its public placements.[183] After the first oil crisis some leading oil producing countries helped this American policy to dry up the dollar component of international liquidity by pouring their ever-expanding dollar-denominated oil revenues into the debt of the IBRD: in 1974 the OPEC countries increased their holding of bonds issued by the IBRD from 5 to 10 percent over the preceding seven years.[184] Therefore, the borrowing policy of the World Bank in the private and public markets tracks its involvement in the Nixon administration's policy to halt the depreciation of the dollar in exchange markets through policies aimed at reducing the dollar component of both liquid and non-liquid international financial assets. Therefore, both macroeconomic thinking and the Bretton Woods institutions' borrowing policies straddled to devise policies aimed at resurrecting the dollar value in exchange markets, and focused attention on the detrimental role of short-term capital markets without linking these developments to the impending termination of cheap oil prices and upward commodity prices. The case was much the same with Washington's gold policies under the new administration early in the new decade.

This string of monetary policies and measures to resurrect the US balance of payments on capital account conducted by the Nixon administration, the Federal Reserve System, and the institutions of Bretton Woods to counteract the balance of payments deficit and the declining strength of the dollar in exchange markets should be put into perspective. In fact, on balance it can be arguably said that from 1969 to 1973 the bulk of balance of payments deficit financing policies rested on the twin pillars of measures to restore equilibrium on the capital account and actions taken to curb the current account deficit. We might certainly say that they were the core of American policies to restore confidence in the dollar and to recast the US international payments position prior to the surge in oil prices and the expansion in transnational capital movements that broke out from 1973 to 1974. As seen in the previous chapters and paragraphs with respect to the Kennedy and Johnson administrations, both growing dollar-denominated financial assets in the domestic and international capital markets, and the increases in gold reserves held at foreign central banks hit hard the confidence in and value of the dollar on exchange markets. On the other hand, since the establishment of SDRs, the White House called on the international economic community for debunking the deep-seated conviction that the central role of gold as reserve unit was irreplaceable. As early as spring of 1969, when the recently established two-tier system was operative, then Under Secretary of the Treasury for Monetary Affairs Paul A. Volcker wrangled over this issue with South African authorities, then the principal gold supplier for both monetary and industrial uses. In light of South Africa's insistence on selling mined gold worldwide to increase monetary reserves irrespective of the price of gold in the private markets, Volcker vigorously made the point "that gold cannot be relied upon to provide the element of growth in official reserve that is needed. Having some arbitrary but uncertain amount of gold come into reserves might divert attention from the more central need, which is to implement the SDR arrangement which we have created to deal with this problem."[185] Likewise, consistently with the approach of the Johnson administration, Volcker ruled out South Africa's request to purchase currencies from the IMF against payments in gold.[186] Therefore, well in advance of the demise of the two-tier system, the new US administration moved from upholding the official gold-pegged monetary system to building up a new international monetary architecture based on new reserve assets and on devising new units of accounts to reduce the volume of dollar liquidity in the international financial system so as to ease pressure on it. Such monetary turn would also reduce the impact of gold movements on exchange rates and on the stability of financial markets.[187] However, consistently with its predecessors, the Nixon administration still focused on the monetary bases of the international system of trade and payments to shield the dollar and restore stability in the system, instead of focusing on the inflationary effects of developments in the international capital markets on either financial transactions and borrowings, or on trade in goods and commodities. Therefore, American authorities continued the pursuit of restoring the balance of payments on capital account without tackling the implication of growing short-term capital market on the price of crude oil and other international commodity markets. The much-heralded new balance of payments program announced at the beginning of 1968 was aimed at curbing capital outflow to improve the capital account balance by roughly $1.5 billion through a string of mandatory controls over US direct investments abroad and the tightening of lending abroad by banks and non-bank financial institutions. In particular, the program focused on scrutinizing investors with respect to the transfers of new capital from the United States, the amount of earnings abroad that could be retained abroad, and the short-term balances that could be retained abroad. This program also entailed a review of overseas US government expenditures.[188] One year later, in early 1969, President-elect Nixon announced a comprehensive balance of payments program mainly aimed at tapping the unfinished weakening of the dollar through the revamp of classical measures to forestall short-term capital outflows and restore equilibrium on the capital account.[189] The US government showed a growingly palpable concern in 1973, when within the EEC arrangements were made to remove controls on capital movements; this was much the case of the British loosening of exchange control restrictions passed by the government of London in 1973 to provide free movement of capital within the EEC.[190] The objective of that policy was to set up essential conditions to rebuild the US trade surplus by restoring stable and non-inflationary economic growth across the US economy.[191] In order to explain this classical policy focused on the capital account it is essential to make reference to the Department of State's approach to the US balance of payments deficit. Even in light of the turn-of-the-decade peaking deficit, American diplomacy made a case for adopting measures that neither violated fundamental foreign political-military responsibilities, nor impaired US foreign assistance policy and its underlying objectives. Within this framework, the Department of State called the White House to undertake sharp restrictions on flows of private capital to industrialized countries, especially Western Europe, but not—quite remarkably—to the balance of payments deficit of non-oil producing less developed countries.[192] Therefore, once again, the shaping of US foreign financial policy to resurrect the dollar intersected with Washington's foreign military and development policies, and revolved around the pillar of the non-oil producing LDCs. Another turn-of-the-decade much-discussed side of American policies to halt capital outflows was certainly the issue of regulatory measures to confront the development of the Eurodollar market. From 1964 to 1973, 445 branches of American banks were located abroad, with half total dollar deposits abroad held by foreign branches of US banks. As the US legislation approved during the 1960s had combined measures to control capital outflows and reserve requirements and interest rate ceilings, this had contributed to the development of Eurodollar deposits in European-based banks as a reaction by the American financial community to the regulatory architecture set off in Washington. As the US Department of the Treasury put it in 1974, "foreign-based banks enjoy an advantage over US-domiciled banks when competing in the Eurodollar markets because they are not subject to required reserves and interest rate ceilings, and they are allowed to pay interest on demand deposits and time deposits held for less than thirty days."[193] The persistence of this legislation under the Nixon administration demonstrates that measures enacted to resurrect the capital account were intended to reduce persisting capital outflows quite consistently with programs to curb the balance of payments deficit conducted in the past, as examined in Chap. 2. Under the Nixon administration the debate on the role and functioning of the Eurodollar market was quite intense owing to the staggering flows that the US money market was subject to from 1968 to 1971, when the outflow of liquid private capital was particularly striking since 1970 and thereafter.[194] This study has tackled the approach of the Fed's Chairman Arthur Burns to the subject; the Standing Committee on the Eurocurrency markets suggested that Group of Ten's central banks did not increase the amount of funds they had placed in the Eurocurrency markets directly or through the BIS, while the Geneva-based multilateral institution should gradually transfer funds received from Group of Ten countries and invested in the Eurodollar market to the United States, to the extent that satisfactory investment opportunities were available there. On the other hand, especially after the market-crushing $5 billion capital movement from the US capital markets to Eurodollar instruments of May 1971, the American financial community led the way in defending the crucible importance of the Eurodollar market in financing the stock markets of multinational corporations, especially in Europe, and international trade, since the 1960s and thereafter. For instance, Rimmer Vries, vice president of the Morgan Guaranty Trust Company of New York, held this view before the US Congress Subcommittee on International Exchange and Payments of the Joint Economic Committee. It is noteworthy that within the Federal Reserve System diverging views arouse, with some high-ranking officials emphasizing the important contribution of the Eurodollar market to the growth of the international economy and the expansion of world trade.[195] This last view is important as it anticipates the approach of the Federal Reserve to the Eurodollar and other Eurocurrency markets with reference to the supply side for fixed capital investments since the first half of 1974, when the mounting oil revenues that accrued to the OPEC countries nurtured short-term capital markets: this turn in the policy of the Fed is explored in the next chapter. In assessing them, it is worth noting that all of these perspectives except the specific view of the Federal Reserve System, as well as all measures adopted under the balance of payments programs since 1968, thereafter focused on whether or not averting further dollar outflows would prevent an expansion in money supply and its inflationary impact within the United States and on the international economy. However, remarkably they did not point to the impact of growing short-term money markets on prices through the pressure exerted on exchange rates. Moreover, quite importantly, such balance of payments deficit financing measures focused on the capital account were not aimed at reducing the current size of Eurodollar assets held by banks in Europe. In so doing, the US monetary and financial authorities working on behalf of the Nixon administration missed a crucial point. As a matter of fact, such reduction in the Eurodollar assets held by banks in Europe was necessary to reduce international borrowing from the Eurodollar market and to contrast the increase in demand for borrowing from that market and the upward movements in yields paid by borrowers of Eurodollars for financing slippages on the current account, governments' deficits, or foreign exchange earnings. Even when in 1971, in light of growing official holdings of Eurodollars by foreign central banks, estimated to amount as of end 1969 at $2.8 billion,[196] the US government borrowed $3 billion directly from the Eurodollar market, Washington did so for balance of payments deficit financing purposes without paying attention to the inflationary strain that US international payments imbalances and the weakness of the dollar caused. It is eye-catching that in so doing the US Department of the Treasury was well aware that "this borrowing tends to weaken rates in the US and strengthen them in the Eurodollar market."[197]

3.6 The US from Western Military Cooperation to Trade and Investments with Middle East Oil Producers 1971–1973

Based on the discussion in the last section, it is worth saying that the newly appointed Nixon presidency showed its underestimation of the effects of patterns in international monetary and capital markets and developments on international commodity and oil prices in so far as it revamped an old-fashioned policy to resurrect the US balance of payments, to prop up the dollar in foreign exchange markets, and to restructure the dollar-pegged system of international trade and payments, focused on tackling the current account deficit. The new administration turned its attention back to the balance of payments on current account to reverse the international payments position of the United States and to strengthen foreign market operations. In the pursuit of policies focused on the current account it first undertook a variety of foreign trade measures. It sought to expand trade bonds with commodity-supplying countries with which, notwithstanding the weakening of the dollar in exchange markets, the purchasing power of US importers prevented US import from further straining the current account deficit. Secondly, the new administration revamped well-established policies to reduce overseas dollar outpayments for military and economic assistance purposes and replaced them with expanded import-financing foreign credit to least developed countries. In addition, it sought preferential trade agreements with the EEC currency areas to minimize the effect of protectionist trade policies, control on exchange markets and unfair competitions with the EEC detrimental to the American balance of trade. Furthermore, the Nixon administration reverted to multilateral burden-sharing by calling its partners in the North Atlantic Treaty Organization (NATO) to raise their contribution to collective security, and it took the lead in reducing overseas military expenditures for the stationing of American forces in NATO countries. Finally, the government of Washington sought a steep increase in the dollar component of US import of commodities, mostly through a combined commitment to reduce US liabilities to foreigners arising out of oil and commodity imports from the Middle East, and a search for trade agreements with commodity supplying currency areas weaker than the dollar or supplying economies with which the US had well-established commercial partnerships. Therefore, the ways in which the Nixon administration revamped and developed a string of measures on the US current account position to reduce the dollar component in Washington's foreign trade are clear. It is worth tackling all of these measures briefly. In the first instance, the case of President-elect Nixon's policy toward the Organization of American States (OAS) and the Latin American countries highlights US efforts to revamp Kennedy's strategy to replace overseas public and military expenditures with US-subsidized foreign export to friendly nations. Nixon's proposal before the OAS for the establishment of an Inter-American Fund for the stabilization of commodity prices and income in Latin American countries and for the creation of a system of trade preferences for Latin American export to the United States, advocated and extended by Nixon as early as 1968, sought to expand US trade relations with currency areas significantly weaker than the dollar to ease the impact of American import of commodities on the US current account.[198] Second, during their appointment, Nixon and the US Department of the Treasury linked their efforts to set in motion a full reform of the international monetary system to restore equilibrium between deficit and surplus countries on the basis of a unilateral reduction of trade restraints by surplus countries and removal of artificial payments as a means of payments.[199] Within the framework of trade imbalances between Washington and its Western European partners, with the former suffering from imbalances and the latter enjoying a substantial trade and capital surplus, such US stance was a striking attempt to improve the US current account position and to raise Washington's foreign exchange earnings. In this context, note Washington's call on its European partners for expanding non-discriminatory preferential trade agreements and seeking trade arrangements with the US before negotiations took place in the General Agreement on Tariffs and Trade (GATT) to minimize the impact of import of manufactured goods and merchandise on the US current account through fair tariff arrangements. From 1971 to 1973 the US engaged in a number of trade negotiations with the EEC to seek a reduction and ultimate elimination of the common external tariff of the EEC, as well as elimination of EEC special trade arrangements contrary to GATT. Likewise, the United States urged the EEC to formulate an industrial policy that did not discriminate against US exports or against US subsidiaries in Europe. As the Department of the Treasury put it in 1973, such trade negotiations "will permit us, within the next few years, to reach a situation under which we will be in equilibrium in our basic balance (i.e., we can finance current external expenditures on aid and military accounts from current earnings in other accounts)." The very target of this firm trade policy toward

European partners was to "encourage countries in surplus on current and overall official account to liberalize trade more rapidly than deficit countries as one acceptable means of adjustments."[200] In order to push forward such a policy of trade liberalization toward the EEC as a way to restore equilibrium in the US balance of payments on current account, the US threatened a swift turn to protectionism through the 1973 Trade Reform Act. This law, soon disowned by the US Chamber of Commerce on behalf of the American business circles,[201] imposed surcharges or temporary quantitative restrictions on imports in instances of serious US balance of payments deficits. All in all, it should be viewed as a set of retaliatory measures passed in the US Congress to advance trade negotiations and liberalization with Washington's Western European economic partners aimed at resurrecting the US current account deficit.[202] Thirdly, a recorded reversal in the US foreign trade position since 1971 led Washington to endlessly pressurize its NATO allies to increase their burden-sharing effort as a way to reduce US foreign military spending. Under the Kennedy administration, Washington straddled to induce its NATO partners to take a larger share of their own defense to reduce the foreign exchange costs of US forces in Europe through both a reduction in the US share of NATO's infrastructure program, and a strong pressure on the Europeans for larger purchases of American military equipment by European allies, which would supposedly trigger an increase in short-term assets in the US balance of payments on current account.[203] Clearly, the Nixon administration specifically chose the route of reshaping US burden-sharing in NATO in the early 1970s in order to achieve the long-standing US ambition to make foreign defense and security policy the bulwark to improve both assets and liabilities in the US current account position. As Nixon put it in his 1973 Foreign Policy Report, the backdrop for this foreign exchange policy was that "as a general principle, we should move toward a lasting solution under which balance of payments consequences from stationing US troops in Europe will not be substantially different from those of maintaining the same forces in the United States."[204] Until 1970, although aggregate US balance of payments showed a large deficit, there had been a surplus trade balance. Although the exchange rate realignments agreed upon at the Smithsonian agreements of December 1971 were expected to stimulate US export as they entailed a de facto devaluation of the dollar, at the end of the year 1971 the US trade deficit was more than $2 billion and had trebled by 1972.[205] Within this framework, the US diplomacy engaged in a relentless effort directed toward Western European allies to strengthen the linkage between international monetary stability, collective defense and security policies, and international trade. In this respect, the role and stance held by the highest US diplomats is clearly apparent. On several occasions during his trips to Europe, Henry Kissinger insisted on the link between money, security and trade as a crucial point in the system of international political and economic relations.[206] Likewise, still in 1973, the interconnectedness between bilateral military cooperation, the stationing of American forces in the Federal Republic of Germany, and the US balance of payments problems thereto, was the subject of bilateral discussions between the United States Secretary of Defense Schlesinger and his German counterpart.[207] It is worth placing this new US stance under the Nixon administration in the framework of Washington's bet on restoring confidence in the dollar, reversing disequilibria in foreign exchange markets and US balance of payments deficit through a sharp reduction in overseas military expenditures and promotion of foreign exchange earnings by means of US military export to friendly nations, first implemented under the Kennedy administration. Therefore, as much as during the 1960s and in particular under the Kennedy administration, under Nixon, US foreign military policy had the twofold objective of reducing US military spending overseas and financing Washington's foreign exchange operations. Therefore, this was an ongoing approach to restore the US external equilibrium and rebuff international confidence in the US dollar consistently pursued during both the 1960s and under the Nixon administration. Finally, the Nixon administration straddled to reshape US import policies to avert adverse effects of import of oil and other commodities on the current account balance through a reduction in the import of oil from producing countries leading the oil price hikes. Likewise, Nixon worked on stemming a staggering reduction in the import from foreign suppliers of both dollar-denominated commodities and merchandise denominated in other hard currencies. Such strategy implied a striking turn toward friendly and trustworthy oil-supplying countries that offered both secure and continued oil supply, and fairly stable posted prices. Within this framework, as early as 1969, in light of increased posted prices of crude oil, the Nixon administration established a government-level Oil Committee, renamed the Shultz Committee, to monitor the international oil situation and formulate possible policies and countermeasures; the Shultz group developed a consensus in favor of a tariff approach to the problem. The basic concept was to switch to a preferential tariff system that would draw the bulk of future imports from secure Western Hemisphere sources[208]: in particular, the Committee stressed the importance of Canada, Venezuela and the rest of Latin America. The very objective of such a change was to establish tariff levels that would bring about a price in the United States per barrel of oil of \$2.50 as against the current world price of \$2.00 and the current price in the United States of \$3.30. According to this plan, the US would have been able to fix a low tariff per barrel for Canada and Venezuela and a much higher tariff for import from Middle Eastern oil producers and other OPEC countries. This plan should be situated within the framework of both a US national security objective to reduce the risk of a rising American dependence on countries like Libya and Kuwait, and a prospective need to ease pressure on the liabilities on the US current account. In either case, according to the Department of State "there was a strong feeling that we should not become dependent upon Middle Eastern suppliers because of the inherent instability in the area and the likelihood of interruption of supply."[209] In this context, certainly US friendly countries such as Saudi Arabia, Iran, Indonesia and Nigeria deserved a better and special treatment that went beyond the scope of restoring equilibrium in the current account balance. In light of the increasing economic wealth of these countries arising out of the very late 1960s expansion in their oil revenues and profits, Washington identified with the promotion of fixed capital investments in these friendly oil producing countries by US manufacturing and American multinationals a workable and feasible alternative to economic aid and military assistance. Yet again, in so far as this strategy was the groundwork for a rise in the export of US instrumental and consumer goods to these economies, the Nixon administration showed its shift toward replacing civilian and military expenditures overseas with export, along the way of its bet on reducing the liabilities in the current account balance and improving the assets. As these oil producing countries were maturing economies, trade and investments should replace economic and military assistance: "For those nations whose economic base is oil production, US oil import policy could play a crucial role in determining our future relationship."[210] The plan, which entailed a tariff on oil import from the Middle Eastern oil producers, posed issues and problems to the US foreign policy. Notwithstanding, US diplomacy approved it to reduce the impact of Washington's foreign oil policy on national security and the US balance of payments.[211] Therefore, the new administration revamped a balance of payments deficit financing policy focused on targeting liabilities on the current account through a commitment to foreign trade and export-promoting policies. The US worries about the impact of surging oil prices on the strength of the dollar and wealth of US balance of payments, were linked to the rising oil posted prices and the deterioration of bilateral economic relations between the United States government, American oil companies, and some key oil producing countries of the Mediterranean basin. Two turn-of-the-decade developments account for this American stance. On the one side, from 1967 to 1970 the posted price of oil hiked up: as a result of the winter 1970 oil tax and price increases, at the end of the year 1970 the posted prices of crude oil exported from Libya, East Mediterranean and Nigerian ports were increased substantially and the tax rates of oil exported from these ports and the Persian Gulf ports were raised from 50 percent to about 55 percent.[212] This steady oil price hike resulted in a staggering increase in the combined current surplus for the four poorest net capital importing oil producers of Saudi Arabia, Kuwait, Libya and Iraq, that between 1970 and 1971 doubled their surplus owing to the effects of oil price increases since the 1967 thereafter on their receipts and payments.[213] By keeping an eye on the performance of these four countries during the period following the quadrupling of oil posted prices in 1974 it is possible to sense that for these four poorest oil producing nations the surplus capacity they attained prior to 1972 was unpaired.[214] On the other hand, more importantly, the rising assertiveness of Arab oil producers since the outbreak of the Arab–Israeli conflict prompted some key oil suppliers to menace oil production cuts and to make arrangements for having military contracts with Western European companies and the Soviets. This new military import policy of Arab oil producers had potentially harmful consequences on the US foreign trade account. In this respect, the case of Libya is of paramount importance. Prior to the Libyan Revolution and the expropriation of the interests of US companies in the country, Libya exerted its leverage power on both lines. In late summer 1970, the Libyan Oil Ministry outspokenly declared that Libya was seriously moving to restrict production as a means of raising oil prices; at the same time the country signed the first in a sequence of contracts to purchase Mirage jet fighters from the French governments that had a spillover on many French and other Western manufacturing sectors and continued through the second half of the 1970s. In the case of some specific manufacturing industries such as radar, computers and communication components the adverse effect of Libyan foreign trade policy on American current account assets was effective in so far as French companies directly competed with American multinationals such as Northrop or ITT. Making matters worse, half of American companies' interests in the country were expropriated a few years later by the Libyan Arab Republic.[215] In either case, Libyan policies represented a threat to the US current account: firstly, the American companies operating in the country brought the US balance of payments up by $800 million; secondly, Libyan military imports from the USSR and Western Europe jeopardized the long-standing US strategy in support for the US dollar in foreign exchange markets through foreign exchange earnings based on military export to friendly nations. As discussed earlier, the June 1967 war triggered remarkable effects on current account assets in the US balance of payments based on the impact that reduced profitability by the oil companies had on Washington's foreign exchange earnings, and consequently, US government leeway to finance foreign markets operations. Consistent with this approach, amid the 1971 concession and tax negotiations between the oil producing countries and the oil companies, a National Security Study Memorandum prepared within the National Security Council at the request of the White House stressed that the decline in profitability by the US international oil companies caused by higher posted prices and tax increases would adversely affect the US balance of payments on current account. Furthermore, making matters worse, unlike in 1968, it would also hit hard the capital account component in so far as reduced profitability and cash generation of multinationals' foreign operations would result in a lower rate of profit remittance and larger capital outflows to finance capital projects. This was in striking contrast with the years that preceded agreements between OPEC and the companies signed since 1970. In fact, according to this study, still in 1969, "the direct investment income from US oil operations abroad amounted to $2.6 billion as compared with a net capital outflow of $1 billion by the oil companies."[216] In this situation, the case of ARAMCO in Saudi Arabia is straightforward: as of the end of 1968, ARAMCO's repatriated profits together with a US favorable trade balance ($129 million) contributed over $535 million to the US balance of payments.[217] It is worth saying in passing that deteriorating bilateral economic relations between the US and the Mediterranean and Gulf area oil producers adversely affected the US balance of payments on capital account in so far as such deterioration triggered a shift in the investment policies of these countries in international money markets. According to a British Economic Intelligence Unit report, the 1972 Arab–Israeli conflict was likely to cause a shift in the investment patters of Arab oil producers out of the United States stock and credit markets and into the Eurocurrency markets.[218] In addition, since the 1967 Arab–Israeli conflict, the US government terminated the selling of arms to Arab governments with which diplomatic relations had been interrupted since the outbreak of the war, and prohibited American private companies from doing business with Arab countries.[219] Therefore, the combined effect of concession negotiations with Western oil companies on posted prices and consolidated taxes, and that of the Arab–Israeli conflict on trade relations between the United States and some OPEC countries, with particular reference to US–Arabian trade in military goods and services, either bilaterally or collectively, had remarkable effects on the US balance of payments on both current and capital accounts. Though the US military industry was prohibited from selling arms and services to Arab countries with which diplomatic relations had been interrupted as a result of the 1967 conflict, American diplomacy and banking made efforts to foster military and civilian export to other Arab countries as part of Nixon's support for the US current account balance and commitment to reverse the combined adverse effects of oil price hikes and deteriorating trade relations following the Arab–Israeli conflict. In this respect Saudi Arabia was the most remarkable case in point: since the beginning of the decade the Export-Import Bank of the United States endorsed an import credit scheme to finance the construction of a number of refinery projects. Such import credit scheme charged the Saudi Arabian General Petroleum and Mineral Organization (Petromin), with constructing a steel mill, and sulfur and phosphate plants that involved American plants, and received collateral support from the Chase Manhattan Bank to finance the transfer of American technology to the country, which increased assets in the US current account balance.[220] It is worth noting that Saudi Arabia's call on the Exim-Bank for funding took place within the context of the Arabian government's heavy placements of oil revenues in the Eurodollar market through the New York-based First National City Bank; this Saudi Arabian government investment policy contributed to the drying up of the local capital market and triggered a tight credit situation.[221] Disregarding the fact that Saudi Arabia was one of the few capital-absorbing Middle Eastern OPEC countries with a potentially growing domestic consumer market, the government of Washington and the financial community of New York devoted most attention to it as Saudi Arabia had a well-tested experience in serving as the bulwark for the stabilization of the region under US umbrella. For instance, by 1970 the country had devoted a considerable percentage of its GDP to provide several unstable countries in the region, such as Jordan, with foreign economic assistance packages tailored to stabilize the entire region in cooperation with economic research people at the CIA.[222] Furthermore, within the framework of the Smithsonian agreements' currency realignments Saudi Arabia showed its propensity to help the US restore the balance of payments by proposing Saudi investments in downstream oil facilities in the United States, in return for setting the US oil import quota from the country.[223] This firm and continuous policy to finance US military and civilian export to the country as a way to increase the assets in the US trade balance had the collateral effect of reducing dollar holdings of OPEC countries: such reduction prevented the oil producers from further running on US gold reserves. In this respect, agreements between the US and the Saudis took place quite consistently with the US relentless search to forestall the outflow of gold and its consequent harmful impact on the value and stability of the US dollar. Likewise, American foreign policy and the US financial community struggled to avoid any further international run on gold detrimental to the convertibility of the US currency. In fact, on many occasions the Nixon administration proved to be sensitive to Arab requests: this was the case with the Saudi Arabian Monetary Authority (SAMA)'s repeated claims on the David Rockefeller-chaired Chase Manhattan Bank to have letters of credit to purchase military equipment either in the United States or, more frequently, from the British defense industry. One instance occurred in 1970, when SAMA made a request for a letter of credit to cover certain Arab purchases of British hardware, in particular British fighters. On this and many other occasions, Chase pleaded to the Department of State for official clearance, stressing that in event that Chase refused to issue letters of clearance to SAMA, the latter would shift abroad some of its balances currently held in New York. In making a case for handling this business, high-ranking officials at Chase Manhattan Bank wished for "Saudi balances not [to] be moved abroad where they would contribute to further gold drain."[224] It is worth saying in passing that Chase Manhattan Bank had long-standing interests in developing and expanding its business bonds in the country: during the 1960s for several years the bank of the Rockefeller family had engaged in lengthy negotiations to obtain permission from the Saudi Arabia government to enter into commercial activities in the country.[225] In 1970, its interest in clearing SAMA's letters of credit should be linked to negotiations at the time underway to finalize an agreement with the Saudi Arabian Monetary Authority regarding the establishment of an industrial bank in Saudi Arabia.[226] Chapter 4 turns the spotlight on how smoothly continuous was the involvement of Chase Manhattan Bank in Saudi Arabia's capital markets in the context of the contributions by American banks in recycling the OPEC countries' bountiful oil revenues in order to stimulate programs of domestic industrialization and economic modernization. Since 1977, Chase Bank joined Saudi Arabia's royal family in underwriting the basic capital of Sarabam and Sarabam M.V., two investment outlets, the latter based in the Netherlands Antilles, jointly established by Arabian and American capital both "to create new enterprises, with an emphasis on project designed to ease the world shortage of food and energy resources," and to promote transfer of American technology to the country, as well as "to help solve a world monetary problem caused by longer-term loans being made to non-oil producing countries, both developing and industrialized, based on short-term Arab bank deposits and investments."[227] Likewise, Chase Manhattan Bank could exhibit a long-standing involvement in Iran: since as early as 1959 the bank of the Rockefeller family cooperated in the setting up of the Industrial and Mining Development Bank of Iran (IMDBI), a shareholding company established to stimulate industrial takeoff in the country through borrowing abroad and lending to private projects in Iran. By the middle of the decade this company established under the aegis of Chase had become a reliable and very useful institution in attracting foreign investors to Iran.[228] In 1968, even as it was committed to building up a new commercial bank in Dubai with capital coming from Chase itself, the Kuwait Commercial Bank, a German bank and some private investors, the bank of the Rockefeller family straddled to pull together a group of American investors to invest in Iran. Along the way, the New York-based First National City Bank (FNCB) went down this route and reached agreements with some Iranian banks to set up a mixed bank with them in the country.[229] Later on, after the first fourfold increase in oil prices, within the framework of the US-Iranian bilateral joint commission for economic cooperation (covered in Chap. 4), FNCB led the way in promoting a growing role for American commercial banks in the Iranian capital market.[230] As for Saudi Arabia, the involvement of American brokerage houses and investment banks in the most important Middle Eastern capital-surplus countries as the litmus for a policy to restore the balance of payments on current account was much the same as the case of Iran. American investment banks and brokerage houses either underwrote foreign borrowings by Saudi Arabia and Iran, or warranted American investments in both countries. Therefore, the involvement of US commercial and investment banks in the Middle Eastern oil producing countries, although well-grounded in the past, was consistent with US policies to develop trade bonds with these countries as a flywheel in the pursuit of Washington's long-lasting aim at restoring equilibrium on the current account. As early as 1966, the Shah and the US government made arrangements for a total US foreign military sales credit of $50 million annually in 1968 and 1969. At the same time, in 1967 the

Shah requested that American firms invest in projects in Iran, especially petrochemical and agriculture; this request met not only the US government's inclination to promote US trade and investments in the country as a way to strengthen with Teheran economic and political bonds as strong as with Saudi Arabia, but also interests and aspirations of the American business community. In cooperation with the US Embassy in Teheran, two prominent figures in the history of US development assistance and foreign economic policy, David Lilienthal and George Ball, led the way in promoting visits by teams of American commercial farmers and American investors to the country.[231] By 1971, the United States had become the largest single investor in Iran.[232] Though debates about investments in new fields like petrochemical and agriculture dominated relations with the US, the quest for credit financing to let Iran import both average capital-intensive military merchandise and modern military items like helicopters, was the centerpiece of bilateral trade relations between the two countries still on the eve of the new decade.[233] This early involvement of leading American banks and brokerage houses in underwriting foreign loans or in warranting foreign investors in the country anticipated their role in recycling the growing oil revenues of Iran and Saudi Arabia since 1974. However, as suggested in the following chapters, their role would change significantly over the course of the 1970s as they moved from the position of underwriters to become investors and lenders. Clearly, this diversification and increase in US business activities in countries such as Iran and Saudi Arabia beyond the scope of American oil companies was to make up for the losses in US foreign exchange earnings caused by the combined weakening of the dollar in foreign exchange markets and reduced profits of oil companies that had resulted from increased taxes and oil prices. Therefore, the role of American banking in the Middle Eastern oil producing countries took place within the framework of the adverse effects on the US balance of payments on both the current and capital accounts in so far as the reduction in profits of US firms and corporations overseas adversely affected US foreign exchange earnings and called to expand multinational foreign investments to compensate for productivity and profit squeeze that could potentially result in a growing US capital account deficit.

Notes

1. Both statistical data can be consulted in Becker et al. 2016, http://www.nber.org/data/nberces.html
2. Board of Governors of the Federal Reserve System, 1971, pp. 269–279.
3. National Archives and Records Administration, Archive II, College Park, MD (henceforth NARA), Record Group 59, General Records of the Department of State (henceforth RG59), Bureau of Near Eastern and South Asian Affairs, Office of Arabian Peninsula Affairs, Records Relating to Saudi Arabia 1955–1974, b. 7, fold. PG and AP Econ-Pet-Petroleum-General, Department of State, "American Economic Opportunities in Arab Oil States," undated.
4. Craft and Toniolo (eds), 1996; Brenner, 2006, chapters 3 and 4; Harvey, 1990, pp. 121–189.
5. Lin, 1984, pp. 781–802. Yergin, 2008; Türk, 2014, pp. 209–213; Painter, 2014, pp. 186–208; Quinlan, 2010, chapter 1.
6. For a like-minded national case study conducted through an econometric approach see Helliwell, 1984, pp. 191–216.
7. See Becker et al. 2016, http://www.nber.org/nberces/
8. This is the case of studies in international political economy: Frieden, 2006; Broz and Frieden, 2001, pp. 317–343.
9. See for reference Skett, 1988; Stork, 1975.
10. In this respect see for instance the Soviet-Iranian arms deal involving non-sophisticated equipment signed by the Shah of Iran: NARA, RG59, Bureau of Near Eastern and South Asian Affairs, Office of the Iran Affairs, Records Relating to Iran 1965–1975, b. 1, fold. E.-Economic Affairs (Gen) IRAN, 1967, Mr. Rockwell (Division of Near Eastern And South Asian Affairs, Department of State) to Mr. Battle, Information Memorandum "Shah's Letter to the President; New Iran-Soviet Arms Deal," November 1, 1967.
11. Schenk, 2010, chapters 5 and 9.
12. Gray, 2010, p. 149; see also a memorandum of conversation between German Finance Minister Strauss and World Bank President McNamara: World Bank Group Archives, Washington, DC (henceforth WBGA), Records of the Office of the President, Records of President Robert McNamara, Contacts with Member Countries: Germany—Correspondence 01, "Visit of Minister Strauss with President McNamara on July, 24, 1968."

13. Department of the Treasury, 1969, p. 39.
14. Gray, 2007, pp. 295–323; Gavin, 2004; Zimmerman, 2010, pp. 127–144.
15. A comprehensive series on real exchange rates is in *Historical Financial Statistics*, http://www.centerforfinancialstability.org/hfs.php? (Accessed June 30, 2016); for the increase in oil prices since 1967 see Board of Governors of the Federal Reserve System, 1974, table A 66.
16. Wachtel, 1990, p. 78; James, 1996, p. 172; Bird, 2003, pp. 267 ff.; Wilkie, 2012, pp. 34 ff.
17. Department of Treasury, Talking Paper on the Basic Pledge, in Position Paper for Gold Pool Negotiations, "Reserve Policies During the Interim Period Prior to Activation of Special Drawing Rights," March 26–27, 1968, in Declassified Documents and Reference System, http://www.gale.com/us-declassified-documents-online/ (henceforth DDRS).
18. Gardner Ackley (Chairman, Council of Economic Advisers), Memorandum for the President "Comments on the Attached Memoranda," January 24, 1968, in DDRS.
19. The National Archives, Kew, Richmond (henceforth TNA), The Cabinet Papers 1915–1988, http://www.nationalarchives.gov.uk/cabinetpapers/ (accessed June 15, 2011), Memorandum by the Ministry of Power "Oil Prices: Devaluation and Surcharge," December 19, 1967.
20. UNCTADstat, Free market commodity price indices, annual, 1960–2010 (price indices 2000=100), http://unctadstat.unctad.org/wds/TableViewer/tableView.aspx?ReportId=30727 (accessed May 20, 2015).
21. WBGA, Records of General Vice Presidents and Managing Directors, Records of Sir Denis Rickett 1970–1974, Oil And Energy, Memos and Reports, 1973 through 1974, Volume 01, John Foster (IBRD) to M. Shoaib (IBRD), Office Memorandum "Projections of Oil Revenues of OPEC Member Countries," January 26, 1973.
22. TNA, The Cabinet Papers 1915–1988, http://www.nationalarchives.gov.uk/cabinetpapers/ (accessed June 12, 2011), UK Government, Minutes of Cabinet Meeting, February 4, 1971.
23. TNA, The Cabinet Papers 1915–1988, http://www.nationalarchives.gov.uk/cabinetpapers/ (accessed June 11, 2011), Memorandum by the Minister of Technology, "The Energy Scene," October 12, 1970.
24. See respectively Selva, 2014, and *idem.*, 2017.
25. Marx, 2014, pp. 251–271.

26. NARA, RG59, Bureau of European Affairs, Office of OECD, European Community and Atlantic Political-Economic Affairs, Records Relating to Economic Matters 1953–1975, b. 13, fold. FSE-OECD Energy 1967–1969, OECD Confrontation on US Energy Policy, Opening Remarks of Assistant Secretary J. Cordell Moore, January 26, 1967, p. 7.
27. Wijnholds, 2015, pp. 69–71.
28. Library of Congress, Manuscript Division, Washington, DC (henceforth LOC), Elliot L. Richardson papers, part 1, b. 292, fold. OECD, Statement by Under Secretary Elliot L. Richardson at the OECD Ministerial Meeting, Paris, February 13, 1969.
29. Solomon, 1976, p. 25; Odell, 1982, pp. 189–190.
30. See La Barca, 2013.
31. NARA, Record Group 56, General Records of the Department of the Treasury (henceforth RG56), Office of the Assistant Secretary for International Affairs (henceforth OASIA), Chronological Files of the Office of Financial Resources and Energy Finance 1974–1977, b. 1, fold. OASIA: Office of Financial Resources and Energy Finance, Permanent Chron. File February 1977, Department of the Treasury, "The Treatment of OPEC Financial Assets," 1977; William Witherell (Office of Financial Resources and Energy Finance), "Saudi Assets and the Link with Saudi Production Policy," February 18, 1977.
32. Mundell, 1989, pp. 64 ff.
33. Council of Economic Advisers, 1960, p. 11.
34. Council of Economic Advisers, 1967, p. 24. See also US Government, 1968, International Statistics, Table B-83-United States Balance of Payments 1947–67, p. 306.
35. Federal Reserve System, 1969, p. 49.
36. McGraw-Hill, Economics Department, 2016. www.nber.org/databases/macrohistory/contents/chapter06 (accessed, January 30, 2016).
37. George Willis, Memorandum of Conversation Fowler-Ackley-Deming-Willis-Colombo-Stammati, "International Monetary Problems and US-European Economic Relations," November 28, 1968, in DDRS.
38. US Government, 1968, Table B-83: United States Balance of Payments 1947–67, pp. 306–307.
39. Department of Commerce, 1967, pp. 17–18.
40. Department of the Treasury, 1968, p. 40.

41. John F. Kennedy Presidential Library and Museum, Boston, Mass. (henceforth JFKPL), Papers of John F. Kennedy, Presidential Papers, National Security Files (henceforth NSF), fold. "Principal Papers Prepared for the Cabinet Committee on Balance of Payments in Connection with its Report to the President, April 6, 1963," Summary Report from the Long Range International Payments Committee "Financial Measures for the US Balance of Payments Deficit 1963–64," March 15, 1963.
42. Federal Reserve Bank of New York Historical Archive, New York City (henceforth FRBNYA), Central Files, Subject Files, Foreign Exchange Control General, b. 35575, B. K. MacLacry to Mr. Coombs, telegram, "Movement of Funds at the Federal Reserve Bank of New York," June 6, 1967; B. K. McLaury, Memo for the Files "Movement of Middle East," June 29, 1967.
43. NARA, RG59, Bureau of European Affairs, Office of OECD, European Community and Atlantic Political Economic Affairs, Records Relating to Economic Matters 1953–1975, b. 13, fold. Finance FN 13 (B) Capital Markets 1967, F. Lisle Widman, Memorandum to the Secretary, "Weekly Bond Buyer Article on Money Rate Gap," April 3, 1967.
44. WBGA, Records of the Office of the President, Records of President Robert S. McNamara, Contacts with member countries: Germany—Correspondence 01, fold. Contacts Germany (1968), Memorandum of conversation McNamara-Aldewereld-Lipfart (GiroZentrale), June 6, 1968; Memorandum of conversation McNamara-Aldewereld-Guth-Kalusens (Deutsche Bank), June 6, 1968.
45. Board of Governors of the Federal Reserve System, Division of International Finance, 1967, charts 2, 3, and 7.
46. NARA, RG56, OASIA, Subject Files of the Office of International Monetary Affairs 1968–1978, b. 3, fold. 3 (Eurodollars), Fred H. Klopstock (Manager, International Research Department, Federal Reserve Bank of New York), "Statement before the Subcommittee on International Exchange and Payments of the Joint Economic Committee," June 22, 1971.
47. FRBNYA, Central Files 765.43.2, Meetings of Secretary of Treasury with NY Financial Men 1958–1981, F.D. Sternlight, Memorandum for the Files "Summary of Discussions between Under Secretary Deming and Market Participants Regarding Treasury Financing," October 17, 1968.
48. Department of the Treasury, 1968, p. 41.

49. Department of the Treasury, 1968, p. XXV.
50. CIA, Directorate of Intelligence, Intelligence Memorandum "French Action in the Recent Gold Crisis," March 20, 1968, retrievable at https://www.cia.gov/library/readingroom/search/site (accessed June 27, 2016).
51. CIA, "The President's Daily Brief," December 18, 1967, retrievable at https://www.cia.gov/library/readingroom/search/site (accessed June 28, 2016).
52. For an estimate elaborated by the Department of the Treasury about future use and production of gold in the United States and the world see Mr. Wolfe to Under Secretary Deming, "Future Production and Industrial Use for gold," December 13, 1967, in DDRS.
53. Frederick L. Deming, Memorandum to the Secretary of Treasury "Plan for Dealing with the Gold Problem," November 10, 1967; attached paper of the Deming Group "Dealing with the Gold Problem," November 10, 1967, both in DDRS.
54. Henry H. Fowler (Secretary of the Treasury), Memorandum for the President "The Gold Situation," November 13, 1967, DDRS.
55. E. V. Rostow, "Next Steps in International Monetary Policy," March 13, 1968, in DDRS.
56. US Department of the Treasury, "Situation Report on Balance of Payments," in DDRS. On such linkage between support for monetary convertibility and domestic economic expansion see also the "Communiqué" issued at the conclusion of the Washington meeting on March 16–17 of the Governors of the Central Banks: "Communiqué notes on US policy," in DDRS.
57. CIA, Directorate of Intelligence, Intelligence Memorandum "Continued Pressure on Sterling and the Dollar," December 12, 1967, retrievable at https://www.cia.gov/library/readingroom/docs/DOC_0005974167.pdf (accessed July 1, 2016).
58. TNA, The Cabinet Papers 1915–1988, http://www.nationalarchives.gov.uk/cabinetpapers (accessed June 9, 2011), Memorandum by the Minister of Power "Oil Prices: Devaluation and Surcharge," December 19, 1967.
59. Board of Governors of the Federal Reserve System, Various issues 1960–1968.
60. NARA, Record Group 82, General Records of the Federal Reserve System, (henceforth RG82), Division of International Finance and Predecessors, International Subject Files 1907–1974, b. 327, Division

of International Finance, Board of Governors of the Federal Reserve System, Capital Market Developments Abroad, 20 December 1967, charts n. 2-3-6-7-8.

61. US Government, 1967, Table B-84-International Reserves, 1949, 1953, and 1961–66, p. 311. The Spanish balance of payments on capital account uninterruptedly improved from 1964 to the end of the decade: International Monetary Fund Archives, Washington, DC (henceforth IMFA), Central Files, C/Italy/810 Mission L. Whittome November 1970, L. A. Whittome to the Managing Director and the Deputy Managing Director of the IMF, "Visits to Portugal, Spain, and Italy," November 20, 1970.
62. US Government, 1969, Table B-89-United States reserve assets: Gold stock, holdings of convertible foreign currencies, and reserve position in the International Monetary Fund 1946–68, p. 330.
63. JFKPL, Papers of John F. Kennedy. Presidential Papers, NSF, fold. Principal Papers Prepared for the Cabinet Committee on Balance of Payments in Connection with its Report to the President, April 6, 1963, Summary Report from the Long Range International Payments Committee, "Financial Measures for the US Balance of Payments Deficit 1963–64," March 15, 1963.
64. The most recent and comprehensive study of SDRs is Wilkie, 2012.
65. Department of State, Position paper for Gold Pool Negotiations, "Reserve Policies During the Interim Period Prior to Activation of Special Drawing Rights," March 16–17, 1968, in DDRS.
66. For these data on gold sales by the IMF to the United States see Federal Reserve System, 1970, p. 53.
67. Federal Reserve System, 1970, p. 53.
68. Memorandum of Conversation Fowler (US Secretary of the Treasury), Under Secretary Barr, Under Secretary Deming, Mr. Ackley (CEA), Martin (Federal Reserve System), Hayes (Federal Reserve Bank of New York), R. Solomon (Federal Reserve), A. Solomon (Department of State), "Highlights of Meeting of Deming Group with Secretary Fowler on Gold Policy," November 24, 1967, in DDRS.
69. For these data and Carli's proposal for activation of SDRs see IMFA, Central Files, Country Files—Italy, b. 7, fold. 17 (C/Italy/820 Member Missions to Washington [1947–1987]), L. A. Whittome, Memorandum for the Files, "Meeting with Mr. Ossola," September 26, 1969; A. Pfeifer, Memorandum for the Files "Discussion with Governor Carli," June 25, 1969.

70. For a thorough discussion of the proposal formulated by Ackley see William B. Dale, Memorandum "The Ackley Alternative," November 27, 1967, in DDRS.
71. On US interventions in foreign exchange markets during the 1960s see Bordo et al. 2015, pp. 120–209.
72. US Department of Treasury, "US Short-Term Liabilities to Foreigners," January 1968, in DDRS.
73. For an overview if this trend see Board of Governors of the Federal Reserve System, 1968, Table A-90 (Foreign Exchange Rates); for the time period from 1967 to 1968 see Board of Governors of the Federal Reserve System, Division of International Finance Europe and British Commonwealth Section, 1970, Table 2A and B. pp. 5–6.
74. The Chase Manhattan Corporation, 1968, p. 8.
75. The US Embassy in Tokyo (Johnson) to the Secretary of State, telegram, "Roundup on Japanese Reaction to Gold Developments," March 13, 1968, in DDRS.
76. On the scaling up expansion in the size of the Eurodollar market in the second half of the 1960s see Altamura, 2017.
77. Mikesell, 1975, p. 2.
78. See for reference Junne, 1976; Storck, 1995.
79. Rockefeller Archive Center, Tarrytown, NY (henceforth RAC), Rockefeller Family Archive (henceforth RFA), Record Group 3 (henceforth RG3) 4L, Nelson A. Rockefeller Personal Project Series, b. 16, fold. 151, Charles Clune (Vice President), to Nelson Rockefeller, March 1, 1967; N. Rockefeller to C. Clune, March 7, 1967.
80. IMFA, Middle Eastern Department Fonds (henceforth Medai), Medai Subject Files, b. 75, fold. 1, A.K. El-Selehdar, Memorandum for the Files "Fund Visit of Mr. M. S. Al Mahdi of OPEC," November 19, 1971.
81. Gilpin, 2009, pp. 268–269; Yergin, 2008, pp. 475–477; from the view point of the British economy see Kochavi, 2016, pp. 91–110; Mitchell, 2011; Shwadran, 1977, pp. 7–16; Venn, 2013, introduction and chapter 3.
82. NARA, RG59, Bureau of European Affairs, Office of OECD, European Community and Atlantic Political Economic Affairs Records Relating to Economic Matters 1953–1975, b. 13, fold. FSE-OECD-Petroleum 1967–1969, LeRoy F. Percival (Department of State) to Mr. Sober, Memorandum "Talking Points for Assistant Secretary Battle at NAC Meeting June 29, 1967," June 29, 1967.

83. *The New York Times*, July 23, 1967.
84. NARA, RG59, Bureau of European Affairs, Office of OECD, European Community and Atlantic Political Economic Affairs Records Relating to Economic Matters 1953–1975, b. 13, fold. FSE-OECD-Petroleum 1967–1969, Abraham Katz (Bureau of European Affairs) to Mr. Springsteen (Bureau of European Affairs), "OECD Oil Committee Meeting: Information Memorandum," July 18, 1967.
85. TNA, Records of the Cabinet Office, Cabinet Minutes and Papers, Cabinet Memoranda, 129/133/9, http://discovery.nationalarchives.gov.uk/details/r/D7660568 (accessed June 8, 2011), Memorandum by the Minister of Power "The Oil Situation," September 12, 1967.
86. NARA, RG59, Bureau of European Affairs, Office of OECD, European Community and Atlantic Political Economic Affairs, Records Relating to Economic Matters 1953–1975, b. 13, fold. FSE-OECD-Petroleum 1967–1969, Department of State, "Western Interests in Arab Oil," November 1, 1967.
87. NARA, Record Group 273, Records of the National Security Council (henceforth RG273), National Security Study Memorandum (NSSM), b. 12, fold. NSSM 114, National Security Study Memorandum 114 "World Oil Situation," January 15, 1971.
88. On the prohibition of selling weapons to Arab countries see NARA, RG59, Bureau of Near Eastern and South Asian Affairs, Office of Algeria, Libya, Morocco, and Tunisia, Records Relating to Libya 1970–1974, b. 1, fold. Chron. January–June Memoranda Libya 1974, Department of State, "US Policy on Arms Sales to Algeria," January 24, 1974.
89. NARA, RG59, Bureau of Near Eastern and South Asian Affairs, Office of Arabian Peninsula Affairs, Records Relating to Saudi Arabia 1955–1974, b. 7, fold. PG and AP Econ-Pet-Petroleum-General, Department of State, "American Economic Opportunities in Arab Oil States," undated.
90. Department of State, Arms Control Group, Memorandum for the Special Committee, "Exceptions to Interim Arms Policy for the Middle East," June 21, 1967, in DDRS.
91. Lyndon Baines Johnson Presidential Library, Austin, TX (henceforth LBJPL), National Security Files (henceforth NSF), Country File-United Kingdom, fold. UK Balance of payments crisis 1965, Thomas Summers to Mr. Hinton, Memorandum "The UK Balance of Payments Crisis," June 21, 1965.

92. WBGA, Records of the Office of the President, Records of President Robert S. McNamara, Contacts with member countries: United Kingdom—General—Correspondence 02, O'Brien to McNamara, cable, September 19, 1968; concerning British measures to counteract the balance of payments crisis during the two years preceding the devaluation of the British pound see *ibid.*, O'Brien to Woods, cable, July 20, 1966.
93. Hauge and Hoffmeyer, 1978: the document is also held in FRBNYA, Presidential papers, papers of Paul A. Volcker 1975–1979, b. 35578, fold. 140A 1977–1978 Annual Meetings of IMF and IBRD.
94. US Government, 1968, table b-88, p. 312.
95. Board of Governors of the Federal Reserve System, 1968, Table A-90.
96. CIA Directorate of Intelligence, Intelligence Memorandum, "French Actions in the Recent Gold Crisis," March 20, 1968, in DDRS.
97. Board of Governors of the Federal Reserve System, 1968, Table A-89.
98. Federal Reserve System, 1969, p. 4.
99. LBJPL, NSF, Country File: United Kingdom, fold. UK Balance of Payments Crisis 1965, George Ball, "British Sterling Crisis," August 6, 1965.
100. Department of the Treasury, 1969, p. 37.
101. FRBNYA, Presidential Papers, Papers of Paul A. Volcker 1975–1979, b. 35607, fold. Wednesday, May 28, 1975—PAV to attend CFR's Survey Discussion on OPEC (Richard Erb to speak), David E. Long, "The Politics of OPEC," Council on Foreign Relations. April 3, 1975, p. 5.
102. IMFA, Executive Board Documents, Secretary's Circular, 1968—Secretary's Circulars, Financial Relations Division, Treasurer's Department, "Report on Foreign Exchange Rates," December 18, 1968.
103. Department of the Treasury, 1968, p. 303.
104. For these figures see NARA, RG82, Division of International Finance and Predecessors, International Subject Files 1907–1974, b. 323, fold. Monetary System Conf. General, Robert F. Emery to Mr. Katz, "Changes in the Proportion of Sterling to International Reserves," May 22, 1968; Robert F. Emery to Mr. Katz, "Estimates of Changes in the Holdings of Sterling of Asian and Middle Eastern Countries," May 22, 1968.
105. Hauge and Hoffmeyer, 1978: the document is also held in FRBNYA, Presidential papers, Papers of Paul A. Volcker, b. 35578, fold. 140A 1977–1978 Annual Meetings of IMF and IBRD.

106. The US Embassy in Madrid to the Secretary of State, March 17, 1968; The US Consul in Frankfurt to the Secretary of State, March 18, 1968, both documents have been reproduced in DDRS.
107. NARA, RG56, OASIA, Subject Files of the Office of International Monetary Affairs 1968–1978, b. 1, fold. Gold (1) to Group of 10 (4), Bernstein (Department of the Treasury), "Gold in a Reformed International Monetary System," May 11, 1973.
108. The US Embassy in Paris to the Secretary of State, March 2, 1968, in DDRS.
109. See, for instance, a letter by Ed Fried to Walt Rostow, December 23, 1967, in DDRS.
110. Regarding such approach by the Council of Economic Advisers, see its chairman's note to the President: G. Ackley, Memorandum for the President "Comments on the Attached Memoranda," January 24, 1968, in DDRS.
111. See Machlup, 1973, p. 25 ff.; on the Rio de Janeiro Annual Meeting see also *Problèmes économiques*, n. 1032 (October 12, 1967); Morse, 1973, p. 242.
112. IMFA, Executive Board Documents, Departmental Memoranda, 1970—Departmental Memoranda, Marcus Fleming (IMF, Research Department), "The SDR: Some Problems and Possibilities," October 1, 1970.
113. Johnson to Kiesinger, March 15, 1968 in DDRS.
114. Comments on Mr. X' views, undated, in DDRS.
115. Department of State, Position Paper for Gold Negotiations March 16–17, 1968, "Reserve Policies During the Interim Period Prior to Activation of Special Drawing Rights," in DDRS.
116. Dean Rusk to all Diplomatic Posts, telegram, March 15, 1968, in DDRS.
117. The US Embassy in Santiago to the Secretary of State, March 16, 1968, in DDRS.
118. The US Secretary of State (Thomas Enders) to all Diplomatic Posts, March 1968, in DDRS; the British Chancellor to Henry Fowler (US Secretary of the Treasury), March 15, 1968, *ibid.*
119. Mayor, 2014, pp. 39 ff.
120. The literature on it in history and international economics is abundant: see, for reference, Eichengreen, 2011;

121. US Department of State, "Position Paper for Gold Pool Negotiations, March 16–17, 1968," in DDRS; for a strong argument against a rise in the official price of gold within the Johnson administration, see Walt Rostow to President Johnson, Memorandum from the President's Special Assistant (Rostow) to President Johnson "Gold," March 14, 1968. In Office of the Historian, 1998, document 189. https://history.state.gov/historicaldocuments/frus1964-68v08/d189
122. NARA, RG56, OASIA, Subject Files of the Office of International Monetary Affairs 1968–1978, b. 1, fold. Gold (3), Rene Larre (Board of Governors of the Federal Reserve System), "Gold and the International Monetary Negotiations," November 9, 1972; G. Willis to Under Secretary Volcker Memorandum "Letter from Mr. Solmssen to Assistant Secretary Fiedler on Gold Policy," August 9, 1972.
123. The US Secretary of State to the US Embassy in Moscow, May 10, 1971, in DDRS. On the Department of the Treasury under Simon see Macavoy, 2003, pp. 213–218.
124. Hawley, 2016, pp. 87–108.
125. IMFA, Executive Board Documents, Departmental Memoranda, 1970—Departmental Memoranda, Marcus Fleming (IMF Research Department), SDRs: Some Problems and Possibilities, October 1, 1970, p. 5.
126. FRBNYA, Presidential papers, Papers of Paul A. Volcker 1975–1979, b. 35607, fold. Wednesday, May 28, 1975-PAV to Attend CFR's Survey Discussion on OPEC (Richard Erb to speak), David E. Long, "The Politics of OPEC," April 3, 1975, p. 7.
127. WBGA, Records of General Vice Presidents and Managing Directors, Records of Sir Denis Rickett 1970–1974, Oil and Energy, Memos and Reports, 1973 through 1974, Volume 01, b. 210672B, M. Shoaib to J. Foster, Office Memorandum "Projections of Oil Revenues of OPEC Member Countries," January 26, 1973.
128. WBGA, Records of General Vice Presidents and Managing Directors, Records Sir Denis Rickett, Oil and Energy, Memo and Reports, 1973 through 1974, Volume 01, b. 210672B, IBRD, Commodities and Export Projections Division-Economic Analysis and Projections Department—Development Policy Staff, "Financial Consequences of Rising Trend in Petroleum Prices for Developing Countries 1970–1985," December 4, 1973.

129. Hoffmeyer and Hauge, 1978: the lecture can be retrieved in FRBNYA, Presidential Papers, Papers of Paul A. Volcker 1975–1979, b. 35578, fold. 740A 1977–1978 Annual Meetings of IMF and IBRD.
130. FRBNYA, Presidential Papers, Papers of Paul A. Volcker 1975–1979, b. 35602, fold. Speech-October 7, 1974-United States Trust Company-C.I.S.-I.C.S. seminar "Petro Money," Remarks by the Honorable Paul A. Volcker, Former Under Secretary of the Treasury for Monetary Affairs, "Petro Money," United States Trust Company C.I.S.-I.C.S. Seminar, October 7, 1974, p. 4.
131. NARA, RG56, OASIA, Subject Files of the Office of International Monetary Affairs 1968–1978, b. 5, fold. International Monetary System General (8), A. B. Hersey (Federal Reserve System, Division of International Affairs) to the Board of Governors of the Federal Reserve System, Memorandum "Reflow of Private Capital after the Realignment of Exchange Rates," January 26, 1972. For a comparison between different prime lending rates in the Eurodollar and national money markets in the three major capital markets, see Morgan Guaranty, *World Financial Markets* 1972–1973.
132. NARA, RG56, OASIA, Office of the Deputy to the Assistant Secretary for International Affairs, Records Relating to International Financial Institutions 1962–1981, b. 8, fold. IM-ID International Monetary: International Capital Flows 1979, Department of the Treasury News, "Statement by the Honorable Anthony M. Solomon, Under Secretary of the Treasury for Monetary Affairs before the Subcommittees of the House Banking, Finance and Urban Affairs Committee," June 12, 1979.
133. NARA, RG56, OASIA, Office of the Deputy to the Assistant Secretary for International Affairs, Records Relating to International Financial Institutions 1962–1981, b. 8, fold. IM-13-7 International Monetary Bank and Banking The Euro-Market 1 of 2, Laurie Goodman to Mr. Kubarych, Federal Reserve Bank of New York Research Memorandum "Eurodollars and the Money Supply," January 10, 1980.
134. Mikesell, 1975, p. 5.
135. Data on borrowings by the LDCs in the Eurobond markets are in NARA, RG56, OASIA, Office of the Deputy to the Assistant Secretary for International Affairs, Records Relating to International Financial Institutions 1962–1981, b. 8, fold. IM-10 International Capital Flows 1977–1978, IMF, Exchange and Trade Relations Department, "Developing Country Access to Capital Markets," January 23, 1973.

See also NARA, RG56, OASIA, Office of the Deputy to the Assistant Secretary for International Affairs, Records Relating to International Financial Institutions 1962–1981, b. 8, fold. IM-10 International Monetary: International Capital Flow 1979, US Department of the Treasury, "Extract from 'The Operation of the International Monetary System July 1977–March 1978: a Treasury Assessment," July 11, 1979.

136. NARA, RG56, OASIA, Subject Files of the Office of International Monetary Affairs 1968–1978, b. 3, fold. 1 (Eurodollars), The Under Secretary of the Treasury for Monetary Affairs, Memorandum for the President, January 15, 1971.
137. Mundell placed this perspective in the framework of his general theory about the absence of an international currency as a reserve asset for the Bretton Woods international trade and payments system. On Mundell's economic theory, see R. Mundell, 1971.
138. NARA, RG82, Division of International Finance and Predecessors, International Subject Files 1907–1974, b. 323, fold. Monetary System Conf. General, S. J. Maisel to the Board of Governors of the Federal Reserve System, "Report on European Trip," June 19, 1968.
139. LOC, Manuscripts Division, R. McNamara Papers, Part I, b. 21, fold. 1 (Bennett, William-Memoranda of McNamara Trips 1968–1971), William L. Bennett to Mr. Clark, Memorandum "Visit to New York City—March 1969."
140. IMFA, Medai, Medai Subject Files, b. 72, Fold. Saudi Arabia, A. K. El Salebdar, "Fund Visit of Mr. M. S. Al-Mahdi of OPEC," November 19, 1971.
141. WBGA, Records of General Vice Presidents and Managing Directors, Records of Sir Denis Rickett 1970–1974, Oil and Energy, Memo and Reports, 1973 through 1974—Volume 01, b. 210672B, IBRD, Commodities and Export Projections Division—Economic Analysis and Projections Department, Development Policy Staff, "Financial Consequences of Rising Trend in Petroleum Prices for Developing Countries 1970–1985," December 4, 1973.
142. NARA, RG56, Records of Secretary of the Treasury George P. Shultz 1971–1974, b. 3, fold. GPS Council on International Economic Policy c-1974, "The LDC Payments Problems Related to Higher Oil Prices. Alternatives for United States Tactics," paper prepared by Ad Hoc Group of IERG Working Group including representatives of State, Treasury, AID, CIEP, CEA, NSC, March 29, 1974.

143. NARA, RG56, OASIA, Subject Files of the Office of International Monetary Affairs 1968–1978, b. 3, fold. 1, Thomas Leddy to Mr. Ryss (Department of the Treasury, Office of the Assistant Secretary for International Affairs), "Background Paper for CIEP on UNCTAD III Issues," January 23, 1972.
144. WBGA, Records of General Vice Presidents and Managing Directors, Records of Sir Denis Rickett 1970–1974, Oil and Energy, Memos and Reports 1973 through 1974, Volume 03, IBRD, "Functions of IBRD and IMF in the Provision of Additional Resources to Developing Countries," 1974.
145. NARA, RG56, OASIA, Office of the Deputy Assistant Secretary for International Monetary and Investment Affairs, Records Relating to OECD Monetary Committees and Working Groups 1961–1974, b. 15, fold. EPC/WP-2 Documents 1973 (Cont'd) 1 of 2, OECD Working Party n. 2 of the Economic Policy Committee, Note by the Secretariat "The Macro-economic impact of higher energy prices over the medium term," December 2, 1974.
146. NARA, RG56, OASIA, Office of the Deputy to the Assistant Secretary for International Affairs, Records Relating to International Financial Institutions 1962–1981, b. 8, fold. IM-10 International Capital Flows 1977–1978, Department of the Treasury, OASIA, "Identification of Future Problem Countries in International Finance," April 4, 1977.
147. FRBNYA, Central Files, Fold. OPEC, Federal Reserve Bank of New York, "Notes on Recycling," July 9, 1974.
148. NARA, RG56, OASIA, Subject Files of the Office of International Monetary Affairs 1968–1978, b. 1, fold. Gold (3), Rene Larre to Arthur Burns, Memorandum "Gold and the International Monetary Negotiations," November 9, 1972.
149. NARA, RG56, OASIA, Subject Files of the Office of International Monetary Affairs 1968–1978, b. 1, fold. Gold (3), Barry Newman (Treasury Department), Memorandum "Reserve Composition and the Adequacy of Reserves," December 14, 1972. As for the hypotheses to correct the growing discrepancy between the official price and the free market price of gold see *ibid.*, T.P. Nelson (Treasury Department) to Under Secretary Volcker, Memorandum "Gold and Monetary Reform," August 4, 1972.
150. FRBNYA, Board of Directors' Minutes, Vol. 78 (January 8, 1970–December 30, 1970), Federal Reserve Banks of New York, Board of Directors Meeting Minutes, January 8, 1970.

151. TNA, FCO 82/277, Trilateral Commission on Relations between the USA, Japan and the EEC, fold. 1 (1973), P. J. L. Popplewell (First Secretary Economic, British Embassy in Tokyo, Commercial Department), cable to London, "Monte Carlo Talks," June 7, 1973.
152. NARA, RG82, Division of International Finance and Predecessors, International Subject Files 1907–1974, b. 323, fold. Monetary System Conf. General, Nathaniel Samuels (Deputy Under Secretary of State for Economic Affairs), Memorandum from Paul Volcker "A Start Toward Negotiating International Monetary Reform," February 22, 1972.
153. NARA, RG56, OASIA, Subject Files of the Office for International Monetary Affairs 1969–1978, b. 1 (Gold (1) to Group of 10 (4), fold. Gold (3), "Gold in a Reformed International Monetary System," May 11, 1973.
154. NARA, RG56, OASIA, Subject Files of the Office for International Monetary Affairs 1969–1978, b. 1, fold. Gold (3), The Secretary of State to all Diplomatic Posts, "Two-Tier Gold System," November 23, 1973; Department of Treasury, Memorandum "Currencies and Exchange," 1973.
155. FRBNYA, Presidential Papers, Papers of Paul A. Volcker, b. 35607, fold. Wednesday, May 28, 1975—PAV to Attend CFR's Survey Discussion on OPEC (Richard Erb to speak), Richard Erb, "Monetary Collaboration. Background paper of the May 28, 1975 Meeting of the Survey Discussion Group on OPEC, Council on Foreign Relations," January 1975.
156. LOC, Manuscript Division, Robert McNamara Papers, Part I, b. 21, fold. 1 (Bennett, William—Memoranda of McNamara Trips 1968–1971), William L. Bennett to Mr. Clark, "Visit to New York," March 16, 1970.
157. See LOC, Manuscript Division, McNamara Papers, Part I, b. 21, fold. 1 (Bennett, William—Memoranda of McNamara Trips 1968–1971), William L. Bennett to Mr. Clark, "Visit to New York City—December 4–6, 1968," December 7, 1968.
158. By R. Mundell, see also Mundell, 1968.
159. Department of the Treasury, 1973, introduction, p. XXXI.
160. US Department of Commerce, 1975, Chapter U, International Transactions and Foreign Commerce, Series U 1-25, p. 866.
161. Federal Reserve System, 1973, pp. 59–60. Council of Economic Advisers, 1971b, p. 25.

162. NARA, RG56, OASIA, Subject Files of the Office of International Monetary Affairs 1968–1978, b. 5, fold. International Monetary System General (8), Department of the Treasury, "Monetary Negotiations 1971–1973," December 5, 1973.
163. NARA, RG56, OASIA, Office of the Deputy Assistant Secretary for International Monetary Affairs, Briefing Books 1971–1980, b. 1, fold. NSSM 168 2. Sum 2/14/73 Flanigan Memo re Economic Objectives Paper, "Summary of February 14, 1973 Memorandum from Peter M. Flanigan on Economic Objectives in Our Relations with Europe."
164. US Government, 1973, p. 116.
165. On the role of foreign trade see NARA, RG56, OASIA, Office of the Deputy Assistant Secretary for International Monetary Affairs, Briefing Books 1971–1980, b. 1, fold. Atlantic Declaration Under Secretary Volcker May 1973, "Summary of February 14, 1973 Memorandum from Peter M. Flanigan on Economic Objectives in our Relations with Europe," February 14, 1973.
166. NARA, RG56, Office of the Secretary, Assistant Secretary for International Affairs, Office of International Investment, Council on International Economic Policy Files 1978–79, b. 1, fold. CFIUS-Early Days 1974, US Department of Commerce, Domestic and International Business Administration, "Initial Survey of Oil Producer Direct Investment in the United States Using Existing Sources," September 10, 1974, p. 3.
167. The US Embassy in Tripoli to the US Secretary of State, telegram, March 15, 1968, in DDRS.
168. The US Embassy in Teheran to the US Secretary of State, telegram, March 16, 1968, in DDRS.
169. IMFA, Medai, Medai Subject Files, b. 72, fold. Saudi Arabia, A.K. El-Selebdar, Memorandum for the Files "Fund Visit of Mr. M.S. Al-Mahdi of OPEC," November 19, 1971.
170. CIA, Intelligence Report "Problems with Growing Arab Wealth," July 1974, in DDRS.
171. Board of Governors of the Federal Reserve System, 1975.
172. FRBNYA, Central Files, fold. OPEC, M. Sakbani (Federal Reserve Bank of New York, Balance of Payments Division) to Mr. Ehrlich, Research Memorandum "Protecting the Real Value of OPEC Revenues and the Dollar Rate of Exchange," March 13, 1975; H. B. Junz to Mr. Bryant, Board of Governors of the Federal Reserve System Office

Correspondence "Changes in OPEC Countries' Valuation of their currencies," March 27, 1975; R.M. Kubarych to Mr. Holmes, Memorandum "Exchange Market Implications of Recent Changes in Valuation of OPEC Currencies," April 15, 1975.

173. NARA, RG56, OASIA, Subject Files of the Office of International Monetary Affairs 1968–1978, b. 3, fold 3 (Eurodollars), Statement by Fred H. Klopstock (Manager, International Research Department, Federal Reserve Bank of New York) before the Subcommittee on International Exchange and Payments of the Joint Economic Committee, undated.
174. NARA, RG56, OASIA, Subject Files of the Office of International Monetary Affairs 1968–1978, b. 3, fold. 3 (Eurodollars), Standing Committee on the Eurocurrency Market, "Report by the Standing Committee on the Eurocurrency Market to the Board of Governors of the Federal Reserve System," June 11, 1971.
175. NARA, RG56, OASIA, Subject Files of the Office of International Monetary Affairs 1968–1978, b. 5, fold. International Monetary System General (8), The US Consulate in Munich to the Secretary of State, telegram, May 27, 1971.
176. For a rather different perspective on Burns' macroeconomic policy, see Wells, 1994.
177. Government Finance Section, Federal Reserve Board, 1967; Government Finance Section, Federal Reserve Board, 1968; As for Johnson's fiscal policy see Sargent, 2014, pp. 33–34.
178. NARA, RG56, OASIA, Subject Files of the Office of International Monetary Affairs 1968–1978, b. 6, fold. Oil (2), Department of the Treasury, OASIA, "Techniques through which the US could obtain the funds for a contribution to the developing countries adversely affected by oil price increases," April 1974. See also LOC, Manuscript Division, Robert McNamara Papers, Part 1, b. 22, fold. 5. (Committees, Board of Governors 1970–1971), Pierre Paul Schmeitzer (Chairman of the Executive Board and Managing Director of the IMF), "Presenting the Twenty-Fifth Annual Report of the Executive Directors to the Board of Governors of the Fund," September 21, 1970; Board of Governors IMF-IBRD 1970 Annual Meetings, Copenhagen, Press Release.
179. Some interpretations suggested that the Nixon administration underestimated the weakness of the dollar in exchange markets: see Wijnholds, 2015, particularly pp. 80–85.

180. LOC, Manuscript Division, Robert McNamara Papers, Part 1, b. 21, fold. 1 (Bennett, William Memoranda of McNamara Trips 1968–1971), W.L. Bennett to Mr. Clark, Memorandum "Summary of New York Visits. October–November 1968."
181. LOC, Manuscript Division, Robert McNamara Papers, Part 1, b. 21, fold. 1 (Bennett, William Memoranda of McNamara Trips 1968–1971), William Bennett to Mr. Clark, Memorandum "Visit to New York City—March 1969."
182. WBGA, Records of the Office of the Presidents, Records of President Robert S. McNamara 1968, Correspondence with Member Countries: Germany. Correspondence 01, fold. Contacts Germany 1968, Memorandum of Conversation McNamara-Aldewereld-Guth-Klausens, June 6, 1968; Memorandum of Conversation Dr. Henkel-Mr. Aldewereld, June 7, 1968; Memo of Conversation Lipfart-Schneider-Schmidt-Anders-Aldewereld, June 10, 1968.
183. LOC, Manuscript Division, Robert McNamara Papers, Part 1, b. 27, fold. 5, IBRD, "Possible Means of Channeling OPEC funds through the World Bank," February 15, 1974. On the use of SDRs to denominate the Bank's interest-yielding bonds see LOC, Manuscript Division, Robert McNamara Papers, Part 1, b. 27, fold. 5 (Energy Crisis), I. P. M. Cargill to Mr. M. Shoalb, "Aid Memoire for Mr. Shoalb," July 19, 1974.
184. NARA, RG56, OASIA, Subject Files of the Office of International Monetary Affairs 1968–1978, b. 6, fold. Oil (2), Background paper "United Nations General Assembly Special Session," April 1974, "Proposal for Use of Surplus Oil Revenues of Petroleum Exporting Countries."
185. NARA, RG56, OASIA, Subject Files of the Office of International Monetary Affairs 1968–1978, b. 1 (Gold (1) to Group of 10 (4)), fold. Gold (1), Memorandum of Conversation Paul Volcker (Under Secretary for Monetary Affairs), William Dale (US Executive Director, IMF), G. P. de Kock (Alternate Executive Director of South Africa, IMF), Daniel Olivier (Minister, Embassy of South Africa), March 8, 1969.
186. *Ibid.*, Department of the Treasury, "Memorandum on Mr. Volcker Proposals of April 1," 1969.
187. On this subject, see some contemporary reflections by Solomon, 1976, pp. 23–27.
188. IMFA, Executive Board Documents, Statements made by Managing Directors and Staff Representatives to Executive Board (BUFF),

Statement by Mr. Dale, Executive Board Meeting 68/1–3 January 1968, "The US Balance of Payments Program," January 2, 1968.

189. See, for instance, US Government, 1969, pp. 14–15.
190. TNA, FCO 82/283 Political Relations between the USA and Europe, fold. 3 (1973), The British Embassy in Washington, DC to Sir Denis Greenhill (GCMG OBE, Foreign and Commonwealth Office), May 9, 1973.
191. Department of the Treasury, 1970, p. 41.
192. Department of State, "Strengthening the International Monetary System," 1968, p. 25, in DDRS.
193. NARA, RG56, Records of Secretary of the Treasury George P. Shultz 1971–1974, b. 3, fold. GPS Council on International Economic Policy c-1974, Department of the Treasury, "The Competitive Position of the United States in the International Money Markets. Foreign Window Option Paper," 1974.
194. Council of Economic Advisers, 1971.
195. NARA, RG56, OASIA, Subject Files of the Office of International Monetary Affairs 1968–1978, b. 3, fold. (3) Eurodollars, Report by the Standing Committee on the Eurocurrency Market, June 13, 1971; "Statement by Rimmer Vries (Vice President, Morgan Guaranty Trust Company of New York) before the Subcommittee on International Exchange and Payments of the Joint Economic Committee," US Congress, June 22, 1971; Fred Klopstock (Manager, International Research Department, Federal Reserve Bank of New York), "Statement before the Subcommittee on International Exchange and Payments of the Joint Economic Committee," June 22, 1971.
196. NARA, RG56, OASIA, Subject Files of the Office of International Monetary Affairs 1968–1978, b. 3, fold. 1 (Eurodollars: Muddling and Piddling), Senn Cross to Mr. Page Nelson, "Proposals for Influencing Eurodollar Flows," February 12, 1971.
197. NARA, RG56, OASIA, Subject Files of the Office of International Monetary Affairs 1968–1978, b. 3, fold. 2 (Eurodollars (1) to IMF General (3), Thomas Leddy, "Klasen's Proposal," April 9, 1971.
198. RAC, RFA, Record Group 4, Nelson A. Rockefeller Personal (henceforth RG4), P.A. A.C. Whitman Politics, b. 10, fold. 245, Address of the Secretary General of the Organization of American States to the National Foreign Trade Council, "Development and Diplomacy in the Hemisphere Today," November 18, 1968.

199. Department of Treasury, 1973, pp. 42–45.
200. NARA, RG56, OASIA, Office of the Deputy Assistant Secretary for International Monetary Affairs, Briefing Books 1971–1980, b. 1, fold. Atlantic Declaration Under Secretary Volcker May 1973, sub fold. NSSM 168 2. Sum 2/14/73 Flanigan Memo re Economic Objectives Paper, quotations are respectively from Department of the Treasury, "US-European Economic Objectives," February 14, 1973; and Department of the Treasury, "U.S. Objectives for Trade Negotiations and Monetary Reform."
201. TNA, FCO 82/283, Political Relations between the USA and Europe, fold. 3 (1973), Foreign and Commonwealth Office, North American Department, "US Policy toward Europe," May 9, 1973.
202. TNA, FCO 82/285, Political Relations between the USA and Europe, fold 5 (1973), Press Release, "Monte Carlo," May 24, 1973.
203. TNA, FCO 82/285, Political Relations between the USA and Europe, fold 5 (1973), Foreign and Commonwealth Office Planning Staff, planning paper "Transatlantic Relations: What Should Europe do?" July 9, 1973.
204. R. Nixon, Fourth Annual Report to the Congress on United States Foreign Policy, May 3, 1973, in Public Papers of the Presidents:, vol. 37, Richard Nixon, 1969–1974. http://www.presidency.ucsb.edu/ws/index.php?pid=3832&st=&st1=
205. TNA, FCO 82/283, Political Relations between the USA and Europe, fold. 3 (1973), Assembly of Western European Union, Nineteenth Ordinary Session, "Evolution of Relations between Europe and the United States," Report submitted on behalf of the General Affairs Committee by Mr. Stewart, Rapporteur, p. 18.
206. TNA, FCO 82/283, Political Relations between the USA and Europe, fold. 3 (1973), B. L. Crowe, "Reactions to Dr. Kissinger's Speech," May 7, 1973; see also the memoranda of conversations and trips by Kissinger held in TNA, FCO 82/307 Visits of Henry Kissinger, US Secretary of State, to the UK (1973), fold. 1.
207. TNA, FCO, 82/285 Political Relations between the USA and Europe, fold 5 (1973), Joint Communiqué after the Meeting between Defense Minister Georg Leber and Defense Secretary Schlesinger, July 30, 1973.
208. Blair, 1977, p. 184.
209. NARA, RG59, Bureau of Near Eastern Affairs and South Asian Affairs, Office of Arabian Peninsula Affairs, Records Relating to Saudi Arabia 1955–1974, b. 4, fold. Saudi Arabia Pet-Petroleum General 1969),

Stuart Mockwell to Mr. Sisco, Memorandum Mr. Samuels Oil Meeting," November 14, 1969; see also J. Katz (Department of State) to D. Szabo (Department of State), "Proposed State Department Position on Oil Imports Review," October 7, 1969.

210. *Ibid.*, Harold Saunders, Memorandum for Mr. Sisco "Iran and Oil," November 6, 1969; quotation from "A Policy for Selective Import of Mid-East Oil."
211. LOC, Manuscript Division, Henry A. Kissinger Papers, Part 1, 1957–1982, telephone conversations 1969–1976, fold. Telephone Conversation Chronological Files 9–16 December 1969, memorandum of telephone conversation Laird (Secretary of Defense), H. Kissinger (national security advisor to the President), December 9, 1969.
212. WBGA, Records of General Vice Presidents and Managing Directors, Records of Sir Denis Rickett 1970–1974, Oil and Energy, Memo and Reports, 1973 through 1974, Volume 01, b. 210672B, IBRD (Commodities and Export Projections Division, Economic Analysis and Projections Department, Development Policy Staff), "Financial Consequences of Rising Trend in Petroleum Prices for Developing Countries 1970–1985," p. 3.
213. IMFA, Medai, Medai Subject Files, b. 75, fold. 1, John W. Gunter (IMF) to M. Yeganeh (IMF), paper "External Payments Outlook for the Oil Producing Countries in the Middle East and Implications for the Reform of the International Monetary System," April 11, 1973.
214. NARA, RG56, Office of the General Counsel. Assistant General Counsel, Records Related to OPEC Financial Affairs 1974–1979, b. 3, fold. O 1975–1978, Alex Lang, Board Briefing "OPEC Trade Balances in 1974 and 1975," March 31, 1975.
215. On the impact of payments to the US companies on the US balance of payments see NARA, RG59, Bureau of Near Eastern and South Asian Affairs, Office of Algeria, Libya, Morocco, and Tunisia, Records Relating to Libya 1970–1974, b. 1, fold. "We told you so" file oil, David D. Newsom to Mr. Samuels, memorandum "Guidelines for US Oil Investment in Libya," September 24, 1970. On the impact of expropriations see *ibid.*, fold. PET 15.2 Nationalizations-Expropriation Libya 1974, L. Carlyle to Mr. Sisco, "A Note to Libya on Its Expropriation of the Remaining Interests of Socal, Texaco and ARCO," March 8, 1974.

216. NARA, RG273, National Security Study Memorandum, Entry 10, b. 12, fold. NSSM 114, National Security Council, NSSM 114 "World Oil Situation," January 15, 1971, pp. 30–31.
217. NARA, RG59, Bureau of Near Eastern and South Asian Affairs, Office of Arabian Peninsula Affairs, Records Relating to Saudi Arabia 1955–1974, b. 4 (Correspondence with Post to V /PPT-Visas and Passports), fold. Saudi Arabia PET-Petroleum General 1969, "A Policy for Selected Import of Mid-East Oil," undated.
218. FRBNYA, Central Files, fold. OPEC.
219. NARA, RG59, Bureau of Near Eastern and South Asian Affairs, Office of Algeria, Libya, Morocco, and Tunisia, Records Relating to Libya 1970–1974, b. 1, fold. DEF 1 Policy, Plans Libya 1974, Department of State, "Recent Libyan Arms Purchases and Negotiations for Purchases," November 21, 1974.
220. NARA, RG59, Bureau of Near Eastern and South Asian Affairs, Office of Arabian Peninsula Affairs, Records Relating to Saudi Arabia 1955–1974, b. 5 (DEF 19 to PET-6-c Tapline), fold. Saudi Arabia Economic FN finance-General 1970, Memorandum of Conversation Kearns-Houston-Bostwick-Morea (Eximbank)—AbsulhadyTaher (Governor, Petromin), "Saudi Arabia-Eximbank Financing for Petromin Refinery Projects," August 10, 1970.
221. See *ibid.*, Memorandum of Conversation C. Grant (Manager, Jidda Branch, First National City Bank), R. Merrick (US Embassy in Jidda), "Saudi Arabian Banking-Credit Availability," January 17, 1970.
222. NARA, RG59, Bureau of Near Eastern and South Asian Affairs, Office of Arabian Peninsula Affairs, Records Relating to Saudi Arabia 1955–1974, b. 5 (DEF 19 to PET-6-c Tapline), fold. Saudi Arabia Economic FN Finance-General 1970, Richard Murphy to Francois Dickman (Counselor of Embassy, US Embassy in Jidda), December 16, 1970.
223. NARA, RG59, Bureau of Near Eastern and South Asian Affairs, Office of Arabian Peninsula Affairs, Records Relating to Saudi Arabia 1955–1974, b. 8 (PET to TEL), fold. Saudi Arabia-PET Petroleum-General 1972, F. Dickman, "Saudi Oil Proposal—My Preliminary Thoughts," October 2, 1972.
224. NARA, RG59, Bureau of Near Eastern and South Asian Affairs, Office of Arabian Peninsula Affairs, Records Relating to Saudi Arabia 1955–1974, b. 5 (DEF 19 to PET-6-c Tapline), fold. Saudi Arabia Def

19 1970 Military Assistance and Sales, US, General, Memorandum of Conversation Alfred R. Wentworth (Senior vice president Chase Manhattan Bank), Mr. Alfred L. Atherton (Department of State), "Chase Request for State Department Letter Approving Financing of Saudi Third-Country Arms Purchases," June 17, 1970.

225. NARA, RG59, Bureau of Near Eastern and South Asian Affairs, Office of Arabian Peninsula Affairs, Records Relating to Saudi Arabia 1955–1974, b. 7 (DEF-12-5-b Saudi Arabia Aerial Tankers to PG and AP), fold. Saudi Arabia, FN-Finance 1971, Memorandum of Conversation Adolph Knul (Vice President and Manager Chase Manhattan Bank, Beirut), Eli W. Bizic (commercial Officer, US Embassy in Beirut), "Saudi Industrial Development Corporation," January 21, 1971.

226. NARA, RG59, Bureau of Near Eastern and South Asian Affairs, Office of Arabian Peninsula Affairs, Records Relating to Saudi Arabia 1955–1974, b. 5, fold. Saudi Arabia Def 19 1970 Military Assistance and Sales, US General, Memorandum of Conversation Anwar Alì (Governor, SAMA), Alfred L. Atherton (Deputy Assistant Secretary of State), "Middle East; Saudi Economic Situation," June 15, 1970.

227. This was the so called "maturity imbalance issue" which the OPEC oil producing lenders and the American commercial banks and intermediaries charged with recycling their financial assets wrangled over. See RAC, RFA, RG3, 4 A (Nelson A. Rockefeller Personal, series A-Activities (hereafter A-Activities), b. 162, fold. 1805, "Sarabam N.V. and Sarabam Corporation. Outline of Corporate Structure," undated, June 1977.

228. NARA, RG56, OASIA, Chronological Files of the Office of Financial Resources and Energy Finance 1974–1977, b. 1, fold. TEFRP: Office of Financial Resources Policy Coordination-Permanent Chronological File, 1974, Department of Treasury, OASIA, "A Saudi Arabian Industrial Development Bank," December 1974.

229. NARA, RG59, Bureau of Near Eastern and South Asian Affairs, Office of the Iran Affairs, Records Relating to Iran 1965–1975, b. 3, fold. FN 6 Bank and Banking, Memorandum of Conversation C. Widney (Representative of Chase Manhattan Bank)—the US Ambassador in Teheran, "Chase Manhattan Activities in the Middle East," October 31, 1968; as for the early activities of First National City Bank in Iran, see *ibid.*, R. Harlan (Counselor of Embassy for Economic Affairs, Teheran) to W. McClelland (Esquire, Department of State, Near Eastern Affairs), July 30, 1968.

230. NARA, RG56, OASIA, Office of the Deputy Assistant Secretary for Developing Nations Finance, Briefing Books on the Middle East 1974–1975, b. 2, fold. Final Subcommittee—Iran 29 September 1975, Economic and Finance Committee, US–Iran Joint Business Commission, "Liason with Joint Business Council On Proposed Financial Conference," September 29–30, 1975.
231. NARA, RG59, Bureau of Near Eastern and South Asian Affairs, Office of the Iran Affairs, Records Relating to Iran 1965–1975, b. 1, fold. E (Economic Affairs General Iran 1967 E1 General Plans. Programs), W. M. McClelland (Department of State, Near Eastern Affairs) to Mr. Battle (Department of State, Near Eastern Affairs), Information Memorandum "Shah Letter to the President," November 1, 1967; Theodore Eliot (Department of State, Near Eastern Affairs) to Ambassador Harriman, Briefing Memorandum "Your Luncheon with Iranian Ambassador Ansary on November 15, 1967," November 14, 1967.
232. NARA, RG59, Bureau of Near Eastern and South Asian Affairs, Office of the Iran Affairs, Records Relating to Iran 1965–1975, b. 6, fold. TP 15 Trade and Investment Opportunities Iran 1971, D. Abshire (Assistant Secretary for Congressional Relations) to W. Scott (House of Representatives), November 6, 1971.
233. NARA, RG59, Bureau of Near Eastern and South Asian Affairs, Office of the Iran Affairs, Records Relating to Iran 1965–1975, b. 9, W. McLelland, Memorandum for the Files, "Sales of Boeing CH-47 Helicopters to Iran," April 15, 1969.

References

Altamura, Carlo Edoardo. 2017. *European Banks and the Rise of International Finance*. Oxford: Routledge.

Becker, Randy, Wayne Gray, and Jordan Marvakov. 2016. *NBER-CES Manufacturing Industry Database*. Cambridge, MA: National Bureau of Economic Research and US Census Bureau's Center for Economic Studies (NBER-CES). www.nber.org/nberces. Accessed 3 Feb 2015.

Bird, Graham. 2003. *The IMF and the Future. Issues and Options Facing the Fund*. London/New York: Routledge.

Blair, John M. 1977. *The Control of Oil*. London/Basingstoke: Macmillan.

Board of Governors of the Federal Reserve System. 1968. *Federal Reserve Bulletin*. 54 (12). Table A-89.

———. 1971. *Federal Reserve Bulletin*. 57 (4).

———. 1974. *Federal Reserve Bulletin*.

———. 1975. *Federal Reserve Statistical Release*, February 28.

Board of Governors of the Federal Reserve System, Division of International Finance. 1967. *Capital Market Developments*. Washington, DC: GPO.

Board of Governors of the Federal Reserve System, Division of International Finance Europe and British Commonwealth Section. 1970. *Selected Interest and Exchange Rates for Major Countries and the US. Weekly Series of Chart*, 431 (December 3, 1969). Washington, DC: GPO.

Bordo, Michael, Owen F. Humpage, and Anna Schwartz. 2015. *Strained Relations. US Foreign-Exchange Operations and Monetary Policy in the Twentieth Century*. Chicago/London: The University of Chicago Press.

Brenner, Robert. 2006. *The Economics of Global Turbulence*. London: Verso.

Broz, Lawrence, and Jeffry Frieden. 2001. The Political Economy of International Monetary Relations. *Annual Review of Political Science* 4: 317–343.

Council of Economic Advisers. 1960. *Economic Indicators, Prepared for the Joint Economic Committee by the Council of Economic Advisers*. Washington, DC: GPO.

———. 1967. *Economic Indicators, Prepared for the Joint Economic Committee by the Council of Economic Advisers*. Washington, DC: GPO.

———. 1971a. *Economic Indicators, Prepared for the Joint Economic Committee by the Council of Economic Advisers*. Washington, DC: GPO.

———. 1971b. *Economic Indicators. December 1971, Prepared for the Joint Committee by the Council of Economic Advisers*. Washington, DC: GPO.

Craft, Nicholas, and Gianni Toniolo, eds. 1996. *Economic Growth in Europe Since 1945*. New York: Center for Economic Policy Research-Cambridge University Press.

Department of Commerce. 1967. *Survey of Current Business*, 47 (12).

———. 1975. *Historical Statistics of the United States Colonial Times to the Present, Part 2*. Washington, DC: GPO.

Department of the Treasury. 1968. *Annual Report of the Secretary of the Treasury on the State of the Finances for the Fiscal Year Ended June 30, 1967*. Washington, DC: GPO.

———. 1969. *Annual Report of the Secretary of the Treasury on the State of the Finances for the Fiscal Year Ended June 30, 1968*. Washington, DC: GPO.

———. 1973. *Annual Report of the Secretary of the Treasury on the State of the Finances for the Fiscal Year Ended June 30, 1973*. Washington, DC: GPO.

Eichengreen, Barry. 2011. *Exorbitant Privilege. The Rise and Fall of the Dollar and the Future of the International Monetary System*. Oxford/New York: Oxford University Press.

Federal Reserve System. 1969. *Annual Report of the Board of Governors of the Federal Reserve System for the Year 1968*. Washington, DC: GPO.

———. 1970. *Annual Report of the Board of Governors of the Federal Reserve System for the Year 1969*. Washington, DC: GPO.

———. 1973. *Annual Report of the Board of Governors of the Federal Reserve System for the Year 1972*. Washington, DC: GPO.

Frieden, Jeffry. 2006. *Global Capitalism: Its Fall and Rise in the Twentieth Century*. New York: W.W. Norton.

Gavin, Francis. 2004. *Gold. Dollars and Power: The Politics of International Monetary Relations 1958–1971*. Chapel Hill: University of North Carolina Press.

Gilpin, Steven G. 2009. *Money, Oil, and Empire. Sterling and Postwar Imperialism 1944–1971*. Cambridge: Cambridge University Press.

Government Finance Section, Federal Reserve Board. 1967. *Federal Reserve Statistical Release*, December 5, 1967.

———. 1968. *Federal Reserve Statistical Release*, December 4, 1968.

Gray, William. 2007. Floating the System: Germany, the United States, and the Breakdown of Bretton Woods 1969–1973. *Diplomatic History* 31 (2): 295–323.

———. 2010. Toward a "Community of Stability"? The Deutsche Mark Between European and Atlantic Priorities 1968–1969. In *The Strained Alliance. US-European Relations from Nixon to Carter*, ed. Matthias Schultz and Thomas Schwartz, 145–168. New York: Cambridge University Press.

Harvey, David. 1990. *The Conditions of Postmodernity*. Cambridge, MA/Oxford: Blackwell.

Hawley, James P. 2016. (or. ed.: 1987). *Dollars and Borders. Us Government Attempts to Restrict Capital Flows 1960–1980*. New York: Routledge.

Helliwell, John F. 1984. Stagflation and Productivity Decline in Canada 1974–1982. *The Canadian Journal of Economics* 17 (2): 191–216.

Hoffmeyer, Erick, and Gabriel Hauge. 1978. *The International Capital Market and the International Monetary System, the 1978 Per Jacobson Lecture*. Washington, DC: The Per Jacobson Foundation-IMF.

James, Harold. 1996. *International Monetary Cooperation Since Bretton Woods*. New York/Washington, DC: Oxford University Press-IMF.

Junne, Gerd. 1976. *Der Eurogeldmarkt. Seine Bedeutungfür Inflation und Inflationsbekämpfung*. Frankfurt: Campus.

Kochavi, Ariel J. 2016. George Brown and British Policy in the Middle East Following the 1967 War. *The Middle East Journal* 10 (1): 91–110.

La Barca, Giuseppe. 2013. *International Trade in the 1970s. The US, the EC and the Growing Pressure of Protectionism*. London: Bloomsbury.

Lin, Ching-Yuan. 1984. Global Patterns of Energy Consumption Before and After the 1974 Oil Crisis. *Economic Development and Cultural Change* 32 (4): 781–802.

Macavoy, Paul W. 2003. "Don't Just Stand There…" Treasury Secretary William E. Simon and Fiscal Policy During Stagflation 1975–1976. *Atlantic Economic Journal* 31 (3): 213–218.

Machlup, Fritz. 1973. The Expanded Role of SDRs and the Possibilities of an SDR Standard. In *Europe and the Evolution of the International Monetary System, Proceedings of the First Conference of the International Center for Monetary and Banking Studies*, ed. Alexander K. Swoboda, 25–34. Geneva: Institut Universitaire de Etudes Internationales.

Marx, Christian. 2014. Failed Solutions to the Energy Crises: Nuclear Power, Coal Conversion, and the Chemical Industry in West Germany Since the 1960s. *Historical Social Research* 39 (4): 251–271.

Mayor, Aaron. 2014. *Architects of Austerity. International Finance and the Politics of Growth*. Stanford: Stanford University Press.

McGraw-Hill, Economics Department. 2016. McGraw-Hill New Orders Index. In *NBER, Macro History Database. VI Distribution of Commodities*. Cambridge, MA: National Bureau of Economic Research. www.nber.org/databases/macrohistory/contents/chapter06. Accessed 30 Jan 2016.

Mikesell, Raymond. 1975. *The Eurocurrency Market and the Recycling of Petrodollars*, National Bureau Report Supplement. New York: National Bureau for Economic Research.

Mitchell, Timothy. 2011. *Carbon Democracy. Political Power in the Age of Oil*. London: Verso.

Morgan Guaranty Trust Company of New York. 1973. *World Financial Markets*. New York: Morgan Guaranty Trust Co.

Morse, Edward. 1973. *Foreign Policy and Interdependence in Gaullist France*. Princeton: Princeton University Press.

Mundell, Robert. 1968. *International Economics*. New York: Macmillan.

———. 1971. *Monetary Theory: Interest, Inflation and Growth in the World Economy*. Pacific Palisades: Goodyear.

———. 1989. The Dollar and the Policy Mix. In *Global Disequilibrium in the World Economy*, ed. Mario Baldassarri and John McCallum, 57–78. New York/Rome: St. Martin's Press-SIPI.

Nixon, Richard. 1973. Fourth Annual Report to the Congress on United States Foreign Policy, May 3, 1973. Online by Gerhard Peters and John T. Woolley, The American Presidency Project. http://www.presidency.ucsb.edu/ws/index.php?pid=3832&st=&st1=. Accessed 8 July 2016.
Odell, John S. 1982. *US International Monetary Policy*. Princeton: Princeton University Press.
Office of the Historian. 1998. In *Foreign Relations of the United States (FRUS), 1964–1968, Volume VIII, International Monetary and Trade Policy*, eds. Evan Duncan, David S. Patterson, Carolyn Yee. Washington, DC: GPO.
Painter, David. 2014. Oil and Geopolitics: The Oil Crises of the 1970s and the Cold War. *Historical Social Research* 39 (4): 186–208.
Problèmeséconomiques. 1967. 1032. October 12, 1967.
Quinlan, Joseph P. 2010. *The Last Economic Superpower: The Retreat of Globalization, the End of American Dominance, and What We Can Do About It*. New York: McGraw-Hill.
Sargent, Daniel. 2014. Lyndon Johnson and the Challenges of Economic Globalization. In *Beyond the Cold War. Lyndon Johnson and the New Global Challenges of the 1960s*, ed. Francis Gavin and Atwood Lawrence, 17–43. New York/Oxford: Oxford University Press.
Schenk, Catherine. 2010. *The Decline of Sterling: Managing the Retreat of an International Currency 1945–1992*. New York: Cambridge University Press.
Selva, Simone. 2014. Capital Intensive Modernization, Internal Expansionary Policies, Competitive Export: The Political Economy of U.S. Nuclear Assistance Programs During Bretton Woods: The Case of Italy Before the End of Fixed Exchange Rates. *Business and Economic History* (12): 1–39. http://www.thebhc.org/sites/default/files/selva1.pdf. Accessed 1 Feb 2016.
———. 2017. Technological Advance, Transatlantic Trade, External Equilibrium. American Financial Assistance to the Italian Nuclear Power Programs from the 1960s Through the First Oil Crisis. In *Contesting Deregulation: Debates and Practices in the West Since the 1970s*, ed. Knud Andresen and Stefan Müller. New York: Berghahn Books.
Shwadran, Benjamin. 1977. *Middle East Oil. Issues and Problems*. Cambridge, MA: Schenkman Publishing.
Skett, Ian. 1988. *OPEC: Twenty-Five Years of Prices and Politics*. Cambridge: Cambridge University Press.
Solomon, Robert. 1976. On the Past and Future of the International Monetary System. *Columbia Journal of World Business* 3: 23–27.

Storck, Ekkehard. 1995. *Euromarkt: Finanz-Drehscheibe der Welt*. Stuttgart: Schäffer-Poeschel.

Stork, Joe. 1975. *Middle East Oil and the Energy Crisis*. New York: Monthly Review Press.

The Chase Manhattan Corporation. 1968. *Euro-Dollar Financing. A Guide for Multinational Companies*. New York: Chase Manhattan Corporation.

Türk, Hening. 2014. Energy Cooperation Among Western Industrialized Countries. *Historical Social Research* 39 (4): 209–213.

US Government. 1967. *Economic Report of the President Transmitted to the Congress January 1967 Together with the Annual Report of the Council of Economic Advisers*. Washington, DC: GPO.

———. 1968. *Economic Report of the President Transmitted to the Congress February 1968 Together with the Annual Report of the Council of Economic Advisers*. Washington, DC: GPO.

———. 1969. *Economic Report of the President Transmitted to the Congress January 1969 Together with the Annual Report of the Council of Economic Advisers*. Washington, DC: GPO.

———. 1973. *Economic Report of the President Transmitted to the Congress January 1973 Together with the Annual Report of the Council of Economic Advisers*. Washington, DC: GPO.

Venn, Fiona. 2013. *The Oil Crisis*. New York: Routledge.

Wachtel, Howard M. 1990. *The Money Mandarins. The Making of a Supranational Economic Order*. London: Pluto Press.

Wells, Wyatt C. 1994. *Economist in an Uncertain World: Arthur Burns and the Federal Reserve 1970–1978*. New York: Columbia University Press.

Wijnholds, Onno de Beaufort. 2015. *Gold, the Dollar and Watergate*. London: Palgrave.

Wilkie, Christopher. 2012. *Special Drawing Rights (SDRs). The First International Money*. Oxford: Oxford University Press.

Yergin, Daniel. 2008. (or. ed.: 1991). *The Prize. The Epic Quest for Oil, Money and Power.* New York: Free Press.

Zimmerman, Hubert. 2010. Unraveling the Ties That Really Bind. The Dissolution of the Transatlantic Monetary Order and the European Monetary Cooperation 1965–1973. In *The Strained Alliance. US-European Relations from Nixon to Carter*, ed. Matthias Schultz and Thomas Schwartz, 125–144. New York: Cambridge University Press.

4

The Rise of Energy Finance and the Quest for Capital Supply in the US Foreign Economic Policy 1973–1976

4.1 Recycling Oil Revenues and Resurrecting International Trade and Payments

A complex jumble of factors added to the structural incapability all through the 1960s to resurrect the balance of payments deficit and to strengthen the dollar and the international payments system. It is worth situating this against the upturn in posted prices of crude oil, other major developments in international commodity markets and the new oil revenues recycling policies, which, in cooperation with the International Monetary Fund (IMF) and the International Bank for Reconstruction and Development (IBRD), the US governments tried relentlessly to set into motion from early 1974 to the termination of the mandate of Jimmy Carter at the White House. All these factors account for the plummeting US balance of payments deficit and the changing trajectory that featured these developments during the following few years. As a matter of fact, the combined appearance of oil price hikes together with the continued depreciation of the dollar in exchange markets that hailed largely from the unfinished capital flows from low-powered reserves in the US into high-powered European reserves and short-term Eurocurrency markets

S. Selva, *Before the Neoliberal Turn*, Palgrave Studies in Economic History,
DOI 10.1057/978-1-137-57443-5_4

pinpointed in the last chapter added to a US balance of payments deficit that throughout the late 1960s ran unchecked. This jungle of developments prompted the US foreign economic policymakers to search for measures other than interventions on the current and capital accounts to restore confidence in the dollar and to stabilize the international trade and payments system. It was at this critical juncture that the US monetary and financial elites turned their attention to the financial resources increasingly accruing to the oil producers united in the Organization of Petroleum Exporting Countries (OPEC). This was in order to devise new ways to resurrect the US external equilibrium and to halt the depreciation of the US dollar. Not coincidentally, since the outbreak of the first oil crisis Washington had worked on involving the OPEC capital-surplus countries in financing the recasting of a dollar-pegged system of international exchange in goods and capital. As Washington moved to get involved in shaping the international investments of the OPEC countries, its political and financial elites straddled to use the oil revenues of the OPEC countries in order to target two objectives. On the one side, such mounting financial assets should be put to resurrect transnational flows in merchandise and capital. On the other, Washington aimed at recasting the US balance of payments by bettering its current and capital account positions and by reducing the liabilities on the capital account. As a matter of fact, from the viewpoint of Washington, the multiple arrangements made since the spring of 1974 to channel the OPEC countries' oil revenues and the way in which the recycling mechanisms were reorganized over the rest of the decade were intended to achieve two results. In the first instance, Washington wished to continue a balance of payments deficit financing policy focused on the current account through open support for US export to the OPEC oil-producing states. This trajectory was consistent with the US strategies conducted in the past few years aimed at strengthening and broadening trade bonds with the Middle East. Such commercial bonds were intended both to bolster the investments of US corporations and the repatriation of profits, and to acquire hard currencies and dollars essential to counteract the run on US gold stock and to prop up the dollar's value in exchange markets. Secondly, the aim was to devise a path-breaking new policy aimed at easing the strains on the US capital account. The recycling mechanism on which the Federal Reserve Bank of New York and the Treasury worked on, with cooperation from leading US banks involved, would stimulate portfolio and equity investments by the OPEC countries in the US. This course of investments would have a positive entry to the US capital account and lessen the outflow of capital directed to more lucrative short-term capital markets that had long plagued the United States throughout the 1960s. In turn, amid the two oil shocks, by and large the US monetary and financial elites made efforts to reshape the international capital markets and to channel the OPEC financial resources to ease pressure on the US payments position. In the pursuit of such target the Washington elites took into account structural developments in the international money markets. The very objective was to resurrect an international trade and payments system based on a global exchange in capital, commodities and consumer goods between the industrialized countries and the non-oil producing Least Developed Countries (LDCs). Therefore, in light of the hiking up of oil prices, the US worked on intersecting capital market developments and international trade to stabilize the system of international economic relations without making the US balance of payments bear the unsustainable cost of such strategy. From the viewpoint of the US financial and monetary policymakers, the mixture of these targets set the framework within which the oil producers would channel their oil revenues in excess of their outpayments to purchase goods and services on foreign markets. Since the spring of 1974 Washington straddled to involve short-term Euro-money markets such as the Eurocurrency markets and the leading US commercial banks traditionally specializing in credit markets, as well as some American investment banks and brokerage houses, in its effort to recast commercial and financial bonds between industrialized economies and the LDCs. The linchpin of this strategy was to induce all of these actors to borrow from the OPEC countries. This US global approach to the restructuring of the international payments system was based on the full involvement of international economic institutions and banking with a global reach. Since the beginning, the US made arrangements to respectively charge the international banking system and the IMF with financing the purchasing power of the LDCs and the industrial economies that suffered the most from the oil price increase and the depreciation of the dollar. Quite remarkably, the involvement of such multilateral institutions and banks would ease pressure on the US foreign financial assistance and reduce overseas American public expenditures for balance of payments and foreign economic assistance purposes. Moreover, it would bring the dollar back to center stage in international financial affairs in so far as such commercial and financial entanglements revolved around world trade and financial transactions usually denominated in US dollar: this was much the case of oil and other commodities payments. To put it another way, as the financial fuel for such entanglement between Western banks and financial institutions, the US capital markets and the non-oil producing LDCs, were the financial assets that accrued to OPEC as a result of dollar-denominated oil transactions, the US currency would retain its central role in international trade and payments. At the same time, however, its share in world money supply would not expand further owing to the investment patterns entailed in the recycling mechanism. This path-breaking new strategy marked a departure from the years so far examined, when Washington engaged in a variety of arrangements to reduce the dollar component of international liquidity as a way to sustain the dollar in exchange markets and restore stability in international trade and payments. In this respect Chap. 3 pointed to the creation and implementation of Special Drawing Rights (SDRs) from the very late 1960s through the dawn of the following decade. Since the launch of the oil revenues recycling mechanism, the US made a departure from this approach to the decline of the dollar, based on identifying units of international account as an alternative to the dollar in order to prop it up. By pressuring oil producers and partners to implement the recycling of oil revenues, Washington turned to place the US currency at center stage: the US focused on combining the centrality of the dollar in international exchanges and investments with its strengthening.

Therefore, this chapter is devoted firstly to exploring the intertwining between the increased financial wealth of the OPEC oil producing countries and developments in the international oil markets from the beginning of the decade through the fall of 1973. At the same time it pays attention to the seamless upward mood in the Eurodollar market and other short-term capital markets within the advanced industrial economies at the beginning of the decade. This was in order to chart the origins of those countries' placements in these kinds of instruments since the first oil shock thereafter. Then, the chapter investigates the twin US strategy to reduce the balance of payments deficit and to restore stability in international trade through the multilateral institutional arrangements set off to recycle the funds of OPEC into long-term investments. Along this line of inquiry, the following pages chart both the involvement in such arrangements of US commercial and investment banks and the IMF, and bilateral arrangements between Washington and the OPEC oil supplying countries. The very objective of all these initiatives was to push forward a balance of payments deficit financing policy based on restoring its current account component through a rise in US trade and investments in the Middle East capital-surplus countries. What is evident is that whether implemented in the non-oil producing LDCs, the oil importing industrial economies, or the least capital absorbing OPEC oil producing countries, what guided the US in the pursuit of such arrangements and measures was to be able to make use of the recycling process to reorganize the supply side of the business cycle. This objective was pursued both in a deflationary environment and against (since 1975) an inflationary backdrop. Finally, the chapter investigates the ways in which the OPEC countries reacted to this US strategy to make the oil producers shift from short-term inflation-sensitive placements to long-term investments. Through a focus on Saudi Arabia, Kuwait and Iran, the centerpiece is that oil producers invested long in the US equity and money markets, as well as in western governments' securities. However, at the same time they refrained from channeling their financial surpluses through institutional arrangements and entities created or managed under US leadership. In so doing, the recycling mechanism is a test case to asscss the course of bilateral economic and financial relations between each of these countries and the US. Contrast to the US approach—does the chapter suggest—they went their way to provide development finance assistance to the non-oil LDCs. The following pages on the one side stress the striking contrast between the positions and interests of oil producing lenders and those of American banking charged with borrowing, trading and relending their financial assets to the LDCs. On the other, the aim is to shed light on the reluctance of the OPEC countries to get involved in multilateral oil recycling arrangements created under the umbrella of the IMF and the IBRD. These contrasts and mischaracterizations between OPEC lenders and western borrowers and intermediaries led OPEC, by the time Carter came to power, to set out a series of unilateral assistance programs to the LDCs. These assistance programs, unlike urged by the western international economic institutions and the US governments, were non concessionary. Such successfulness of OPEC in sidetracking the US recycling policy and in developing direct financial assistance bonds with deficit countries sheds light on the extent to which the rise of the so called energy finance of oil producers on the world economic stage was decisive in striking the balance between them and the US in the field of international economic relations and economic diplomacy. The following chapter is devoted to chart the persistence and final demise of this strategy under the Carter administration. In Chap. 5 the very argument is that in light of failing policies to get the OPEC countries involved in either multilateral recycling mechanism or in bilateral concessionary assistant programs to the LDCs, the US government pushed forward a demand management strategy to combine a fight on inflation within the advanced industrial economies with full support for the LDCs purchasing power through the outbreak of the second oil crisis and the collapse of the Shah regime in Iran. At the same time, Chap. 5 explores the pushing forward of policies to reduce the US balance of payments deficit focused on restoring equilibrium on the current account position. In this respect, attention is given to inward investments by the OPEC countries to stimulate American export in support for the industrial modernization and economic development of the highest capital absorbing oil producers. In this perspective, the activities of bilateral technical cooperation commissions set up between Washington and the main OPEC counterparts (Iran, Saudi Arabia, Kuwait) are also investigated. From around 1977 through 1979, in order to attain these targets quite consistently with the previous years, the US monetary and financial authorities turned back to the IMF and the IBRD to carry over the recycling of OPEC oil revenues and to shape the international credit and money markets accordingly.

4.2 US Current Account Policies, the Dollar, and Capital-Surplus Oil Producers at the End of Bretton Woods

As seen in Chap. 3, Middle Eastern oil posted price and tax concessions began surging at the turn of the decade and the multiple American attempts to restore international confidence in the dollar and to stabilize its value in foreign exchange markets always involved more often the two largest and highest capital-absorbing oil producing members of OPEC. Both policies focused on the recasting of the balance of payments on capital account, and initiatives to reform the international monetary system through the search for new reserve units of account to ease pressure on the dollar and toss aside the gold rule established at Bretton Woods, as well as—more importantly—the string of policies on the current account component of the US balance of payments, took place against the backdrop of the rising role of Saudi Arabia and Iran. These two countries became increasingly influential to US foreign economic relations, and it is possible to track an increasing interconnection between their economies and the forces of US capitalism and banking. It is plausible to argue that the quest for restoring equilibrium in the US balance of payments and in foreign exchange markets was increasingly intertwined with the shaping of international investment patterns to channel the OPEC oil producing countries' growing oil revenues and financial assets in the international capital markets. The increase in the posted price of oil and tax concessions early in the decade, as outlined in this study, had by 1973 triggered a sweeping increase in the oil revenues of the OPEC members, which increased further the year after and contributed to make the surpluses on the current accounts of the OPEC countries in the aggregate reach an all-time peak by 1974 (see Table 4.1).[1]

Analogous to this trend, US export to the Middle East rose accordingly. By 1973 US sales of merchandise, consumer goods and investment goods to the Near East Arab countries and to Iran totaled $2 billion, up about 50 percent from the 1972 figures, with Iran and Saudi Arabia leading the way as the two largest markets. In light of these noticeable developments, as a study drafted on behalf of the US National Association of

Table 4.1 OPEC oil revenues and surpluses

	US dollars/billions—Bank of England data			
	Surplus on current account	Cash surplus	Oil revenue	Investment income
1974	60.9	57.0	89.8	4.0
1975	32.6	35.7	96.8	7.1
1976	36.6	33.2	113.2	7.8

Source: World Bank Group Archives

Manufacturers (NAM) put it, "as worldwide attention had been irresistibly drawn to the massive oil revenues accruing to the petroleum producing countries of the area, have Americans begun to realize the potential for doing business in the Near East."[2] The late 1960s combined growth in the volume of world money supply and of short-term capital markets, and sluggish growth rates across the advanced industrial economies compared with the postwar heydays of growth of the early 1960s, had a prominent and enduring effect. The rate of increase in capital supply ran faster than the rate of increase in aggregate demand.[3] In the quest to strike a balance between oversupply in capital in the international capital markets, and shortage in aggregate demand and consumer demand across the advanced industrial economies, Washington turned its attention to the development of the oil producing countries' domestic economies. The aim was to make these countries invest their oil revenues to foster domestic investments in order to target two problems. The first issue was the potential deflationary impact of growing Arab capital assets at international level, which could cause an oversupply of capital to demand for fixed capital formation across the oil consuming countries. Second, Washington struggled to make use of the OPEC financial assets in the oil producing economies in support of the US balance of payments on current account through a prompt promotion of US export and foreign investments. Since the spring of 1974 the international monetary policy conducted by the Federal Reserve Bank of New York was convincingly aimed at charging the American banking system with promoting long-term fixed capital investments and at encouraging capital-surplus OPEC countries to carry out a policy of investment diversification. Such policy should be based on investments in US government securities and equity investments in the US stock markets. This move is the subject of the following sections of this chapter. In striking contrast with this strategy, at an early stage the US monetary authorities favored the involvement of US investment banks and brokerage houses in the local capital markets of Iran and Saudi Arabia. Furthermore they promoted, as far back as 1974, domestic development policies in oil-supplying capital-surplus countries.[4] In striking contrast with the following years, prior to the first oil crisis the Federal Reserve Bank of New York and the US government fiercely opposed Arab investments in US government securities, US real estate markets or in the American equity markets. The Department of State, for instance, made a strong case for promoting the creation of mixed banks in Kuwait and Saudi Arabia to stimulate US trade and investments with these two countries and their neighbors in the Gulf. For a number of years the two countries had maintained official balances in the US, placed with major American banks and invested primarily in US government securities. Moreover, since the 1960s both countries had set up investment institutions and companies to raise private capital and government funds for placements in various forms of investments, which included equity participations in the United States. This was, for instance, the case of Kuwait Investment Company, which during the decade made some purchases in US real estate and invested in the New York Stock Exchange.[5] Then, within the framework of the pre-oil shock rise in profits of the oil producing countries, the combined eagerness to promote US export credit financing, and fear "that at some point one or more of the Arab oil states for some politically motivated reason would [...] abruptly shift large amounts of foreign exchange holdings to the detriment of international financial stability," led the Department of State to suggest the opening of local branches of American banks. The opening of local branches in the region would stimulate American export of instrumental and consumer goods and enhance industrial modernization and technological upgrade across these Middle Eastern economies. Therefore, prior to 1974 the US diplomacy discouraged countries as Saudi Arabia and Iran from investing in the United States and other Western equity and money markets. At the same time, Washington encouraged them to invest their booming financial assets to modernize their economies in joint partnership with American manufacturing and banking. Within this framework, unlike the experience so far conducted by the American brokerage houses and investment banks operating in the Gulf area to facilitate Saudi dealings in American securities, the government of Washington promoted the presence and activities of US banking in the region. A larger presence of US banks in the area would stimulate the development of local banks and capital markets to finance local fixed capital investments and imports. The other side of this strategy was to prevent the reinvestment of oil profits in the Lebanese, British and Swiss capital markets on which the United States had no control. Against this backdrop, the US diplomacy encouraged the opening of local branches not only in Iran, Saudi Arabia and Kuwait, where the only one active in 1972 was Merrill Lynch, but also in smaller capital-surplus oil states like Abu Dhabi, Bahrain and Qatar.[6] This early activism of US diplomacy to combine the modernization of these key oil-supplying economies with support for American export to the Gulf area as a way to absorb the capital-surplus financial assets of OPEC countries and sustain the US current account is noteworthy. It was, clearly, a twofold way to prop up the balance of payments and the US dollar: an upsurge of US export to dollar-holding countries would contrast against a growth of dollar-denominated share in world money supply and contribute to lessening the run on US gold stock. Besides, it was likely to increase the foreign profits of US corporations and to uphold their repatriation, seen as being a means of propping up the US capital account position. Such policy laid the groundwork for the establishment of bilateral technical cooperation commissions between Washington and each leading Middle Eastern OPEC member state. Since 1974 and thereafter the Department of State, led by Henry Kissinger, relentlessly worked on the buildup of these commissions, widely documented in the American federal and monetary archives. In order to investigate the linkage between international oil relations and capital markets developments it is worth stressing that the OPEC oil producing countries that took advantage of rising posted prices, consolidated taxes and other concessions agreements since the turn of the decade, showed their propensity to invest a substantial share of their oil revenues not only in the national financial markets of New York and London, in interbank deposits, in multilateral arrangements such as the IMF facilities, or in the oil consumer countries' financial outlets and stock markets.[7] Indeed, they massively invested into the least regulated

European money markets. This investment path developed since the fourfold oil price rise but began way before: most capital-surplus countries started investing in short-term highly liquid placements by the turn of the decade.[8] In this respect, the case of Saudi Arabia stands out once again: according to the American First National City Bank representative in Jeddah, in 1970 the two most important Saudi Arabian national banks were making heavy placements into the Eurodollar market. These investment patterns dwarfed domestic credit for fixed capital investments and imports.[9] This attitude of most OPEC surplus countries to place their oil revenues into short-term Euro-money markets was a clear hindrance to the Nixon administration's strategy to stimulate the development of Middle Eastern national markets. The US exports to the Gulf area mentioned above were also hindered. Therefore, prior to 1973 there was a short circuit between the placements of the OPEC countries in the Eurocurrency markets, and capital supply for productive investments in the developing oil-supplying OPEC states and in the industrialized economies. Understandably, owing to their inflation-sensitive features and short-term maturity, the Eurodollar and other Eurocurrency markets were unfit to fuel fixed capital investments and the supply side of the oil producing countries' production chain. Another issue peculiar to the period prior to the quadrupling of oil prices and the meteoric ascendance of OPEC countries on the world financial stage was at stake. Prior to the first oil price hikes, in Washington a much-discussed issue in connection with the development of short-term unregulated Eurocurrency assets was certainly the highly stigmatized tendency of Western central banks to place their foreign currency holdings into the Eurocurrency markets. According to the US authorities, at that time most OPEC oil producing countries were still borrowing heavily into those markets to finance their lending programs to other oil producing OPEC states or—more frequently—to non-oil producing LDCs.[10] As charted below, after the first quadrupling of oil posted prices, the role of the main capital-surplus oil states in the Eurocurrency markets changed altogether. In the context of the oil revenues recycling process begun in the spring of 1974 these nations invested short instead of borrowing short. This tendency triggered the so called "maturity imbalance" issue on which the OPEC nations and commercial banks—that used to borrow from the OPEC capital-surplus countries through the investment banks and brokerage houses that traded in the Eurocurrency markets—wrangled over. This point is also covered in this chapter.[11] Therefore, prior to the second half of 1973, the uneven expansion of the OPEC countries' financial assets anticipated a major development typical of the following few years. As a matter of fact, even then Washington straddled to make the oil states and the American brokerage houses reinvest the assets placed with them by the oil producers into the Middle Eastern economies themselves in support for the US balance of payments on current account. As stressed, the oil producers' inclination to invest in the Eurocurrency markets and to borrow from them to finance their development assistance programs to the non-oil LDCs ran counter to such American strategy. On the other hand, however, compared to the oil revenues' recycling mechanism that began in 1974, the contribution of the OPEC countries to the Euro-money markets during this early period was totally different. In fact, at this early stage they also borrowed from them. Finally, and remarkably, it is unwise to identify any connection between the surge in Eurocurrency markets and the long-established US strategy to combine the recasting of the US international payments position, with the crucial problem of preventing the non-oil producing LDCs from slipping away from the international trade system that revolved around the European manufacturing and consumer markets. In other words, prior to the fourfold oil price increase, Eurocurrency deposits were not substantially reflowed to the non-oil LDCs through the largest American banks that used to trading in that market. In striking contrast with this tendency, from around 1970 to 1973 the Euro-money market had largely financed Western European corporations and the international trade of Western European countries.

It is widely known that by 1971 the US balance of trade turned into deficit for the first time since 1891, while even prior to the de facto devaluation of the dollar agreed on at the Smithsonian meetings, the par value of the US currency against any leading Western currency had deteriorated. In order to face up to such twin deterioration, among other measures the Nixon administration placed importance on rebounding military and civilian exports to the Gulf area countries. This was a way to prop up the US currency at a time of increasing trade deficit and deteriorating dollar rate in exchange markets.[12] Such US tendency is further demonstrated by the inner debate held in Washington about the reclassification of friendly Arab countries into the categories of developed and developing countries proper to the US Foreign Military Sales Act of 1968. On the occasion of a correspondence with the US Embassy in Jeddah, the Near Eastern division of the Department of State went for listing Saudi Arabia among the "non-developed countries" to bypass restrictions to furnish credits for foreign military sales to economically less developed countries and to stimulate American trade and investments with the country.[13] Moreover, it is crucial to sense the importance of Saudi Arabia, along with Iran, to the US diplomatic commitment to establish bilateral technical cooperation bodies with these countries after the first oil crisis as a way not only to channel their surplus oil revenues, but also to tighten diplomatic relations with Jeddah and Teheran. This was part of US Secretary of State Henry Kissinger's oil policy toward OPEC. As for Iran, it is worth just stressing that as early as 1969 the US Treasury and the Department of State agreed on the Shah's request for preferential treatments with respect to the US oil import policy from Iran. Rather than a source for dollar outflow, Washington viewed the import of oil from Iran as a means of financing the security interests of Iran without losses to the US balance of payments. By increasing Washington's oil import from Teheran, the oil revenues that accrued to the Iranian state would be put as dollar credits to finance military import by Teheran from the United States and to better the US export to the country and the US trade balance.[14] Against this backdrop, in 1970 the National Security Council approved a general strategy for the near-term: the Council recommended the promotion of cooperation between Iran and Saudi Arabia "as the desirable basis for maintaining stability in the Persian Gulf" and for strengthening trade and financial bonds between the United States and the two countries.[15] Therefore, the case of military and civilian exports to Saudi Arabia and Iran before the quadrupling of crude oil prices in 1973 highlights the intertwining between US friendly OPEC member countries, a commitment by the Nixon administration to promote manufacturing export to improve the balance of payments deficit on current account, and the early Arab inclination to invest their oil revenues into the Eurodollar market way before the fourfold oil price increase. These investments in the Eurodollar market brought about a drying up of domestic capital markets and fixed capital investments in these capital-surplus countries. Besides, they prompted Washington to make arrangements to finance US export to these countries through the involvement of American investment banks and brokerage houses in the Gulf area. Likewise, the case of Iran's oil export sheds light on the use of oil revenues to finance import and domestic economic development programs. This strategy lay at the center of US financial diplomacy amid the two oil crises of the 1970s, when the Department of State straddled to make Arab capital, American commercial banks, and US manufacturers build up a virtuous circuit between the oil crisis-induced developments in international financial markets and new ways to finance development assistance programs in the largest oil producing economies; a policy that clung to the new American diplomatic stance to strengthen political and economic bonds with some of the most powerful Middle Eastern member countries of OPEC through investments and trade.[16]

Notwithstanding such sweeping turn to connect international capital market developments and the increasingly powerful stance of the Arab oil producing states to the ongoing issue of US balance of payments deficit, and irrespective of the de facto devaluation of the dollar agreed on at the Smithsonian summit of December 1971, on the eve of the first oil crisis the US balance of payments continued to dwindle and the value of the dollar in exchange markets went through an ongoing downturn (see Tables 4.2 and 4.3).[17] These adverse developments came about as the combined effect of short-term transnational capital movements prior to the Smithsonian Agreements through 1973 and a record-setting US current account deficit during this period. The long-standing tendency to growing interest rates differentials between Wall Street and the Euromoney markets, that had laid at the origins of the prolonged shift in transnational capital movements out of the US national credit markets to the Eurocurrency markets and the Western European national credit markets, accelerated since fiscal year 1970. This came about as a result of strikingly diverging national economic policies between the US and its western European partners (see Table 4.4).[18] During calendar year 1970 and the early months of the following year, the appearance of much more attractive interest rate conditions abroad than in the United States were attributable to the attempts by the Western European countries to

Table 4.2 Foreign exchange rates—averages based on daily non-buying rates for cable transfers in New York City

Country	Monetary unit	November 1973	October 1973	September 1973
Belgium	Franc	2.58817	2.73283	2.70892
France	Franc	22.6865	23.7181	23.4663
Germany	D. Mark	38.7640	41.4281	41.2458
Japan	Yen	0.359410	0.375467	0.376679
Switzerland	Franc	31.6040	33.0190	33.1458
United Kingdom	Pound	238.6985	242.9186	241.8279

Country	Monetary unit	November 1972	December 1971
Belgium	Franc	2.26851	2.19862
France	Franc	19.8392	18.5494
Germany	D. Mark	31.2154	30.5928
Japan	Yen	0.332235	0.312490
Switzerland	Franc	26.3465	25.6147
United Kingdom	Pound	235.1530	252.6641

Rates in US cents per units of foreign currency
Source: Federal Reserve Statistical Release, 1972, 1973

Table 4.3 US overall balances on international transactions in millions of US dollars

	Long-term private capital flows, net	Balance on current account and long-term capital	Non-liquid short-term private capital flows, net
1967	−2932	−3304	−522
1968	1191	−1935	231
1969	−70	−3637	−640
1970	−1429	−3778	−482
1971	−4381	−10,559	−2347
1972	−98	−11,235	−1541
1973	62	−1026	−4276
1974-1st quarter	506	1795	−3966
1974-2nd quarter	−973	−2479	−5429
1974-3rd quarter	−1998	−3581	−1668

	Net liquidity balance	Net balance on merchandizes excluding military grants	Military transactions direct expenditures
1967	−4683	3800	−4378
1968	−1611	635	−4535
1969	−6081	607	−4856
1970	−3851	2159	−4855
1971	−21,965	−2722	−4819
1972	−13,856	−6986	−4759
1973	−7606	471	−4620
1974-1st quarter	−1053	−74	−1166
1974-2nd quarter	−6222	1631	−1319
1974-3rd quarter	−4466	−2557	−1257

Table 4.4 OPEC member countries investments in the USA

Type of asset	$ billion year-end 1977
Government securities	
Short-term treasury issues	5.7
Long-term treasury issues	9.5
Other government securities	3.3
Bank liabilities	
Short-term bank liabilities	7.9
Long-term bank liabilities	1.1
Corporate securities	
Bonds	1.8
Stocks	4.9
Other investments	2.3
Total	36.5
Short-term (one year and under)	15.3
Long-term (over one year)	21.2

Source: NARA, RG56, OASIA, Office of the Deputy to the Assistant Secretary for International Affairs, Records Relating to International Financial Institutions 1962–1981, b. 6, fold. International Monetary 1978, Michael Blumenthal (Secretary of the Treasury) to Henry Reuss (Chairman, Committee on Banking, Finance and Urban Affairs, House of Representatives)

restrain inflationary pressures and to the expansionary policies implemented in the United States. On the other hand, the US trade position, which had rebounded temporarily in 1970, deteriorated again in the first two quarters of 1971: by mid-year 1971, the US balance of payments was in deficit by nearly $23 billion on the official settlements basis in the first half of the year. The US Secretary of the Treasury announced that, "the secular deterioration in the underlying position of the United States and the exacerbating factor of massive shifts of liquid capital had converged, bringing the international payments system and the United States to a critical point."[19] As anticipated, then, the Smithsonian agreements did not help reverse this trend; in striking contrast to expectations, the change in the dollar's par value, effective in May 1972, did not help rebound the US balance of payments deficit and Washington's losses in official foreign reserves. Considering all the functions that the dollar had performed in the international financial system since the end of World War II, from the time exchange rates were realigned to the outbreak of the first oil crisis, the US currency progressively weakened (see Table 4.2).

Among other functions, the dollar was the unit of account in international trade: from the viewpoint of this study, that was the most interesting role the dollar played as amid the two oil crises, the continuing depreciation of the US currency was a crucial issue. In fact, it accounted for the collapse of both the oil revenues' recycling mechanism and the financial dependence of the oil-consuming countries on OPEC. While prior to 1971 exporters in many countries other than the United States drew sales contracts in dollars and asked to be paid in dollars, in this sense beginning with the devaluation of 1971 the dollar had become much less important. According to several studies produced at the request of the Department of the Treasury, since 1972 many foreign firms did not use the dollar in contracts and transactions. Rather, they began shifting either to their national currencies or priced merchandise to a basket of currencies.[20] In the case of commodities, this could prop up the real value of the dollar in exchange markets by reducing the volume of dollar-denominated international transactions. As highlighted in the following pages of this study, the OPEC oil producers repeatedly threatened to set oil prices in currencies other than the dollar. Such a move would not only sustain their purchasing power in foreign markets, but also prop up the value of the US dollar. However, a shift away from the dollar in international transactions also reduced international investments and capital flows to the United States, thus hitting the US capital account and hurting US foreign currency earnings. Even if one considers the function of the dollar as the unit of account in international financial transactions, although the largest part of Eurocurrency lending was in dollars, the next few years following the Smithsonian agreements recorded a decline in the amount of newly issued international bond markets denominated in dollar. Finally, considering the reserve role of the dollar, from the end of 1971 foreign official holdings of dollars by non-US private individuals and institutions declined. On the other hand, with the beginning of the floating currency system, most countries with large dollar holdings turned to hold diversified portfolios by driving down the price of the dollar in order to shift their assets out of dollars.[21]

Shortly after the decision of OPEC to cut production and following the quadrupling of oil prices, a meteoric expansion was recorded in the capital surplus of oil producers: in calendar year 1974 the OPEC nations accumulated an estimated $60 billion in revenues in excess of their payments for imports of goods and services.[22] This rapid ascendancy of the OPEC oil producing countries marked a breakthrough in the policies so far conducted by the US governments and the Washington-based Bretton Woods sister institutions aimed at restoring a dollar-pegged system of international trade and payments. The combined ascendancy of OPEC and the devaluation of the dollar set off the change in US policies. In fact, since the devaluation of the dollar and the birth of a floating currency system, Washington tore apart its long-standing command to restore international confidence in the dollar and to prop up its value in foreign exchange markets as the groundwork for stabilizing international commodity prices and payments. As seen in this study, certainly the termination of fixed exchange rates and the devaluation of the dollar had crimping effects on the role of the US currency. The end of Bretton Woods hit not only the role of the US currency as unit of account in international trade and international financial transactions, but also its well-established role as store of value and as reserve for market interventions and foreign exchange operations. This tangle of effects hailing from its de facto devaluation contributed to its depreciation substantially. However, it is noteworthy to pinpoint a jumble of other fundamental transformations that occurred in the national and international capital markets over the preceding few years in conjunction with the continued flows of the dollar from the US to the unregulated short-term Eurocurrency markets. Much the same as under the Kennedy and Johnson administrations, prior to 1974 continued dollar outflows and the shift of funds from long-term financial assets to short-term financial instruments—as the cases of Saudi Arabia and Kuwait highlight—pushed forward the decade-long structural weakening of the dollar that neither US foreign trade policies nor measures designed to control capital movements proved to be able to revert. This process continued through 1974; by this year, 40 percent of total OPEC surpluses had been placed in the Euro-banking markets, including UK and other European banks, and a substantial amount of offshore banks.[23] In the first instance, from 1970 to 1971 a number of leading American banks such as, among others, Bankers Trust Company, Bank of America and Chase National Bank, that had borrowed from the Eurodollar market over the past few years, repaid about $10 billion to the market. These scheduled repayments induced US monetary authorities to expect a decline in the Eurodollar rates. Contrary to these expectations, through 1973 a further upswing movement in borrowings from the Eurodollar market was recorded. Three main reasons accounted for this continued surge in demand for Eurodollar credits. Firstly, shortly after the repayments by American banks, from 1971 to 1972 the Eurodollar market lent this money to Germany, Italy, Japan, the UK and other countries to finance international investments and trading. This relending met increasing demand from German multinational corporations, Italian state-shareholding institutions, Japanese international trade financing and British speculation in gilt-edged securities.[24] Such increased borrowings from the Eurodollar market reflected sharply increasing interest rates differential between Eurodollar rates and the cost of money in the national capital markets of most advanced industrial economies.[25] In this context, very tight monetary conditions in certain European countries induced residents of those countries to seek external sources of funds for domestic use. Most notably this was the case of Germany, where tight money and higher interest rates made it attractive to German banks and corporations to borrow in the Eurodollar market.[26] Secondly, it is worth noting that since the turn of the decade a number of restrictions on the inflow of short-term funds were in force in countries like the United Kingdom or the Federal Republic of Germany.[27] However, some member countries of the European Economic Community (EEC) made efforts to attract Eurocurrency and other short-term assets to reduce their balance of payments deficit. This was, for instance, the case of Italy, where national regulatory measures were used to induce the inflow of funds. Since June 1971, both Italian banks and certain public-sector institutions, such as the Istituto Mobiliare Italiano (IMI), have been directly encouraged to take highly liquid shorter funds abroad to help finance Italy's payments deficit.[28] Thirdly, the aforementioned early tendency by the OPEC surplus countries to place their growing financial resources in the Euromoney markets increased borrowers' expectations and triggered an upturn in short-term loan rates.[29] This string of overlapping dynamics had a staggering impact on both the Eurodollar interest rates and commodity prices, thus contributing to set off the inflationary course of the decade. By the second half of 1973, it was apparent that the US balance of payments policies geared to the 1960s failed in meeting their target. In particular, net liquidity balance and net liquid private capital flows, and net non-liquid short-term private capital flows continued to plummet, while the balance on current account and long-term capital did not recover from its recent falloff (See Table 4.3). This jumble of complex developments fully accounted for and tracked the intertwining between dynamics in capital markets and the upsurge in commodity prices, the unfettered weakening of the US dollar in exchange markets, and the upturn in the cost of money for short-term lending in the US and across the main Western financial centers.

At the same time, the meteoric ascendancy of the Arab capital-surplus countries on the international financial stage added to these trends. It induced Washington to reshape the agenda of its foreign economic relations to devise different means of curbing the depreciation of the US dollar and of reversing the final crumbling of a faltering system of international payments. In the first instance, the appearance of powerful capital-surplus countries, such as the Arab and non-Arab oil producing economies, engulfed with dollar-denominated financial assets, shifted to the OPEC the issue of the expansion in dollar-denominated financial assets in international markets. In the second instance, this shift changed the place and role of the Eurocurrency markets with respect to international investments. Throughout the early 1970s, in the context of still-fixed exchange rates, dollar placements in the Eurocurrency markets, largely made by Western central banks, had been heavily drawn by governments for balance of payments deficit financing purposes, rarely for foreign lending and international investments. From the second half of 1973, with the drying-up of American and other Western local credit markets, even as the OPEC capital-surplus countries began increasing their dollar placements into the Eurocurrency markets, the focal issue became the ratio between the Euro-money and Euro credit markets to fixed capital investments. The topicality of this issue came about irrespective of the deflationary or inflationary framework that followed one another during the 1970s. To put it another way, the extent and limits to which short-term capital markets, currently fueled by the oil producers, could trigger the supply side and sustain productive investments came to center stage in the US policies to combine the stabilization of the balance of payments with domestic growth. Not coincidentally, by this time the debate on borrowing in the Eurocurrency markets and the Eurodollar market to fuel fixed capital investments was a much-discussed issue in the ongoing debate that involved the highest ranking US monetary and financial elites on the interconnectedness between short-term capital markets and the reshuffling of productive investments.[30] This point slips into the topicality of two issues fundamental to better understand the US foreign economic policies under the Ford administration, and the development and financial assistance programs of the IMF and the IBRD. On the one side the crucial ratio of transnational capital supply to aggregate demand: this became a pressing issue as the combined result of the worldwide decade-long downswing economic mode, and the rapid expansion in the capital supply that hailed from the long-term increase in commodity prices and the financial resources that accrued to the OPEC countries since prior to the 1973 oil price hikes. As soon as the Western elites realized the scale of the OPEC states' financial resources in spring of 1974, a much-discussed issue within the US government and the OECD was the substantial shift in financial resources from industrial economies traditionally inclined to investments and private consumption, to oil producing countries apt to financial investments and hedge activities.[31] This shift might have potential macroeconomic effects on the ratio of capital supply to aggregate demand in the international economy.[32] On the other hand, as the oil producers began engulfing short-term capital markets, such a shift in financial resources placed against a new and different backdrop the issue of non-oil LDCs external equilibrium. What had been seen as a well-established issue in Washington since the early 1960s, was now a pivot to the restructuring of a fairly stable international trade and payments system. The next sections will focus on exploring the debates and negotiations involving the OPEC countries, the US governments and monetary authorities, and the IMF on the recycling of the oil producing countries' oil revenues before the Carter administration's policy shift.

4.3 Inflationary Strains Before the First Oil Shock

The time has come to assess the scale of the increases in oil prices and its overlapping with a depreciating dollar in exchange markets to then pinpoint two developments. These are, firstly, the inclination of the OPEC countries to pour money into the Eurocurrency markets; secondly, the initiatives by the Ford administration, the IMF, and the Federal Reserve Bank of New York to make institutional arrangements in order to set off an oil revenues recycling mechanism, the reactions to it of OPEC as a community, and the reactions of the most powerful OPEC member states individually. This research trajectory helps to better understand two points: on the one side the attempts by the US and the international economic institutions to direct the reshuffling of international capital markets that hailed from the first oil crisis; on the other, the opening up of new opportunities to reshape both the balance of power between oil producers and the Western powers, and power relations among the leading oil producers united in the OPEC. Over the following three years the OPEC capital-surplus members implemented a policy of diversification of their investments that shifted their funds from short-term money markets to US marketable obligations and investments in the London and New York credit markets, as well as in the equity markets of other advanced industrial economies. By contrast, at this stage the varying institutional arrangements set up to channel oil revenues to non-oil supplying LDCs under the umbrella of Bretton Woods institutions failed. Such failure continued until later, under the Carter administration, the American and Western banking system came under strains. By that time, the malfunctioning of recycling through private markets and the abortive institutionalization of the recycling process led Washington to call on the IMF and the IBRD to carry out the recycling process. Prior to 1977, the failure to get OPEC involved in the recycling process with regard to institutional arrangements prolonged the role of the Eurocurrency markets and led OPEC to directly engage in lending to poor but creditworthy non-oil LDCs. The sequential upsurge in the cost of borrowing and upward inflation prior to the first oil shock owing to the continuing outflow of funds from the US money markets to the Eurocurrency markets before 1973 (see Sect. 4.2), and the failure to build up multilateral arrangements to make the OPEC countries fund the non-oil supplying LDCs' balance of payments, account for the sluggish US balance of payments deficit (see Table 4.3). This sequence of events also accounts for the continued weakening of the dollar in foreign exchange markets up to the arrival at the White House of Carter (see Table 4.2). On the other hand, the failure of this balance of payments deficit financing policy led

Secretary of State Henry Kissinger and the Ford administration to establish bilateral economic commissions with the leading Middle Eastern oil producers to support the dollar and the US balance of payments on current account through an export-based policy briefly explored in Chap. 5. Such strategy, as already stressed, was consistent with the US balance of payments deficit financing policies revolving around the current account and carried out over the past decade. Within this framework, it revamped well-established bilateral commercial bonds and financial relations between Washington and the leading Middle Eastern oil producers pinpointed in the previous pages of this study.

The timeline of the first oil crisis has long been the subject of historical reconstructions, in particular from the viewpoint of its impact on the system of international relations.[33] In this work it is worth chronicling the main developments in the international oil markets before the meteoric rise of the oil receipts of OPEC began exceeding their expenditures on imports of goods and services for domestic investments. Likewise, it is noteworthy to pinpoint connections and asymmetries between these early developments in commodity markets and the course of the US balance of payments deficit, the cost of borrowing money, and consumer goods prices. This is in order to better assess the ratio of oil price increases to inflation in capital markets and in the real economy, the falloff of the dollar in exchange markets and the course of the US balance of payments deficit from prior to 1973 and the following three years. Thereafter, the focal point of this investigation would be the recycling process and its linkage to the US balance of payments deficit financing policies under the Ford administration.

As is widely known, from 1950 to 1972 total world energy consumption increased by 179 percent, equal to a doubling of per capita energy consumption: oil accounted for much of this increase, jumping from 29 percent of world energy consumption in 1950 to 46 percent in 1972. Likewise, the oil consumption share of total energy consumption rose both in the Unites States and, more strikingly, in Western Europe and Japan: oil consumption peaked to roughly 60 percent of total energy consumption in Western Europe and to over 70 percent in Japan.[34] However, over the postwar period the US share of incremental world energy and oil consumption declined, while the combined share of Western Europe increased, particularly from 1955 to 1972.[35] In light of the unmet demand in domestic oil supply, by the early 1970s Western Europe and Japan came to depend on foreign oil supply much more substantially than earlier in the postwar international economic order. Moreover, as charted in Chap. 3, the increasing assertiveness of the Organization of Arab Petroleum Exporting Countries (OAPEC) from the deterioration of fixed exchange rates to the wide-ranging agreements reached at the Teheran conference, and the profit squeeze and increased foreign investments of American oil industry to make up for the losses in profits, adversely affected the US balance of payments on current and capital accounts respectively.

Against the backdrop of these long-term developments in the international oil markets, the quadrupling of oil prices in the winter of 1973 followed a series of measures to cut production and restrain supply. A few days after the outbreak of the 1973 Arab–Israeli war, the Organization's members met in Kuwait and announced a series of measures designed to curtail oil exports in order to put pressure on Western nations to limit Washington's support for Israel. Beginning in October, OAPEC reduced supplies by 5 percent per month until Israel withdrew from occupied territories, and oil prices were increased substantially, some by as much as 70 percent. A few days later, in order to retaliate against US economic and military support for Israel, the OAPEC instituted a total embargo against the United States, the Netherlands and locations known to be processing oil for the US, and approved a 10 percent reduction on the net output during the remainder of October.[36] At a second conference held on November 5, the Arab oil states escalated their measures by reducing November production to 75 percent of the September level, with a further 5 percent cut slated for December. According to a report prepared by the Balance of Payments Division of the Federal Reserve Bank of New York in mid-November, with the embargo remaining in effect, and taking into account the disruption of refining and shipping facilities because of the war, as early as November Arab oil production was cut back by an estimated 30 percent.[37]

Finally, at the Teheran OPEC meeting held in December 1973 the Organization decided to increase the price of crude oil fourfold.[38] Therefore, far-reaching increases in oil prices and restraints on supply came about before the fourfold oil price increase of December, whose mechanism became operative only as of January 1974.[39] Despite this peak in the prices of crude oil, it is certainly plausible to detect a sequential correlation of events that stretched from the preceding few years when capital markets and Western banks were engulfed with short-term funds, to the subsequent overheating of the international economy prior to the fall and winter of 1973 international oil developments. In turn, such late developments put under further pressure the international business cycle and exchange markets. In particular, a number of events are worth recalling: the timing and scale of transnational capital flows and the loan rate of short-term loans in the Eurocurrency markets and business borrowings loan rates; a parallel trend in the dollar's value in exchange markets and the US balance of payments; and, yet again, the pace of wholesale and commodity prices in the US and international markets. This chapter has charted the constant rise of Eurodollar rates from the 1960s through the early 1970s: although many observers expected that the repayment of outstanding US banks' liabilities to the Eurodollar market in 1971 would have put Eurodollar rates down, this did not occur, owing to the rise in demand for loans by European corporations, for international trade financing, and other reasons mentioned earlier in this section.[40] From the suspension of dollar's convertibility in the fall of 1973, notwithstanding a temporarily decline in the cost of short-term lending,[41] demand for short-term loans rose as new borrowers drew from the highly liquid Eurocurrency assets. Such rise in demand for short-term loans fostered continued outflow of non-liquid assets from the United States, which from 1971 to 1972 increased by over 50 percent and contributed to drive down the capital account position in the US balance of payments deficit.[42] Therefore, the linkage between short-term capital markets and borrowing for fixed capital formation turned out to be a breaking new issue way before the OPEC countries fueled the Eurocurrency markets with their mounting oil revenues. Such upward trend on the demand side triggered an increase in the loan rates in the Eurocurrency markets. From 1972 to 1973 it was registered a general widening of interest margins over the LIBOR index in international banking, with an increase in the spread over London Interbank Eurodollar deposits doomed to peak further from 1974 to 1975.[43] Chapter 3 pointed to the growing borrowings in these markets by Western governments for balance of payments deficit financing purposes. Besides this, other borrowers pulled out short-term funds. This increased number of borrowers accounts for the increase in the Eurodollar loans rate. First, Eurocurrency lending to then non-oil producing LDCs had surged since 1974, but in fact had begun over the preceding few years. Countries such as Mexico, Brazil and Korea borrowed from the international money markets for balance of payments financing purposes from 1971 onward within the framework of expansive national monetary policies to finance domestic development programs and to avert a decline in official reserves.[44] On the other hand, from January through October 1973 Eurocurrency liabilities of European banks increased at a monthly average of $2.71 billion.[45] Moreover, following the fourfold increase in oil prices, the interest margins of Eurodollar rates over the LIBOR index widened as both most non-oil producing LDCs and a number of the smaller OECD countries continued to foster expansion via heavy reliance on borrowing for consumption purposes from either resident or non-resident banks.[46] In 1973, a significant inflow of foreign direct investments was registered in the United States, spurred by the increased relative advantage of producing goods in the US, caused by the lower exchange value of the US dollar. Despite this, the outflows from the United States of short-term private capital continued uninterruptedly from 1972 through the October 1973 international oil developments. Such pace engulfed further the Eurocurrency markets and contributed to putting pressure on the US balance of payments. The combined outflow of funds from the US and the rising borrowing for fixed capital investment in the Eurocurrency markets accounts for the widening of interest margins between national capital markets and the Eurodollar market: as shown in Fig. 4.1, this development in interest rates was well on track from 1971 to 1972.

Interestingly, at the same time, this trend drove down the value of the dollar and pushed up loan rates on short-term lending. As stressed in Chap. 3, since the beginning of the decade this lending was much used to finance fixed capital formation and international trade. The monthly average market exchange rate of the US dollar against 10 major foreign currencies plummeted from the first quarter of 1972 to the third quarter of 1974,[47] while continued short-term outflows from the US made

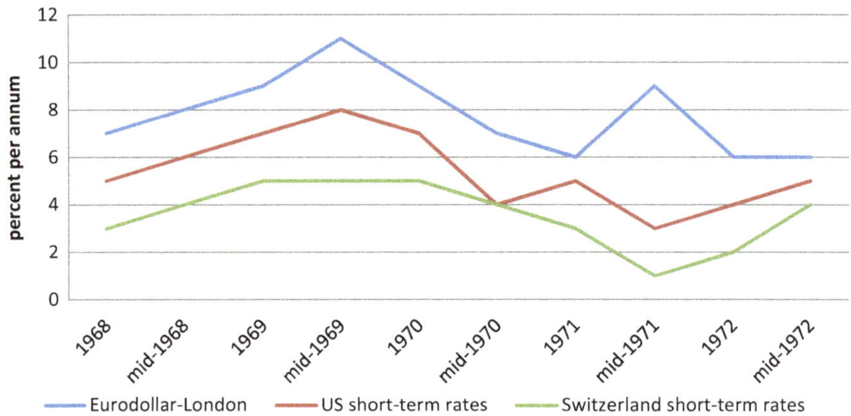

Fig. 4.1 Selected short-term interest rates from 1968 to mid-1972 (Source: Board of Governors of the Federal Reserve System. 1972. *Selected Interest and Exchange Rates for Major Countries and the US. Weekly Series and Charts*. Washington, DC: GPO, Chart 12B)

the US balance of payments and the trade balance remain in substantial deficit despite the devaluation of the dollar (see Table 4.3).[48] During roughly the same time frame, marked by a combined tremendous dynamism in short-term capital markets on the demand side, and a plunging dollar rate, the international economy overheated. If one keeps focusing attention on the US economy, from the beginning of 1972 to the fall of 1973, seasonally adjusted commercial and industrial loans at commercial banks and in non-bank-related commercial papers issued through dealers rose constantly and steadily, alongside surging wholesale prices of industrial commodities and consumer prices of all commodities with the exception of food.[49] Likewise, if one considers in the aggregate the consumer price index in all advanced industrial economies it is quite easy to identify a clear upswing from 1971 to 1973. This pace eloquently shows the interconnectedness between short-term capital markets developments and inflationary strains on the supply side of the manufacturing production chain. In addition, it also sheds light on the consequences of US failures in both reverting capital outflows from the US and in tapping international capital flows to the non-oil producing LDCs and to industrial countries like Italy and Japan that, as stressed, borrowed in those markets in support of their corporations' investments or for international trade financing.[50] Therefore, as Paul Volcker himself recalled one year later at a lecture given in London, although "there is no doubt that the abrupt jump in oil prices has sharpened the inflation-recession dilemma, inflation long antedates the oil crisis."[51] As a matter of fact, in 1974, the oil component of international inflation was modest, accounting for as little as 0.45 percent of the rate of inflation in the United States and 1.5 percent of the inflationary trend in other countries, while the general increase in prices approximated an average of 12 percent. Therefore, the outburst in loan rates owing to the developments in the international capital markets charted in these pages, and a rising pressure on the demand side by business borrowers and governments not only further depressed the dollar in exchange markets. Indeed, it also triggered the overheating of the international economy well before the outbreak of the December 1973 fourfold increase in oil prices. In addressing the 29th session of the United Nations General Assembly in the early fall of 1974 the Foreign Ministry of Iran summarized this sequential course of events: "disorder in the world economy and money market preceded the oil price rise and was mainly due to mismanagement of the economy in European States and America, as well as excessive consumption in the more advanced countries."[52]

Therefore, growing demand for short-term loans pushed up the rates of business borrowings and international trade financing and caused an upward trend in prices. On the other hand, continuous capital outflows from the United States and the engulfment of the Eurocurrency markets prior to the unprecedented impact of the first oil crisis on the international investment patterns of the OPEC countries, certainly interacted with a deteriorating US balance of payments deficit and mounting pressure on the dollar's value in exchange markets. As suggested in the following paragraphs, such interaction was the long-term cause for the failure of Washington's strategy to recast a dollar-centered international trade and payments system through massive borrowing from the OPEC Arab countries and Iran. By taking into account the ongoing appreciation in the Eurodollar rate since the beginning of the new decade and considering that the first wave of flows of OPEC surplus oil revenues was largely invested in the Eurocurrency markets,[53] it is noteworthy to draw attention to the combined importance of growing short-term capital markets, the plummeting of stable exchange rates and the hiking up of wholesale and consumer prices. This came about irrespective of developments in oil and other commodity prices. Such linkage between capital market developments, foreign exchange rates, and prices featured in the international economy from the period preceding the first oil crisis through to the few months that followed the fourfold price hike, when oil prices had an increasing impact on the 1974 cost-push inflation.

4.4 American Banks, the Eurocurrency Markets, and the Recycling of Oil Money to the Non-OPEC LDCs 1974–1975

From the quadrupling of oil prices in the winter of 1973 to the following September, oil prices increased further by some 20 percent; then, the September 1974 OPEC meeting froze posted prices to the end of the year but imposed increased royalties and tax rates which were estimated to raise average prices by over 3.5 percent estimated by OPEC at the time.[54] Since the beginning, in the United States this process stemmed fear for a deflationary spiral on both commodity prices and consumer goods prices: the most popular interpretation of this price policy was that a surge in oil prices and consumer prices would dwarf demand for consumer goods and trigger a stunning imbalance between an oversupply and a sluggish aggregate demand. Likewise, the outlook was for a slump in the cost of borrowing from US commercial banks caused by capital supply exceeding aggregate demand and demand for fixed capital investments.[55] On the other hand, since January 1974 the Federal Reserve Bank of New York suggested that the rise in oil prices might reduce demand for goods and services and create unemployment.[56] This twofold concern draws attention to the twin ways in which the US administrations tried to use the international financial consequences of the oil price hikes in the context of Washington's driving objective of resurrecting the dollar and the US balance of payments. The US linked the oil revenues that accrued to the oil supplying countries to the payments imbalances of oil importing nations and to the development of domestic markets in the oil producing countries. It also promoted demand management expansionary policies through a support for the US export to oil-rich nations. From 1974 to 1976 the US financial and monetary authorities focused on the first issue, whereas under the Carter administration Washington focused most attention on the latter one.

Within this framework, OPEC's total oil revenues registered an unprecedented increase; in 1972, before OPEC began its peak price policy, receipts of the OPEC group from international oil sales totaled less than $14 billion,[57] while one year later total payments to OPEC nations for oil amounted to $22 billion.[58] During calendar year 1974 OPEC oil revenues jumped from $23 billion in 1973 to $94 billion by year-end, with the volume of oil export in 1974 being 5 percent less than in 1973. As a result, during 1974 OPEC countries' receipts from the sale of oil and other products exceeded their import payments by about $63 billion, up from less than $5 billion in 1973.[59] In the context of these booming oil profits and foreign exchange earnings that chronicled the year 1974, since the quadrupling of oil prices the Persian Gulf oil producers showed their incapacity to spend on additional import as much as they had earned from increased export earnings. This gap between receipts on dollar-denominated oil export and foreign expenditures on imports, soon being dubbed as petrodollars, was mostly the case of small oil producers as Kuwait, the United Arab Emirates, and Qatar, featuring small low capital-absorbing domestic consumer markets.[60] Contrasting with those, since the winter of 1973–74 Iraq and, more importantly, Iran, proved to be much more capital-absorbing economies. In letting alone for a while any single case, in the aggregate their financial surpluses substantially increased their holdings of international reserves. For instance, by the end of 1973 Saudi Arabia, an average capital-absorbing economy, had official reserves holdings of $3.2 billion and $21 billion at the end of the third quarter of 1975.[61] However, a breakdown of the figure concerning the holding of international reserves by high-absorbing and low-absorbing OPEC countries in the aggregate leads to the deduction that both oil states with potentially large domestic consumer markets and small states with little import requirements engulfed with oil revenues, contributed to the recycling process. During calendar year 1974 the current account surplus of the high-absorbing OPEC states peaked at over $23 billion, while the current account surplus of the low absorbers run at over $36 billion[62] for a total of up to $60 billion by the late fall of 1974.[63] Therefore, both small oil producing economies and the largest and most important countries like Iran provided the financial groundwork to the American objective, among others, of resorting to their capital surpluses to strike the balance between capital oversupply and borrowing for fixed capital investments. It is worth situating within this framework the equal importance paid by Washington over the following years to a potentially high absorber like Iran and to a typically high capital-surplus country such as Kuwait, as well as to an average capital-absorbing oil producer like Saudi Arabia. In either case, long-standing economic bonds with these countries and the involvement of American commercial and investment banks in the local economies of these states intersected with large capital surplus in both the highest absorbing and the low absorbing Middle Eastern economies. Chapter 3 covered the increasing involvement of American capital into Saudi Arabia and Iran since as early as the late 1950s and thereafter. In exploring the dynamics of the recycling process, this and the next chapter focus on both countries, and Kuwait, an extremely current account surplus economy. As much as for the case of Saudi Arabia and Iran, foreign economic policymakers based in Washington could count on well-established bonds between the American banking system and the country. For instance, since as early as the mid-1960s Chase Manhattan Bank had helped as agent or broker the government of Kuwait to make investments in the US real estate market,[64] while Citibank both established branches in Saudi Arabia, Dubai and Abu Dhabi, and completed joint ventures with the Kuwaitis in Beirut.[65]

Since the beginning of 1973, the immediate consequence of this capital surplus that rapidly piled up on the assets of such a variety of OPEC member countries was a steady rise in their foreign investments in the form of either foreign direct or portfolio investments. As outlined in this study, they diversified their investments since their oil profits boomed. However, by breaking down the course of their foreign investments as they stood a few months after the quadrupling of oil prices, it is possible to conclude that during the first few months that followed the first fourfold oil price hikes, a large share of their oil profits were invested in short-term funds and call deposits. Only later on, and gradually, did they begin placing more money always at the longer-term, even for as much as three to five years.[66] If one looks closer at calendar year 1974, all sources available concur to estimate that the share of OPEC current account surplus invested in the Eurodollar and other Eurocurrency markets amounted up to 40 percent of total oil revenues invested by OPEC countries abroad.[67] Moreover, considering the total of OPEC investments in short-term financial instruments, the percentage peaked to over 50 percent. As a whole, investments in the US money markets, the sterling money market based in London, and the Eurocurrency markets, came to about 60 percent of total OPEC investments of all types.[68] Although this figure included investments in Treasury bills, most of these investments were highly liquid and callable money market placements, with Eurocurrency deposits of no more than 6-month maturity. It is also worth taking into account that since the beginning the OPEC nations made significant placements with the Swiss private capital markets, which invested these deposits in the Eurocurrency markets. As early as the first quarter of 1974, Swiss capital provided the Eurocurrency markets with a total of $3.5 billion including a significant portion from oil producing countries.[69] Based on all these data it is evident that the OPEC countries' tendency throughout the first year since the first oil shock was to invest short. Clearly, such investment attitude was at variance with and jeopardized the US government's move to redress the balance between capital oversupply and a fall-off on the demand side. This occurred because highly liquid short-term financial instruments were unfit to re-launch fixed capital formation and employment across the US and major advanced industrial economies. On the other hand, as anticipated with respect to the attitude by the non-oil LDCs to borrow from the Eurocurrency markets to finance their external debt and balance of payments deficit, the early engulfing of short-term private capital markets represented an opportunity for the non-oil producing LDCs. For a comprehensive and as much well-founded as possible estimate of OPEC investments in short-term financial assets and the scale of US banks' lending to the LDCs, it would be essential to figure out the OPEC investments in the offshore centers of American commercial banks, most of which were established at the Bahamas and in the Cayman Islands during the 1960s. At that time the US maintained controls on the outflow of capital to reduce capital flight to the Eurodollar market. Within that regulatory framework the US commercial banks established these offshore centers to bypass it and to keep providing services to their large (primarily US) overseas corporate customers. In a report to the White House a few years later under the Carter Presidency, Secretary of the Treasury Blumenthal recalled "the activities of the Bahamian branches in terms of Arab deposits and lending to LDCs," calling on the Federal Reserve Board to regulate such flow of funds.[70] To better understand the importance of these offshore centers of US banks it is worth saying that by 1976 as much as 44 percent out of total US banks' international lending was provided by these US banks' branches in the offshore centers of the Caribbean and Far East.[71] If one leaves out this last issue and considers the currency denomination of oil payments, at year-end 1974 about two-thirds of the total increase in the OPEC countries' official foreign assets were invested in US dollar-denominated assets. However, while the dollar component of OPEC surplus invested abroad was predominant, the course of investments of the OPEC countries changed over the course of the year with a shift from short-term financial instruments to longer-term assets. From the end of 1973 through to early 1975 the largest US commercial banks involved in reinvesting the OPEC financial assets reshuffled their international lending significantly. In the aggregate, during that time frame purchases of debt securities and financial assets by the home branches of American banks rose from $26 billion to $45 billion, equal to 70 percent. At the same time purchases by foreign subsidiaries of US banks surged from $36 million to $51 million, equal to a yearly rise of only 41 percent.[72] Considering that foreign subsidiaries traditionally specialized in trading in the Euro-money markets, it is quite easy to infer the relative decrease of OPEC investments in short-term financial instruments and their growing attitude to make longer placements. However, over the decade highly liquid placements continued to comprise a large share of total OPEC international investments: in the aggregate, they grew from $160 billion in 1973 to $485 billion at the end of 1978, to peak at $600 billion in 1980.[73] The implication of such massive Arab investments in short-term Eurocurrency markets and other short-term assets was a rare stance by OPEC to finance the US economy and its business cycle. As of early April 1974, Chase's officers reported to the Federal Reserve Bank of New York that since oil prices had been hiked up, there had been no evidence of large scale, direct inflow of OPEC oil money into the United States under the form of equity or portfolio investments. By contrast, Chase's officers reported that as a result of the limited capacity of credit markets to absorb funds, the OPEC member countries were heavily placing their money in the Eurodollar market, with money going since the beginning of the year into very short-term placements in a number of European banks including the European branches of American banks.[74] Therefore, it is evident that the adverse impact of short-term investments by OPEC on the American policy to draw upon the OPEC's capital surplus to restore equilibrium between capital supply and aggregate demand, in order to avert a deflationary spiral, did apply to the US equity market. This chapter has stressed that the investments in the Eurocurrency markets and other short-term markets were a substantial share of the OPEC countries' international investments during the first two quarters of the year. By contrast, during the third and fourth quarters they declined in connection with, among other reasons, the falloff in short-term interest rates recorded since midsummer. In the midsummer of 1974, according to the Executive Director of the US Council on International Economic Policy, though most of the OPEC surpluses had gone into short-term, highly liquid Eurodollar assets, the oil producing states were increasingly willing to move into long-term investments, both financial and direct. They were supposed to be willing to invest both in the United States and across other industrial nations, under the form of either portfolio or direct investments.[75] However, at the end of the year, the investment of oil revenues surpluses in Eurocurrency assets peaked again, notwithstanding the recalcitrance of American commercial and investment banks to channel OPEC funds into short-term placements discussed further here.[76] Although they diversified their investments, the following year the OPEC nations persisted in pouring an impressive share of their capital surplus into the Eurocurrency and other short-term financial instruments: at the end of March 1975 roughly 80 percent of total OPEC financial assets held in official accounts consisted of short-term assets.[77] Over the following four years, the OPEC countries went down the route of diversifying into long-term instruments. Consider their investments in the United States: at year-end 1977 their investment behavior showed a gradual diversification toward long-term assets doomed to continue the following year (see Table 4.4).[78]

Therefore, the kickoff to the recycling process revolved by and large around short-term Eurocurrency assets and the US dollar, the currency in which the largest amount of OPEC surplus investments were denominated. Earlier in this chapter it was stressed that prior to the first quadrupling of oil prices the development of short-term capital markets had long been the subject of skepticism and negative speculation among US economic policymakers as it had intersected with capital outflow from the US money markets and the long-term weakening of the dollar. By contrast, since the first oil shock the increasing tendency by OPEC to make investments in the Eurocurrency markets was serviceable to Washington's twin project to draw upon the OPEC financial resources to ease the pressure of development assistance policies to the LDCs on the US capital account position, and to resurrect the current account position through the financing of US export to the oil producing countries. To put it another way, the involvement of American banks and the Eurodollar market in the early phase of the recycling process of dollar-denominated oil revenues was considered in Washington as a means of financing both development assistance to the non-oil LDCs, and the export of US manufacturers to the OPEC nations. Washington aimed to reach these two targets by drawing from the dollar capital markets. This US attempt to link the growing capital surplus of OPEC countries to a long-standing Washington effort to prevent the non-oil-rich LDCs from sliding away from the international payments system is consistent with past American policies. Based on our study so far on the 1960s and the first half of the 1970s, it is evident that throughout the two decades Washington established a linkage between reducing the US balance of payments deficit and making any reasonable effort to keep the non-oil LDCs in the loop of multilateral trade and payments. During the 1960s, the US governments resorted to domestic fiscal policy in order to finance foreign economic assistance and decided upon improving the US terms of trade and the US current account position. This was in order to partially make up for the losses of a costly commitment to sustain the non-oil LDCs' external balance and their purchasing power in foreign markets. In the last two chapters the historical origins of such US foreign financial policy were covered. Over the course of the 1970s the Ford and Carter administrations seamlessly resorted to the OPEC financial assets to finance the trade and balance of payments deficits of the non-oil supplying LDCs through a variety of different channels: the early prominent role of US banking was followed by a number of projects following the same route. Among other things, it is worth mentioning the US commitment to establish new multilateral institutional or private arrangements, the idea of getting the IBRD involved in the pursuit of such target, as well as the promotion of concessionary loans by the OPEC nations themselves. Therefore, it is worth beginning this reconstruction of the recycling mechanism through close attention to the intertwining between the Eurocurrency markets and the OPEC financial resources that exceeded their domestic investments and the out-payments on imports of goods and services. As seen in this book, prior to the first energy crisis some leading capital-surplus countries such as Saudi Arabia had been used to alternating placements in the Euro-money markets, and borrowing from it to finance other small oil states' balance of payments deficits. However, at that time a substantial share of the Eurocurrency markets had been financed through deposits by Western central banks. Thereafter, as widely anticipated in this chapter, US banking came to center stage in the process of reflowing the oil producers' assets. As a matter of fact, what makes the financial history of the OPEC capital-surplus countries since the first oil crisis a distinctive new chapter in the history of their involvement in the international financial arena is on the one side the meteoric expansion in their surplus financial assets, and on the other, the intertwining, for a few years ahead, between the course of their foreign investments and the history of Western, mostly Wall Street based commercial banks, investment banks and brokerage houses. Likewise, as from 1973 to early 1974, the OPEC countries quickly moved from the position of borrowers to that of lenders, some Western central banks went the other way around. A country whose current account deficit was worryingly and quickly affected by the increase in oil prices, such as the United Kingdom, moved to borrow in the Eurodollar market as early as January 1974 to finance its balance of payments deficit[79] even as surplus countries such as Iran made offers to directly finance London's current account deficit.[80] In addition to borrowing from the Eurocurrency markets by Western central banks, since the fourfold increase in oil prices other causes triggered an uptick in demand for short-term borrowing. On the one hand, as outlined, this surge in Arab investments in the Eurodollar market through the largest Wall Street banks should be situated within the framework of peaking loan rates caused by the growing demand for Euro-bank credit from international corporations, advanced and developing countries, and for international trade financing from 1971 through 1973. These OPEC investment patterns that followed the December 1973 increase in oil prices should also be placed against the backdrop of the US legislation under operation from the mid-1960s through the first oil crisis. The US voluntary restraint programs, introduced as a balance of payments measure in 1965 and strengthened in 1968, contributed to stimulate the runaway of American and international investors from Wall Street to the Eurocurrency markets. They were removed only in 1974; notwithstanding, reserve requirements and interest regulations imposed on domestic deposits remained "as reasons for re-establishing a foreign branch."[81] As, a few years later, the then Under Secretary of the Treasury Anthony Solomon stressed, by the time the oil payments-induced current account imbalances put further pressure on the dollar, "the overseas branching operations of US banks had been well established."[82] All these aforementioned factors and trends contributed to get the US commercial banks involved, mostly through their foreign branches operating in Europe and their offshore centers, in the recycling process.

Therefore, against this clearly outstanding interconnectedness between growing oil revenues surpluses in excess of import requirements, and peaking Eurocurrency deposits from the very outset of the oil crisis, it is worth charting the role of American commercial and investment banks, whose involvements was substantial during the first part of 1974 and came under strain since the end of the year through the 1975 recession. As already remarked, giant American banks such as Citibank or Chase Manhattan Bank had long been involved in the national credit markets of important OPEC member states mostly either to underwrite import credit requirements or to finance national industrial or economic ventures as it was the case of Iran since as early as 1959. Since the end of 1973, the OPEC governments received payments in New York dollar deposits held at the five largest US commercial banks residing in Wall Street, and funds were invested into the circa 30 banks they trusted in the Eurodollar market, primarily in extremely short maturities: call money, seven-day money, 1-month money or 3-month certificates, available to oil importing countries that suffered from liquidity problems. For instance, in early January 1974 Chase Manhattan Bank received and reflowed Arab countries' deposits through a number of accounts of Arab agency banks it held.[83] The reflowing of these funds from these Wall Street-based foreign agency banks' accounts to the banks in the Eurodollar market was the way in which the oil revenues surpluses were poured into the Euro-money market. These Euro deposits were backed by New York dollar deposits "so that the original underlying dollar deposits never leave New York or the US domestic money supply, even though their ownership changes from that of a US oil company to that of an Arab government or Eurodollar bank."[84] Thereafter, these deposits were used to a great extent to lend short and to a rather limited amount to finance some long-term capital markets, mostly the Euro-bond market.[85] Therefore, the very mechanism on which the process of reflowing oil money was based essentially contrasted with the American policy to draw on the OPEC countries' capital surplus to finance productive investments and to sustain aggregate demand. This because it technically poured petrodollars into liquid placements. The scale of these deposits in the Eurocurrency markets cannot be tidily estimated as long as statistical and archival sources fail to provide evidence as to the course of investments of OPEC member states. Two reasons undermine the possibility of unfolding reliable statistical data and figures: as already stressed, the role of US banks' offshore centers in accepting Arab deposits and relending their funds to the LDCs. Furthermore, reasoning along this line, it is worth making a detour in relation to OPEC's lending to the Swiss capital market. According to the Office of Financial Resources and Energy Finance, the unit established within the US Department of the Treasury to manage any money, credit and equity issue that arose from the recycling process, as of fall of 1974 the Swiss banks reinvested the Arab deposits they held into the US money market or the London-based Eurodollar market. American economic policymakers wrangled over this issue: in contrast with the Department of the Treasury, the Federal Reserve Bank of

New York argued that the Swiss and Netherlands Antilles financial centers, which handled money from investors from around the world, had changed little the scale of their international lending and portfolio investments from the levels that prevailed prior to 1974.[86] Therefore, according to the Fed the Swiss banking system played a negligible role in reflowing the OPEC assets across the globe. Irrespective of this, a thorough estimate of the OPEC deposits in the Eurocurrency markets should take into account their deposits in the offshore centers of US banks and in the Swiss capital markets. In either case, the trajectory of reflowing was into short-term inflation-sensitive assets. This said, disregard any quantitative estimate of these investments of the OPEC countries' resources by offshore centers and Swiss banks. Instead, consider that the oil producers engaged in these investment patterns at a time of trouble for the US and European commercial banks. Since the US Congress amended the Bank Holding Company Act in 1970, the debt ratio of US banks, namely the ratios of short- and long-term debt to invested equity capital, had deteriorated significantly. The setting up of bank-owned holding companies had induced banks to raise money for the new entities through the issuance of debt, primarily through the sale of commercial paper and long-term debt securities. In order to finance secondary borrowing by the holding companies, American banks issued off-the-balance sheet obligations not backed by the reserve requirements imposed by the Federal Reserve Board.[87] Therefore, investments in the Eurocurrency markets and off-shore centers surged at a time when US banking suffered most from liquidity shortage and poorly performing capital adequacy. In tight money markets the hazardous move of issuing off-the-balance sheet obligations not backed by reserve requirements increased reliance of banks on the banking system for capital and brought under severe strains the capital adequacy of banks. In this framework, during fall 1973 the failure of the US National Bank of San Diego, which defaulted on $ 93 million of stand-by letters of credit, set out a roughly year-long series of banking failures in both the United States and continental Europe. From fall 1973 to late summer 1974, when Franklin National Bank, the largest bank to ever fail, collapsed, nine large US banks and the German giant Herstatt,[88] which defaulted in spring 1974, undermined the western banking system.[89] This turmoil occurred even as the OPEC countries' mounting capital surpluses induced several Wall Street bankers to forecast a gloomy deflationary spiral and urged large-scale programs to channel oil revenues to strike the balance between capital supply and demand for fixed capital formation across the advanced industrial economies. Therefore, from 1973 to 1974 the weakness of the US and international banking system and the steady development of short-term investments by the oil producers or those national capital markets as the Swiss banks working on their behalf interacted each other in a complex fashion. This interaction undermined further the balance between capital supply and aggregate demand. Since the quadrupling of oil posted prices crushed the purchasing power of the oil importing industrial countries, demand for industrial loans soared and national credit markets began slipping into a stiff drying up. As commodity and oil prices went up, manufacturers expanded their borrowing from the national capital markets to compensate for the uptick in prices and maintain their purchasing power level in foreign markets. Although the effects of the increase in oil prices on the US import requirements were much less in proportion to other Western countries as France, Italy or Japan, during the first half of 1974 within the United States it was registered a drying up of the market for new capital that led corporations to borrow from the nation's banks as never before. As a result of it, the so called prime lending rate of banks, the rate that banks charged for their most creditworthy customers, soared to record-setting levels.[90] It was in this jumble of banking fragile and rising rates that foreign branches of the six largest American banks operating in the Eurocurrency markets began relending the OPEC countries' expanding surplus capital and continued through the 1975 recession. Since its inception, this process of relending the OPEC financial assets through Wall Street showed a string of palpable shortcomings. A few months later these concerns and hindrances led the US government to change the way in which Washington made use of the oil revenues' recycling process to confront the US capital account deficit through pressure on the OPEC countries to move to long-term investments. The six largest US banks that poured the OPEC countries' financial assets in their foreign branches operating in the Eurocurrency market, and mostly in the Eurodollar portion of it, were Chase Manhattan Bank, Bank of America, Chemical Bank, Citibank, Manufacturers Hanover and Morgan Guaranty.[91] As of

April 1974 the bulk of oil payments deposited in the Eurocurrency markets were mainly in dollar and British pound.[92] In the aggregate, during the first 8 months of the year, Eurocurrency lending by US banks including both lending by domestic offices and portfolio investments by foreign subsidiaries located in the Eurocurrency markets increased by roughly over 3 percent a month.[93] If one disaggregates this data by foreign subsidiaries specializing in short-term lending and US-based domestic offices trading in long-term financial instruments, it is possible to deduce that the recycling of OPEC nations' financial assets in short-term Euro-money markets peaked during the first quarter of the year. Thereafter, US domestic offices took the lead in shaping the international investments of the largest American banks in longer and less inflation-sensitive capital markets.[94] Therefore, the investment shift was paired with a shift from foreign branches to domestic offices of US banks. Besides, since the beginning six countries (Algeria, Qatar, Abu Dhabi, Kuwait, Bahrain and Iraq) chose to have their oil payments in British pounds, while Saudi Arabia kept only 25 percent of its payments in British currency. Most of these British sterling payments were deposited through banks operating in the Eurocurrency markets other than the US banks, with few of the oil countries placing much in the way of sterling deposits with any London branch of US banks, one of which was Chase Manhattan.[95] Notwithstanding a decline in the OPEC countries' short-term placements with these commercial banks over the rest of the decade, at the end of the 1970s OPEC deposits at foreign branches of American banks were larger than OPEC deposits at domestic offices in Wall Street or other US-based financial centers. In 1979, the OPEC deposits at the eight largest New York banks amounted to over 11 percent of their total deposits in domestic and foreign offices: just over half of total OPEC deposits were liabilities of Citibank. More importantly, OPEC deposits at domestic offices of those eight largest banks amounted to over 21 percent of these banks' net Federal Funds position, while at foreign branches and subsidiaries of the banks these deposits were still over 54 percent of the banks' Eurocurrency placements with foreign banks.[96] From December 1975 to December 1978 the deposits of Middle East oil producing countries in foreign branches of the six largest US banks peaked from $197.5 billion to $274 billion.[97] Therefore, although the role of American banks

Table 4.5 Outstanding Eurocurrency loans by currency denomination, percentage of total

Currency denomination	1975	1976	1977	1978
Dollars	75.4	76.8	56.9	63.0
Deutsch Mark	18.6	12.1	24.2	18.1
Swiss Franc	1.0	4.2	7.9	4.5
Yen	0.3	0.6	1.3	2.2
Others	4.7	6.3	9.7	12.2
Total	100	100	100	100

Source: NARA, RG56, Office of the Under Secretary for Monetary Affairs, Subject Files of Anthony Solomon Under Secretary for Monetary Affairs 1977–1980, b. 2, fold. International Banking, F. Lisle Widman to Assistant Secretary Bergsten, Memorandum 'Currency Denomination of International Borrowing', October 24, 1979

in reflowing OPEC deposits paved the way for multilateral arrangements and direct or portfolio investments, as well as direct loans by each OPEC member state, the role of US banks did not fade away throughout the decade. Their private placements in the Eurocurrency markets continued to represent a significant share of total world capital supply; Table 4.5 shows trends in private banks placements in the Eurocurrency markets in the aggregate, including their short-term lending financed by the OPEC countries, from 1973 to 1979, broken down by currency denomination.

By and large, since the beginning of the recycling process American commercial and investment banks turned to finance the non-oil producing LDCs. As detailed below, since early spring of 1974 several multilateral financial arrangements were discussed among the industrial nations and between them and the non-oil supplying LDCs. Among others, within such supranational bodies as the Committee of Twenty Deputies, the LDCs, at the time led by Brazil, and the advanced industrial economies, wrangled over the setting up of an extended fund facility under the aegis of the IMF to permit real resources transfer to the non-oil LDCs.[98] Such disputes and negotiations on the establishing of the extended fund facility is a case in point that sheds light on the ill-functioning American attempt to lock OPEC's financial resources into multilateral bodies under US leadership and the oil producers' recalcitrant reaction. In this framework, the foreign branches of US commercial and investment banks as well as the brokerage houses, operating in the London-based Eurodollar market, drew upon the short-term OPEC deposits to lend mid-term and longer-term in the Eurobond and Eurocredit markets. This in the aim to finance the balance of payments deficit of oil importing industrial nations and the current imbalances of the non-oil producing LDCs. Since shortly after the quadrupling of oil prices through the first quarter of the year the United Kingdom, France and Italy borrowed a total of over $10 billion medium- and long-term credit from the Eurobanks, while at the same time non-oil LDC countries borrowed as little as $4 billion.[99] Based on this data it is worth noting that even at this early time the role of Western central banks had already moved from that of net lenders to net borrowers from the Euro-money markets. However, over the following two years the share of industrial nations' borrowing in total Eurocurrency lending declined, while borrowing by the non-oil LDCs surged. As a matter of fact, over the course of 1974 and thereafter the latter course of investments gained momentum: during the first 8 months of 1974, the developing countries as a group borrowed about $5.5 billion in the Euromarkets.[100] Eurocurrency banks were particularly active in channeling credits to developing nations in 1976. As many as 20 developing countries each borrowed $100 million or more during that single year: this amount accounted for a sizable part of the $11.3 billion raised by non-oil LDCs through the Euromarket. This group increased its share of total Eurocurrency loans from 39 percent in 1975 to about 41 percent in 1976.[101] In the four years ending in 1979, commercial banks made net loans amounting to 70 percent of the non-oil producing developing countries' total financing needs.[102] Against this general backdrop, according to the statistical series provided by the OECD, the non-oil producing LDCs increasingly issued bonds in the Eurobond market. From 1973 to 1975 their foreign issues were equally divided between the foreign and Eurobond markets, while by June 1977 three-quarters of such foreign credit had been borrowed from the Eurobond market.[103] Therefore, it is clear that the US commercial banks strikingly moved to reflow the OPEC investments into the non-oil LDCs, thus making the oil producers' capital surplus a source of development financial assistance useful to ease pressure on the US overseas expenditures and reduce liabilities in the US balance of payments. Likewise, it is evident that such activism by the US commercial banks and other Western banks that operated in the

Eurocurrency markets highlighted the unsuccessfulness of the efforts by the Ford administration and the Bretton Woods economic institutions to establish multilateral financial arrangements to channel the OPEC financial resources. In this respect, it is worth considering the increasing tendency of OPEC to make placements in the Eurocurrency markets, and the corresponding borrowing from them by the non-oil LDCs, a litmus test of the failure of Washington to keep the recycling policy under its full control.

On the other hand, the size of the OPEC placements with Western monetary institutions and governments should not be underestimated. Since the beginning of the recycling process US commercial banks worked on tapping the payments imbalances met by the United Kingdom, France and Italy. As of early spring of 1974 Chase and other US banks had already provided sizable credits to these three countries to finance their heavy borrowings in foreign markets for balance of payments deficit financing purposes. In these circumstances, the US banks drew call money from the Eurodollar market deposited either by the banks themselves or by the oil companies, which, since shortly after the increase in oil prices, had begun to place their profits into both US and British Treasury bills, Eurodollars and Eurosterling.[104]

4.5 The Consequences of OPEC Short-Term Investments: Eurocurrency Markets, Inflation, and US External Disequilibria. American Debates and Policies

Under both the Ford and Carter administrations, the US monetary and financial authorities held the view that from the beginning American banks had served the purpose of depositing OPEC financial resources through the recycling mechanism revolving around the Eurocurrency markets (outlined in the previous section) in a workable manner. This was in order both to weigh the balance between capital supply and aggregate demand that deteriorated as a result of the fourfold upsurge in oil prices, and to face up to the deflationary scenario caused by diminishing demand and growth rates. Moreover, according to the US authorities this role of the US banking was serviceable in order to curb the current account imbalances, which most oil importing nations began suffering from. The Federal Reserve System was in the forefront in reckoning the role of the Eurocurrency markets in pouring short-term deposits into mid- and short-term lending to the non-oil producing LDCs. In so doing, the highest-ranking US economic policymakers recognized the importance of the largest commercial banks involved in the recycling process in replacing the US development financial assistance programs necessary to prevent the oil crisis from pushing the non-oil LDCs away from international trade. According to Board of Governors member, Henry Wallich, while US banks had pioneered the development of lending to non-oil-rich developing countries "well before the 1973 rise in the price of oil," such flow of money increased in volume and economic significance as recycling of the OPEC surplus became necessary to finance the purchasing power and terms of trade of developing nations. Borrowing from him, "the developing countries in large part were unable to maintain a good rate of growth during the difficult years that followed. It is not easy to visualize how that result could have been achieved without the activities of American banks" in recycling OPEC funds for LDCs lending purposes.[105] A few years later, the then Under Secretary of the Treasury for Monetary Affairs Anthony Solomon stressed that "the Eurocurrency market has become a very important element in a global system. We want this market to remain strong and to continue to fulfill its intermediary function without eroding domestic money and credit policies." This approach is noteworthy in that it made a substantial departure from the way in which US monetary authorities viewed and managed the development of short-term capital markets and the unfettered outflow of dollars from Wall Street during the 1960s. It is worth recalling that under the Kennedy and Johnson administrations the outflow of capital from the United States to short-term Eurocurrency markets had been viewed as a development harmful to the dollar's strength and worth curbing. The change of approach to the Eurocurrency markets in the early 1970s and particularly since the first oil crisis was stubborn. It can be linked to the US changing view on the role of the Eurocurrency markets in propping up the balance of payments deficit of the non-oil LDCs and in sustaining their purchasing power in foreign markets as already described. In fact, in making such a case for the role of the Eurodollar and Eurocurrency markets, Solomon tellingly maintained that their development did not put pressure on the value of the dollar in exchange markets, nor did it trigger any inflationary upswing. In his view, such pressure depended on the changing market demand for dollars relative to other major currencies, while the level of dollar deposits in the Eurocurrency markets was not a measure of dollar overhang and as such a cause for its depreciation. In his view the depreciation of the US currency depended on the yields that could be obtained there compared to the US money markets rates.[106] This issue is worth exploring as it is at variance with one of the most prominent concepts maintained in this study. As suggested in this chapter and earlier in Chap. 3, it is plausible to establish a sequential correlation between the continued rise in Eurocurrency and Eurodollar deposits since the early 1960s through the Nixon administration and the growing demand for borrowings from those markets from the turn of the decade to the first oil price rise, and the unfettered depreciation of the US dollar in foreign exchange markets, the soaring US balance of payments deficit, and the upswing movement in the loan rate of short-term money markets. The debate that developed at the time in the United States about the nature and impact of such continuous outflows of dollars from the US and its further development since the largest American commercial and investment banks accepted short-term highly liquid deposits from the OPEC countries and rechanneled these oil revenues into the inflation-sensitive Eurocurrency markets, is worth exploring to better assess the thesis maintained in this study. Besides, this theme was the first in a number of issues that from 1974 to the following international recession of 1975 the US Congress, some leading American policymakers and US bankers focused on. In the economic literature of the time, it was quite a widely shared view that insofar as they were unregulated, the Eurocurrency deposits caused an expansion in deposits. As neither the foreign branches of American commercial banks nor the Eurobanks in which the OPEC financial assets were deposited through the Wall Street banks were subject to any reserve requirements, the expansion in Eurodollar deposits could potentially run unchecked and skyrocket. However, owing to the investment attitude of the Eurobanks and that of the foreign branches of US resident banks involved in the recycling process, according to the US monetary and financial authorities this was unlikely to happen. The dollars deposited with the Eurobanks or in the foreign branches of US banks were assets of the depository banks that might form the basis for an extension of a dollar-denominated loan. The proceeds of such a loan, after being spent, would be deposited once more in the recipient's bank: this secondary deposit formed the basis for another loan that was the basis for another loan and further proceeds. This process of loans and deposits from the original primary deposit was the basis for such Eurodollar deposits expansion.[107] However, insofar as neither the Eurobanks re-lent their available dollar deposits or the proceeds on outstanding loans, nor did any foreign branch of US banks choose to repatriate such proceeds through the purchasing of securities from a United States resident or other investments, such process did not trigger an expansion in Eurodollar deposits. Both academics and US monetary and financial authorities debated the inflationary impact of such supposed expansion in Eurodollar deposits. This topic is all the more remarkable as it sheds light on the linkage between short-term capital markets and two important macroeconomic dynamics of the time. In the first instance, the recycling of OPEC funds in the Eurodollar market preceded the inflationary upswing recorded in the second half of 1974 and the decline in the value of the dollar in foreign exchange markets from the fall of 1974 to the beginning of 1975.[108] Secondly, as charted in this book, prior to the first increase in oil prices the development of the Eurocurrency markets anticipated the early decade upswing in short-term loan rates and commodity prices (see Chap. 3). The debate about the ratio of Eurodollar expansion to inflation and the depreciation of the dollar revolved around the linkage between the Eurodollar markets and the US money supply. As anticipated, the bulk of this debate depended on whether or not the proceeds of Eurodollar deposits and investments were repatriated. In contrast to Solomon's view, influential Austrian-American economist Fritz Machlup argued that the flow of short-term funds from the United States to the foreign countries were expansionary in themselves in that they increased US money supply.[109] Taking a perspective larger than the United States, several studies that appeared prior to the first oil crisis sought to discover how much the Eurodollar market added to the global money supply and what proportion of world inflation could be attributed to growth of that market. Besides, some scholars also linked the growth of the Eurodollar market to the US balance of payments deficit and to the changing position of the dollar in foreign exchange markets.[110] The research department of the IMF worked on the subject even as, at the highest international financial monetary diplomacy level, the Western community straddled to lay a shift in the investment patterns of the OPEC nations away from short-term investments. The IMF took a balanced view on the problem: the Eurocurrency deposits would not count as money supply, both because the larger portion was held by banks and owing to the fact that they were deposits not transferable, for the most part, by check. Reasoning along these lines, the economists of the Fund argued that the inflationary effects of the Eurocurrency deposits depended on the extent of national monetary restraints by central banks.[111]

However, although such perspective held within the IMF was widely shared, some highly influential bankers and economists working in the field of US foreign economic assistance and charged with leading some federal agencies took a different perspective on the subject. The first issue on which they focused their attention was the case of acceptance by American banks of dollar-denominated Arab deposits and the pouring of money into the Eurocurrency markets that would follow on. According to them, this process might potentially put pressure on the dollar. Reflecting on the issue in 1975, Eugene Black stressed that "the overhang of petrodollars in the Eurodollar and other related markets [...] could cause pressure on the dollar and other currencies." On the other hand, Black exhibited his palpable concern about the likely unsuccessfulness of any multilateral recycling program being discussed in 1974 and 1975 to distribute the oil producers' financial wealth across the most seriously affected oil importers. According to him, in the case that a large portion of the \$80 billion of OPEC external assets accumulated during 1974, plus some \$50 billion more accrued to the oil producers in 1975 and 1976, was not usefully invested in the Western financial and monetary system, this would cause an increase in the dollar-denominated component of world money supply. In his view such pace of events would drive down the strength of the dollar staggeringly and might destabilize further world payments. To put it another way, Black argued that the recent weakening of the dollar stemmed from the growing dollar liquidity in the international monetary system caused by the Saudis' announcement that they would accept no more sterling for their oil selling.[112]

Against the backdrop of this intense debate both in the academic environment and among the highest economic policymakers of Washington, the timeline that linked the growth of the Eurocurrency market and its loan rates prior to and after the fourfold oil price rise to the growing US balance of payments deficit, the surge in inflation, and the dwindling dollar exchange rates against all major currencies, help to best track this causal relation.[113] As detailed in this chapter and Chap. 3, from the end of convertibility to 1973 the Eurodollar loan rates steadily increased, while since early 1974 the OPEC nations placed a substantial portion of their oil revenues into the Eurocurrency markets through the largest US banks. In the spring of 1974, as the OPEC nations heavily pumped money into Eurodollar and other Eurocurrency deposits through the Wall Street banks, it was registered a downward pressure on short-term Eurodollar rates.[114] However, from the second quarter to the end of the third quarter of the year the cost of Eurodollar loans again soared at an unpaired rate.

Throughout the second half of 1974 this increase in the cost of short-term borrowings was combined with a plummeting value of the dollar in exchange markets and the onset of inflationary strains on the real economy. Insofar as the oil revenues' recycling mechanism accelerated the process of capital flows into short-term Eurodollar and other Eurocurrency markets, the dollar depreciated while prices began flaring up. Based on London mid-day rates, from October 1974 to February 1975 the dollar rates declined further,[115] while the international inflation on world commodities and consumer goods had begun. Therefore, keeping attention focused on the first half of the recycling process, one can establish a sequential correlation between the growth of the Eurocurrency deposits as a result of the reflowing of OPEC's capital surplus, the upswing in the loan rates of short-term Eurocurrency markets, the continued tottering of the dollar in foreign exchange markets, and the inflationary strains that hit the real economy and ushered in the 1975 recession. These developments had short-term consequences on the central role of the US currency to international oil payments. Until early 1975 all OPEC countries had tied the foreign exchange value of their currencies to that of the

US dollar: they fixed official buying and selling rates for their currencies against the US dollar. Therefore, they received the bulk of their payments in dollars and held most of their reserves in dollar-denominated assets, diversifying into the major continental currencies out of new revenues and without any restructuring of their existing portfolios. As the dollar plummeted, this dollar-pegged currency denomination made the OPEC nations suffer from such depreciation of the dollar. Reacting to the situation, on February 12, 1975, Iran cut its link to the dollar and established a mechanism for adjusting the riyal/dollar rate to take into account variations in the SDR value of the dollar. Soon thereafter, in March, Saudi Arabia and Qatar adopted an SDR-link, while other key oil producers as Kuwait pegged their currencies to a basket of currencies reflecting the composition of their trade.[116]

This unquestionably quick reaction from the leading capital-surplus oil producers best confirm the inflationary bias and the downward effects on the value of the dollar of short-term capital markets as a result of their constant expansion throughout 1976 and their further expansion as a result of the international reflowing of OPEC countries' capital surpluses from 1973 to the beginning of 1974. Another way to chart the inflationary implications of short-term investments by the oil-producing countries was the doldrums in which the Eurobond market, a traditional stronghold of mid-term and long-term investments much less dependent on inflation, lay over the first half of 1974: the Department of the Treasury correctly blamed its weakness on continuing inflation, high short-term interest rates, and funds more readily available on the Eurocurrency bank credit market.[117]

As pointed out above, since the beginning, the intermediary role of the largest US banks and other Western banking in rechanneling the OPEC countries' capital surplus had been as much pivotal as risky, owing to the poorly performing creditworthiness of most non-oil LDCs. For the remainder of 1974 the issue of bank exposure was deepened as a result of the multiple failures that churned the banking system across the United States and Western Europe. Reporting on the situation before the representatives of the OECD Committee on Financial Markets in September 1974, a group of Western private bankers stressed that private bank intermediaries were unwilling to take on the risk of lending to countries or companies where ultimate repayment was in doubt. They stated that bank credit flows to such areas had fallen off sharply and some withdrawals of prior commitments were reported: "banks have become increasingly reluctant to accept large deposits from OPEC sources, partly because their capital and liquidity positions have become strained and partly because of the exposure to sudden subsequent withdrawals."[118] Morgan Guarantee Vice President Rimmer de Vries went into the technicalities of this impending issue. According to a speech he gave in September 1974, the rapid pace of expansion of foreign loans undertaken by the American banks in recent months—by some $12.5 billion over the first half of the year according to his calculations—were not to continue for two fundamental reasons. On the one side he declared that the banks' normal prudential approach to risk management on the liability side of their balance sheets was increasingly inhibiting their acceptance of large short-term deposits from oil exporters, often accepted only at a discount. On the other hand, he pointed out that the banks' deposit to capital ratios was increasingly out of line, and banks were reluctant to expand their equity base at present price-earnings multiples.[119] On his part, in the summer of 1974, Bank of America President Clausen went so far as to directly call on the IMF and other official institutions to find alternative channels for recycling oil money with the aim of using the surplus of the oil producing countries to finance the deficit of oil importing nations. Without calling into question the bank exposure of American banks committed to lending to the LDCs, he made the point that a larger involvement of the international institutions in the process would ease the pressure of the recycling process on the Euromarkets.[120] In contrast to this early approach by the US banks, as already remarked in this study, over the following few years the role of commercial banks and the Eurocurrency markets in distributing the financial resources of oil producers increased in connection with the failure of international institutional arrangements set up under US leadership in order to keep the non-oil LDCs in the loop of world exchanges in goods and capital. It also increased owing to the role of American bankers in promoting financial bonds and trade partnership between the US and the oil-producing largest consumer markets.

One further problem that the 1974 recycling of OPEC's oil revenues through American commercial banks posed was the so called "maturity imbalance." This issue was the source of conflicts between OPEC members and the few leading US commercial and investment banks committed to placing their funds in international assets. In light of the development of such conflicts it is worth exploring these developments. In early July the research section of the Federal Reserve Board called attention to the oil producers that made short-term deposits in European and foreign branches of US banks mainly through the Eurodollar market. As these banks made longer-term loans to official, semi-official, and private borrowers, studies produced within the Fed underlined the "exposure of banks borrowing short loans" and lending long.[121] This mismatch between the OPEC countries and the largest commercial banks charged with investing their financial resources was all the more a sticky issue in the recycling process as over time it was not overcome. By early fall of 1974 in the Eurocurrency markets it was a widely followed practice to adjust at frequent intervals the interest rate on loans to that on deposits: this measure was thought to virtually eliminate any concern as the interest rate risk inherent in maturity imbalance appeared to be taken care of. Indeed, with an increasing differentiation in the interest rate structure, some banks at the time of renewing their deposits had to pay interest rates on deposits higher than what they could charge on existing loan contracts.[122] Besides, since the beginning any attempt by American bankers to negotiate the issue with the Arab oil producers failed. For instance, as early as spring of 1974 an unidentified large commercial bank tried to convince the OPEC investors that it was not able to accept more call money except at a discount rate from the market rate of interest; despite such pleading the OPEC countries insisted on call deposits, conceding only the possibility of accepting 6-month deposits.[123] Although the sources of debates and disputes, the mighty inflationary effects and the maturity imbalance issue triggered by the recycling of the OPEC funds into the Eurocurrency and Eurodollar markets were just two out of many issues posed by such course of the recycling process.

In fact, in 1975, nerve-racking conflicts between US banks and the OPEC countries added to a long-lasting and widely shared concern about the risk posed by sudden large-scale withdrawals by the OPEC countries from their foreign investments. In American eyes such scenario would threaten the solvency of US banks or hamper the independence of

US foreign policy. A widespread alarm about the risk of large-scale withdrawals of funds from the American banks, combined with concern that US banks might extend credit to countries which could be forced to default on these loans due to the burden of increasing oil prices, explains a long-lasting investigation initiated in April 1975 by the Subcommittee on Multinational Corporations of the Foreign Relations Committee, the so-called Church Subcommittee of the US Congress. The Subcommittee collected data from the largest US commercial banks on their foreign assets and liabilities; this collection of data, relentlessly opposed by all five largest US banks throughout the year, was clearly related to their involvement in channeling the OPEC investments into the Eurocurrency markets. It sheds light on the widespread concern in Washington about the possibility of OPEC withdrawals from their investments and deposits with the US banking system.[124] At variance with the Congress view, the Federal Reserve took a rather different position. Henry Wallich, a renowned advocate of capital market integration, tossed aside any concern about the likelihood of banking withdrawals. In addressing the Committee on Government Operations of the US Senate, he vigorously contended that fears expressed that the banking system could be threatened by sudden withdrawals by the OPEC countries were exaggerated. In explaining his opinion he argued that as the American banks suffered from such outflows, these financial assets would flow into banks of other nationalities since the owners of these funds had to deposit them somewhere: "The banks that had lost the petrodollar deposits would be able to bid for funds from the banks that had received the large and relatively sudden inflow of petrodollar deposits."[125] Irrespective of its individual members' opinions, the Federal Reserve Board pointed attention to the interbank market and the exchange rate costs of large Eurodollar selling. In so doing, the Fed wished to warn against such concern and encouraged to promote the investment of OPEC oil revenues in short-term Eurodollar assets. In addition to observing that withdrawals from dollar-denominated assets resulted in exchange costs to invest in assets denominated in currencies other than the US dollar, the Federal Reserve Board Staff noted that "if a group of large depositors withdrew their deposits from any US bank or group of banks, and transferred them to non-US banks, the banks receiving the funds will have resources to invest and may well offer them in the interbank market," suggesting that US banks could repurchase those funds in the interbank market.[126] A few years later, under the Carter administration, in light of deteriorating economic relations between the OPEC capital-surplus lending countries and Washington in the context of a dramatic depreciation of the dollar in exchange markets, the US Department of the Treasury adopted a similar approach with respect to the Iranian and other major oil producers' direct and portfolio investments in the United States. Coherently, the Carter administration made the argument that the proceeds from any divestitures of US government securities, portfolio or direct investments in the United States by the Arab oil producers could be repurchased in the interbank market.[127]

Another much-discussed issue that called into question the workability of the investments of OPEC in the Eurocurrency markets was the absence of any lender of last resort for Eurocurrency depositors in either the United States or the European countries that hosted the Eurocurrency markets. The absence of lender of last resort institutions and facilities, a long-lasting issue in the economic and political debate about the Eurocurrency markets, blew up and became a top issue in US banking circles when the Israel-British Bank of Tel Aviv defaulted in July 1974.[128] This case raised questions and concerns as to the support that central banks were ready to give since it was reported that the Israeli authorities argued that the London office was a subsidiary subject to British regulations rather than a branch controlled by the parent in Israel. Therefore, the Israelis were unwilling to provide the backing, while the Bank of England maintained that the subsidiary was indeed controlled by the parent bank in Israel, and so refused to rescue it.[129]

One more reason that undermined confidence about the involvement of American banking in recycling OPEC surpluses through the Eurodollar market as a means of financing the current account position of the non-oil producing LDCs, and of easing pressure on the US balance of payments and the dollar, was suggested by the US Comptroller General in 1979. In reckoning that the Eurodollar market was very large and efficient and posed no liquidity problem to the American banks, he stressed that the "US banks might incur the cost to the American bank of replacing deposits through borrowing on the Eurodollar market is likely to be a few basis points above the interest it would have paid on the direct deposit."[130]

Finally, but no less importantly, as already stressed in the previous pages such large-scale investments by the OPEC nations in the Eurodollar and other Eurocurrency markets hit hard the US balance of payments, the value of the dollar and the competitive edge of US manufacturing. Consider the case of the US balance of payments insofar as it is affected by repatriation of profits by US corporations' foreign investments and foreign direct investments in the United States. Based on a rough breakdown of contributions by the Middle East oil producing countries to the US balance of payments during the three years following the first increase in oil prices, the relevance of the recycling process and the shift from short-term to long-term OPEC investments from 1974 to 1975 is clear. The repatriation of profits by American oil companies in $ million peaked in 1974 as a result of the upswing in the value of oil transactions and then declined as a result of the 1975 international recession and the decline in demand for oil by the US and other advanced industrial economies.[131] In contrast, capital flows to the United States resulting from the first oil shocks had a rather different impact on the US balance of payments. In fact, apparently the flow of money to the US capital market from the Middle Eastern oil producers increased substantially from 1974 to 1975, jumping from $5.5 million to over $6.5 million. However, nearly $4 million out of $5.5 million were short-term bank deposits, which shared the largest portion of capital flows to the US.[132] Considering that a substantial fraction of it was reflowed by the US commercial and investment banks into the Eurocurrency markets through the mechanism described in this study, the picture is rather different. In a flexible exchange rate system such as the one typical of the mid-1970s, a significant flow of funds from the oil countries to the United States tended to strengthen the value of the US dollar in foreign exchange markets, to reduce interest rates in the US, and to better the purchasing power of US importers with positive effects on the competitive position of American firms in foreign markets. Such losses of short-term assets to the Euro-money markets reversed such scenario. In the floating currency system of the time the outflow of funds deposited by the oil producers in the Eurocurrency markets through the foreign subsidiaries of US banks put pressure on the dollar, weakened the US importers and plummeted further the US capital account position. On the whole, such reversal laid the groundwork for the widely known overheating of the international economy. It also complicated further Washington's long-term commitment to recast international trade and payments under a strong dollar and a stable US balance of payments.

Therefore, owing to the string of issues charted above, the recycling of the oil producing countries' oil revenues into short-term capital markets posited to the US a number of macroeconomic problems that made it increasingly difficult to draw on the OPEC oil revenues. In turn, this might complicate the attempt both to target disequilibria in the balance of payments stability of the LDCs and the hardest hit industrial nations, and to ease pressure on the US balance of payments on current account. As seen, insofar as the reflowing of the OPEC financial assets into the Eurocurrency and other short-term private capital markets triggered an upswing in the cost of borrowing for fixed capital formation and put under further strain the US currency in exchange markets, this development set the stage for the overheating of the US economy that ravaged the competitive position of US manufacturing and jeopardized the stability of international trade and payments. Therefore, not only did the ill-functioning of the recycling process through the US commercial banks fail due to the scarce creditworthiness of LDCs and the problems arising from relations with the OPEC oil producers. Indeed, it also contributed to wreck the competitive position of Western economies and to accelerate the crisis of the US dollar in international exchange markets. It would be wise to question why this process, as tracked by data about the surge in the share of Eurocurrency deposits in total foreign investments by oil producers over the rest of the decade, continued over the following years. The failure of US-led multilateral financial arrangements to take over the oil money, explored in Chap. 5, helps to better understand this point.

Against the backdrop of this jumble of problems Washington, its Western partners and the most important international organizations born out of the Bretton Woods conference discussed lengthily the problems related to recycling since as early as the oil price hikes triggered a meteoric upturn in the surplus financial assets of the oil producers.

4.6 From the Eurocurrency Markets to Long-Term Investments: Institutionalizing the Recycling Process

Therefore, since the outset, the history of the process of recycling the oil revenues was closely intertwined with that of American banking and its wealth. As anticipated in these pages, over the course of 1974 and 1975 the concentration of OPEC investments in the Eurocurrency markets and the prominent role of American commercial and investments banks in it declined, while a policy of diversification of investments gained ground. The US federal and monetary authorities charged with striking the balance between a falloff in industrial output and international trade, and the oversupply of capital that stemmed from the December 1973 fourfold increase in oil prices, concurred to set off this turn. The US authorities made a plea to the OPEC countries on the basis of the negative impacts of OPEC's short-term investments on the stability of the dollar and the international financial system, whereas the decline of the dollar in exchange markets itself and a downward pressure on their dollar-denominated international investments made the OPEC countries undertake such diversification policy.[133]

The previous section has tracked a number of issues and hindrances that stemmed from the OPEC investments in the Eurocurrency markets and other short-term assets. From the viewpoint of the US monetary authorities and American financiers, since early 1974 through the following year two diverging views had emerged. With important exceptions such as Anthony Solomon and the US Congress Church Committee, the leading economic policymakers on the Federal Reserve Board and at the Federal Reserve Bank of New York favored such course of OPEC short-term investments on the basis that it was supposed neither to put further pressure on the dollar and the US balance of payments, nor to cause large OPEC withdrawals from the US stock and securities markets. Furthermore, they assumed that the Federal Reserve Bank and other central banks could do some market interventions as lenders of last resort to the commercial and investment banks that traded in the Eurocurrency markets in case of need. On the other hand, from the viewpoint of American financiers largely involved in the history of financial assistance to the non-oil producing LDCs like Bank of America President Clausen, as well as other high-ranking officials of the largest commercial banks involved in reflowing the assets deposited by OPEC into the Eurocurrency markets like De Vries, as early as the fall of 1974 the recycling of OPEC deposits into short-term assets looked like an experiment close to termination. The string of banking failures that churned away at US national and regional banks such as Franklin National Bank of New York , as well as European giants such as Herstatt, from the fall of 1973 through 1975, the issue of banks' exposure to non-oil producing LDCs borrowers, and the stiff controversy with the OPEC countries over the so-called maturity imbalance issue pushed American bankers to call for terminating such a transnational flow of funds.[134] As a result of diminished confidence in the stability of the international money markets, after the collapse of Herstatt and Franklin banks, the third and fourth quarters of 1974 showed a decline in both US banks' lending and Eurocurrency credits.[135] On his part, in early 1975 de Vries repeated once more, that "in the last part of 1974, banks were no longer willing or able to provide anywhere near the portion of the financing required by oil-importing countries that they did earlier in the year."[136] Moreover, from the standpoint of the US balance of payments deficit financing policies, American bankers argued that such reflowing patterns drove further down the value of the dollar in exchange markets and contributed to the upswing movements in the international commodity and consumer goods prices and in the cost of money for productive investments. These concerns were palpably exhibited by bankers formerly working for the federal agencies such as Eugene Black for the destabilizing inflationary and monetary effects of growing capital flows into short-term assets: his viewpoint helps track this widely advocated disappointment within the Washington elites. Such widespread disappointments and worries about the financial and macroeconomic effects of short-term investments represented the first cause for a shift in the policy of the US monetary authorities toward the OPEC countries. During the second half of 1974 and the following two years Washington made arrangements to convince its closest OPEC members to make a shift from highly liquid short-term investments to long-term investments: investments should be directed into the equity markets of the United States and western Europe, and in public and private security markets, and portfolio investments.

This shift came about through attempts to set up institutional arrangements arranged by the Washington elites and their European partners, especially Germany, to lock such change in the investment patterns by the OPEC nations into multilateral financial arrangements to be established under the aegis of existing institutions like the IBRD, the IMF or the multilateral regional institutions. Considering the steady development of OPEC resources reflowing into the Eurocurrency markets over the rest of the decade, it is worth charting this American strategy and its demise. This is in order to even better understand the uneven long-lasting development of OPEC investments in the Euro-money markets all along the decade. This section explores the interaction between the OPEC countries' inclination to make direct loans to the non-oil LDCs and to invest in the equity and security markets of Western nations, and such attempt by the Western elites, particularly the US Department of the Treasury, the Federal Reserve Board, and the IMF, to reposition OPEC's investments into long-term assets through institutionalized multilateral entities. This dispute is placed within the framework of a persistent and much-heralded US need to ease off the pressure of development assistance to the non-oil LDCs on the dollar and US balance of payments.

The second cause for such a shift in the way in which the OPEC countries' oil revenues were reinvested was a pressing need by the US to finance its current account deficit through a rise in US export and investments to the largest absorbing OPEC countries. Reducing the portion of the OPEC foreign investments to total surplus oil revenues and increasing the disposable liquidity of OPEC countries was certainly a move in this direction. The more the OPEC nations invested in long-term financial instruments in the United States, such as equity and portfolio investments, and the largest the portion of oil revenues they retained and added to their liquidity, the more US export to and commercial bonds with the LDCs could develop in the framework of an increased purchasing power by the LDCs in the US market.

This chapter has stressed that the largest American commercial banks became involved in reflowing the oil revenues into short-term Euro-money markets and, through them, in supporting the non-oil LDCs' current account deficit since as early as the OPEC's far-reaching capital surplus outstripped demand for fixed capital formation in early 1974. By that time, Washington held a two-pronged approach to the recycling of the oil revenues; as the Department of the Treasury pointed out in early March 1974, over the next few years the OPEC capital-surplus countries were expected to provide a substantial amount of concessionary aid to the non-oil LDCs. In this perspective, it was worth devising some forms of institutional arrangements in cooperation with the EEC in order to offer new help to the LDCs within the framework of existing international organizations as the IMF, the World Bank and the EEC. The first point was at the top of the US agenda in negotiating with the OPEC countries their international investments during the following years. In placing such importance on this point, Washington assumed that to "many of the poorer LDCs who are hard hit and who do not have access to world capital markets" such financing was meaningful only on highly concessionary terms.[137] The latter issue was more short-lived; by the time President Ford left the White House the OPEC nations had relentlessly shown their unwillingness to channel their resources under US and Western leadership. Under the Carter administration the role of IBRD and IMF in the recycling process was revamped and it was much discussed in the setting up of co-financing schemes involving both private capital and public international organizations. However, Washington's attempts to institutionalize the recycling process deserves a thorough investigation as it began prior to the development of the Eurocurrency markets described in the previous pages and developed further after the US commercial and investment banks showed their recalcitrance to share the costs and risks of channeling the "energy finance" in view of the extremely fragile international banking environment characteristic of 1974. In addition, such attempt to institutionalize the recycling process overlapped with the OPEC's oil producing countries move to shift their investments from short-term loans to long-term financial instruments. Furthermore, such American position combined with the early activism by some leading oil producing countries, which on the one side went their own way on investing their oil surplus on the international bond and securities markets of either the developing or industrial nations; on the other, oil producers made efforts to set up brand-new large multilateral arrangements in partnership with the US and OECD. The case of Iran's proposal for a multilateral development fund tackled below highlights the aspiration of Teheran to exploit the oil revenues issue in order to establish a special bilateral relationship with the OECD and its community of member nations.

It is important to consider this string of efforts by the United States to place the issue of the non-oil LDCs in the framework of Washington's differing strategies to ease off the US capital account deficit and to halt a weakening dollar from bearing the cost of recasting the international trade and payments system, and to prevent the non-oil LDCs from sliding away from it. Owing to the aforementioned number of issues and hindrances that channeling the financial resources of OPEC through commercial and investment banks posed, as early as January 1974 at the highest economic diplomacy level the advanced industrial economies and some leading supranational organizations began debating and negotiating the most suitable way to drain the flow of oil money into short-term liquid assets. The very topical issue was how to make a shift in the investment patterns of the OPEC nations towards long-term investments bound to be better placed to uphold the terms of trade of the non-oil producing LDCs and the current account deficit of the industrial economies that suffered the most from the increase in oil prices.

Since its inception, this turn in investment patterns took place in the framework of soon-institutionalized multilateral financing schemes. As early as February 1974 the IMF, and some leading multilateral regional banks as the Inter-American Bank and the Asian Development Bank "agreed in principle to a joint approach of our institutions to OPEC countries with view of exploring possibilities of utilizing existing financial institutions as intermediaries for channeling excess OPEC resources into development financing."[138] The first one and best-known in order of appearance was the so-called IMF oil facility. Within the framework of a joint declaration by the IMF's Committee on Reform of the International Monetary System and Related Issues, the so-called Committee of Twenty (C-20), gathered in Rome in early 1974 to discuss a pressing need for closer international cooperation in connection with the oil crisis[139]; the creation of the oil facility was first proposed by the IMF before the Committee, from which it received approval, in January 1974.[140] The

IMF oil facility was thought to be a financial fund, related to oil deficits, on which all deficit countries, both industrial and developing nations, might draw to cover those deficits. Apparently, based on the early story of this facility OPEC appeared inclined to cooperate with Washington in shaping the recycling process. After lengthy negotiations, the OPEC countries finally agreed on providing their financial assistance to the facility since its creation, with a contribution of some $3.5 billion, at the less-than-market rate of 7 percent. Indeed, such amount would be equal to the needs of the non-oil producing developing countries.[141] The first proposal elaborated by the IMF Managing Director Witteveen in January and February of 1974 was aimed at providing temporary and limited assistance for developed and less developed countries facing difficult financial prospects due to the oil price rise, with the amount a country could borrow determined by a formula based on increased oil costs, reserves and IMF quotas. On behalf of the US government, Paul Volcker opposed this proposal since the beginning. In February he told Witteveen that "the United States' main reservation about the proposal concerned the ability of poorer countries to repay." In his view the proposal did not meet the need of hard-pressed LDCs with limited debt service capacity for highly concessional assistance.[142] In so doing, he exhibited Washington's constant and repeated concern for the implications of the increases in oil prices on the LDCs and their full participation to the existing system of international trade and payments. Volcker's position also sheds light on the US firm call on the OPEC countries to offer concessional assistance. It was only with Witteveen's trip to the Middle East in April 1974 that the US government and the IMF convincingly began straddling to attract the OPEC nations' financial assets into long-term financing schemes. Such arrangements had the primary objective of offsetting the effects of the oil crisis on the LDCs' current account deficit, and relieving the US balance of payments on capital account from bearing the cost of it. In turn, this was essential in order to sustain the non-oil LDCs' import of manufactured goods from the industrial nations and their export of commodities to Western Europe. Therefore, the oil facility highlights the close intertwining between the US effort to establish multilateral recycling schemes and the upmost American support for the LCDs' international payments position. In the pursuit of this objective, Witteveen broadened his institutional bonds with the Middle Eastern OPEC producers. Prior to Witteveen's visit to the Middle East, during bilateral meetings with high-ranking officials of the IMF, several low-absorbing oil producing countries, including Kuwait, the United Arab Emirates (UAE), Libya and to a lesser extent Saudi Arabia, had reacted positively to the prospect of financing the IMF but insisted on both the commercial attractiveness of lending to the Fund, and their aspiration to get greater voting power in the Fund. The Government and the Central Bank of Iran itself showed their propensity to finance the facility and to accept some sacrifices with respect to interest rates. Since these early negotiations, the government of Iran and the Governor of the Bank Markazi showed a position much more pro-Western, exhibiting their efforts to reach agreements, compared to other OPEC nations.[143] During his visit to the Middle East, Witteveen reached important agreements but also faced a number of hindrances and disappointments on the part of other key oil producing nations. The two most important countries at the center of his trip were Kuwait and Saudi Arabia. Reporting to the Executive Board of the Fund upon his return from the Middle East, Witteveen stated that all the oil producing countries with which he spoke expressed their willingness to cooperate with the Fund to assist in the financing of the projected balance of payments deficit of oil-importing nations. On that occasion he settled agreements with Saudi Arabia for the equivalent of SDR 1 billion loan at 7 percent, and for smaller amounts with Kuwait, Libya, and the United Arab Emirates. The claim on the Fund would be expressed in SDRs valued in terms of a basket of currencies, an arrangement bound both to protect lenders from further downswings that might occur in the value of the dollar, and to prevent the financing of the IMF oil facility from expanding the dollar component of world money supply: a dynamic that in turn would nurture the depreciation of the US currency.[144] In either case, the oil facility was thought to support the dollar in foreign exchange markets without letting the balance of payments deficit of the non-oil producing LDCs run unchecked. Indeed, the birth of the oil facility was laborious due to skepticism by both Volcker and other Washington high-ranking monetary policymakers about its likely impact on the non-oil LDCs. Furthermore, key lenders such as Kuwait took a hard stance. Irrespective of the amount on which it reached agreements with Witteveen, over the course of their bilateral meetings with him, the government of Kuwait and the governor of Kuwaiti Central Bank opposed large-scale lending and called into question the terms of their economic relations with both the Fund and the leading industrial nations. Such a tough position anticipated the country's stance a few years later under the Carter administration, which is explored in the next chapter. In 1974, the Kuwaiti Prime Minister called on the Fund to get assurances that there would be satisfactory investment outlets when lending countries came to be repaid, while the Minister of Finance and Oil Al-Ateeqy firmly opposed large-scale lending to the Fund. In taking such a harsh stance, Al-Ateeqy stated that the World Bank and other leading development assistance institutions were portraying the Arabs "as devils" irrespective of their constructive cooperation; he stressed that Kuwait was already extending a lot of bilateral assistance and was making its surplus available to the world economy through a substantial level of foreign investments.[145] Therefore, the creation of multilateral arrangements to channel the financial assets accruing to the oil producing countries to the LDCs and the deficit industrial nations through a substantial shift in their investments patterns from short-term lending through the private capital markets to long-term investments was difficult and teetered on multiple occasions. It raised the issue of reshuffling the conditions for a well-functioning trade and payments system through the institutions of Bretton Woods. At the same time it highlighted the long-term US objective of drawing on the OPEC financial resources to ease off the US balance of payments from bearing the hammering cost of recasting the system of international commerce and finance. In contrast to the oil producers' attitude to make investments into the Eurocurrency and other short-term private capital markets, the government of Washington identified with the Bretton Woods' sister institutions the ideal existing venues to redirect the investments of the oil producing countries into long-term financial assets. As early as January 1974, under guidance of Witteveen, the IMF fine-tuned the creation of an Extended Fund facility to provide resources with extended maturity and in larger amounts for serious payments imbalances and structural maladjustments with repayments in three years following a four-year grace period: a maturity structure that was clearly premised over longer-term lending on the part of the OPEC countries.[146] The project was successful and the IMF could secure financial resources for the following years from the Arab oil producing countries, in particular from the Saudi Arabian Monetary Authority (SAMA), the Central Bank of the Kingdom of Saudi Arabia, and the main repositories of the country's oil revenues.[147] Consistently with this approach, during the following three years the Fund managed to set up a number of financial arrangements to provide the LDCs with long-term lending. This was the case of the Supplementary Financing facility to be funded by the OPEC countries discussed in 1977 and fiercely opposed by some private investment bankers whom, relieved from the 1974 banking failures, identified in it an obstacle to their investments. The Supplementary facility, finally funded by Libya, Saudi Arabia and Kuwait, was thought by the Fund to "provide exactly the sort of longer-term scope for adjustment that is desired" for the LDCs.[148] Despite most oil producing countries showed their recalcitrance to lock their money into institutional arrangements under US leadership and straddled to invest long through investments in the equity and security markets of the West, to some extent they trusted the recycling mechanism built up under the aegis of the IMF. This was, for instance, the case of the Fund's second oil facility set up in 1975, the investment approach of Kuwait since its oil revenues skyrocketed, or that underpinning the Iranian proposals to channel the OPEC nations' oil revenues within the framework of multilateral schemes involving the OPEC and the OECD nations. As for the second oil facility, the case of Saudi Arabia is striking: from early on in the negotiations the Saudis saw no objections to lending to the IMF oil facility throughout 1975 and favored the Fund as a recycler of their assets. At the same time they firmly opposed some proposals put forward by the US and the OECD to fund a sort of safety net for the industrialized oil importing countries in support for their purchasing power in the international commodity markets and their import of commodities from the non-oil producing LDCs.[149] Kuwait itself, since as early as the late winter of 1974 showed its inclination to provide the non-oil producing LDCs with bilateral assistance or to cooperate with the IBRD.[150]

Consistently with the Fund, the World Bank itself had made early moves to draw on the oil producing countries' surpluses to provide near-concessionary assistance to the non-oil producing LDCs. As early as January 1974, IBRD President McNamara had proposed Kuwait, Saudi Arabia and Iran to finance the Bank's long-term borrowings.[151] Over the course of the spring, in the Western world a string of proposals were elaborated to make the mounting financial assets of OPEC compensate for the shaking rise in the current account imbalances of the LDCs and of some oil-scarce industrial nations, most notably Italy, the UK and Japan, such as the EEC's Commission proposal to establish a one-shot fund worth up to $3 billion designed to provide concessional assistance to the poorest oil importing LDCs.[152] On its part, the IBRD ventured on fine-tuning some financial arrangements to finance its development assistance programs through OPEC. As early as April the Washington-based institution had already reached agreements to secure the purchases of IBRD bonds by Libya, Iran, Venezuela and Oman.[153] At the same time, the IBRD engaged in discussions and plans aimed at shaping the most suitable ways "to provide assistance to developing countries in order to prevent the disruption of their development programs by higher oil prices." While the Bank called on the IMF to help them tide over the LDCs' balance of payments difficulties stemming from the oil crisis, it shaped a plan to establish a Special Fund financed and under the policy control of the OPEC countries. According to the project crafted within the IBRD, such Special Fund would be administered by the Bank under guidelines of all OPEC contributors and designed to provide assistance on concessional terms with a five-year grace period and a 15-year repayment period to developing countries as an alternative to the issuing of IBRD bonds and to an increase in the LDCs capital subscriptions.[154]

According to IBRD data, during the first 8 months of the year, commitments and disbursements to the IBRD by the oil producing countries through the purchases of IBRD bonds amounted to $1 billion and circa $7 billion respectively.[155]

Therefore, based on these efforts by the IMF and the IBRD, the search by the United States and the Bretton Woods institutions for multilateral recycling schemes under an institutional umbrella were aimed both at securing development financial assistance to the non-oil LDCs, and at triggering a shift in the investment patterns of the OPEC members from highly liquid placements into long-term capital markets.

In fact, owing to large investments in short-term Euro-money assets that drove the OPEC countries investment attitudes throughout the second and third quarter of 1974,[156] these early moves to institutionalize the reflowing of their assets in order to cope with the outburst of the LDCs' current account deficit and to prevent the US balance of payments from bearing the cost of adjusting the international payments system, contributed little to the recycling process. As seen in this book, the linkage between the OPEC countries capital surplus and the largest US banks that traded on the Eurocurrency markets was the pivot of the recycling process. At the same time, as detailed here, the soon process of institutionalization met opposition by a number of key oil producers that contributed to delay its introduction.

All institutional and financial arrangements discussed and negotiated during the spring within the IMF or the IBRD entailed long-term concessional assistance funded through the oil revenues that piled up on the OPEC nations' bank accounts: they were aimed at locking such assistance into either an institutional framework or a structure of bonds and securities tapped by the two Washington-based international economic institutions.

By the early summer the US commercial banks began suffering from the string of bank failures that had begun since the fall of 1973 and put pressure on the banks' capacity to bear responsibility for channeling the OPEC countries' resources. The situation was complicated by widespread risks for trade and payments restrictions: in early June the IMF's ad hoc Committee on Reform of the International Monetary System and Related Issues stressed the importance of avoiding the escalation of restrictions on trade and payments for balance of payments purposes.[157] In this context the international debate about the setting up of institutional recycling arrangements and a better coordination between the maturity of investments and needs of the LDCs intensified. This debate demonstrates further that the struggle to build up a multilateral reflowing of the OPEC financial resources was intended in Washington to serve the twofold aim of bolstering long-term capital markets and fueling financial assistance to the non-oil LDCs. In early July 1974, over the course of bilateral US–UK meetings, the government of London suggested that a big multilateral facility be established to issue high-yielding interest rates to the Middle Eastern oil producers.[158]

According to London's Foreign Office, the collapse of Herstatt in Germany had led many investors to shift their investments to London and New York; that process coincided with considerable sales of gilt-edged securities by the authorities in London. Based on such view by the British authorities that these investment patterns were a sign that the OPEC nations were investing their surpluses in long-term British securities, it is possible to argue that the Middle East oil producers began shifting their placements as early as that period of the year. Within this framework, both at the highest diplomatic level and among Washington's monetary elites charged with international financial matters, pressure to pour the financial resources of OPEC into long-term investments began in early summer. In June, although the former was less pessimistic about the strength and functioning of the Eurocurrency markets than the latter,[159] the British Prime Minister Harold Wilson together with US Vice President Nelson Rockefeller agreed on favoring the Arab oil producers interested in long-term investments of their surpluses in other forms of energy. In early July, US Secretary of State Kissinger told the British Prime Minister that although Washington was about to set up bilateral commissions with some oil producing countries, in particular Saudi Arabia, he strongly supported a multilateral approach to coordinate the pumping of the OPEC's capital surplus into transnational capital supply and in order to support the current account deficit of the non-oil LDCs. This was in view of the effects of the increases in oil prices on the aggregate demand and growth rates of developed nations.[160] At the same time, the German government showed its increasing nervousness about the capacity of the Eurodollar market to distribute the oil money: by the early summer the Germans had revised somewhat their earlier relaxed attitude concerning the Eurodollar market's ability to handle the OPEC countries' short-term investments.[161] In 1974, the issue of drawing on the OPEC financial assets to recast the growth rates of the industrial nations was not quite as far at the top of the agendas of Washington's economic policymakers as it would be under the Carter administration. At this time the Ford administration focused most attention on the current account deficit of the non-oil producing LDCs. However, since the summer of 1974 the falloffs in growth rates and aggregate demand were already a timely issue insofar as most oil importing developing and developed nations reacted to the first oil shock by upholding their pre-oil-shock growth rates. In pursuit of this target, they engaged in expansionary policies to uphold consumption levels and accelerated external borrowing: this policy eventually resulted in increased budget deficit, and upswings in current account imbalances, as well as soaring inflation.[162] The shift of OPEC assets from highly liquid and inflation-sensitive financial instruments to long-term deposits was essential to supply fixed-term capital yielding stable returns ideal to finance fixed-capital investment and to uphold consumption levels. Therefore, in the Western world these debates and policies to create a shift in the investment patterns of the OPEC countries from short- to long-term assets was bound to make up for the downward business cycle caused by capital market developments and the oil shock. The concept resorted to demand side policies, with full support for international financial policies aimed at striking the balance between transnational capital flows and domestic aggregate demand in the industrial economies. As suggested in Chap. 5, under the Carter administration this objective became a top priority foreign economic policy target. Prior to that, it had been part of a general policy in Washington to avert the LDCs from sliding away from the global system of international trade and payments. Over the course of the summer of 1974 such discussions on the international investments of OPEC led Washington and its Western partners to devise a string of projects. For instance, following a first proposal, which appeared as early as March, in July the Shell Oil Company discussed with the BIS a plan to have the BIS serve as a sort of clearing house for oil payments that would prevent the oil surpluses from going into the hands of commercial banks and would reduce the volume of dollar-denominated oil payments, thus curbing the effects of oil trade on the international supply of dollars and its stability in exchange markets.[163]

Notwithstanding these early plans to pour the OPEC surplus into long-term financial instruments, over the course of summer the firmest stance against the recycling of OPEC assets through private commercial banks was taken by the Federal Reserve Bank of New York. The Fed was concerned not so much about the implications of recycling the oil revenues through inflation-sensitive liquid placements on the economic stability of the oil importing countries. Rather, the most pressing concern in

New York was the difficulty and danger of financing very large balance of payments deficits through short-term financing, especially in light of the recent falloff in foreign exchange transactions, which declined by 30–50 percent since the collapse of Herstatt. Reasoning along the lines of the BIS project, the Fed called for a greater role by central banks and encouraged the oil producers to invest in US government securities and other Western bond and securities markets, while for his part Rockefeller consistently pleaded for the setting up of some form of official recycling.[164]

In the same way as the Fed's proposal, the Department of the Treasury called on the oil producing countries to increase their investments in US government securities to bolster the supply of capital within the US economy. Unlike the Fed's ambition to attract the oil producing countries to fuel the US balance of payments deficit, during his July visit to the Middle East, US Secretary of the Treasury George Simon did his best to convince the Arab oil producing nations to invest in non-marketable US government securities with the aim of lessening the Federal Government's demand for funds in the domestic market and to make more credit available to private borrowers.[165]

By late summer, this turn to stem the shift in the investment patterns of the oil producing countries to long-term financial instruments in support for the capital supply side coincided with a wide-ranging awareness about the growing reluctance and unsuitability of private capital markets, as well as a pressing need to set up some form of capital controls and surveillance.[166] In fact, American commercial bankers relentlessly repeated their unwillingness to bear the cost of recycling even as the Federal Reserve Bank of New York and the Comptroller of the Currency pressed them to adopt a much more strict lending policy and to scrutinize the creditworthiness of borrowers.[167]

Likewise, a similar approach focused on fostering a shift in investment patterns gained momentum on the opposite shores of the Atlantic Sea. The British government made a case for better tailoring the international investments of the OPEC nations to the imbalances that strained the oil consuming nations at the end of the summer of 1974. During a late September meeting with Kissinger, UK Secretary of State for Foreign and Commonwealth Affairs James Callaghan reckoned the important role that was played by both the national financial markets of London and New York, and the Eurocurrency markets in offering a wide range of flexible investment instruments to the large flow of oil money that was moving into their markets. At the same time, he called for greater surveillance of the Eurocurrency markets along the lines set out in the September 9 meeting of BIS central banks' governors. Moreover, he pointed to the pressing need to let consumer countries with mounting balance of payments deficit "have access to the funds locked in New York," stressing that "some means will have to be found of recycling these funds."[168] At the same time, more importantly, Callaghan made his case for setting up some functioning multilateral arrangements to overcome the recycling of OPEC resources through the intermediation of Western private capital markets: "I did not think it is satisfactory in the long-term that Arab funds should flow into London and, more particularly, into America, [...], nor were bilateral deals between an individual producer and an individual consumer a sufficient answer. I thought that there must be some intermediary organization sufficiently attractive to the producers, which would bear the main responsibility of recycling funds."[169]

During the fall of 1974, from the Chairman of the Board of Governors of the Federal Reserve System Arthur Burns to the Bundesbank's highest-ranking officers, a cohort of central bankers called Western governments to focus their attention on narrowing the burden of payments imbalances through a reduction in the price of oil, rather than on the recycling of petrodollars.[170] Meanwhile, at the highest diplomatic level the debate about the institutionalization of OPEC's foreign exchange surpluses and their investments in long-term financial instruments in the Western world developed further. Within the Ford administration, there was an intense dispute over the issue of whether borrowings by the IBRD from the OPEC countries increased the influence of OPEC on the Bank's decisions on loans, or whether it was a Bank's instrument to persuade the poorest oil producing countries to commit to offset arrangements, such as bond purchases, as a conditions for receiving these loans. Afterward, all federal agencies represented in the US National Advisory Council on International Monetary and Financial Policies (NAC) shared the view "that the OPEC countries should increase their purchase of shares in the

Bank but this should be conditioned on the undertaking to make associated commensurate contributions of concessional funds to IDA," the World Bank's branch specializing in concessional development finance.[171] On the other hand, the IMF took a step further: in his wide range of contacts with the highest US policymakers, IMF Managing Director Witteveen stressed that any Fund's financial facility was to reach the twin target of creating a shift in the investment patterns of the OPEC countries and preventing private capital markets from taking the lead in channeling the oil revenues. The Managing Director made his stance clear in September to Secretary of the Treasury Simon: his proposal for a second oil facility funded by the Fund's members placed the bulk of the default risk of borrowers on the IMF's largest shareholders and gave the oil producers an attractive, guaranteed asset. At the same time it lessened the pressure on them to provide concessional assistance. In so doing, the scheme allowed the oil producers to bypass the risks inherent in dealing with private market and tended "to short-circuit the private market's role in recycling and emphasize official financing."[172] By the first half of 1975 only some high-ranking officers in the Department of State, and Arthur Burns, were still concerned about the political implications on the US foreign policy and the OECD countries as a whole of direct borrowings from these countries. Such concern led, for instance, Thomas Enders, Under Secretary of State for Economic and Business Affairs, to continue his support for OPEC investments in the Western private capital markets and to bid for making the OECD Financial Support Fund, an OECD facility established to offset its member countries' payments imbalances, tap the private market to finance its emergency activities.[173]

In light of these mounting pressures to induce the OPEC nations to shift their investments from short-term instruments to less liquid long-term assets, and as a reaction to the recalcitrance of American banks to bear thc burden of the recycling process in support for the LDCs imbalances, the Unites States made a case for institutionalizing the reflowing of the oil revenues. This was in order to shape twin assistance programs directed to relieve both the LDCs and the heaviest affected industrial economies from the effect of the oil price increase on their purchasing power in foreign markets. Speaking in Chicago in mid-November 1974,

Kissinger proposed to set up a new financial mechanism in association with the OECD to provide stand-by financial support to any participating country in trouble. At the same time he made a case for setting up a Special Trust Fund managed by the IMF to help developing countries that were suffering the most and necessitated financing on concessionary terms. Kissinger's concept of "financial solidarity" among consumer nations was intended to reckon the role that private financial institutions had played so far in redistributing the OPEC funds so as to meet the needs of the industrial and the developing countries, and to buttress these efforts through central banks cooperation. The US diplomat called on its Western partners' monetary authorities and governments to establish a common law and guaranty facility to redistribute up to $25 billion in 1975 and as much as necessary over the following year. This special fund would be a multilateral framework involving the industrial economies but it was not thought to be an institution. In other words, in his plan, rather than an entity to be funded through taxes, he thought about a mechanism for recycling, at commercial interest rates, funds flowing back to the industrial world from the oil producers. In making a case for creating such a Fund, Kissinger's objective was to protect the stability of the international financial system, the creditworthiness of participating governments, the purchasing power and terms of trade of the non-oil producing LDCs and, last but not least, to complement the role of private capital markets with a multilateral scheme.[174] In elaborating his proposal, clearly Kissinger reckoned at the same time the role so far played by the private banking system and the ill-functioning of purely institutional arrangements in stabilizing international payments between developed and developing nations and in striking the balance between capital supply and growth rates within the Western world. A few days after Kissinger's proposal the Secretary of the Treasury Simon clarified that the objective was to maintain open economies at appropriate levels of activity any time the international private financial system proved to be unable to sustain needed credit, assuming the pivotal role of the non-oil LDCs in order to attain such objective.[175] As at the top-ranking US economic policymaking level, the non-oil LDCs was a theme that soon thereafter, in spring 1975, led Kissinger's approach to stabilize the international economy at the United Nations. At that venue, he repeatedly stressed the unmistakable importance of development finance to the stability of the international system. In the winter of 1974, the creation of a mutual financial support fund among the major industrial countries and a trust fund for the LDCs was discussed in the Group of Ten (G-10) machinery, with the US preferring the establishment of such a new fund over the extension of existing IMF facilities such as the second Witteveen oil facility.[176] It is important to note the continued search for institutional arrangements to channel the OPEC nations' financial resources in the fall and winter. Either the British government, or the private banking institutions proposed by the Germans, as well as this twin proposal to target the global consequences of the increases in oil prices both in the LDCs and in the advanced economies of the West, represented different projects to replace the role of the largest US banks with a tight institutional environment locked in the postwar Western institutions. Furthermore—and more importantly—with the reflowing of OPEC funds through Wall Street, the involvement of the IMF and other institutions was to ease the capital account component of the US balance of payments from the effect of Washington's commitment to pour money into the LDCs.

To round off, it is important to stress that as much as the development of the OPEC's investments into the Eurocurrency markets after 1974 helped track the failure of the multilateral institutional arrangements explored in this section, and the US recycling policy, the continued quest of the Ford administration, the IMF, the IBRD and the BIS to establish such schemes sheds some light on the widespread conviction in Washington that the meteoric expansion in the OPEC members' capital surplus was a unique opportunity to target the long unmet twofold American objective. More precisely, in straddling to channel OPEC's financial assets, Washington aimed at recasting the US international payments position and the dollar's strength in foreign exchange markets without letting the non-oil LDCs slip away from world trade and payments. This was a prerequisite to prevent the developing nations of the globe from retrenching into protectionist national economic policies detrimental to the Western nations' foreign trade and wealth.

Notes

1. Rockefeller Archive Center, Tarrytown, NY (Henceforth RAC), Rockefeller Family Archive (henceforth RFA), Record Group 3 (Henceforth RG3), 4 A (N. A. Rockefeller Personal), A-Activities, b. 162, fold. 1805, "OPEC Surpluses and the Disequilibrium in International Payments"; World Bank Group Archives, Washington, DC (henceforth WBGA), Records of General Vice Presidents and Managing Directors, Records of Sir Denis Rickett, Oil and Energy, Memos and Reports, 1973 through 1974, Volume 1, IBRD Commodities and Export Projections Division, Economic Analysis and Projections Department, Development Policy Staff, "The Financial Consequences of Rising Trend in Petroleum Prices for Developing Countries 1970–1985," December 4, 1973, pp. 17–18.
2. National Archives and Records Administration, Archive II, College Park, MD (henceforth NARA), General Records of the Department of Commerce (henceforth RG40), Office of the Secretary, Executive Secretariat's Subject File 1953–1974, b. 309, fold. Commerce Action Group on the Near East (DIB), "The Near East Markets. A Report to the US Business," prepared by BIC Near East Study Group, p. 4, May 17, 1974.
3. On the mismatch between capital flows and GDP growth see Library of Congress, Manuscript Division, Washington, DC (henceforth LOC), Elliot Richardson papers, Part I, b. 292, fold. OECD, "Statement by the Under Secretary Elliot L. Richardson at the OECD Ministerial Meeting," Paris, February 13, 1969. For a theoretical fine-tuning on the interconnectedness between transnational capital supply and domestic investments and growth see Kindleberger, 1987, p. 14. See also id., 1978, pp. 207–209. For an overview of the macroeconomic framework in the US and international financial developments see Department of the Treasury, 1972.
4. The economic and historical literature on the petrodollar cycle of the 1970s has by and large focused attention on this side of the recycling process. See, for instance, El-Gamal and Jaffe, 2010, p. 29.
5. Federal Reserve Bank of New York Historical Archive, New York City (henceforth FRBNYA), Central Files, b. 107333.
6. NARA, General Records of the Department of State (henceforth RG59), Bureau of Near Eastern and South Asian Affairs, Office of Arabian Peninsula Affairs, Records Relating to Saudi Arabia 1955–1974, b. 7, fold. PG and AP Econ-PET-Petroleum General, Department of State, "American Economic Opportunities in Arab Oil States," 1973.

7. The National Archives, Kew, Richmond (henceforth TNA), FCO 82/466, Meeting between James Callaghan, Secretary of State for Foreign Commonwealth Affairs and Dr. Henry Kissinger, US Secretary of State, 1974, Secretary of State Discussions with Dr. Kissinger in New York, "Recycling the Financial Surpluses of Oil Producers," September 24, 1974.
8. NARA, General Records of the Department of the Treasury (henceforth RG56), Office of the Assistant Secretary for International Affairs (henceforth OASIA), Subject Files of the Office of International Monetary Affairs 1968–1978, b. 3, fold. Eurodollars, Statement by Fred H. Klopstock (International Research Department, Federal Reserve Bank of New York) before the Subcommittee on International Exchange and Payments of the Joint Economic Committee, June 22, 1971.
9. NARA, RG59, Bureau of Near Eastern and South Asian Affairs, Office of Arabian Peninsula Affairs, Records Relating to Saudi Arabia 1955–1974, b. 5, fold. Saudi Arabia Economic FN Finance-General 1970, Memorandum of Conversation Cedric Grant (First National City Bank Jidda Branch)—Roger B. Merrick (Commercial Attaché (US Embassy), January 17, 1970.
10. NARA, RG56, OASIA, Subject Files of the Office of International Monetary Affairs 1968–1978, b. 3, fold. 1, T. Nelson to Under Secretary Volcker "Euro-dollar Interest Rates," January 27, 1971.
11. See, generally, NARA, RG56, OASIA, Subject Files of the Office of International Monetary Affairs 1968–1978, b. 7, fold. 4, IMF, "Ability of Private Financial Markets to Handle OPEC Surpluses," January 28, 1975.
12. See respectively Westra, 2010, p. 190, and Board of Governors of the Federal Reserve System, 1976, table 15.24, pp. 1035–1047.
13. NARA, RG59, Bureau of Near Eastern and South Asian Affairs, Office of Arabian Peninsula Affairs, Records Relating to Saudi Arabia 1955–1974, b. 5, fold. Saudi Arabia Def 191970 Military Assistance and Sales-US-General, Richard Murphy (Office of Arabian Peninsula Affairs), to Francois M. Dickman, telegram, July 20, 1970.
14. NARA, RG59, Bureau of Near Eastern and South Asian Affairs, Office of Arabian Peninsula Affairs, Records Relating to Saudi Arabia 1955–1974, b. 4, fold. Saudi Arabia Pet-Petroleum General 1969, Department of State, "A Policy for Selective Import of Mid-East Oil," p. 5; *ibid.*, Harold H. Saunders, Memorandum for Mr. Sisco, "Iran and Oil," November 5, 1969.

15. NARA, RG56, OASIA, Subject Files of the Deputy Assistant Secretary for Developing Nations Finance 1976–1977, b. 3, fold. Boards, Committees, Organizations, Panels, Working Groups, National Security Council (H. Kissinger), National Security Decision Memorandum 92, "US Policy Toward the Persian Gulf," November 7, 1970.
16. NARA, RG56, OASIA, Chronological Files of the Office of Financial Resources and Energy Finance 1974–1977, b. 1, Briefing Paper, "Oil Producing Governments' External Investment of Surplus Revenue," January 15, 1975.
17. Department of Commerce, 1973, p. 41.
18. Federal Reserve System, 1971, pp. 16–20.
19. Department of the Treasury, 1973, p. 46.
20. NARA, RG56, OASIA, Chronological Files of the Office of Financial Resources and Energy Finance 1974–1977, b. 2, fold. OASIA/OFREF Perm. Chron. OCT 1976, Robert M. Dunn and Sara Krulwich, "The Petrodollar Problem," July 1976.
21. NARA, RG56, OASIA, Office of the Deputy to the Assistant Secretary for International Affairs, Records Relating to International Financial Institutions 1962–1981, b. 2, fold. IM-5 Boards, Committees, Organizations, Panels, Working Groups 1977–1978, J. Karlik and P. Kenen to Under Secretary Solomon, Memorandum "The International Role of the Dollar and Related Issues," August 2, 1978.
22. NARA, RG56, OASIA, Chronological Files of the Office of Financial Resources and Energy Finance 1974–1977, b. 1, Department of the Treasury, Briefing paper for Secretary Shultz "Oil Producing Governments' External Investment of Surplus Revenue," January 15, 1975.
23. Lea, 1975, Exhibit 6; Bank of England, 1975.
24. NARA, RG56, OASIA, Office of the Deputy to the Assistant Secretary for International Affairs, Records Relating to International Financial Institutions 1962–1981, b. 8, fold. IM-13-7 International Monetary Bank and Banking The Euro-Market 2 of 2, George H. Willis to Under Secretary Volcker through Assistant Secretary Petty, Memorandum "The Euro-Dollar Market: Entering a Third Phase?" March 29, 1971.
25. NARA, RG56, OASIA, Office of the Deputy to the Assistant Secretary for International Affairs, Records Relating to International Financial Institutions 1962–1981, b. 2.
26. Department of the Treasury, 1971, pp. 42–44.

27. On British monetary and financial policy during the period see Needham, 2014, pp. 46–78.
28. NARA, RG56, OASIA, Office of the Deputy to the Assistant Secretary for International Affairs, Records Relating to International Financial Institutions 1962–1981, b. 8, fold. IM-13-7 International Monetary Bank and Banking The Euro-Market 2 of 2, Department of the Treasury, "Controls on the Euro-currency Market."
29. NARA, RG56, OASIA, Subject Files of the Office of International Monetary Affairs 1968–1978, b. 3, fold. Eurodollars, Statement by Fred Klopstock (Manager, Research Department, Federal Reserve Bank of New York) before the Subcommittee on International Exchange and Payments of the Joint Economic Committee, June 22, 1971.
30. FRBNYA, Rosemary Lazenby-Mr. Kubarych's Files, b. 114512, fold. Rosenthal Sub-Committee (OPEC Financial Holdings), Statement by the Honorable Fred Bergsten (Assistant Secretary of the Treasury for International Affairs) before the Subcommittee on Commerce, Consumers and Monetary Affairs, Committee on Government Operations, House of Representatives, July 18, 1979.
31. On the OECD in the 1970s economic downturn and oil crises, see Schmelzer, 2016, pp. 313–328.
32. NARA, RG56, OASIA, Office of the Deputy Assistant Secretary for International Monetary and Investment Affairs, Records Relating to OECD Monetary Committees and Working Groups 1961–1974, b. 15, fold. EPC/WP-2 Documents 1973 (cont'd) 1 of 2, OECD, Working Party II of the Economic Policy Committee, note by the Secretariat "The Macro-economic Impact of Higher Energy Prices over the Medium Term," December 2, 1974.
33. Gfeller, 2012, pp. 285–287; Hughes, 2008, pp. 3–40; Randall, 2005; Cooper, 2011; Venn, 2013; Trachtenberg, 2012; Dietrich, 2016; Jacobs 2016; see also the essays published in Leffler and Westad, 2010. Recently a collective work has brought much more into focus the linkage between transformation in international relations and the macroeconomic consequences of the first oil shock: Bini, Garavini and Romero (eds), 2016.
34. Painter, 2014, pp. 189–190. See also British Petroleum, 1972.
35. Lin, 1984, pp. 783–784.
36. WBGA, Records of General Vice Presidents and Managing Directors, Records of Sir Denis Rickett, Oil and Energy, Memos and Reports,

1973 through 1974 Volume 01, IBRD (Commodities and Export Projections Division, Economic Analysis and Projections Department, Development Policy Staff), "Financial Consequences of Rising Trend in Petroleum Prices for Developed Countries 1970–1985," December 4, 1973, p. 10.

37. FRBNYA, b. 35575, fold. Foreign Exchange Control-General 1956–1975, B. Schneider (Federal Reserve Bank of New York, Balance of Payments Division) to Mr. Garvy, "Export Controls as a Retaliatory Weapon Against Arab Oil Producing Countries," November 13, 1973.
38. For a discussion of the debate within the December OPEC meeting see Venn, 2013.
39. Chalabi, 2010, p. 113.
40. NARA, RG56, OASIA, Subject Files of the Office of International Monetary Affairs 1968–1978, b. 3, fold. Eurodollars, Statement by Fred Klopstock (Manager, Research Department, Federal Reserve Bank of New York) before the Subcommittee on International Exchange and Payments of the Joint Economic Committee, June 22, 1971.
41. NARA, RG56, OASIA, Subject Files of the Office of International Monetary Affairs 1968–78, b. 3, fold. 1; Board of the Governors of the Federal Reserve System, Selected Interest and Exchange Rates for Major Countries and the US, Weekly Series of Charts, n. 520 (1971), T. Nelson to Under Secretary Volcker, "Eurodollar interest rates," January 27, 1971.
42. Department of Commerce, 1972a, b.
43. OECD, February 1, 1975, CMF (75) 2. See also NARA, RG56, Office of the General Counsel. Assistant General Counsel, Records Related to OPEC Financial Affairs 1974–1979, b. 2, fold. G Part 1 of 3 1974–1975, Department of Treasury, "Outlook for International Lending by Banks in 1975," March 24, 1975.
44. Cleveland and Brittain, 1977, pp. 737–747.
45. Bank for International Settlements, 2012.
46. NARA, RG56, OASIA, Office of the Deputy to the Assistant Secretary for International Affairs, Records Relating to International Financial Institutions 1962–1981, b. 8, fold. IM-10 International Capital Flows 1977–1978, H. Willis (Department of the Treasury), "Identification of Future Problem Countries in International Finance," February 4, 1977.

47. See Federal Reserve System, 1973.
48. Department of the Treasury, 1973, pp. 48–49.
49. Council of Economic Advisers, 1973, pp. 26–27, 33.
50. As for the wholesale commodity price index and the consumer price index see Council of Economic Advisers, 1973, pp. 26–27. As mentioned, data on short-term business borrowings are drawn from Federal Reserve System, 1974, p. 40. Concerning CPI in each of the advanced industrial economy, see Castaneda, 2012.
51. FRBNYA, Presidential Papers, Papers of Paul A. Volcker (1975–1979), b. 35602, fold. Speech—November 27, 1974, Paul A. Volcker, Paul A. Volcker "The Laurie Milbank Centenary Lecture Sponsored by the City University," London, November 27, 1974, p. 18.
52. NARA, RG59, Bureau of Near Eastern and South Asian Affairs, Office of the Iran Affairs, Records Relating to Iran 1965–1975, b. 9, fold. POL 3-2 UNGA Oct. 1974 Iran 1974, "Statement by His Excellency Mr. Abbas Ali Khalatbari Foreign Minister of Iran at the 29th Session of the United Nations General Assembly," October 10, 1974, p. 4.
53. On OPEC's aggregate investment patterns see Storck, 1995; Kopper, 2009, pp. 40–41. For a breakdown of OPEC's early investments that sheds light on the pouring of money into Eurocurrency assets, see NARA, RG56, OASIA, Office of the Deputy to the Assistant Secretary for International Affairs, Records Relating to International Financial Institutions 1962–1981, b. 8, fold. IM-13-7 International Monetary Bank and Banking The Euro-market 1 of 2, Paul A. Volcker, "The Recycling Problem Revisited. Remarks by Paul A. Volcker, Chairman, Board of Governors of the Federal Reserve System, before the Graduate School of Business Administration, New York University," March 1, 1980, table 3.
54. TNA, FCO 82/446, "Secretary of State's discussions with Dr. Kissinger in New York on September 24, 1974."
55. NARA, Office of the General Counsel. Assistant General Counsel, Records Related to OPEC Financial Affairs 1974–1979, b. 1, fold. E Part 1 of 2 1974–1979, D. Keyser to T. Willett, Memorandum "Contingency Planning: Consultations with Bankers," August 5, 1974.
56. FRBNYA, Central Files, b. 114512, fold. OPEC, W. M. Corden (Oxford University), "Oil Scenarios: The Implications of a Risk in the Price of Oil," January 1974.

57. NARA, RG56, OASIA, Office of the Deputy Assistant Secretary for International Monetary Affairs, Briefing Books 1971–1980, b. 1, fold. Advisory Committee for International Monetary Reform April 19, 1977 Secretary Blumenthal, "The Need for Order in International Finance," Address by Arthur F. Burns (Chairman, Board of Governors of the Federal Reserve System) at the Annual Dinner of the Columbia University Graduate School of Business, New York, April 12, 1977. A revised version of this speech was published in Burns, 1977, pp. 5–12.
58. NARA, RG56, OASIA, Office of the Deputy Assistant Secretary for International Monetary Affairs, Briefing Books 1971–1980, b. 1, fold. G-10 Deputies' Working Group, Paris 5–6 December 1974, "Address of the Honorable William Simon Secretary of the Treasury before the 61st National Foreign Trade Convention Sponsored by the National Foreign Trade Council," New York, November 18, 1974.
59. NARA, RG56, RG56, Office of the General Counsel. Assistant General Counsel, Records Relating to OPEC Financial Affairs 1974–1979, b. 3, fold. O 1975–1978, A. Lang, Board Briefing, "OPEC Trade Balance in 1974 and 1975," March 31, 1975. As regards data on the OPEC countries' oil revenues see also NARA, RG56, OASIA, Chronological Files of the Office of Financial Resources and Energy Finance 1974–1977, b. 1, B. Witherell to G. Parsky, Shultz Briefing Paper "Oil Producing Governments' External Investment of Surplus Revenue," January 15, 1975.
60. FRBNYA, Central Files, fold. OPEC, D. Beek (Federal Reserve Bank of New York Balance of Payments Division) to W. Gasser, Research Memorandum "Import and Expenditure Plans of Individual OPEC Countries," March 14, 1975, p. 12.
61. NARA, RG56, Office of the General Counsel. Assistant General Counsel, Records Related to OPEC Financial Affairs 1974–1979, b. 2, fold. F Part 4 of 4 1974–1978, Department of the Treasury, "International Monetary Role," undated.
62. NARA, RG56, OASIA, Chronological Files of the Office of Financial Resources and Energy Finance 1974–1977, b. 1, fold. Apr–May 1975, Department of the Treasury Special Reports, "Submission by the US Representative to the Temporary Working Party of the Economic Policy Committee on Problems Related to Investment of Financial Surpluses by Oil Producers," May 12, 1975.
63. TNA, FCO 42/865, "An Address by US Secretary of State Henry Kissinger at the University of Chicago," November 14, 1974.

64. NARA, RG56, Office of the General Counsel. Assistant General Counsel, Records Related to OPEC Financial Affairs 1974–1979, b. 3, fold. L 1978, The US Embassy in Teheran to the Secretary of State Washington, DC, "Cooper Visit to Kuwait: US Tax Treatment of Kuwait Direct Investment," telegram, October 27, 1978.
65. NARA, RG56, OASIA, Chronological Files of the Office of Financial Resources and Energy Finance 1974–1977, b. 1, fold. TERFP: Office of Financial Resources Policy Coordination-Permanent Chron. File, June 1975, O'Connor (Department of the Treasury), "Notes on Conversation in New York Concerning Middle Eastern Financial Matters," June 16, 1975.
66. NARA, RG56, Office of the General Counsel. Assistant General Counsel, Records Related to OPEC Financial Affairs 1974–1979, b. 2, fold. I 1977–79, Memorandum of Conversation D. Urech (First Vice President Swiss Bank Corporation)—C. Ellis (American Counsel General, Zurich), "OPEC Investment and the US Dollar," December 7, 1977.
67. FRBNYA, Rosemary Lazenby-Mr. Kubarich's Files, b. 114512, fold. Rosenthal Sub-Committee (OPEC Financial Holdings), Office of International Banking and Portfolio Investment, "Estimated Disposition of OPEC Investible Surplus 1974–1978," July 16, 1979; NARA, RG56, OASIA, Chronological Files of the Office of Financial Resources and Energy Finance 1974–1977, b. 1, fold. TEFRP: Office of Financial Resources Policy Coordination-Permanent Chron. File 1974, Department of Treasury, "OPEC Investments in the United States."
68. For similar estimates, see Kopper, 2009, p. 42.
69. NARA, RG56, Office of the General Counsel. Assistant General Counsel, Records Related to OPEC Financial Affairs 1974–1979, b. 2, fold. F Part 4 of 4 1974–1978, "Trends in the Euro-Banking Market."
70. NARA, RG56, OASIA, Office of the Deputy to the Assistant Secretary for International Affairs, Records Relating to International Financial Institutions 1962–1981, b. 8, fold. IM-13-1 International Monetary 1977–1980 Bank Regulatory Agencies, M. Blumenthal, Memorandum for the President "Bahamian Banks," March 31, 1977; on the Cayman Islands and Bahamas offshore centers see also *ibid.*, Department of the Treasury, Treasury Staff, "Caribbean Branches of US Banks," April 12, 1977.
71. Bank for International Settlements, 1976.

72. NARA, RG56, Office of the General Counsel, Assistant General Counsel, Records Relating to OPEC Financial Affairs 1974–1979, b. 2, f. G Part 1 of 3 1974–1975, "Outlook for International Lending by Banks in 1975," March 24, 1975.
73. NARA, RG56, OASIA, Office of the Deputy to the Assistant Secretary for International Affairs, Records Relating to International Financial Institutions 1962–1981, b. 8, fold. IM-13-7 International Monetary Bank and Banking The Euro-Market 1 of 2, P.A. Volcker, "The Recycling Problem Revisited. Remarks by the Chairman of the Board of Governors of the Federal Reserve System before the Graduate School of Business Administration, New York University," March 1, 1980.
74. FRBNYA, Presidential Papers, Paul Volcker Papers 1975–1979, b. 142572 (President Paul Volcker Material. Annual Report-Presidents' Office to Survey of 1978—Budget Outlook Second Federal Reserve District 1963–1977), fold. President's Office. Chase Manhattan Bank 1961–1977, F. Schadrack to Mr. Hayes, "Discussion with Senior Officers of the Chase Manhattan Bank," April 2, 1974.
75. CIEP Executive Director, Memorandum for the Secretaries of State, Treasury and Defense, "Proposed CIEP Working Group Review of Direct Investment in the US by Oil Producers," July 29, 1974, in DDRS.
76. NARA, RG56, Office of the General Counsel. Assistant General Counsel, Records Related to OPEC Financial Affairs 1974–79, b. 3, fold. O 1975–1978, R.H. Mills, "Board Presentation," March 31, 1975.
77. FRBNYA, Central Files, fold. OPEC, T. J. Giletti (FED New York, Balance of Payments Division) to Mr. Klopstock, "OPEC Funds Flows for January–April 1975," May 6, 1975.
78. FRBNYA, Central Files, b. 114512, fold. Energy, Y. Benari, (Fed New York, Industrial Economics Division, International Research Department) to Mr. Kubarych "Comments on Energy: Managing the Transition," March 9, 1978.
79. FRBNYA, Presidential Papers, Papers of Paul Volcker (1975–1979), Annual Report-President's Office to Survey of 1978, b. 142572, fold. President's Office. Chase Manhattan Bank 1961–1977, D. Willey (Federal Reserve Bank of New York), Memorandum "The Chase Manhattan Bank," January 28, 1974.
80. WBGA, Records of General Vice-Presidents and Managing Directors, Records of Sir Denis Rickett, Oil and Energy, Memos and Reports,

1973 through 1974, Volume 03, "Note on an Interview with the Shah Appeared in the Daily Telegraph on February 6, 1974."
81. NARA, RG56, Records of Secretary of the Treasury George P. Shultz 1971–1974, b. 3 (Commerce 73/74c to GPS Energy Problems 1972), fold. c, "The competitive Position of the United States in the International Money Market. Foreign Window, Option Paper."
82. NARA, RG56, OASIA, Office of the Deputy to the Assistant Secretary for International Affairs, Records Relating to International Financial Institutions 1962–1981, b. 8, fold. IM-ID International Monetary: International Capital Flow 1979, "Statement by the Honorable Anthony Solomon Under Secretary of the Treasury for Monetary Affairs Before Subcommittees of The House Banking, Finance and Urban Affairs Committee," July 12, 1979.
83. FRBNYA, Presidential Papers, Papers of Paul Volcker (1975–1979), Annual Report-President's Office to Survey of 1978, b. 142572, fold. President's Office. Chase Manhattan Bank 1961–1977, H. Willey (Federal Reserve Bank of New York), Memorandum "The Chase Manhattan Bank," January 28, 1974.
84. NARA, RG56, Office of the General Counsel. Assistant General Counsel, Records Related to OPEC Financial Affairs 1974–1979, b. 1, fold. E Part 1 of 2 1974–1979, Thomas Willett to Under Secretary Bennett and Assistant Secretary Cooper, Memorandum "Report on Discussions with New York Bankers Concerning Prospective Problems in International Financial Markets," August 7, 1974, p. 5.
85. NARA, RG56, OASIA, Chronological Files of the Office of Financial Resources and Energy Finance 1974–1977, b. 2, fold. TEFRP: Office of Financial Resources Policy Coordination-Permanent Chron. File, December 1975, "US Estimates of OPEC Investments," undated.
86. FRBNYA, Rosemary Lazenby—Mr. Kubarich's Files, b. 114512, fold. Rosenthal Sub-Committee (OPEC Financial Holdings), Russell Munk to Assistant Secretary Bergsten Memorandum "Disclosure of Information Concerning Saudi Arabian Investments in the United States," October 13, 1978.
87. Metz, 1974, p. 42.
88. On the failure of Herstatt, see now Mourlon-Druol, 2015, pp. 311–334.
89. Pettway, 1976, pp. 465–477; Sinkey, 1977, pp. 779–800; NARA, RG56, Office of the General Counsel. Assistant General Counsel, Records Related to OPEC Financial Affairs 1974–1979, b. 2, fold. F Part 4 of 4. 1974–1978, "Problems faced by Banks," September 4, 1974.

90. McCracken, 1974, p. 8.
91. FRBNYA, Central Files, Meetings of Secretary of Treasury with New York Financial Men 1958–1981.
92. At year-end 1974 the share of OPEC's dollar-denominated investments in the United States and that of sterling-denominated investments excluding the Euro-banking market in the United States on total OPEC placements amounted to 19 and over 10 percent respectively: see NARA, RG56, OASIA, Chronological Files of the Office of Financial Resources and Energy Finance 1974–1977, b. 2, fold. TERFP: Office of Financial Resources Policy Coordination Permanent Chron. File, December 1975, Department of the Treasury, "US Estimates of OPEC Investments," undated (1975).
93. Board of Governors of the Federal Reserve System, 1975a, p. A72.
94. NARA, RG56, Office of the General Counsel. Assistant General Counsel, Records Related to OPEC Financial Affairs 1974–1975, b. 2, fold. G Part 1 of 3 1974–1975, "Outlook for International Lending by Banks in 1975," March 24, 1975. See also Treasury Bulletin, March and April 1976.
95. FRBNYA, Central Files, b. 107333, fold. OPEC, Edna E. Ehrlich to Messrs. Coombs Holmes and Davis, "Petrodollars. Discussion with Charles Fiero of Chase," April 24, 1974.
96. FRBNYA, Central Files, b. 107333, fold. OPEC, D. Holdeworth (Fed New York Banking Studies Department) to Mr. Timlan (Fed New York), "OPEC Deposits in Selected New York Banks'," November 30, 1979.
97. FRBNYA, Central Files, b. 114512, fold. OPEC, P. Coldwell (Member, Board of Governors of the Federal Reserve System), Statement before the Commerce, Consumer, and Monetary Affairs Subcommittee, Committee on Government Operations, House of Representatives, Table 3, July 18, 1979.
98. NARA, RG56, OASIA, Office of the Deputy Assistant Secretary for International Monetary Affairs, Briefing Books 1971–1980, b. 1, fold. ADB Annual Meeting Monetary Reform April 1974, Under Secretary Volcker, Briefing Material, "International Monetary Reform," April 1974.
99. NARA, RG56, Office of the General Counsel. Assistant General Counsel, Records Related to OPEC Financial Affairs 1974–1979, b. 2, fold. F Part 4 of 4. 1974–1979, C. Callender to W. Morell, Memorandum "Report on Dollar Holdings of OPEC Countries. Trends in the Euro-Bank Loan, and the Euro-bond Market," August 30, 1974.

100. International Monetary Fund Archives, Washington, DC (henceforth IMFA), Central Files S 1184 Oil Crisis, Address by Otto Emminger (Deputy Governor of the Deutsche Bundesbank) at the Bank of Spain, "The Monetary Consequences of the Oil Price Explosion and the Implications for the Euro-currency Markets," p. 7, October 14, 1974.
101. NARA, RG56, OASIA, Secretary for International Affairs, Office of the Deputy Assistant Secretary for International Monetary Affairs, Briefing Books 1971–1980, b. 1, fold. Department of the Treasury, OASIA, Advisory Committee on International Monetary Reform, Secretary Blumenthal, Fowler Committee Meeting, "Private International Financing," April 19, 1977.
102. The First National Bank of Chicago, 1980, p. 1.
103. NARA, RG56, OASIA, Office of the Deputy to the Assistant Secretary for International Affairs, Records Relating to International Financial Institutions 1962–1981, b. 8, fold. IM-ID International Capital Flows 1977–1978, IMF, "Developing Country Access to Capital Markets," prepared by the Exchange and Trade Relations Department, Approved by E. Sturc, January 23, 1978, p. 6.
104. FRBNYA, Central Files, b. 107333, fold. OPEC, Edna E. Ehrlich to Messrs. Coombs Holmes and Davis, "Petrodollars. Discussion with Charles Fiero of Chase," April 24, 1974.
105. NARA, RG56, OASIA, Office of the Deputy to the Assistant Secretary for International Affairs, Records Relating to International Financial Institutions 1962–1981, b. 8, fold. IM-13-8 International Monetary Country Risk 1978–1980, 1 of 3, p. 3, "American Banks during the 1970s and Beyond," Remarks by Henry Wallich (Member, Board of Governors of the Federal Reserve System) at the Roundtable on Credit Systems in the 1970s Sponsored by the Ente per gli Studi Monetary Bancari e Finanziari Luigi Einaudi, September 3–7, 1980.
106. NARA, RG56, OASIA, Office of the Deputy to the Assistant Secretary for International Affairs, Records Relating to International Financial Institutions 1962–1981, b. 8, fold. IM-ID International Monetary: International Capital Flow 1979, Statement by the Honorable Anthony Solomon Under Secretary of the Treasury for Monetary Affairs before Subcommittees of the House Banking, Finance and Urban Affairs Committee, July 12, 1979, pp. 4 and 6.
107. Friedman, 1969; Little, 1969; Lewis and Hoskins, 1970, pp. 49–50.
108. Department of the Treasury, 1975, Introduction, p. XXXI.
109. Machlup, 1972, pp. 11–14.

110. Giddy, 1979, pp. 5–6.
111. IMFA, OMD, Witteveen Chronological Files, b. 1, fold. 8, A. Crockett, Memorandum for Files "Euro-Currency Committee," August 8, 1974. For a view on the problem by the US monetary authorities see NARA, RG56, OASIA, Office of the Deputy to the Assistant Secretary for International Affairs, Records Relating to International Financial Institutions 1962–1981, b. 8, fold. IM-13-7 International Monetary Bank and Banking The Euro-market 1 of 2, L. Goodmar (Fed New York), Research Memorandum "Eurodollars and the Money Supply," February 10, 1980.
112. RAC, RFA, Record Group 26 (henceforth RG26), Nelson Rockefeller Vice Presidential Records, Series 3, Central Files 1974–1977, b. 167, fold. FI 9, E. Black to J. Bennett (Under Secretary of the Treasury for Monetary Affairs), March 21, 1975.
113. On the dollar's dwindling see Chap. 5, Table 5.1. Regarding the wobbling of the US balance of payments from 1971 through the two trimesters that followed the first oil shock in 1974 see Board of Governors of the Federal Reserve System, 1975a, table A 60.
114. FRBNYA, Presidential Papers, Papers of Paul Volcker, b. 142572, fold. President's Office. Chase Manhattan Bank 1961–1977, Schadrack to Mr. Hayes, "Discussion with Senior Officers of the Chase Manhattan Bank," April 2, 1974.
115. NARA, RG56, Office of the Under Secretary for Monetary Affairs, Subject Files of Anthony M. Solomon Under Secretary for Monetary Affairs 1977–1980, b. 2, fold. Gold.
116. On this important issue see FRBNYA, Central Files, fold. OPEC, R. Kubarych (FED New York) to Mr. Holmes (FED New York), "Exchange Market Implications of Recent Changes in Valuation of OPEC Currencies," April 15, 1975; *ibid.*, H. Juntz (Fed New York) to Bryant (Fed New York), "Changes in OPEC countries' valuation of their currencies," March 27, 1975.
117. NARA, RG56, Office of the General Counsel. Assistant General Counsel, Records Related to OPEC Financial Affairs 1974–1979, b. 2 fold. F Part 4 of 4 1974–1978, C. Callender to W. Morell, "Report on Dollar Holdings of OPEC Countries. Trends in the Euro-Bank Loan, and the Euro-bond Market," August 30, 1974.
118. NARA, RG56, OASIA, Chronological Files of the Office of Financial Resources and Energy Finance 1974–1977, b. 1, fold. TERFP: Office

of Financial Resources Policy Coordination-Permanent Chron. File 1974, telegram, The Department of State to OECD Paris, telegram, "OECD Committee on Financial Markets Meeting," December 11, 1974.

119. NARA, RG56, OASIA, Office of the General Counsel. Assistant General Counsel, Records Related to OPEC Financial Affairs 1094–1979, b. 1, fold. G Part 2 of 3 1974–1975, D. Keyser to T. Willet, Memorandum "Recycling Petrodollars: Aspects of Financial Market Behavior," September 23, 1974. See also *The Financial Times* 1974. September 24.
120. *Euromoney*, 1974, p. 4.
121. FRBNYA, Central Files, fold. OPEC, Fed New York, Research Department, "Notes on Recycling," July 9, 1974.
122. International Monetary Fund, 1974, p. 4.
123. NARA, RG56, OASIA, Office of the General Counsel. Assistant General Counsel. Records Related to OPEC Financial Affairs 1974–1979, b. 1, fold. E Part 1 of 2 1974–1979, Memorandum of Conversation (partly classified) C. Keyser (US Treasury Department), US banker, July 26, 1974.
124. FRBNYA, Rosemary Lazenby, Mr. Kubarich's Files, b. 114512, A. Burns (Chairman, Board of Governors of the Federal Reserve System) to Honorable Frank Church (Chairman, the Subcommittee on Multinational Corporations of the Foreign Relations Committee), March 9, 1975; Request by Church Subcommittee Chronology', November 11, 1975; P. E. Coldwell (Board of Governors member) to Sen. B. Rosenthal (Chairman, Commerce, Consumer, and Monetary Affairs Subcommittee of the Committee on Government Operations), July 13, 1979. See also NARA, RG56, Office of the General Counsel. Assistant General Counsel, Records Related to OPEC Financial Affairs 1974–79, b. 3, fold. N Part 1 of 2 1977–1978, C. Cooper-G. Parsky, Memorandum for Under Secretary Yeo "Church Subcommittee Request for Bank Data," undated (but 1975). As for resistance to divulgate requested data by all major New York City banks (Manufacturers Hanover, Chase Manhattan Bank, Citibank, Morgan Guarantee) see correspondence with bankers by the Board of Governors of the Federal Reserve System held in NARA, RG56, Office of the General Counsel. Assistant General Counsel, Records Related to OPEC Financial Affairs 1974–79, b. 2.

125. Statement by Henry C. Wallich, Member, Board of Governors of the Federal Reserve System, before the Permanent Subcommittee on Investigations, Committee on Government Operations, US Senate, 16 October 1974, Statement to Congress, in Board of Governors of the Federal Reserve System, 1974, p. 760.
126. FRBNYA, Rosemary Lazenby, Mr. Kubarich's Files, b. 114512, fold. Rosenthal Sub-committee (OPEC Financial Holdings), "Memorandum on Foreign Assets and Liabilities of US Banks Prepared for Subcommittee on Multinational Corporations by Staff of the Federal Reserve Board."
127. NARA, RG56, Office of the General Counsel. Assistant General Counsel, Records Related to OPEC Financial Affairs 1974–1979, b. 3.
128. Schenk, 2014, pp. 1150–1151.
129. NARA, RG56, Office of the General Counsel. Assistant General Counsel, Records Related to OPEC Financial Affairs 1974–79, b. 1, fold. E Part 1 of 2 1974–1979, D. Keyser to T. Willett, Memorandum "Contingency Planning: Consultation with Bankers," August 5, 1974.
130. FRBNYA, Rosemary Lazenby, Mr. Kubarych's Files, b. 114512, fold. Rosenthal's Sub-committee (OPEC Financial Holdings), Report by the Comptroller General of the United States "Are OPEC Financial Holdings a Danger to US Banks or the Economy," June 11, 1979.
131. Department of Commerce, 1976.
132. IMFA, OMD, Witteeven Correspondence, b. 3 (General Correspondence), fold. 6, O. Aburdene (the First National Bank of Chicago), "The Financial Flows from the Oil Producing Countries of the Middle East to US for the Period 1974–1976," March 1977.
133. FRBNYA, Central Files, fold. OPEC, Paul Meek (Fed New York), Office Correspondence, "Discussion with Robert Bennett of FNMA," December 31, 1974.
134. NARA, RG56, Office of the General Counsel. Assistant General Counsel, Records Related to OPEC Financial Affairs 1974–1979, b. 2, fold. F Part 4 of 4 1974–1978, "Problems Faced by Banks," September 4, 1974.
135. NARA, RG56, Office of the General Counsel. Assistant General Counsel, Records Related to OPEC Financial Affairs 1974–1979, b. 2, fold. G Part 1 of 3 1974–1975, Department of the Treasury, Office of Statistical Reports, "Outlook for International Lending by Banks in 1975," March 24, 1975, p. 11; see also Board of Governors of the Federal Reserve System, 1975b.

136. Morgan Guaranty Trust Company, 1975, p. 5.
137. NARA, RG56, Records of Secretary of the Treasury George P. Shultz 1971–1974, b. 3, fold. GPS. Council on International Economic Policy C-1974, Department of the Treasury, "The Energy Crisis and the LDCs: The Problem," undated; *idem.*, "US Policy Towards Financing Proposals to Assist LDCs to Meet Oil and Other Import Requirements," March 1974.
138. IMFA, Middle Eastern Department Fonds (henceforth Medai), Medai Subject Files, b. 71, fold. 1 (January 1974–February 1974), A. Labidi President AFDEV to Witteveen, telegram, February 6, 1974.
139. IMFA, Middle Eastern Department Fonds, Medai Subject Files, b. 71, fold. 1 (January 1974–February 1974), The IMF to the Governor of Bank Markazi and Governor of the IMF for Iran, telegram, January 30, 1974.
140. Scharrer, 1974, p. 198.
141. NARA, RG56, OASIA, Office of the Deputy Assistant Secretary for International Monetary Affairs, Briefing Books 1971–1980, b. 1, fold. Briefing Material G-10 Deputies' Meeting, November 20–21, 1974, A.K. Rawlinson (the British Embassy in Washington) to W. Simon (The US Secretary of the Treasury), note, September 17, 1974.
142. IMFA, OMD files, Witteveen Papers, Chronological Files, b. 1, A.D. Crockett, Memorandum for Files, "New Oil Facility," February 14, 1974. See also NARA, RG56, OASIA, Office of the Deputy Assistant Secretary for International Monetary Affairs, Briefing Books 1971–1980, b. 1, fold. ADB Annual Meeting Monetary Reform April 1974. Under Secretary Volcker, "Briefing Material. International Monetary Reform," April 10, 1974.
143. IMFA, OMD Files, Witteveen papers, Chronological Files, b. 1, A.D. Crockett, Memorandum for the Files "Managing Director's Trip to Middle East," March 12, 1974; *idem.*, A.D. Crockett, Memorandum for the Files, "Managing Director's Conversation with Mr. Yeganeh," February 26, 1974.
144. NARA, RG56, OASIA, Subject Files of the Office of International Monetary Affairs 1968–1978, b. 6, fold. oil, "Statement by Managing Director on Visit to Member Countries in North Africa and the Middle East at Executive Board Meeting 74/37," April 22, 1974; IMFA, OMD Files, Witteveen papers, Chronological Files, b. 1, fold. 2, A.D. Crockett, Memorandum for Files, "Saudi Arabia: Conversations with Authorities," April 19, 1974.

145. IMFA, OMD Files, Witteveen papers, Chronological Files, b. 1, fold. 2, A.D. Crockett, Memorandum for Files, "Conversation with Authorities," April 24, 1974.
146. NARA, RG56, Records of Secretary of the Treasury George Shultz 1971–1974, b. 3, fold. GPS. Council on International Economic Policy C-1974, Department of the Treasury, "Proposed Lending Institutions," April 1974.
147. See documentation in NARA, RG56, Office of the General Counsel. Assistant General Counsel, Records Related to OPEC Financial Affairs 1974–1979, b. 3.
148. IMFA, OMD Files. Witteveen papers, Chronological Files, b. 2, fold. 15, IMF Memorandum for Files, "Managing Director's Visit to Various Bankers in New York," August 24, 1977. Regarding the negotiations between the Fund and the Arab oil producing countries on their lending to this facility see IMFA, Middle Eastern Departments Fonds, Medai Subject Files, b. 87, fold. 6 (February–July 1977).
149. On Saudi Arabia see IMFA, OMD Files, Witteveen papers, Chronological Files, b. 1, fold. 4, Managing Director's Meeting with Chancellor Healey on December 16, 1974.
150. IMFA, Medai, Medai Subject Files, b. 71, fold. 1 (January–February 1974), The representative in Kuwait to IMF Washington, DC, telegram, February 2, 1974.
151. IMFA, Medai, b. 75, fold. 3 (OPEC 1972–1979), D.K. Palmer to Mr. Finch, Oil Problem. IMRD Plans, January 16, 1974.
152. NARA, RG56, Records of Secretary of the Treasury George P. Shultz 1971–1974, b. 3, fold. GPS Council on International Economic Policy C-1974, Department of the Treasury, "EC Commission Suggestion," April 1974.
153. NARA, RG56, OASIA, Subject Files of the Office of International Monetary Affairs 1968–1978, b. 6, fold. Oil, OASIA to Under Secretary Volcker, Memorandum "Summary of Various Proposals to Assist Developing Countries to Deal with Oil-Induced Development and Financial Problems," April 9, 1974; *idem,* Department of the Treasury, "Background Paper United Nations General Assembly Special Session," April 1974.
154. WBGA, Records of General Vice Presidents and Managing Directors, Records of Sir Denis Rickett, Oil and Energy, Memos and Reports, 1973 through 1974–Volume 03, IBRD, "Possible Means of Channeling

OPEC Funds Through the World Bank," February 15, 1974; *ibid.*, IBRD, "Functions of IBRD and IMF in the Provision of Additional Resources to Developing Countries."

155. IMFA, September 25, 1974, Medai, Medai Subject Files, b. 75, fold. 1, "Financial Arrangements of Certain Oil-Exporting Countries in 1974."
156. NARA, RG56, Office of the General Counsel. Assistant General Counsel, Records Related to OPEC Financial Affairs 1974–79, b. 3, fold. O 1975–1978, R. Mills, Board Presentation, March 31, 1975.
157. IMFA, Central Files, Country Files—Italy, b. 6, fold. 26 (C/Italy/810-Mission Rose and Staff June–July 1974), IMF, "Voluntary Declaration on Trade and Other Current Account Measures. Executive Board Decision," June 26, 1974; *ibid.*, J. Witteveen, Letter to Members, July 8, 1974.
158. TNA, FCO 82/442, Visits of Dr. Henry Kissinger US Secretary of State, to UK, March 28, May 14 and 8 July, fold. 3, Record of Conversation between the Foreign and -Commonwealth Secretary and Dr. Henry Kissinger at the Foreign and Commonwealth Office, July 8, 1974.
159. IMFA, OMD Files, Witteveen Papers, Chronological Files, b. 1, fold. 2, A.D. Crockett, Memorandum for Files, "Managing Director's Conversation with Mr. Healey, Chancellor of the Exchequer," June 11, 1974.
160. TNA, FCO 82/442, Record of a Conversation between the Prime Minister and the United States Secretary of State, Dr. Henry Kissinger, at 10 Downing Street on July 8, 1974.
161. IMFA, OMD Files, Witteveen papers, Chronological Files, b. 1, fold. 2, A.D. Crockett, Memorandum for Files, "The Managing Director's Trip to Europe," June 4, 1974.
162. NARA, RG56, OASIA, Office of the Deputy to the Assistant Secretary for International Affairs, Records Relating to International Financial Institutions 1962–1981, b. 8, fold. IM-10 International Capital Flows 1977–1978, Department of the Treasury, OASIA, Deputy to the Assistant Secretary G. Willis, "Identification of Future Problem Countries in International Finance," April 2, 1977.
163. IMFA, Medai, Medai Subject Files, b. 71, fold. 3 (June 1974–August 1974), G. Gunter to Witteveen "Proposed Recycling Scheme through BIS," August 1, 1974; *ibid.*, Shell Oil Company, "Aid Memoire," March 13, 1974.

164. IMFA, OMD Files, Witteveen Chronological Files, b. 1, fold. 8, The IMF Managing Director, "Notes on Discussions with New York Bankers, Mr. Hayes (Fed New York), Mr. Coombs (Fed New York), Mr. Rockefeller (Chase Manhattan Bank), Mr. Kaufman (Solomon Brother)," July 25, 1974.
165. NARA, RG56, OASIA, Chronological Files of the Office of Financial Resources and Energy Finance 1974–1977, b. 1, fold. TEFRP: Office of Financial Policy Coordination. Permanent Chron. File 1974, G. Simon to R. Taft Jr., December 16, 1974.
166. NARA, RG56, OASIA, Office of the General Counsel. Assistant General Counsel, Records Related to OPEC Financial Affairs 1974–79, b. 2, fold. F Part 4 of 4 1974–78, Department of the Treasury, "Problems Faced by Banks," September 4, 1974.
167. NARA, RG56, OASIA, Office of the General Counsel. Assistant General Counsel, Records Related to OPEC Financial Affairs 1974–1979, b. 1, fold. G Part 2 of 3 1974–1975, D. Keyser to T. Willet, Memorandum "Recycling Petrodollars: Aspects of Financial Market Behavior," September 23, 1974.
168. TNA, FCO 82/446, "Secretary of State's Discussions with Dr. Kissinger in New York on 24 September 1974," brief no. 3.
169. TNA, FCO 82/446, fold. Meeting between James Callaghan, Secretary of State for Foreign and Commonwealth Affairs, and Dr. H. Kissinger, US Secretary of State, New York, September 24, 1974, The Secretary of State for Foreign and Commonwealth Affairs in New York to the UK Prime Minister, the UK Ministers for Energy and the Treasury, telegram.
170. See, for instance, a speech by the Deutsche Bundesbank Deputy Governor Otto Emminger: IMFA, Central Files, S 1184 Oil Crisis, Otto Emminger, "The Monetary Consequences of the Oil Price Explosion and its Implications for the Euro-currency Markets," October 14, 1974.
171. NARA, RG56, National Advisory Council on International Monetary and Financial Policies (NAC), NAC Alternates Minutes and Agenda, b. 1, fold. Meeting n. 75-1 Through Meeting n. 75-8, National Advisory Council Alternates Meeting Minutes, Meeting 75-1, January 16, 1975.
172. NARA, RG56, OASIA, Chronological Files of the Office of Financial Resources and Energy Finance 1974–1977, b. 1, fold. TEFRP: Office of Financial Policy Coordination. Permanent Chron. File 1974, "General Comment on Healey Proposal for Witteveen Mark II," November 14, 1974.

173. RAC, RFA, RG26, Nelson Rockefeller, Vice Presidential Records, Series 3, Central Files 1974–1977, b. 167, fold. FI 9, T. Enders to E. Black, May 17, 1975; A. Burns to E. Black, April 14, 1975.
174. TNA, FCO 82/465, Energy Policy of USA (1974), "The Energy Crisis. An Address by US Secretary of State Henry Kissinger, at the University of Chicago," pp. 8–9, November 15, 1974.
175. NARA, RG56, OASIA, Office of the Deputy Assistant Secretary for International Monetary Affairs, Briefing Books 1971–1980, b. 1, fold. G-10 Deputies' Working Group, December 5–6, 1974, "Address of the Honorable William Simon, Secretary of the Treasury before the 61st National Foreign Trade Convention Sponsored by the National Foreign Trade Council," November 18, 1974.
176. TNA, FCO 82/436, Monthly Meeting of UK Permanent Secretaries on Coordinating Relations between UK and USA Chaired by Sir John Hunt, Secretary to the Cabinet (1974), P. Ramsbotham (UK Embassy in Washington), "United Kingdom-United States Relations: Monthly meeting of Permanent Secretaries," December 3, 1974.

References

Bank for International Settlements. 1976. *Annual Report 1976*. Basle: Bank for International Settlements.

———. 2012. *Multilateral Surveillance Statistics*. Basle: BIS.

Bank of England. 1975. *Quarterly Bulletin*. June and September.

Bini, Elisabetta, Giuliano Garavini, and Federico Romero, eds. 2016. *Oil Shock. The 1973 Crisis and Its Economic Legacy*. London: IB Tauris.

Board of Governors of the Federal Reserve System. 1973. *Federal Reserve Bulletin* 59 (12).

———. 1974. *Federal Reserve Bulletin* 60 (11).

———. 1975a. *Federal Reserve Bulletin* 61 (1).

———. 1975b. *Federal Reserve Bulletin* 61 (2).

———. 1976. *Banking and Monetary Statistics 1941–1970*. Washington, DC: GPO.

Board of the Governors of the Federal Reserve System. 1971. Selected Interest and Exchange Rates for Major Countries and the US, Weekly Series of Charts, n. 520. Washington, DC: GPO.

British Petroleum. 1972. *Statistical Review of the World Oil Industry*. London: British Petroleum Co.

Burns, Arthur. 1977. The Need for Order in International Finance. *Columbia Journal of World Business* 2: 5–12.

Castaneda, Juan. 2012. *Statistical Gold Analysis Worldwide*. Madrid: Gold Money Foundation.

Chalabi, Fadhil J. 2010. *Oil Policies, Oil Myths: Observations of an OPEC Insider*. London/New York: I.B. Tauris.

Cleveland, Harold Van B., and Bruce W.H. Brittain. 1977. Debt and the Banks: Are the LDCS in Over the Heads? *Foreign Affairs* 55 (4): 737–747.

Cooper, Andrew Scott. 2011. *The Oil Kings. How the US, Iran and Saudi Arabia Changed the Balance of Power in the Middle East*. New York: Simon and Schuster.

Council of Economic Advisers. 1973. *Economic Indicators. October 1973, Prepared for the Joint Economic Committee by the Council of Economic Advisers*. Washington, DC: GPO.

Department of Commerce. 1972a. The US Balance of Payments: Revised Presentation. *Survey of Current Business* 52 (6).

———. 1972b. The US Balance of Payments: Revised Presentation. *Survey of Current Business* 52 (9).

———. 1973. *Survey of Current Business*. 53 (12).

———. 1976. *Survey of Current Business*. 56 (8).

Department of the Treasury. 1971. *Annual Report of the Secretary of the Treasury on the State of the Finances for the Fiscal Year Ended June 30, 1971*. Washington, DC: GPO.

———. 1972. *Annual Report of the Secretary of the Treasury on the State of the Finances for the Fiscal Year Ended June 30, 1972*. Washington, DC: GPO.

———. 1973. *Annual Report of the Secretary of the Treasury on the State of the Finances for the Fiscal Year Ended June 30, 1973*. Washington, DC: GPO.

———. 1975. *Annual Report of the Secretary of the Treasury on the State of the Finances for the Fiscal Year Ended June 30, 1975*. Washington, DC: GPO.

Dietrich, Christopher R. 2016. Oil Power and Economic Theologies: The United States and the Third World in the Wake of the Energy Crisis. *Diplomatic History* 40 (3): 500–529.

Federal Reserve System. 1971. *Annual Report of the Board of Governors of the Federal Reserve System for the Year 1970*. Washington, DC: GPO.

———. 1974. *Annual Report of the Board of Governors of the Federal Reserve System for the Year 1973*. Washington, DC: GPO.

Friedman, Milton. 1969. The Eurodollar Market: Some First Principles. *The Morgan Guaranty Survey* 12: 4–14.

Gamal, El, A. Mahmoud, and Amy Myers Jaffe. 2010. *Oil, Dollars, Debt, and Crises. The Global Curse of Black Gold*. New York: Cambridge University Press.

Gfeller, Aurélie Elisa. 2012. *Building a European Identity. France, the United States, and the Oil Shock 1973–1974*. New York: Berghahn.

Giddy, Ian. 1979. The Public Policy Implications of the Eurocurrency Markets. *Columbia Journal of World Business* 14 (3): 4–7.

Hughes, Geraint. 2008. Britain, the Transatlantic Alliance, and the Arab-Israeli War of 1973. *Journal of Cold War Studies* 10 (2): 3–40.

International Monetary Fund. 1974. *IMF Staff Paper SM/74/232*. September 26.

Jacobs, Meg. 2016. *Panic at the Pump. The Energy Crisis and the Transformation of American Politics in the 1970s*. New York: Farrar, Straus and Giroux.

Kindleberger, Charles. 1978. *Economic Response. Comparative Studies in Trade, Finance and Growth*. Cambridge, MA: Harvard University Press.

———. 1987. *International Capital Movements. Based on the Marshall Lectures given at Cambridge in 1985*. New York: Cambridge University Press.

Kopper, Christopher. 2009. Le recyclage du Pétrodollars. *Revue d'économie Financière* 9 (1): 39–48.

Lea, Sperry. 1975. *Higher Oil Prices: Worldwide Financial Implications*. Washington, DC: British-North American Committee.

Leffler, Melvyn P., and Odd A. Westad, eds. 2010. *The Cambridge History of the Cold War, Volume 2*. New York: Cambridge University Press.

Lewis, Furman, and W.H. Hoskins. 1970. The Eurodollar Markets: Their Nature, Role, and Future. *Business Horizons* 13 (2): 49–55.

Lin, Ching-yuan. 1984. Global Pattern of Energy Consumption Before and After the 1974 Oil Crisis. *Economic and Cultural Change* 32 (4): 781–802.

Little, Jane Sneddon. 1969. The Eurodollar Market: Its Nature and Impact. *New England Economic Review* 3: 2–31. Federal Reserve Bank of Boston.

Machlup, Fritz. 1972. The Eurodollar System and Its Control. In *International Monetary Problems. A Conference Sponsored by American Enterprise Institute for Public Policy Research*, 3–36. Washington, DC: American Enterprise Institute.

McCracken, Paul. 1974. Are the Latter Days Upon Us? *The Wall Street Journal*, July 22.

Metz, Robert. 1974. Market Place: Banks Raise Debt Ratios. *The New York Times*, July 31.

Morgan Guaranty Trust Company. 1975. *World Financial Markets*, January 21.

Mourlon-Druol, Emmanuel. 2015. Trust Is Good, Control Is Better: The 1974 Herstatt-Bank Crisis and Its Implications for International Regulatory Reform. *Business History* 57 (2): 311–334.

Needham, Duncan. 2014. *UK Monetary Policy from Devaluation to Thatcher 1967–1982*. London: Palgrave.

OECD. 1975. *Financial Markets Trends* (75): 2. February 1, 1975, CMF.

Painter, David. 2014. Oil and Geopolitics: The Oil Crises of the 1970s and the Cold War. *Historical Social Research* 39 (4): 186–208.

Pettway, Richard H. 1976. The Effects of Large Bank Failures Upon Investors' Risk Cognizance in the Commercial Banking Industry. *Journal of Financial and Quantitative Analysis* 11 (9): 465–477.

Randall, Stephen J. 2005. *United States Foreign Oil Policy Since WWI*. Montreal/London: McGill-Queen's University Press.

Roundtable. 1974. How Precarious Are the Euromarkets? *Euromoney*, July 1974, p. 4.

Scharrer, Hans-Eckart. 1974. The Heritage of the Committee of Twenty. *Intereconomics* 9 (7): 198.

Schenk. Catherine R. 2014. Summer in the City: Banking Failures of 1974 and the Development of International Banking Supervision. *English Historical Review* CXXIX (540): 1129–1156.

Schmelzer, Matthias. 2016. *The Hegemony of Growth. The OECD and the Making of the Economic Growth Paradigm*. Cambridge: Cambridge University Press.

Sinkey, Joseph F. 1977. Identifying Large Problem/Failed Banks: The Case of Franklin National Bank of New York. *Journal of Financial and Quantitative Analysis* 12 (5): 779–800.

Storck, Ekkehard. 1995. *Euromarkt: Finanz-Drehscheibe der Welt*. Stuttgart: Schäffer-Poeschel.

The Financial Times. 1974. September 24.

The First National Bank of Chicago. 1980. Recycling and the Commercial Banks. *World Report*, September–October.

Trachtenberg, Marc. 2012. *The Cold War and After. History, Theory, and the Logic of International Politics*. Princeton: Princeton University Press.

Venn, Fiona. 2013. *The Oil Crisis*. New York: Routledge.

Westra, Richard. 2010. *Political Economy and Globalization*. New York/London: Routledge.

5

The Linkage Between Petrodollar Recycling and Demand Side Policies: Its Rise and Fall Under the Carter Administration

5.1 The OPEC Response to the US: Investment Diversifications and Unilateral Assistance to the LDCs

Irrespective of Washington's strategies, as examined in the last paragraph of Chap. 4, the Organization of Petroleum Exporting Countries (OPEC) had proceeded to invest its surplus foreign exchange earnings in long-term investments, mostly securities issued by Western governments, as well as equity and bond markets, since as early as the beginning of 1974. Since shortly after the oil crisis, the OPEC nations considered both loans to the non-oil Least Developed Countries (LDCs), and investments in the Western world. Chapter 4 has shed some light on the borrowings by the LDCs from the OPEC countries through the intermediation of the Eurocurrency markets. In this chapter it is worth focusing firstly on the OPEC contribution to the shift from short-term investments to longer investments over the course of the year. Secondly, the aim is to understand why the disparity between the process of institutionalization (explored in Chap. 4) and foreign direct investments by the oil producers contributed, along with other components, to cause a fundamental shift

S. Selva, *Before the Neoliberal Turn*, Palgrave Studies in Economic History,
DOI 10.1057/978-1-137-57443-5_5

in the US oil revenues recycling policies from balance of payments deficit financing targets on the capital account to measures aimed at increasing commercial bonds with OPEC and at stimulating expansionary policies within the US and other leading industrial economies. In order to comprehend this tangle of interconnections it is worth focusing attention on the OPEC investments in the industrial economies. As seen in this study, as long as the absorbing capacity of the Eurocurrency markets was not saturated over the course of the summer of 1974,[1] the investments of the OPEC nations in the Western world were channeled through the Euromoney markets. However, as early as the first half of 1974 the oil producers engaged in direct investments in debt securities, equities and other long-term financial instruments in the Western world. Such course of investments peaked since the summer of that same year in conjunction with mounting pressure on the part of the largest American banks, US monetary authorities, and the highest American and British economic policymakers, to devise ways to reflow their oil revenues so as to bypass the stream of hindrances—pinpointed in Chap. 4—posed by the distribution of large amounts of oil money through short-term financial instruments. In trying to push the OPEC members in this direction, the Western monetary and political elites also wished for facing up to and overcoming the banking recalcitrance, restated by prominent Western bankers in early 1975,[2] to drive the process of recycling. In so doing, the Arab and non-Arab capital-surplus countries showed a bilateral approach, while some of them—most notably Iran, showed an aspiration to exploit the recycling mechanism in order to emerge as leading oil producers within the framework of supposedly multilateral new arrangements. This study has charted how the early OPEC recycling policies through the Eurocurrency markets posited a string of issues that ranged from the negative impact on the dollar exchange rate to the inflationary strains and increased world money supply that they triggered. As seen in the last section of Chap. 4, the US and the Washington-backed Bretton Woods institutions struggled to create a shift in the investment patterns of oil producers in order to tackle this jumble of problems. From the viewpoint of the US monetary and federal authorities a reshuffling of the recycling process was by and large aimed at stabilizing exchange markets and reducing payments imbalances. This chapter first points to the reaction of the OPEC countries to such a push by the Americans. In the framework of the OPEC countries' bilateral assistance to the LDCs, and their direct and portfolio investments in the US, Washington's strategy to direct the recasting of the US balance of payments on capital account proved to be unsuccessful. Against this backdrop, it is worth situating the early Ford administration's turn to improve the current account position through a gamble on the US export to the oil producers through technical and industrial cooperation.[3] Likewise, and more importantly from the viewpoint of this study, it is possible to situate and interpret the Carter administration's striking turn to draw on the OPEC surplus capital to promote demand management policies in support for a restructuring of the business cycle on the demand side in both the US and other advanced industrial nations.

Consider first the bilateral investments of the OPEC countries to industrial and LDCs economies. From May 1974 to June 1974 Iran reached agreements with Egypt on a loan of $850 million, with Syria for $150 million, and with France for a loan of $1 billion. Shortly thereafter, in July, Teheran signed loan commitments with Pakistan for $850 million, with the UK for $1.2 billion, and bought a one-quarter interest in West Germany's Krupp steelworks.[4] At the same time, the Japanese government, the UK, and the US entered in negotiations with Saudi Arabia on large loans,[5] while the government of London and Kuwait began discussions on the purchase of British bonds worth up to $1.8 billion.[6] The US Department of the Treasury estimated that OPEC countries invested during the eight-month period about $7 billion in the US, about $3 billion in the UK, and about $2 billion in other European countries in various types of government securities, corporate bonds, and commercial banks deposits. Of the $7 billion invested in the US, $4 billion were poured into US government securities, with most of the remainder being placed in commercial banks, corporate securities and real estate.[7] The cases of Iran, Saudi Arabia and Kuwait are crucial to better catch the American strategy to reshuffle the US balance of payments on capital account. Likewise, for a variety of reasons, explored in this book, that ranged from their outstanding bonds with US banks and corporations to their capital-surplus status or their high-absorbing capacity, not to mention their well-established political and economic bonds with Washington, the financial relations of these three oil producing countries with the Carter administration deserve attention insofar as Washington turned to draw on the OPEC assets to improve its current account position and to finance demand side expansionary policies. However, as detailed in the next two sections, during the Carter administration such massive bilateral investments in the US by these OPEC nations became the source of disputes over the terms and conditions of such investments. At the same time, they used their investments as a means of trading off their financial support to demand management policies and to the US export for protection of both their purchasing power in world trade and of their dollar-denominated investments from the continuing depreciation of the dollar in foreign exchange markets, which sharpened from September 1977 through late 1978 against the Dutch guilder, the Japanese yen, the German Deutschmark, and the Swiss franc (Table 5.1).[8]

Therefore, during the Carter administration the OPEC countries could potentially enjoy more leverage power toward Washington and used this to try to fix the long-standing issue of the implication of a weaker US dollar on their purchasing power and the value of their foreign investments. The deterioration of such bilateral economic and financial relations on which was based the Carter administration's recycling policy aimed at financing American export and domestic aggregate demand through demand side policies began in 1978 with a worsening in US–Saudi relations. Then, such bilateral relations crumbled from the destabilizing effects of the Iranian Revolution on the US economic relations in the Gulf to the appointment of Paul A. Volcker to the chairmanship of the Federal Reserve Board in 1979. Such course of events cannot be charted but by outlining the early commitments by Iran, Saudi Arabia and Kuwait to large investments in the United States, and the attitude by US authorities to such investments in connection with the US balance of payments deficit financing policies. Consider first the case of Kuwait. By late summer of 1974, the Department of the Treasury approached the Kuwaiti authorities to let them know that the US market could absorb up to $750 million for three to six months.[9] At this early stage in the recycling process Kuwait focused its investments on non-US entities: its acquisition of 14.5 percent interest in Daimler Benz tracked this Kuwaiti investment policy. From 1975, Kuwait showed its increasing propensity

Table 5.1 Exchange rate movements 1970–1978, percentage change

	May 29, 1970 to June 2, 1978	March 20, 1973 to June 2, 1978	Year-end 1974	Year-end 1975	Year-end 1976	Year-end 1977	September 1977 to June 2, 1978
Value in terms of dollar							
Swiss franc	+130.1	+72.3	+27.7	−3.1	+6.9	+22.0	+24.4
German mark	+74.7	+35.7	+12.2	−8.1	+11.0	+12.0	+12.4
Dutch guilder	+62.8	+29.4	+12.7	−6.8	+9.4	+8.2	+10.2
Japanese yen	+63.5	+20.2	−7.0	−1.4	+4.2	+22.2	+20.9
French franc	+20.4	−1.4	+5.9	−0.9	−9.7	+5.7	+6.9
Canadian dollar	−4.1	−10.9	+0.5	−2.5	+0.7	−7.6	−4.1
Pound sterling	−24.3	−26.2	+1.1	−13.8	−15.9	+11.9	−4.1
Italian lira	−27.0	−34.4	−6.4	−5.0	−21.9	+0.5	+2.5

Rate source: London mid-day rates, in NARA, RG56, Office of the General Counsel. Assistant General Counsel, Records Related to OPEC Financial Affairs 1974–1979, b. 1 fold. F Part 1 of 4 1978–1979

to make equity investments in the United States: in the spring of 1975 the Kuwaiti government engaged in a wide-ranging study about the most feasible and profitable investment opportunities in US corporations to best place its oil revenues. On that occasion the Kuwaiti government declared that such a search for equity investments was thought to shift the country's foreign investments to long-term financial outlets. This outspoken declaration cast light on the Kuwaiti attitude to follow up the course of investments suggested by the US monetary and financial authorities since the year before. At the same time, Kuwait expanded its well-established investments in the US real estate markets: in the summer of 1975 the Kuwaitis joined forces with Bank of America and Chase Manhattan subsidiaries to channel funds into a diversified portfolio of East and West coastal US real estates. At year-end 1975 such course of investments had developed further: over the second half of the year the Kuwaitis' inclination to invest long in the US stock and real estate markets had consolidated long-lasting business relations with the largest American banks that served as intermediaries. Among other duties, American banks had injected Kuwaiti oil revenues into the liquidity portion of large investment accounts they were used to managing on behalf of some OPEC oil producing countries, including Kuwait, in offshore countries. Such was the case of the Bahamas, where US banks poured into local offshore accounts a significant portion of financial resources held by the Government of Kuwait, which was never included in US statistics on US banks' reported liabilities to foreigners.[10] The role of Kuwait in the US capital and stock markets increased from 1975 through the following few years: as David Rockefeller himself pointed out, this occurred in the framework of the decline in short-term interest rates that the drying up of American commercial banks' liquidity to absorb short-term deposits triggered from the second half of 1974 through to the following years. It is worth saying in passing that this declaration of Rockefeller highlights his disappointment about the development of short-term capital markets and the attitude of the OPEC countries to nurture it: considering his pivotal role as representative of the American banking community at the highest US political level, it is easily understandable that firm opposition to such pattern of investments was widely shared in Washington and New York.[11] Following on the heels of Kuwait, Saudi Arabia got involved in the American economy quite early after the first oil shock and its commitment increased over the following three years. The role of Saudi Arabia was prominent since 1974 and US monetary authorities showed their willingness to favor it; as of December 1974 special arrangements favorable to the Saudi central bank, the Saudi Arabian Monetary Authority (SAMA), had been made in connection with the purchase and sale of US Treasury securities having maturities of one year or more. According to these agreements, the Federal Reserve Bank of New York committed to tender on behalf of SAMA on a non-competitive basis and on completion of the auction informed SAMA of the average price of the accepted public tenders. Among other agreed conditions, Washington conceded that in the event that SAMA "wishes to sell the securities purchased under these arrangements prior to their maturity, it would give two days' notice to the [Federal Reserve] Bank. In such event, the Treasury would be in a position to make an offer to purchase such securities from SAMA at market prices."[12] Before the depreciation of the US dollar in exchange markets worsened and crushed the value of the OPEC countries' dollar-denominated portfolio and equity investments since the very end of 1977 (see Table 5.2),[13] from 1975 to 1976, Saudi Arabia increased such long-term investment policy through the acquisition of important shares, such as in the American telecommunications giant AT&T, in which the Saudis made a portfolio investment of $100 million openly approved by the Ford Administration.[14]

It is important to notice that inclination by the US governments and monetary authorities to trigger a shift in the investment patterns of the OPEC countries to overcome the string of issues inherent to the OPEC short-term investments took place within the framework of Washington's balance of payments deficit financing policies under the floating currency system under operation at the time. US authorities did not have a shared view on it. As seen in the previous pages of this study, Arthur Burns wished for a tossing aside of the recycling process and favored a decrease in oil prices to strengthen international financial stability and the US balance of payments. In the fall of 1974, for instance, at Congressional Hearings before the Joint Economic Committee he favored early hearings

Table 5.2 Movements in relative purchasing power of OPEC dollar-denominated assets

Movements in relative purchasing power of OPEC dollar-denominated assets						
	January	February	March	April	May	June
1973			0.0	0.6	−1.1	−3.6
1974	3.3	−1.4	−5.1	−5.5	−4.5	−4.8
1975	−2.1	−4.6	−2.7	−2.3	−1.7	−2.9
1976	5.4	4.8	6.1	7.0	6.6	5.9
1977	5.7	5.7	5.6	6.3	5.7	3.5
1978	−1.9	−2.3	−4.1	−2.0	−2.2	−5.7
	July	**August**	**September**	**October**	**November**	**December**
1973	−6.2	0.0	−3.2	−5.2	−1.8	−1.0
1974	−2.2	2.0	0.3	1.2	1.6	−0.8
1975	3.1	3.9	6.2	4.6	5.6	5.1
1976	5.9	4.9	5.1	6.0	6.0	4.3
1977	2.8	2.8	2.1	−0.1	0.2	−3.5
1978	−9.9	−8.8	−8.9			

Source: See endnote 12

on legislation to restrict direct investments in the US by OPEC nations. Reasoning along these lines, he aligned with a large number of Congressmen and businessmen,[15] not to mention the American Jewish community,[16] who repeatedly exhibited their palpable and wide-ranging concern for massive Arab investments in the United States. By contrast, in light of public disclosure in the American newspapers about Arab attempts to invest in Lockheed that spring, the US Department of the Treasury reaffirmed the US open door policy and dismissed any concern about Arab control of key national industries, emphasizing US need for capital from abroad. In light of such widespread Congressional concerns about the growth of Arab investments in the US, US Treasury Assistant Secretary Parsky repeatedly and convincingly stressed that the United States must continue to hold its basic policy of freely admitting foreign capital on a nondiscriminatory basis, whether from oil producing nations or from other countries, and that "the investments of such funds in the United States can also make available additional capital to finance domestic investment and thereby to improve our long-term growth and productive potential."[17] The Working Group on foreign investments established in 1974 within the US Council on International Economic Policy favored direct investments by the OPEC countries in the US: the Council made the argument that OPEC direct investments were a positive entry in the US balance of payments accounts both in the short-run and in the long-run. Based on the expected increase in the oil revenues of OPEC over the following few years, the Working Group maintained that direct investments by the OPEC countries in the US were likely to be financed from abroad in the following few years as well, thus making the recycling of oil money a positive entry in the US capital account.[18] The Office of Financial Resources and Energy Finance established by the US Department of the Treasury upheld this view on a positive correlation between OPEC investments in the US and the US balance of payments through a focus on the intertwining between the inflow of oil money and US inflation. According to that office, with a flexible exchange rate for the dollar, the inflow of dollar-denominated oil money to the US would cause the price of the dollar to rise against other currencies, and so reduce the price of import, decrease prices and improve the US current account position.[19] Chapter 4 has pointed to the correlation between the increase in the short-term foreign investments of the OPEC countries, particularly in short-term Eurocurrency assets during the first half of 1974, and the depreciation of the dollar in exchange markets. To put it another way, in the new context of floating currencies, OPEC investments in the US and in the Eurocurrency markets had exactly opposite effects on the value of the dollar in real exchange markets, on the US balance of payments in the aggregate, and on the cost of money and inflation. While investments in the Eurocurrency markets, as suggested in Chaps. 3 and 4, expanded the dollar component of world money supply, contributed to depreciate the value of the dollar, increased the rates of interest on loans as a reaction to peaking Eurocurrency rates and pushed up the cost of US imports, the reverse did occur somewhat in the case of OPEC investments in the US stock and security markets. In general, Arab investments in the United States contributed to dry up the monetary bubble of growing dollar holdings in world capital markets, lessened the race to peaking interest rates and rising consumer prices, and would be a positive entry in the US balance of payments. Against this backdrop, if one points to the US balance of payments, it is easy to understand this debate on the correlation between OPEC portfolio and direct investments in the US and the process of recycling oil money that preceded it. In the aggregate, during fiscal year 1974, the US balance of payments improved compared to the previous three years.[20] However, considering US banking activities and its entry to the US capital account position, the picture is far more complex than expected. As stressed in Chap. 4, over the course of 1974 a shift was registered in the investment patterns of US banks: over the first three quarters of the year they registered an upswing in the foreign lending managed by their overseas subsidiaries based in Europe and a stagnant level of financial intermediation by their US domestic branches and affiliates. This pace clearly reflected the active involvement of the largest US banks in recycling oil money in the Eurodollar market. In contrast to this early investment attitude, during the December 1974 quarter a $ 4.6 billion rise was registered in the net outflow of private US capital that exceeded the $2.9 billion rise in the inflow of foreign funds by $1.9 billion.[21] On a yearly average, net liabilities on assets reported by US banks, which reached their lowest point at year-end 1974, slightly contracted during fiscal year 1975, reflecting in part a reduced exposure of US banks to high-risk debt borrowing countries.[22] Therefore, the early OPEC countries' short-term investments in the Eurocurrency and other short-term maturities not only positively contributed to the US capital position because they triggered a reduction in the US foreign expenditures to finance development assistance to the LDCs insofar as the latter heavily borrowed from the Eurocurrency markets. Rather, by contrast, such investments had cumbersome effects on the US economy, both owing to the pressure they posited on the value of the dollar, and for the crushing effect on the total balance of capital flows, which were, as stressed in this research, the bulk of Washington's recycling strategy during 1974 and 1975. This helps to explain Washington's debate on the opportunity to stimulate OPEC investments in the US and why a majority of US economic policymakers and financial elites convincingly supported it.

Along with investments in the US economy, the other cornerstone of OPEC countries' direct and bilateral financial assistance packages as they developed from 1974 through the following years was precisely represented by their multilateral assistance schemes to the LDCs,[23] either directly or through the Bretton Woods institutions, just mentioned. From the viewpoint of the US government, while their direct or portfolio investments in the United States did pertain to the possibility of raising the assets in the US balance of payments on capital account, the flow of their capital surplus through direct and indirect assistance to the LDCs was all about reducing the liabilities in the capital account component.

Therefore, consider this second pattern of investment by the three OPEC oil producers at the center of this investigation. Since the beginning of the decade Iran, Kuwait and Saudi Arabia had been in the forefront in providing some non-oil producing Middle Eastern and Mediterranean countries with lines of credit. As soon as the fourfold oil price increase triggered a rise in the investible resources of OPEC capital-surplus countries, the government of Venezuela proposed that OPEC establish a special fund to help LDCs meet higher petroleum costs. By the September 1974 quarter, Saudi Arabia, Iran and Kuwait bore the largest share of concessional aid to the non-oil LDCs; by that time Egypt and Syria received about 60 percent of total concessionary aid by the OPEC countries to non-oil exporting LDCs, followed by India and Pakistan.[24] These early moves by the largest OPEC oil producers to connect the meteoric rise in their financial resources to the LDCs' imbalances caused by the oil crisis highlight their attitude towards directly extending loans across the globe and to bypass the Western world. Such an early move is quite important as it helps explain the way the OPEC countries reacted to the Western attempt to lock their funds in multilateral arrangements under US leadership, mentioned in the previous pages of this work. Notwithstanding this attitude, in the following months and years they had to confront such institutionalization of the recycling process under Western financial arrangements: in this context the focal issue for the OPEC surplus countries was the worthiness and scale of financing such schemes fine-tuned in Washington. In this respect, Iran led the way. The case of Iran highlights the repositioning of oil producing countries in the system of international economic relations since the fourfold oil price hike: by early 1974 Teheran had already begun plans to sell bonds to other oil producing countries.[25] On February 21, 1974, the Shah discussed with Robert McNamara, President of the International Bank for Reconstruction and Development (IBRD), and Johannes Witteveen, Managing Director of the International Monetary Fund (IMF), three proposals for the recycling of OPEC oil revenues. On the one side he proposed to buy IBRD bonds and to finance the IMF oil facility whose creation Witteveen had recently brought before the international community and its public opinion. Such proposal for lending to the IBRD was immediately approved by the US government.[26] On the other side, more importantly, the Shah envisioned the creation of a new development institution to be founded by contributions from up to 24 oil exporting and industrialized countries. Such a fund was thought to be, according to him, a neutral institution aimed at providing the poorest LDCs with both concessional aid to finance investments in those countries and funds to offset the balance of payments impact of their higher prices of imported oil.[27] Therefore, such early activism of Iran to promote multilateral assistance to the non-oil LDCs was consistent with the very aim of US global financial policy of coping with the impact of the oil crisis on the system of international trade and payments. It suggests Teheran's ambition to establish special economic and financial bonds with the US irrespective of OPEC policies. The way in which Saudi Arabia reacted to the Shah's proposal further proves this ambitious Iranian strategy to make the recycling of OPEC financial assets a way to distance itself from OPEC in order to entertain ever closer economic bonds with Washington.[28] As detailed in the previous chapters, the tangle of business and financial relations between Washington on the one side and Saudi Arabia and Kuwait on the other were long-lasting and well established. These multiple economic bonds between the US and these three countries drove the recycling process through the second half of the decade and marked a string of issues and problems. From the taxation of Arab investments in the US to the fall in value of their foreign investments caused by the depreciation of the dollar in exchange markets, through to the reliability of their portfolio and stock market investments from the 1975 recession onward, from 1976 to 1979 this string of issues undermined the financial relations between the United States and these three Middle Eastern members of OPEC. The teetering of these relations eventually triggered a collapse of the US government's strategy to borrow from the oil producing countries in order to bolster the US balance of payments previously pursued under the Ford administration. Likewise, these hindrances jeopardized the US attempt to prop up the US current account position through export-oriented policies and to set up demand management domestic economic policies aimed at resurrecting the US and other advanced industrial economies from the sluggish economic downturn of the decade that came to center stage in the recycling policies of the Carter administration.

Against the backdrop of plans and debates within the American political and financial elite about making the OPEC nations shift their investments from the Euro-money markets into longer assets to better fix the nerve-wracking problem of payments imbalances that afflicted the non-oil LDCs, by the fall of 1974 several OPEC countries had gone their own way. Along these lines, the Iranian initiatives were only the first and most remarkable case in point. During his late fall trip to Saudi Arabia, British Chancellor had been assured about the intention of the Saudis to continue their investments in sterling and their strong desire to move more into medium- and long-term investments.[29] In the aggregate, at year-end 1975 the OPEC investments in IBRD bonds and in the IMF oil facility had increased by 10 percent compared with 6 percent in 1974.[30]

Along the lines of the American strategy to heavily borrow from the oil producing countries to finance both the non-oil LDCs current account deficit and the industrial countries' purchasing power developed under Ford and even more under the Carter administration, over the following years the IMF oil facility came to depend always more upon the oil producing countries and the emerging industrial economies: after a first lot of borrowings from a number of central banks in 1974 including SAMA, the Central Bank of Iran and those of Kuwait and the United Arab Emirates,[31] in 1975 the Fund made arrangements to borrow from SAMA, the Central Bank of Kuwait and the Deutsche Bundesbank.[32] On the other hand the IBRD itself increasingly bid for assistance with the surplus OPEC nations, in particular with regard to Saudi Arabia: in December 1974 the Saudis reached agreements with the World Bank and the US government on a Saudi loan to the bank.[33]

In light of both this prompt shift to diversify their investments beyond the scope of short-term assets, and the aforesaid negative effects of recycling the OPEC nations' oil revenues into the Euromarkets on the value of the US dollar and the all international payments systems, since 1975 several authorities in Washington started thinking about new arrangements to favor such shift in the investment patterns of capital-surplus OPEC nations from short-term assets to long-term investments. In the pursuit of continued Washington policy to make the OPEC financial resources ease off the US capital account from the strains of massive financial assistance to the non-oil LDCs, a widely held view in Washington was that such a path-breaking turn to long-term investments should be framed into institutionalized multilateral financial arrangements under US leadership. Within this broader framework, in early 1975 the Federal Reserve Bank of New York called for monetary collaboration among Western governments and made a strong case for giving some of the oil producing nations, and in particular Saudi Arabia, a stronger voice within those institutions to which they belonged, including the World Bank and the IMF. The Fed also called for allowing these countries access to those institutions to which they did not belong, such as the Organization for Economic Cooperation and Development (OECD) and the Bank for International Settlements (BIS).[34] This approach gained consensus in Washington, as the recession that crushed the advanced industrial economies in 1975 affected the purchasing power in the foreign markets of the OECD member states and began jeopardizing their commercial bonds with commodity and raw material producing LDCs.[35] In fact, this loss in the competitive edge and purchasing power of the OECD economies triggered a falloff in their import from the LDCs and a decline in commodity prices in world markets (see Fig. 5.1).[36] According to the Department of State and the OECD, during the first half of calendar 1975 the non-oil producing LDCs run a current account deficit at an annual rate of some $40 billion. In this context the Department of State exhibited its palpable concern about the effects of this deficit running "at an alarming and unsustainable rate" on both the development objectives of the countries and their creditworthy stance before private lenders, which were supposed to "take a harder look at LDC loan applications in view of their mounting indebtedness."[37]

Despite the US attempt to trigger a shift in the investment patterns of the oil producing countries from short-term investments to longer financial instruments, leading to a substantial policy of investment diversification from the second half of 1974 to the end of 1975, neither its predicted positive impact on the dollar's value in exchange markets

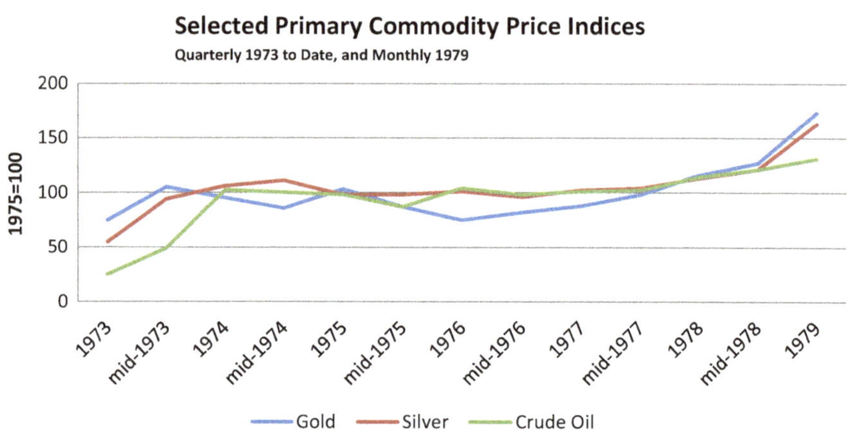

Fig. 5.1 Commodity prices in world markets (Source: IMF quoted in NARA, RG56, Office of the Under Secretary for Monetary Affairs, subject files of Anthony M. Solomon, Under Secretary for Monetary Affairs 1977–1980, b. 2, fold. gold)

and on the US balance of payments, nor its institutionalization through the IMF and World Bank programs, produced the expected outcomes. It has already been stressed in this study the downward trend in the depreciation of the dollar from the fall of 1974 to spring of 1975 and the sluggish balance of payments trend in 1975. Likewise, Washington's strategy proved to be unsuccessful with respect to the latter point as well. Although the increase in the OPEC nations' contribution to the IMF facilities and the IBRD development assistance programs for the LDCs,[38] the OPEC countries were successful in averting such institutionalization of the recycling process. In January 1976 the oil producing countries established the OPEC Special Fund, a multilateral assistance agency to provide concessionary balance of payments and development finance as well as grants to the least-developed third-world nations. The Fund, which started operations in August 1976, received contributions from all 13 OPEC members, with Saudi Arabia and Iran being the largest contributors, followed by Kuwait and Venezuela. As of 31 December 1978, the Fund had committed $1.6 billion in aid activities to the LDCs, which were increased in 1979, and had become the main venue to channels the OPEC member states' financial contributions to the IMF.[39] The budget and assistance provided by the Special Fund to the LDCs was modest compared to total external assets of the OPEC countries over the second half of the decade. To better understand such discrepancy, it is worth recalling that at year-end 1977 the bulk of the OPEC members' investments were still in the Eurocurrency markets and in the five largest industrial economies (Canada, Germany, Japan, United Kingdom, United States) under the form of Treasury bills, notes and bonds, equity investments, direct loans, and bank deposits denominated in domestic currencies.[40] However, the establishment and functioning of the Fund is noteworthy as it was the litmus test of Washington's failure to make the Arab countries turn to long-term investments in support for the assets in the US balance of payments on the capital account through direct investments in the US. By the second half of 1976 the multiple initiatives devised in Washington to link the recycling of the OPEC capital surplus to the preservation of a high level of exchange in goods and capital among the LDCs and the Western industrial economies, under the political and institutional umbrella of the Western world, proved to be unsuccessful in making the OPEC countries share the financial burden. Likewise, it sheds light on the failure to lessen the liabilities in the US balance of payments through the financing of Bretton Woods institutions' multilateral balance of payments and development assistance programs for the hardest hit least-developed non-oil LDCs. The creation of the OPEC Special Fund sheds light on the capability of OPEC to contrast such course of financing multilateral payments imbalances, while the growing importance of borrowing by the LDCs from the Eurocurrency and Euro-money markets during 1976 highlights the limited importance of the institutional arrangements fine-tuned by the US governments and set up under guidance of the Bretton Woods institutions. During 1976, the current account deficit of non-oil LDCs stood at $28 billion, equal to $10 billion less than the 1975 peak. Remarkably, borrowing from private capital markets accounted for such substantial improvements far more than institutional financial arrangements: over the course of 1976, twenty developing countries each borrowed $100 million or more, which accounted for a sizable part of the $11.3 billion raised by non-oil LDCs through the Euromarket. This group of countries increased its share of total Eurocurrency loans from 39 percent in 1975 to about 41 percent in 1976.[41] On the other hand, based on data on US foreign aid commitments over the following years the failure of such US strategy found full confirmation insofar as it was aimed at squeezing the liabilities in the US balance of payments through a substantial reduction of balance of payments deficit financing assistance programs to the non-oil LDCs: instead of decelerating, from 1977 to 1979 both total overseas bilateral assistance and US contribution to multilateral assistance programs increased further.[42]

The remaining sections of this chapter are devoted to demonstrating that, as a result of this American unsuccessfulness, under the Carter administration Washington changed its policy altogether to link the financial assets of the oil producing countries to its policy to resurrect US international monetary might, and the international trade and payments system under its guidance.

5.2 Oil Recycling and International Payments: At the Origins of Demand Management Policies 1975–1977

These last two paragraphs chart a fundamental shift in the American policies aimed at targeting the US balance of payments deficit and at linking it to the recycling of the oil revenues of the OPEC countries. Such a turn occurred in connection with both the failure of the recycling mechanism set up since 1973, which led the OPEC countries to try go their way in rechanneling their financial assets, and a totally new approach to the unfettered depreciation of the dollar and US balance of payments deficit (see Table 5.1). This new approach identified the origins and causes of this twofold malaise with the seemingly intractable problems that afflicted the domestic economy and a fundamental imbalance between capital supply and aggregate demand. It paved the way for intensifying US pressure on its allies to set up anti-inflationary demand management policies based on striking the balance between capital supply for fixed capital formation and domestic aggregate demand through full capacity utilization in industry, the lessening of tight monetary policy and the fueling of capital supply based on the combining of a quota of GNP and a portion of the OPEC countries' oil revenues reinvested in the Western industrial economies. At the same time, these last few pages investigate the reshaping of international lending to the non-oil LDCs since US-led multilateral financial institutions and arrangements failed to accomplish their target. Under the Carter administration and through the end of the decade the role of the IMF in backing lending by private capital markets to countries with poor debt service capacity was revamped. The IMF began complementing the involvement of private capital markets in channeling the oil revenues to the non-oil producing LDCs. At the same time the OPEC countries were permitted to finance the non-oil LDCs directly.[43]

On the one hand, certainly the establishing of the OPEC Special Fund signaled the failure of US government's policy based on drawing on OPEC's capital surpluses to resurrect the current account position and foreign reserve assets in the non-oil producing LDCs, and the capital account position in the advanced economies, through existing or newly established international financial arrangements under US leadership. On the other hand, the persistence through the middle of the decade of conflicts between OPEC investors and the largest US commercial banks charged with recycling petrodollars over the so called "maturity imbalance" issue came at variance with and undermined the objective of the Federal Reserve to create a shift in the investment policies of the OPEC countries from short-term highly liquid assets to long-term equity and security markets. To put it another way, the Federal Reserve failed in its ambition to make petrodollars nurture fixed capital investments required to re-launch the supply side and the business cycle. Moreover, from 1976 to 1977 a jumble of other events jeopardized the US strategy to connect the recycling of oil revenues to the resurrecting at the same time of the US balance of payments, the strength of the dollar, and the permanence of the least wealthy non-oil LDCs in the loop of the international trade and payments system within the framework of Washington-led multilateral or bilateral financial and trade arrangements. For sure, the end of cooperation on energy matters, raw materials and development policies among the European Community, the United States, most leading industrial countries and the developing countries, united in the Conference on International Economic Cooperation (CIEC) that terminated its activities in June 1977, marked a step forward in this direction.[44] More importantly from the viewpoint of this book, under the Carter administration Washington's betting on the reflowing of OPEC financial resources to the largest capital absorbing oil producing OPEC members to finance American export of services, instrumental goods and consumer goods slowed down significantly, marking the collapse of this US policy to resurrect its current account position. The previous chapters pointed to the tangle of economic and financial bonds between the United States, its manufacturing and banking system, and the most capital absorbing oil producing economies of the Middle East, and the jumble of effects that such relations had on the US balance of payments through the rise in US export and the potentially positive repatriation of profits of US corporations' overseas investments. With the outburst of financial wealth accruing to these countries that followed the first quadrupling of oil prices since the beginning of 1974, Washington carried forward this way to sustain the US current account position. In this respect, the Ford administration was consistent with policies implemented in the past few years analyzed in this study. As a matter of fact, Ford strove to improve the US current account position through a rise in its export to the Middle Eastern oil producers quite consistent with the strategies to raise export and decrease overseas military expenditures by the Kennedy and Johnson administrations charted in the previous chapters of this study. Since the summer of 1974 the US established a series of bilateral technical cooperation commissions with some oil producing Middle Eastern countries, first and foremost Saudi Arabia and Iran, to promote industrial modernization and the mechanization of agriculture, as well as manpower training, the development of science and technology and of technical and educational institutions in these countries.[45] In establishing these bilateral venues, Washington pursued a twofold objective: in the first instance, the aim was to sustain the US balance of payments on current account and to uphold the value of the US currency through an increase in US exports to the largest OPEC consumer economies. Instead of investing short abroad, in this case the OPEC countries were expected to finance US foreign currency operations: US oil and other corporations' overseas investments in the oil producing largest economies would be achieved without an increase in foreign expenditures by US firms. This would in turn prevent American foreign investments from hurting further the US current account deficit. Besides, resorting to the OPEC capital surplus to finance US exports to those countries was intended to prop up the value of the dollar in exchange markets by letting the US acquire dollars and by reducing the dollar component of international liquidity. If one takes a look back to the 1960s, this was a long-standing US policy to counter the depreciation of the dollar in foreign exchange markets. In this last case the oil-rich OPEC countries were expected to use their financial might to import merchandise, services and technology from the US in this perspective. The increase in US export, direct fixed capital investments by US manufacturing firms in these oil producing economies, as well as technological transfer and technical assistance was to be based on the involvement of the largest US investment and commercial banks. In some sense, the involvement of US banking in developing such commercial relations was a means of keeping them involved in the oil revenues recycling process and relieving them from sharing the risky burden imposed on them by the lack of creditworthiness and low repayment prospects of the LDCs seen in the previous chapters. As stressed, most leading US banks as Chase Manhattan and First National City Bank (FNCB) featured a long-lasting involvement in the capital markets of these countries. From just prior to the first oil crisis through the following few years the number of foreign branches of these US banks in the Middle East and the Mediterranean basin increased substantially.[46] Since the establishment in the late spring of 1974 of the first technical cooperation commission between Washington and Saudi Arabia, the US–Saudi Arabian Joint Commission on Economic Cooperation, co-chaired by the US Secretary of State Kissinger and Saudi Prince Fahd, the US banks were involved in underwriting the Saudis' borrowings and warranting American investors in the country.[47] Likewise, the creation and implementation of a US–Iranian bilateral cooperation body capitalized on past involvement of US investment and commercial banks in the country.[48] In addition to reducing the dollar component in international liquidity and bolstering the value of the dollar, the development of bilateral commercial bonds with these high capital absorbing oil producers was clearly expected to also benefit the US trade balance and the current account position. However, the establishment of these bilateral commissions was also aimed—in the eyes of Washington—at increasing the leverage power the United States could exert on them to attain a number of diplomatic objectives. To be specific, the architect of these bilateral commissions, the then Secretary of State Henry Kissinger, mastered its development to make Washington's Middle Eastern partners pursue an oil price policy consistent with US objectives. This was particularly the case of Saudi Arabia: Kissinger sponsored the creation of the first bilateral commission during 1974 within this framework. Notwithstanding this commitment in Washington to develop such bilateral economic and financial bonds, since the beginning these bilateral commissions proved to be ill-functioning. At the end of the decade the US Secretary of the Treasury Henry Miller wrote to Secretary of State Cyrus Vance that "recent history suggests that an effective joint commission in not easy to attain. Saudi Arabia is the exception, and not the rule."[49]

This stream of overlapping events marked the failure of US policy to restore balance of payments equilibrium and to appreciate the dollar in exchange markets through a long-standing American commitment to focus the US foreign financial policy on the capital or current account portion of the US balance of payments deficit as the main cause for the malaise of the dollar. This jumble of overlapping problems prompted Washington to abandon such balance of payments deficit financing strategy. In other words, under Carter the sticky and mounting issue of transnational capital flows and the unparalleled growth of the Eurocurrency markets that had ravaged the value of the dollar was no longer identified as the origin of the depreciation of the US currency. Washington reappraised the idea that the OPEC countries were viable world lenders to reverse the weakening of the dollar in exchange markets and the dismissal of the idea that the deterioration in the international payments system was linked either to external pressure that capital outflows exerted on the US capital account, or to a sluggish current account position traceable back to federal foreign spending or sluggish American export. This argument paved the way for a new course in the history of US balance of payments deficit financing policies. Since his appointment to the White House, in cooperation with the IMF, Carter undertook a shift away from such previously-held interpretation: as pinpointed in these last few pages, from 1977 to the end of 1979 Washington associated the soaring inflation and plummeting dollar with domestic economic doldrums and productivity lags. To counter these disequilibria the newly appointed US government engaged in promoting expansionary policies that lay at the center of multilateral economic negotiations with Washington's Western European partners and drove the US to let the OPEC oil producers take responsibility for directly financing the external equilibrium of the non-oil LDCs.[50]

The abandonment of that long-lasting strategy to resurrect the dollar and to curb the balance of payments deficit based on measures on the capital and current accounts took place in the gloomy context of poorly performing macroeconomic data about the American recovery from the 1975 recession. More importantly, the context in which such a shift took place was also the seemingly intractable depreciation of the dollar, the persistence of US external imbalances and the pace of soaring inflation and downward sloping competitive edge, which the US and all major industrial economies suffered from. In the beginning of 1977, a surge in US energy demand for fuel imports and unchanged US exports put under pressure the US trade balance and shifted the US net balance on goods and services into a deficit, which during the year peaked at $11 billion. The ensuing depreciation of the dollar against most major US trading partners (see Table 5.1) triggered a surge in the price of a wide range of imported goods that added to the US inflation rate.[51] Such surge in prices came with an increase in income and consumer demand. On the other hand labor productivity in industry showed a mild downturn; as widely recognized in the economic literature, in 1976 it began a decade-long falloff in productivity growth.[52] At the same time, personal income and wages rose: as the Board of Governors of the Federal Reserve System reckoned at year-end, from 1976 to the new year "hourly compensation in the private nonfarm business sector rose about 8 and a half percent during 1977. At the same time, growth in productivity slowed from the cyclically advanced rate of 1976."[53] This macroeconomic framework had a stunning impact on unemployment: from 1976 to 1977 total US employment in 1000s declined sharply,[54] whereas by the time the Western economic powers gathered at the London Summit in May 1977 unemployment in the Western world soared to an aggregate total of 15 million people, and in most Western industrial economies the rate of unemployment was higher than in 1975 or 1976.[55] Making matters worse, world-based growth rates felt the pinch of decline; solely in the OECD the average growth rates were expected to decline from 5 percent in 1976 to 4.5 percent in 1977.[56] All of these economic indicators in the US and the international economy were plausible reasons that prompted Washington to take the lead once more in enhancing the resurrection of the international economy on a multilateral basis. This was in order to avert any recovery in the Western world based on either deflationary policies or trade restrictions as well as external borrowings and mounting debt, which would mark a striking departure from an interdependent international economy. The worsening economic picture of the industrial economies clearly jeopardized economic recovery against an orderly international economic framework. On the other hand, the failure to resurrect the dollar hit the international payments system: as the

IMF itself pointed out, under the fixed exchange rate system under operation prior to 1973 the weakening of the dollar had led other central banks to resort to reserves to support foreign exchange operations; in the floating currency system of the mid-1970s they were likely to resort to exchange rate movements and, more importantly, to private capital movements.[57] The incapability to resurrect the US dollar and to restore order in the international payments system hindered such a move and let the current account deficit run unchecked: at year-end 1976, in the aggregate the OECD current account deficits included the largest deficit countries (Italy, the UK, Canada and France) run at $98 billion, while the aggregate current account deficit of the non-oil LDCs had surged to $72 billion.[58] Therefore, by the time Carter took office, the combined sluggish industrial recovery and prolonged depreciation of the US dollar in international exchange markets, and persistently ravaging current account deficits and inflationary strains across the world, led the new US administration to phase out a strategy based on reshuffling the US external balance through continued focus on capital account and a shift in the investment patterns of the OPEC nations from short-term assets to longer financial instruments consistently pursued since the first oil price hike. Rather, owing to the new picture, the reshuffling of the international payments and monetary system needed to be coordinated as much as possible, with a pressing quest for resurrecting aggregate demand and competitive edge across the advanced industrial economies.

One further problem that stemmed from the strategy of US governments and the Federal Reserve System to make the OPEC oil revenues finance the recasting of the international trade and payments system added to this jumble of issues in the early stages of the Carter administration. It was the faltering of the US strategy to induce the OPEC countries to channel their money to both capital deficit industrial nations and the poorest LDCs. Based on available data, a rough estimate of the scale and scope of the OPEC long-term investments in the US and other Western economies makes it possible to better understand the correlation between OPEC foreign investments, the soaring US balance of payments deficit and the dollar's depreciation at the beginning of the Carter administration, and the ensuing movement to embrace a totally different macroeconomic interpretation about the causes of the dollar's depreciation and continued deterioration in the US external balance. A continuous depreciation from 1977 was associated with domestic recession, inflation, and striking losses in the competitive edge of US manufacturing. In the United States during the two-year period from 1974 to 1975, net placements by the Persian Gulf countries in bank deposits and portfolio holdings of governments and corporate securities totaled over $12 billion, in addition to a total inflow of direct investments not much more, according to Treasury's estimates, than $1 billion. By making a comparison between the investments of the Middle Eastern oil producing countries in the US from 1974 to 1975, it is clear that OPEC investments in the United States in support for a decrease in US foreign borrowing to nurture domestic investments and import requirements, did not make substantial improvements: investments in bank deposits and US Treasury bills declined from roughly $4 million to $1.8 million, while a quintupling of investments in corporate stocks, and a stunning surge in domestic corporate bonds and long-term deposits barely outstripped losses in bank deposits in absolute values.[59] According to the Office of Financial Resources and Energy Finance in the Treasury Department, "in aggregate, those investments were not particularly significant, although they were important to specific sectors of our capital market, particularly to certain international banks and in 1975, to the domestic corporate equity market."[60] A 1975 report by the Fed to the Senate Subcommittee on Multinational Corporations confirmed these figures: the six largest US banks (Chase Manhattan Bank, FNCB, Hannover Trust Corporation, Morgan Guaranty, Bank of America, Chemical Bank) had $11.3 billion in deposits from Middle East and North African oil producers, equal to 4.5 percent of the banks' total assets, in addition to the roughly $2.57 billion in deposits from other members of OPEC, including Venezuela and Indonesia. The total deposits of the six largest banks from oil producers were roughly equal to their total deposit liabilities to the financial centers of non-oil producing countries, including Panama, the Bahamas, Singapore and Switzerland.[61] At year-end 1975 these banks' deposits and portfolio holdings from the OPEC countries in the US were just a little over twice as much as the loans and grants of the Persian Gulf oil producers to the non-oil LDCs, which amounted to short of $5 billion.[62] Such modest contribution of the OPEC countries' surplus capital to the US external equilibrium through equity and portfolio investments is all the more striking if one places it within the framework of OPEC's total foreign official assets. To borrow from the example of Saudi Arabia, still in spring 1975 the largest contributor to long-term investments in the United States,[63] by early summer 1976 the total foreign official financial holdings of the largest supplier of crude oil to the US was estimated to have reached $43.100 billion.[64] From 1975 to late 1976 this decline in the OPEC countries' investment position in the US, paired with a sloping down US current account balance defined as the total amount of goods, services and official and private transfers of funds that are not considered capital transfers. During the first half of 1977 the current account position of the United States moved to a deficit at an annual rate of $17.5 billion, seasonally adjusted, as against $1.3 billion in the full calendar year 1976.[65] Considering that as a result of the 1975 recession in the US a stark reduction in merchandise import and a $12 billion current account surplus were registered, and that the current account was close to balance in 1976,[66] the malaise in which the US balance of payments lagged over the period was undoubtedly associated with transnational capital movements. Against this backdrop it is easy to get a sound fix on the small contribution of OPEC's Middle Eastern oil producers to the resurrection of US balance of payments. Such scanty contribution undermined the American strategy to bet on the OPEC portfolio and equity investments in the United States to drain the depreciation of the dollar in international exchange markets. However, if one points at the same time to trends in the value of the dollar in exchange markets (Table 5.1), the value of the OPEC countries' dollar-denominated investments abroad (Table 5.2), the slowly increasing growth rates and declining competitive edge with increased labor costs and prices in the US and major advanced industrial economies from the outbreak of the 1975 recession to early 1977,[67] and the pace of the non-oil LDCs balance of payments deficit during the same time frame, it is reasonable to establish a correlation between the recession in the largest consumer economies of the West, the falloff in international demand for OPEC oil, a significant reduction in size of

OPEC's dollar-denominated investible surplus, the value of their dollar-denominated investments in the US and other international portfolio and equity markets, and the pace of current account deficit for the non-oil producing LDCs. As shown by data on the change in the value of the US dollar against major currencies reported in Table 5.1, amid the 1975 recession and its strains over the following two years, a decline in international demand for oil and the ensuing contraction in the share of dollar-denominated financial assets in total private capital markets on world level, eased the pressure on the value of the dollar in international exchange markets. At the same time such course propped up the value of the OPEC member states' international investments and their purchasing power in foreign markets[68] in a way similar to the increase in the purchasing power of a country following the appreciation of its currency.[69] As the case of Saudi Arabia in Table 5.2 demonstrates, the value of OPEC investments recovered; at the same time, the unfettered decline in the purchasing power of oil prices in foreign markets, which plummeted both in 1974 and since 1976 as a result of the weakening of the US dollar within the framework of floating real exchange rates, registered a tempered reduction during 1976 compared to the collapse registered shortly before and thereafter (Fig. 5.2). It is worth establishing a linkage between such course and the mild recovery

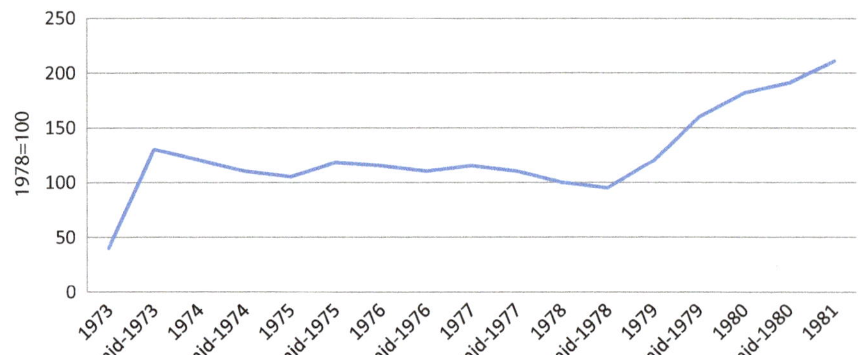

Fig. 5.2 Real oil prices: purchasing power of OPEC oil (Source: Federal Reserve Bank of New York Historical Archive)

in the value of the dollar in exchange markets as a result of the 1975 recession, with its ensuing decrease in international demand for oil, OPEC investible capital surplus, and dollar-denominated placements by the oil producers in international markets. To put it another way, the rate of economic growth was inverse to the value and strength of the dollar in international markets.

However, it was only with the 1979 increase in the price of crude oil that OPEC could counter the impact of the inflation of the decade and the continuous depreciation of the dollar on its purchasing power in the international consumer market and on the real value of its foreign capital investments. By contrast, the non-oil LDCs suffered from the 1975 recession insofar as they used to finance their import of consumer goods from the Western advanced industrial economies through the export of raw material and strategic goods[70]: the 1975 recession triggered a decrease in the international demand for non-oil LDCs-produced commodities and a general decline in commodity prices in world markets (see Fig. 5.1). Many developing countries, whose current account deficit and growth rates had continuously worsened since 1970, throughout the first half of the decade had borrowed heavily in foreign markets to maintain the flow of import of Western instrumental and consumer goods and to sustain the development programs and their current production level of commodities.[71] This triggered an unchecked increase in their external debt and debt service payments since as early as 1970 thereafter.[72] After a mild recovery during 1976 in connection with that year's mild industrial recovery in the US and most leading Western economies, at the beginning of 1977 two large supplying countries like Brazil and Mexico suffered from a stiff drawback in their current account deficit: in the aggregate the current account deficit of the non-oil LDCs dropped in 1977 from about $3 billion to about $25 billion.[73] This correlation helps make sense of a causal relation between the 1975 recession in the Western economies and the modest contribution of the international investments of oil revenues from the OPEC countries to the restoration of the dollar's strength and US balance of payments stability. At the same time, from 1975 through the spring of 1976 the recession in the advanced industrial economies cooled off new OPEC investments in the equity and portfolio markets in the US and added to the limited contribution of petrodollars to the fight to forestall the decline of the dollar and to reverse the US balance of payments deficit through investments in the US equity and money markets. Based on data on the value of the dollar in exchange markets, the purchasing power of oil-selling producers and the value of their international investments, the linkage between on the one side OPEC dollar-denominated long-term investments in the US and other financial markets and the financing of US export to the Middle East, and on the other the stabilization of the dollar's exchange rate and the US international payments position, seems a faltering argument widely shared in Washington. Furthermore, such development suggests the very weakness of the soon-to-be-implemented Carter administration's approach to link the OPEC's countries capital surplus to the nurturing of demand side policies in the US and other leading consumer economies through the financing of fixed capital formation and other productive-oriented long-term investments. The mid-decade story of recession in the West demonstrated that any temporary falloff in the volume of oil revenues accruing to the OPEC countries jeopardized a bolstering of the supply side revolving around the capital surplus of oil producers. In turn, at the time the decline in the OPEC countries' long-term investments triggered a decrease in the dollar component of world money supply that helped restore the value of OPEC's dollar-denominated international investments and the stability of monetary relations between the US and the leading OPEC oil producers. In addition to data charted in Table 5.2, the stunning upswing in relative purchasing power of the Saudi Arabian dollar-denominated assets registered since the 1975 western recession that followed a rough two-year period of decline in the real value of Saudi foreign investments charted in Table 5.3 is an exemplary case in point.

However, the early 1976 industrial upswing in the United States and other advanced industrial economies began reversing this trend. This work had already paid attention to the growing US current account deficit since the economy rebounded. Within this framework, international demand for crude oil surged again: at year-end 1976 the earnings

Table 5.3 Real value of Saudi Arabia's foreign investments

Movements in relative purchasing power of Saudi Arabian dollar-denominated assets

	January	February	March	April	May	June
1973			0	0.5	−1.2	−4.0
1974	2.2	−2.4	−6.8	−7.8	−6.4	−6.5
1975	−3.6	−5.9	−3.6	−2.8	−1.9	−3.2
1976	5.7	4.9	5.9	6.9	6.6	5.8
1977	4.8	4.7	4.8	5.4	4.9	2.7
1978	−3.8	−4.8	−6.1	−3.7		

	July	August	September	October	November	December
1973	−7.0	−0.5	−3.7	−5.5	−2.1	−1.5
1974	−3.4	0.8	−0.8	−0.1	0.1	−2.3
1975	3.2	4.0	6.5	4.8	6.0	5.3
1976	5.2	4.1	4.1	5.0	4.8	3.7
1977	1.8	1.9	1.1	−1.4	−1.4	−4.8
1978						

Source: Department of the Treasury, OASIA, Memorandum, in NARA. Office of the General Counsel. Assistant General Counsel, Records Related to OPEC Financial Affairs 1974–1979, b. 1, fold. F Part 1 of 4 1978–1979
Date: June 7, 1978

of OPEC countries on the accumulated invested surpluses from previous years reached an estimated $9 billion. This pace helped to push the combined OPEC current-account surplus in 1976 to an estimated $40 billion compared with $33 billion in 1975.[74] From 1975 to year-end 1976 all the three leading OPEC capital-surplus countries increased their assets generated by oil payments: as early as mid-spring 1976, they all began increasing their investments in US bank deposits and portfolio holdings. Saudi Arabia increased its purchases of government securities, while Kuwait boosted investments in commercial banks, especially its large concentrations of funds at Citibank.[75]

Therefore, shortly before Carter took office a sloping down dollar rate in international exchange markets was recorded, while the US balance of payments deficit run unchecked, most LDCs suffered from current account deficit once more, and the expected role of OPEC's surpluses in financing the US current and capital account position through long-term investments in US securities and equity markets was not as satisfactory as expected a few years earlier.

5.3 The Deterioration of US–Middle Eastern Financial Relations and the Demise of Demand Side Policies

In this jumble of overlapping dynamics, in cooperation with the IMF President-elect Carter made a turn to sustain expansionary policies as part of the new strategy to curb the US balance of payments deficit and the continuous decline of the dollar, which included successful economic and financial relations with Saudi Arabia and Iran to moderate oil prices. The combined failure manifested itself since as early as 1978; such two-fold strategy to reverse the weakening of the dollar, unfettered imbalances in international payments and the overheating of the international economy, and the ensuing crumbling of US relations with its key OPEC partners, led US monetary authorities and the government to phase it out. Within this framework Washington embarked upon the use of monetary policy to stabilize the US international payments position and the international economy.

Since early January 1977 the option for expansion was on the top of the agenda of the Western industrial economies as a prominent way to stabilize the international payments system. Since it came to office, the Carter administration planned to spend 1 percent of US GNP in 1977 to finance a domestic stimulus policy, while during his visit to Western Europe US Vice President Mondale received encouraging feedbacks from the European Commission, the Dutch and the Belgian authorities about a stimulus policy as a viable way to resurrect the international economy.[76] During the January Tokyo meeting of the Trilateral Commission, such perspective was discussed further. The very concept that emerged from the conference was to make the three leading industrial nations of the time (United States, Japan, Germany) the engine of international economic revival: on that occasion there was a general consensus that these three countries should pursue more expansionary domestic economic policies and refrain from an export-led growth, to reduce pressure on the industrial and developing countries that suffered the most from current international payments imbalances. At the same time, these countries should commit to coordinating their macroeconomic policies.[77] In was a clear turn to associate the restructuring of the international payments system and the rebuilding of sound trade exchanges with the reorganization of competitive industrial economies and wealthy domestic consumer markets.

In preparing for the Seven Nation Summit of late spring 1977, the White House put pressure on the Preparatory Group set up with the other participating powers to coordinate discussion, in order to confirm commitment by the US, Germany and Japan to keep their policies under review to ensure that they achieved moderately expansionist rates of growth; while the UK, France, Italy and Canada, as deficit countries, pledged to continue their stabilization policies until they had brought inflation under control.[78] The outspokenly stated objective of such stimulus policies was to drive a surge in the export of deficit countries to capital-surplus economies as German and Japan to enhance the adjustment process in the international payments system. At the London Summit of May 1977 a general consensus and commitment to strike the balance between surplus and deficit countries in which the former pledged to expand domestic aggregate demand and imports, while the latter countries went for enforcing domestic stabilization policies required to attract foreign investments and to borrow from international institutions and private lenders, was reached. Likewise, in London it was a widely shared view to consider revamping the role of the IMF in financing imbalances.[79] However, tellingly, most industrial nations linked such expanded role of the Fund to its imposition on the borrowing countries of adoption of domestic stabilization policies milder than what it usually required: otherwise, so went this argument, "countries might prefer not to borrow from it and resort instead to protectionism or induced recessions."[80] Later on, from 1978 to 1979, this policy was further implemented and extended to the creation of compensatory financing facilities, established under the United Nations agency UNCTAD at the request of the joint IMF/IBRD Development Committee, in support for commodity producing developing countries that felt the pinch of a continuous and unchecked decrease in commodity prices to compensate commodity producers of shortfalls in earning of each commodity.[81] Therefore, clearly the Fund and the US government established a linkage between domestic economic growth and external economic openness and integration, whether through support for export by, and attractiveness to, international investors in the non-oil LDCs or through fully-fledged support for growing fixed capital investments and increased aggregate demand across the advanced industrial economies. The Carter administration and the Washington-based Bretton Woods institution would pursue such course of action through the very end of the decade until the US monetary authorities inaugurated monetary tightness.

At the International Monetary Conference held in Tokyo in May 1977 the US Secretary of the Treasury better pinpointed the very general objective of such domestic stimulus policies discussed in London: capital-surplus countries and industrial economies suffering from sticky current account deficit should "collaborate to assure that the deficits which remain are distributed among countries in a pattern compatible with their ability to attract capital on a continuing basis. The present pattern does not achieve that balance. Substantial redistribution is required."[82] By the spring of that same year such target could count on a renewed role of the IMF in financing payments imbalances as desired by London, and on American support for the underwriting by the IBRD of developing countries' bonds.[83] On the other hand, by that time the US authorities clearly went for encouraging the oil producers to lend directly to the non-oil LDCs and the OECD industrial nations to self-finance their current account deficit.[84] In so doing, Washington aimed at lessening the financial dependence of the advanced industrial economies as a group on the oil producing lenders of OPEC. After turning down proposals to use a share of the industrial countries' GNP to finance the current account deficit of non-oil LDCs, such as the so-called "Carter Plan" presented by foreign monetary authorities to the US government,[85] the Carter administration turned its attention to making a clear distinction between the financing of non-oil LDCs and that of industrial countries. On the one side, the Executive Branch made a case for increasing the IMF resources by seeking arrangements under which countries in a relatively strong financial position, including both OPEC members and industrial nations, would lend money to the Fund. On the other hand, the US administration and—more fiercely—the US Congress, supported the idea of stabilizing international exchanges and payments within the Western world with the corollary implementation of stimulus policies in the USA, Germany and

Japan, and stabilization policies in current account deficit countries, such as the UK or Canada, by resorting to the OECD Financial Support Fund, better known at the time as the Safety Net, a financing scheme based only on contributions from the OECD member countries. The very objective of such policy was to strike the balance between orderly domestic growth and a sound international payments system revolving around a healthy US dollar without resorting to the financial might of oil producers.[86] Reasoning along these lines, the Carter administration strove to prevent a resurrecting of the international trade and payments system based on high level of domestic growth in the advanced industrial economies from a cursing financial dependence on the oil producing OPEC nations.

Certainly, the centerpiece of Carter's new foreign financial and monetary policy was to achieve non-inflationary domestic expansion in the US and across most advanced industrial economies to tear apart the linkage between domestic inflation and international financial instability. The core argument was that inflationary strains and their consequences on the dollar and the stability of the international payments system stemmed from a fundamental imbalance between the supply side and aggregate demand, whereby the latter outstripped production and productivity levels. According to the Carter administration, such imbalance reflected both underutilized industrial capacity as a result of the 1975 recession, and the impact of upward oil prices on the competitive edge of US industry and on wages and consumers prices, as well as tight credit policies. Under Secretary of State for Monetary Affairs Richard Cooper made this strategy clear to his German counterparts when he visited Bonn along with Vice President Mondale in January 1977: a stimulus package based on a reduction in payroll taxes would prop up aggregate demand, which in turn could stimulate fixed capital investments. This policy should be complemented with a shift from monetary tightening to fiscal tightening to ease the cost of money, to fuel fixed capital investments and to foster consumers demand.[87]

Significantly, the IMF shared such inward-looking interpretation of disorderly international payments and intractable current account deficits, and the idea of implementing domestic expansionary policies. Even in the floating exchange rate system under operation, did the Fund's Research Department pin down, income effects dominated relative price effects in the short and medium term, so much so that the relative cyclical positions of the various industrial countries significantly affected their current account position with disturbing effect on exchange rates. The way suggested by the Fund was exactly the same the White House embarked upon, though the Fund made a bet on combined expansionary policy and below average capacity utilization: "discretionary demand management policies can be used to increase the rate of growth without excessive costs in terms of higher inflation as long as the country remains significantly below capacity."[88]

The US strategy, consistently endorsed by Secretary of the Treasury Blumenthal throughout 1977,[89] met with two hindrances: resistance within the Western world to carry over unfettered expansionary policies by Germany and Japan, and the deterioration of bilateral relations between Washington and Iran and Saudi Arabia. Making matters worse, the stimulus policies triggered little positive effect on all macroeconomic data they were supposed to tackle: the depreciation of the dollar, the current account balance of deficit countries, the pace of international inflation and the corresponding competitive edge of the American economy all became worse during Carter's tenure in office. Therefore, the new strategy to resurrect the dollar and the US international payments position through replacing the investments of OPEC dollar-denominated assets in long-term financial instruments and an increase of US corporations' investments and export to oil producing economies with higher levels of economic growth and productivity across the US and most advanced industrial economies proved to be short-lived. In all of these respects, it is worth pointing to 1978 as the watershed year, and it is worth focusing on all of these issues.

Although German Chancellor Schmidt repeatedly reckoned the need to reverse "the decline in investment and capital expenditure in recent years,"[90] from 1977 to 1979 Germany followed the Carter administration's idea of fostering domestic expansion to raise import and reduce the German current account surplus only to a very limited extent.[91] In fact, even if during 1979 the German and Japanese surplus diminished during the previous two years Bonn carried over limited domestic stimulus policies. Since he met the US Vice-President in early 1977, Schmidt pledged to develop a domestic infrastructure program but linked it to the possibility of borrowing without raising interest rates.[92] At that early stage Carter himself urged the German chancellor to stimulate the national economy more than he had planned to do.[93] Notwithstanding such American pressures, over the following two years Bonn pledged to such course on many occasions with little results. On its part, at the end of the decade the Japanese authorities relentlessly showed their worries about the inflationary implication of any stimulus policy, whether fiscal or commercial in nature: on many occasions they stressed that monetary tightening and relaxation should be mixed to avert strong domestic demand and accelerated inflation.[94]

Throughout 1977 and the first half of 1978 the Carter administration could promote before the other Western powers such expansionary pace to curb inflation and the decline of the dollar in exchange markets because Iran and, more consistently, Saudi Arabia exhibited a palpable concern about the international political impact of an economic downturn in the West and committed to make a case within OPEC to moderate the price of crude oil. According to a prominent interpretation, the two countries took a rather different perspective on the subject, and the Saudi decision to moderate oil prices laid down the economic origins of the Iranian revolution.[95] Based on the archival documentation consulted during the writing of this chapter, it is worth saying that for a limited period of time until 1977 both giant oil producers shared a policy of moderate increases in oil prices. The prospective recessionary effects of a skyrocketing increase in oil prices on the US economy and other advanced industrial nations were viewed as a precondition for an American retreat from the Gulf. Since Nelson Rockefeller visited Saudi Arabia in the spring of 1977, Saudi authorities had expressed concern about the implication on growth and stability of rising oil and food prices in world trade markets, stressing the risk of a Soviet takeover in the Persian Gulf. The Saudi authorities linked their support for moderate price increases to their deep-seated concern for the US balance of payments deficit, the growth of the Western economies and the threat of inflation.[96]

However, the combined concern by Saudi Arabia and Iran about the security implications in the Middle East of a recession in the US and the ensuing oil price moderation, melted down from 1977 to 1978 over the issue of the dollar's value in international exchange markets, was considered crucial both to Washington and to Jeddah and Teheran. During this period, such issue drove the foreign financial policy of the two countries toward Washington and checked the hazardousness of going for an upswing in oil prices for the security and freedom of the Gulf's member countries of OPEC.

As already stressed in this study, the worse the US economy performed, the better the purchasing power of oil producing countries and the value of their dollar-denominated foreign investments were as a result of a falloff in Western demand for oil and the ensuing decline of dollar-denominated assets in world financial markets. On the other hand, as remarked, this trend hit hard the external debt and balance of payments deficit of LDCs used to import instrumental and consumer goods from the industrial nations. Punctually, when the strain of the 1975 recession faded away, the value of the dollar in exchange markets began tottering again: the case of bilateral exchange rates between the dollar and the Saudi Riyal charted in Table 5.2 is a case in point as they are bilateral exchange rates with Saudi dinars and other leading oil producers.[97] This was clear by the fall of 1976: the curse of bilateral relations between the US and Kuwait, which, as the least capital absorbing country suffered the most from the dollar's depreciation, helps chart this. During his visit to Kuwait in late October, Under Secretary Cooper had to cope with complaints by the Kuwaiti oil and finance ministers about the fact that the US had so far failed to curb a downward spiraling dollar. Cooper stressed the consistent US commitment agreed upon in London to expand the US and world economy: he pointed to the improvements achieved since Carter arrived to the White House in terms of commodity prices, and the current account deficit of primary producing countries. Both had improved, he insisted, while temporary US measures such as increased gold sales and interest rates accounted for the recent increase in the US trade balance.[98] Notwithstanding that, the value of the dollar in exchange markets began plummeting: at year-end 1977 the dollar had depreciated over 10 percent over its October level against the German, Swiss and Japanese currencies.[99] During the first quarter of 1978 the US current account deficit run at an annual rate of $28 billion, almost twice the 1977 level.[100] From 1977 to 1978 US incapability to keep under control the value of its currency and its balance of payments deficit coupled with the modest effects of the American strategy to try to tackle the problem of the dollar and international payments through measures to enhance domestic growth. In the summer of 1977 such unsatisfactory results were clear to the Western economic establishment: for instance, in commenting the US trade deficit, de Vries declared that "while energy is a large part of the problem, the competitive position has also eroded."[101] The pace of US–Kuwaiti relations since the fall of 1976 anticipated the deterioration of Washington's economic bonds with Teheran and Saudi Arabia. It is worth focusing on the latter due to its long lasting relations with the US.

As anticipated, certainly the turning point that marked the unsuccessfulness of Carter's strategy to counter the depreciation of the dollar and the US balance of payments deficit through the combined fighting of domestic economic downswing and inflation, and stable relations with the largest oil producers of the Middle East ensuring affordable oil prices to the overheated Western economies, was the year 1978. By the first half of 1978 in the aggregate the current account deficit of the industrial countries and that of the LDCs had worsened staggeringly.[102]

Against this backdrop, US–Saudi relations began deteriorating: in January 1978 Saudi oil Minister Yamani complained about the lack of US commitment to successfully devise energy policies alternative to oil and the Saudi need for much more technological transfer and manpower training.[103] In May, Yamani linked the proposed sale of 60 fighters F15 by the United States to the Saudis to continued Saudi support of the United States economy in the form of increased oil production and continued support for the dollar.[104] However, certainly the most disturbing issue to the Saudis was lack of US commitment to undertake plans for energy diversifications aimed at reducing demand for oil in international markets.[105] If one recalls the linkage between oil trade and the growth of the US economy, the pace of international oil transactions, and the real value of the OPEC countries' international investments, it is easy to grasp the position of the Saudis. A firm call on the West for energy diversification prevented the OPEC countries from facing up to the alternative between a depreciation of their financial assets and foreign investments, and a recession in the West that might jeopardize Washington's firm presence in the Persian Gulf and make way for a Soviet takeover of the region.

Washington's promises to craft new energy policies proved to be fallacious throughout the following one and a half years, and hazardously coupled with the continued faltering of the dollar in exchange markets during 1978, and the Iranian Revolution that from the fall of 1978 to the demise of the Shah in Teheran in early 1979 reduced international oil supply and increased stockpiling and oil hoardings. The development of the situation in Iran stirred expectation for further increase in the price of posted oil and expected inflationary strains in the international economy.

Therefore, the oil policy of Iran and Saudi Arabia changed substantially from 1977 to 1978, adding strains to the international payments and trade system. In the fall of 1977, high-ranking officials of the Saudi Arabian Monetary Authority (SAMA) reckoned that the Saudi government had "overcome its initial grave concerns over the growing weakness of the dollar" and was waiting to see how the US economy performed.[106] Still in early 1978, the Shah and Saudi Crown Prince Fahd reached a Saudi–Iranian Agreement to maintain a crude oil price freeze for the entire year of 1978.[107] However, in light of continued lack of effective measures on the part of Washington to forestall the collapse of the dollar in exchange markets in the spring and summer of that same year, in the fall, within OPEC, Saudi Arabia traded a crude oil price hike in return for not shifting away from the dollar as the medium for pricing oil to a basket of currencies.[108] At that time, the price of oil was determined by a basket of currencies against the fluctuation of the dollar: within OPEC some countries like Algeria and Libya, later on led by Iran, called for leaving the dollar. Therefore, on the eve of Secretary Blumenthal's visit to the Middle East in early November 1978, the Department of State briefed the White House and the National Security Council about the criticality of Washington's relations with Jeddah: "with a significant portion of Saudi reserves invested in dollars and oil priced in dollars, the Saudi's concern for the dollar and the economic health of the US is very real."[109] Such a path-breaking turn in Saudi policies followed a continued depreciation of the dollar; from April to November the dollar depreciated substantially against the Japanese yen, which during this period was the strongest currency: during those seven months the dollar rate for the yen rose by 16 percent.[110] This tottering of the dollar added pressure to the weakened relations between Washington and Jeddah. As anticipated in this chapter, the collapse of the Iranian regime increased stockpiling and oil hoarding: the uncertainty about oil prices that stemmed from such pace coupled with further deteriorating political stability in the Persian Gulf. Over the course of their visit to the Middle Eastern oil producing countries, both Blumenthal, in November, and the new Secretary of the Treasury Miller one year later, pledged to restrain energy consumption and to implement alternative energy policies: either commitment would be proved to be faltering in light of a depreciation of the dollar that ran unchecked.[111] A growing Saudi concern about the future of the area,[112] coupled with plummeting financial relations between the US and Kuwait: as a retaliation against the Iranian regime, which in November 1979 declared that it did not plan to meet its financial obligations incurred under the Shah's regime, the US decided to freeze the Iranian assets and to declare Teheran on default on a number of syndicated dollar loans raised by Teheran with the American banks when the Shah was in power.[113] At the same time, Morgan Guaranty went for attaching the Iranian shares in the German Krupp company. Following such events, the Kuwaiti government condemned this array of sanctions.[114] In this framework of precipitating financial relations with oil producers that deprived the Carter expansionary method of stabilizing the dollar and the international payments system of the fundamental pillar of moderate increases in oil prices, stimulus policies proved to be unsuccessful insofar as by 1979 international payments, inflation, US industrial productivity and the dollar did not improve substantially. Although in early 1979 the international payments system showed signs of recovery demonstrated by a reduction in the Japanese current account surplus and improvements in the US current account deficit by and large owed to exchange rate adjustments,[115] the global outlook for international payments among the oil producers, the OECD economies and the non-oil LDCs was decidedly bad-looking.[116] In the framework of a major downswing in the international economy and soaring international inflation in 1980, when in the OECD countries inflation run at 13 percent in the second half of the year,[117] the US domestic economy and industrial productivity were on a decidedly downward spiral: in the first quarter of the year compensation per hour increased at a 10 percent annual rate, productivity declined over 4 percent, and unit labor costs soared by a staggering 15 percent, while both consumer prices and wholesale prices continued to experience an upswing mode.[118] On the other hand, the strength of the dollar and the US external balance confirmed the incapability to restore the competitive edge of the US and the strength of its currency through the fight of domestic inflation and the enhancement of demand side policies. In the first quarter of 1979 the current account surplus reflected a sharp increase in net investment income that offset the continued deficit on merchandise trade and sluggish export and competitive edge of US manufacturing, while during the same quarter the gross outflow of private capital decreased substantially compared to the first quarter of 1978.[119] This worsening in the competitive position of US manufacturing paired with the decline of the dollar. This combined negative outcome tracked the unsuccessfulness of the Carter administration's strategy to pair the rebounding of the US international payments position and the dollar's strength with a recasting of country's domestic growth and competitive edge in the framework of Washington's increase financial independence from the OPEC oil producers. A rough comparison between the value of the US currency against the eight most important Western currencies from 1974 to 1978, based on London mid-day rates, shows that in 1978 the US currency depreciated against all but the Canadian dollar as worse as it never did since 1973.[120]

On the other hand, the intractable weakening of the dollar in exchange markets was reflected in the continued decline in the role of the dollar in international finance: from 1976 to 1978 the volume of Eurocurrency deposits in other currencies had been rising, and as of mid-1978, approximately 25 percent of the liabilities of Eurocurrency banks were in non-dollar currencies and 75 percent in dollars.[121] Therefore, notwithstanding the expansionary policies and the rescue package put into place by the Carter administration to defend the dollar in November 1978, the US currency and the national economy lost ground and proved the failure of Carter's fight to strike the balance between capital supply and aggregate demand as a way to fight inflation and to restore confidence in the dollar as a prerequisite to rebuild an orderly international payments system based on the US currency.

These unfixed issues and the staggering oil price increase decided by OPEC that year added to deteriorating financial relations between the US, and Saudi Arabia and Iran. This book has pointed to the course of Washington's relations with these key partners: the taking of the US Embassy and the kidnapping of US citizens in Iran for 444 days, which led the Carter administration to undertake further retaliatory economic measures in addition to the freezing of Iranian assets a few months earlier, made matters even worse and deprived the Carter administration's strategy to resurrect the balance of payments deficit and the dollar of a fundamental pillar.

Such deterioration of financial relations between the United States and its most important partners in the Middle East was aggravated by the sticky issue of US taxation of foreign investments in the US. Since the fall of 1976, the proposed revision by the US IRS of American tax regulations to cover some of the investments of foreign governments in the US stirred a string of vivid reactions in Kuwait, where finance and oil ministers warned the US government that provision of such regulation, "by discouraging Kuwaiti investments in the US, could also discourage Kuwaiti oil production."[122] Far from being fixed, this issue blew up over the course of 1978 and 1979 and contributed, along with Kuwait's fierce reaction to the US decision to declare Iran on default on several credit lines in the fall of 1979,[123] to deteriorate bilateral relations between the two countries and to reduce the positive contribution of Kuwaiti investments in the US to the American current account balance. In particular, the two countries wrangled over the inclusion of Kuwait real estate investments in the US, which the Middle East oil producer had expanded in California in partnership with Chase Manhattan and Bank of America,[124] under the taxable "commercial" category: such investments had traditionally been tax-exempt because US tax regulation considered them as investments, not commercial activities.[125] While the problem of taxation of real estate investments by foreign governments still shook bilateral relations between the US and Kuwait in early 1979,[126] the problem of taxation undermined Washington's relations even with Saudi Arabia. In 1978, the Saudi Minister of Finance cabled Blumenthal to express his concern regarding the application of the US foreign tax credit to Saudi Arabia, stressing that it was "a retrogressive step inimical to the growing commercial relationship between the two countries."[127]

Such intricacy of cumbersome issues provided the framework against which the US government appointed Paul Volcker to the head of the

Federal Reserve Board in August 1979: his appointment marked not simply—as correctly pointed out in the literature[128]—the end of Carter's bet to ease international credit to restore equilibrium in the international trade and payments system and to fight inflation.[129] Shortly after he took office, Volcker undertook a series of monetary measures to dramatically tighten money and credit: by mid-1981 the US prime lending rate exceeded 20 percent. Certainly, the new chairman did reverse a policy that since the early 1970s proved to be unable to finance the explosion in current account imbalances of all countries in a deficit position.[130] From the research perspective of this study it marked the end of Carter's inward-looking interpretation about the causes and nature of the US balance of payments deficit and of the unfettered and long-standing depreciation of the dollar.

For sure, over the course of the fall of 1979, the Carter administration had already taken a departure from the expansionary strategy followed over the last two years: in early September of that year a widening gap between high interest rates in Germany and Japan and the rates on dollar loans chronicled the international financial scenario. In the light of these developments, the Chairman of the House of Representatives Banking Committee Reuss suggested President Carter urge other countries to change their anti-inflationary mix so as to rely less on monetary tightness and more on fiscal tightness. On behalf of the White House, Secretary Miller responded that monetary policy should not be eased: "to fight inflation, continued discipline is called for in both fiscal and monetary policy."[131]

Notes

1. Coombs, 1974. On Iran's loan to the UK see also *Financial Times*, July 23, 1974.
2. National Archives and Records Administration, Archive II, College Park, MD (henceforth NARA), General Records of the Department of the Treasury (henceforth RG56), Office of the General Counsel. Assistant General Counsel, Records Related to OPEC Financial Affairs 1974–1979, b. 2, fold. G Part 1 of 3 1974–1975, D. Keyser to L. Widman, "Recycling: Banks' 1975 Projection," February 18, 1975.

3. On the policies of the Ford administration aimed to promote export and international trade see also Macavoy, 2003, pp. 216–217.
4. Declassified Documents and Reference System. http://www.gale.com/us-declassified-documents-online/ (henceforth DDRS), CIA, Intelligence Memorandum "Iran: The Shah's Lending Binge," December 15, 1974.
5. The National Archives, Kew, Richmond (henceforth TNA), FCO 82/446, Meeting between James Callaghan, Secretary of State for Foreign and Commonwealth Affairs, and Dr. Henry Kissinger, US Secretary of State, September 24 (1974), Secretary of State's Discussion with Dr. Kissinger in New York on September 24, 1974 "Recycling the Financial Surpluses of the Oil Producers."
6. *The Wall Street Journal*, August 24, 1974.
7. International Monetary Fund Archives, Washington DC (henceforth IMFA), Middle Eastern Department Immediate Office (henceforth Medai), Medai Subject Files, b. 75, fold. 1, E. Sturc to the IMF Managing Director, Memorandum "Financial Arrangements of Certain Oil-Exporting Countries in 1974."
8. NARA, RG56, Office of the General Counsel. Assistant General Counsel, Records Related to OPEC Financial Affairs 1974–1979, b. 1, fold. F Part 1 of 4 1978–1979, Memorandum of Conversation Blumenthal (US Treasury Secretary)-Solomon (Under Secretary of the Treasury)-Bergsten (Assistant Secretary US Department of the Treasury)-Abalkhail (Saudi Arabia Finance Minister)- al-Quraishi (SAMA Governor)-Alturki (Saudi Deputy Finance Minister), October 29, 1977; data about the exchange movements of the dollar through mid-1978 based on the London mid-day rates in *ibid.,* "Draft Briefing material for the Solomon/Quarishi (Sama Governor) meeting scheduled for June 13," June 7, 1978, annexed table.
9. *The New York Times*, August 28, 1974.
10. NARA, RG56, Office of the Assistant Secretary for International Affairs (henceforth OASIA), Chronological Files of the Office of Financial Resources and Energy Finance 1974–1977, b. 1, fold. TEFRP: Office of Financial Resources Policy Coordination-Permanent Chron. File June 1975, Declaration of Mr. Khalid Abu al-Sa'ud, Director of Investment at Kuwait Ministry of Finance, Financial and Banking News, "Middle East Economic Survey," May 1975; ivi, fold. TEFRP: Office of Financial Resources Policy Coordination-Permanent Chron. File August 1975, M. O'Connor (Treasury /TEFRP Financial Resources) "US Attitude Toward Kuwaiti Investment Issue," August 1975.

11. IMFA, Office of the Managing Director Fonds (henceforth OMD), Witteveen Sous-Fond, b. 3 (correspondence), fold. 3, D. Rockefeller (Chairman, Chase Manhattan Bank), "Comments To Woodrow Wilson Center on: Monetary Aspects of the Oil Problem," February 6, 1975.
12. NARA, RG56, Office of the General Counsel. Assistant General Counsel, Records Related to OPEC Financial Affairs 1974–1979, b. 3, fold. K 1977, R. Debs (Federal Reserve Bank of New York) to A. Aziz al-Quraishi (Governor, SAMA), December 24, 1974; ivi, fold. O 1975–1978, Debs to Al-Quraishi, January 13, 1975. On these special arrangements see also Federal Reserve Bank of New York Historical Archive, New York City (henceforth FRBNYA), Mr. Kubarych's Files, b. 114512, fold. Rosenthal Sub Committee (OPEC Financial Holdings), Summary of Letters of January 13 and 14, 1974.
13. NARA, RG56, Office of the General Counsel. Assistant General Counsel, Records Related to OPEC Financial Affairs 1974–79, b. 2, fold. F Part 4 of 4. 1974–1978, Department of the Treasury, "The Dollar and the Pricing Unit for Oil," October 23, 1978.
14. Rockefeller Archive Center, Tarrytown, NY (henceforth RAC), Rockefeller Family Archive (henceforth RFA), Record Group III 4 A, Nelson A. Rockefeller Personal (henceforth RG III 4 A), Series C-Business, b. 161, fold. 1791, "Economic Perspective. Point B"; NARA, RG56, Office of the General Counsel. Assistant General Counsel, Records Related to OPEC Financial Affairs 1974–1979, b. 1, fold. D 1974–1975, Memorandum of Conversation W. Simon-Under Secretary E. Yeo-Assistant Secretary G. Parsky-Governor Abdul Aziz al Qurayshi (SAMA)- Abdul Aziz al-Dukhayyel (Saudi Minister of Finance), "Saudi Investments in the US," September 2, 1975.
15. See among other sources the documents held in NARA, RG56, OASIA, Office of International Investment, Council on International Economic Policy Files 1978–1979, b. 1; see also FRBNYA, Mr. Kubarych's Files, b. 114,512, fold. Rosenthal Sub Committee (OPEC Financial Holdings).
16. NARA, RG56, OASIA, Chronological Files of the Office of Financial Resources and Energy Finance 1974–1977, b. 1.
17. NARA, RG56, OASIA, Chronological Files of the Office of Financial Resources and Energy Finance 1974–1977, b. 1, fold. TEFRP: Office of Financial Resources Policy Coordination. Permanent Chron. File 1974, G. Parsky to P. Grasso (House of Representatives).

18. NARA, RG56, OASIA, Office of International Investment, Council on International Economic Policy Files 1978–79, b. 1, fold. CFIUS Early Days 1974, J. Niehuss to W. Eberle, Memorandum "Mid-East Investment in the US," December 6, 1974; see also ivi, Council on International Economic Policy (CIEP), "International Economic Considerations."
19. NARA, RG56, OASIA, Chronological Files of the Office of Financial Resources and Energy Finance 1974–1977, b. 1, fold. TEFRP: Office of Financial Resources Policy Coordination. Permanent Chron. File 1974, M. O'Connor to Assistant Secretary Worthington "Responses to McCracken Memo," September 24, 1974.
20. Department of Commerce, 1975c, 55 (8). table S 3 and 1975a, 55 (1).
21. Department of the Treasury, 1975, p. 97.
22. Department of Commerce, 1975b, 55 (6) and 1975d, 55 (9).
23. On this shift in the investment pattern of the oil producers in the literature, see Bell, 1976, p. 31.
24. DDRS, Department of the Treasury, OASIA, "OPEC aid Commitments to non-Oil Exporting LDCs," September 20, 1974.
25. IMFA, OMD, Witteveen Papers, Chronological Files, b. 1, A.D. Crockett, Memorandum for Files, "Financing Oil in the Medium Term," February 11, 1974.
26. NARA, RG56, National Advisory Council on International Monetary and Financial Policies (henceforth NAC), NAC Staff Committee Minutes 1974, b. 2, fold. Meeting n. 74-1 through 74-21, NAC, NAC Staff Committee Minutes, Meeting 74-14, March 19, 1974.
27. NARA, RG56, OASIA, Subject Files of the Office of International Monetary Affairs 1968–1978, b. 6, fold. Oil, Department of the Treasury, Background Paper "United Nations General Assembly Special Session" April 1974.
28. IMFA, Medai, Medai Subject Files, b. 72.
29. IMFA, OMD, Witteveen papers, Chronological Files, b. 1, fold. 4, "Managing Director's Meeting with Chancellor Healey," December 16, 1974.
30. NARA, RG56, OASIA, Chronological Files of the Office of Financial Resources and Energy Finance 1974–1977, b. 2, fold. TEFRP: Office of Financial Resources Policy Coordination. Permanent Chron. File December 1975, Office of Financial Resources and Energy Finance, "US Estimates of OPEC Investments," December 1975.

31. *IMF Press Release* 74/41, August 22, 1974.
32. IMFA, Central Files, Economic Subject Files, b. 471, fold. 9(S 1781 Oil Facility. Borrowing from Germany 1974–1978), Draft Minutes of Meeting 75/12 and 75/13; The IMF to Karl Klasen (President Deutsche Bundesbank), telegram, May 16, 1975; O. Emminger to Witteveen, May 23, 1975; The IMF Secretary to Members of the Executive Board, "Federal Republic of Germany—Borrowing in Connection with the Oil Facility," May 27, 1975; J. Witteveen to K. Klasen, April 25, 1975. See also IMFA, OMD Files, Witteveen papers, Chronological Files, b. 1, fold. 5, Witteveen to Klasen (President of the Deutsche Bundesbank), January 23, 1975.
33. NARA, National Advisory Council on International Monetary and Financial Policies (NAC), NAC Actions 1974, b. 4, fold. n. 74-451 Through n. 74-609, NAC, "IBRD. Proposed $750 Million Borrowing Outside the United States-Saudi Arabia," December 10, 1974.
34. FRBNYA, b. 35607, fold. PAV to Attend CRF's Survey Discussion on OPEC (Richard Erb to Speak), R. Erb, Background paper "Monetary Collaboration," May 28, 1975.
35. World Bank Group Archives, Washington DC (henceforth WBGA), Records of the Office of the President, Records of President Robert S. McNamara, Contacts with Member Countries. Germany-Correspondence 05, "Notes for Meetings with Poehl, Gentcher (Federal Republic of Germany Foreign Minister), and Chancellor Schmidt," January 29, 1975.
36. NARA, RG56, Office of the Under Secretary for Monetary Affairs, Subject Files of Anthony M. Solomon Under Secretary for Monetary Affairs 1977–1980, b. 2, fold. Gold, F. Lisle Widman to Under Secretary Solomon, "Possible Initiatives by the Brandt Commission on an IMF Gold Sales Program," table 3, April 27, 1979.
37. NARA, RG56, OASIA, Office of the Deputy Assistant Secretary for International Monetary Affairs, Briefing Books 1971–1980, b. 1, Department of State, Briefing Paper, Position Paper "Effect of LDC International Payments Imbalances on the Dialogue" October 1975.
38. See documentation in NARA, RG56, OASIA, Office of Regional and Resources Policy, Briefing Books 1975–1982, b. 1.
39. IMFA, Medai, Medai Subject Files, b. 75 (OPEC), fold. 4 (OPEC 1977–1981), Briefing Paper for the Managing Director's Meeting with Dr. Ibrahim Shihata, Director General of the OPEC Special Fund, October 29, 1979.

40. Morgan Guaranty Trust Company of New York, *World Financial Markets*, November 1977; see also IMFA, Medai, Medai Subject Files, b. 75 (OPEC), fold. 4 (OPEC 1977–1981), E. Maciajewski to Engstrom, Memorandum "OPEC Countries: External Assets and Investment Flows," December 13, 1977.
41. NARA, RG56, OASIA, Office of the Deputy Assistant Secretary for International Monetary Affairs, Briefing Books 1971–1980, b. 1, fold. Advisory Committee for International Monetary Reform Secretary Blumenthal, Fowler Committee Meeting, Meeting Agenda, April 19, 1977.
42. NARA, RG56, OASIA, Subject Files of the Deputy Assistant Secretary for Developing Nations Finance 1976–1977, b. 3, fold. DA 9-6, Department of the Treasury, Office of Development Policy, February 26, 1977, US Annual Aid Commitments with Intermediate Increase of Bilateral Commitments and Intermediate Increase of Multilateral Commitments FY 1977–1982.
43. In support for such cooperation between private capital markets and the IMF see IMFA, OMD, Witteveen Papers, Chronological Files, b. 1, fold. 6 (April–June 1975), IMF to Yemen Arab Republic Prime Minister, telegram, June 22, 1977.
44. Conference on International Economic Cooperation, 1977, pp. 970–976; *US Department of State Bulletin*, June 20, 1977, pp. 650–652. On the CIEC, see for reference, in the literature Coffey, 1979, pp. 192–193.
45. For further insights and research on the subject see NARA, RG56, OASIA, Office of the Deputy Assistant Secretary for Developing Nations Finance, Briefing Books on the Middle East 1974–1975, b. 2; NARA, RG56, OASIA, Office of Regional and Resources Policy, Briefing Books 1975–1982, b. 1; NARA, RG56, OASIA, Subject Files of the Deputy Assistant Secretary for Developing Nations Finance 1976–1977, b. 2; FRBNYA, Presidential Papers, Paul A. Volcker Papers, b. 35,604.
46. NARA, General Records of the Department of Commerce (henceforth RG40), Office of the Secretary, Executive Secretariat's Subject File 1953–1974, b. 309, fold. Commerce Action Group on the Near East (DIB), "The Near East Markets: A Report to US Business, prepared by BIC Near East Study Group," May 17, 1974, p. 57.
47. On the establishment of this commission, see RAC, RFA, Record Group 26, Nelson A. Rockefeller, Vice Presidential (henceforth RG26),

Foreign Affairs and National Security, b. 3, fold. 53, Department of State, "Joint Statement on Saudi Arabian–United States Cooperation," June 10, 1974; Joint Communiqué on the First Session of the US–Saudi Arabian Joint Commission on Economic Cooperation, undated; Department of State, Briefing Paper "Secretary Robinson's Visit to Saudi Arabia, February 1975."

48. See, among other sources, documents held in NARA, RG56, OASIA, Office of the Deputy Assistant Secretary for Developing Nations Finance, Briefing Books on the Middle East 1974–1975, b. 2.
49. Jimmy Carter Presidential Library and Museum, Atlanta, GA (henceforth JCPL), Anthony M. Solomon Collection, Chronological File, b. 8, fold. 1/18/80-1/31/80, Miller to Vance.
50. NARA, RG56, OASIA, Subject Files of the Deputy Assistant Secretary for Developing Nations Finance 1976–1977, b. 3, fold. DA 9-6, R. G. Pelikan to Under Secretary Solomon, interoffice memorandum "EPG Deputies' Meeting February 22—North/South Relations—The Financial Issues," February 21, 1977.
51. Federal Reserve System, 1977, pp. 6 ff.
52. Peden, 1991, p. 159.
53. Federal Reserve System, 1977, pp. 6–7.
54. Becker, Gray and Marvakov, 2016, http://www.nber.org/nberces/
55. Department of the Treasury, 1978, introduction, p. XXVI.
56. Minutes of the London Economic Summit Meeting. First Session, May 7, 1977. In Office of the Historian, 2013, pp. 82 and 88.
57. IMFA, J. Polak Papers Fonds, Polak Chronological Series, b. 4, fold. 17 (Coordination of Demand Policies 1978), J. Polak to Mr. Artus, "Coordination of Demand Policies," November 8, 1978.
58. RAC, RFA, RGIII 4A, Series A-Activities, b. 162, fold. 1805, N. Rockefeller, "OPEC Surpluses and the Disequilibrium in International Payments," April 1977.
59. NARA, RG56, OASIA, Chronological Files of the Office of Financial Resources and Energy Finance 1974–1977, b. 3, fold. OASIA: Office of Financial Resources and Energy Finance, Permanent Chron. File November 1976, Odeh Aburdene (The First National Bank of Chicago), "The Financial Impact of OPEC and its Middle East Members on the US Balance of Payments and the Disposition of Surplus Oil Funds," October 1976; see also *Treasury Bulletin*, June 1976.

60. NARA, RG56, OASIA, Chronological Files of the Office of Financial Resources and Energy Finance 1974–1977, b. 2, fold. OASIA/OFREF Perm. Chron. Mar. 1976, Office of Financial Resources and Energy Finance, "Confidential Noform," December 1975.
61. Fed Shows Scope of US Deposits from Oil Lands 1976. *The Wall Street Journal* March 12, p. 4.
62. NARA, RG56, OASIA, Chronological Files of the Office of Financial Resources and Energy Finance 1974–1977, b. 2, fold. OASIA: Office of Financial Resources and Energy Finance, Permanent Chron. File, April 1976, D. V. Pritchett (Department of the Treasury) to W. Witherell, Memorandum "Importance of the Persian Gulf to the US over the next Decade," April 5, 1976.
63. FRBNYA, Central Files, fold. OPEC, T.J. Gilletti, (Balance of Payments Division), "OPEC Funds Flows for January–April 1975."
64. CIA Intelligence Memorandum "OPEC Countries: Size and Distribution of Official Foreign Assets on 30 June 1976," ER 77-10023, February 1977. https://www.cia.gov/library/readingroom/historical-collections (accessed July 3, 2015).
65. Department of the Treasury, 1978, introduction, p. XXVI.
66. Federal Reserve System, 1977, p. 69.
67. Federal Reserve System, 1978, pp. 3–10, 56–58.
68. FRBNYA, Central Files, b. 114,512, fold. OPEC, B. Nunemaker to Mr. Kubarich, Office Memorandum "OPEC Price and Production Cuts," September 28, 1981, table annexed.
69. Frieden, 2016, p. 6.
70. Street, 1978, pp. 61–62.
71. NARA, RG56, OASIA, Subject Files of the Deputy Assistant Secretary for Developing Nations Finance 1976–1977, b. 1, fold. D-A-9-2 OECD 1976, Joint Ministerial Committee of the Board of Governors of the Bank and the Fund on the Transfer of Real Resources to Developing Countries, Press Communiqué, October 3, 1976.
72. See data in FRBNYA, Presidential Papers, Papers of Paul A. Volcker, b. 35,578, fold. 74OA 1977–1978 Annual Meeting of IMF and IBRD, R. McNamara, "Address to the Board of Governors," September 25, 1978, Annex 1, Capital Flows to and Debt Status of the Poorest Nations.
73. JCPL, NLC-15-108-2-3-1, "US Relations with the Developing Countries 1978."
74. Federal Reserve System, 1977, p. 69.

75. FRBNYA, Central Files, fold. OPEC, P. Winder to Mr. Willey, "Review of OPEC Accounts. Notes for Period 3 March–7 April 1976," April 13, 1976; as for the OPEC payments position in 1975 and 1976, a breakdown by nation is in Federal Reserve Bank of New York, OPEC Payments Position—1975, and OPEC Payments Position—1976.
76. JCPL, NLC-23-27-7-2-8, The Vice President to Dr. Brzezinski, telegram "My first day of Meetings in Europe," January 1977.
77. RAC, Trilateral Commission Collection, Series 1, b. 72, fold. 801, C. Heck to Commission Members (US) who did not participate in the Tokyo Meeting, "Recent Tokyo Meeting," January 28, 1977.
78. JCPL, NLC-4-1-3-12-0, Henry Owen to the President, "Seven Nation Summit," April 29, 1977.
79. On this see also Basosi 2012, pp. 159–160.
80. NARA, RG56, OASIA, Deputy Director of the Office of International Monetary Affairs, Subject Files 1977–1979, b. 2, fold. London Summit 1 of 4, London Summit. First Session (May 7, 1977)—Morning Session.
81. IMFA, Medai, Medai Subject Files, b. 44, Statement by the President of the Bank and the Managing Director of the Fund after the Discussions by the Executive Boards of the Fund and the Bank, "Financial Flows to Developing Countries and the Adjustment Process," August 6, 1979.
82. JCPL, Solomon Collection, Speech File, b. 9, fold. Discussion with Morgan Guaranty 6 July 1977, Remarks by Michael Blumenthal "Toward International Equilibrium: A Strategy for the Longer Pull," International Monetary Conference, Tokyo, May 25, 1977.
83. NARA, RG56, OASIA, Subject Files of the Deputy Assistant Secretary for Developing Nations Finance 1976–1977, b. 2, fold. D-A 7-1, Robert G. Pelikan to Deputy Assistant Secretary Nachmanoff, Office Memorandum "World Bank Underwriting of LDC Bond Issues," July 6, 1977.
84. NARA, RG56, OASIA, Subject Files of Deputy Assistant Secretary for Developing Nations Finance 1976–1977, b. 3, fold. D-A 9-6, Robert G. Pelikan to Under Secretary-designate Solomon, Office Memorandum "EPG Deputies' Meeting February 22. North/South Relations. Financial Issues," February 21, 1977.
85. NARA, RG56, OASIA, Subject Files of the Deputy Assistant Secretary for Developing Nations Finance 1976–1977, b. 2, fold. DA 7-1-1, Angelos Angelopoulos (Governor of the National Bank of Greece): "A "Carter Plan" for International Economic Cooperation," March 1977; Fred Bergsten to A. Angelopoulos, May 20, 1977.

86. JCPL, White House Central Files, Subject File, Foreign Affairs, b. FO-44, fold. FO 6-5 1/2077-1/20/81, Inter office paper "International Financial Issues," Spring 1977.
87. JCPL, NLC-23-2772-8, The Am Embassy Bonn to the Secretary of State, telegram "Vice President-Chancellor Discussions," January 25, 1977.
88. IMFA, J. Polak Papers Fonds, Polak Chronological Series, b. 4, fold. 17, J. R. Artus to Mr. Polak, Office Memorandum "Coordination of Demand Management Policies," October 31, 1978.
89. JCPL, NLC-126-10-14-1-4, Stu Eizenstat-Kitty Schirmer, Memorandum for the President "Decision Memorandum on Balance of Payments Options," December 19, 1977.
90. Schmidt, 1978, p. 6.
91. On the international economic relations of Germany under the Chancellorship of Schmidt, see Spohr, 2016.
92. JCPL, NLC-23-27-7-2-8, The Vice President to Dr. Brzezinski, telegram "My first day of Meetings in Europe," January 1977.
93. Carter, 2010, p. 17.
94. NARA, RG56, OASIA, Office of the Deputy to the Assistant Secretary for International Affairs, Records Relating to International Financial Institutions 1962–1981, b. 6, fold. 9-1 Reform International Monetary 1978–1980, The US Embassy in Paris to the Secretary of State, telegram, July 8, 1980.
95. Cooper, 2008, pp. 567–570. On the fall of the Shah, see also Cooper, 2016.
96. RAC, RFA, RG III 4A, Series C-Business interest, b. 161, fold. 1789, Nelson Rockefeller to Crown Prince Fahd, April 18, 1977. For a different interpretation of Saudi Arabia's oil price freezing policy see Rustow, 1977, pp. 504–505.
97. Data on the purchasing power of dollar-denominated assets of Kuwait is also held in NARA. Office of the General Counsel. Assistant General Counsel, Records Related to OPEC Financial Affairs 1974–1979, b. 1, fold. F Part 1 of 4 1978–1979, Department of the Treasury, OASIA, Memorandum.
98. NARA, RG56, Office of the General Counsel. Assistant General Counsel, Records Related to OPEC Financial Affairs 1974–1979, b. 2, Am Embassy Kuwait to the Secretary of State, telegram, "Visit of Under Secretary Cooper to Kuwait," November 2, 1976.

99. As for the depreciation of the dollar see JCPL, NLC-126-10-14-1-4, Eizenstat-Schirmer Memorandum for the President "Decision Memorandum on Balance of Payments Options," December 19, 1977.
100. Memorandum from John Renner of the National Security Council Staff to the President's Assistant for National Security Affairs (Brzezinski) and the Special Representative for Economic Summits (Owen), "International Economic Policy Balance Sheet," July 19, 1978, in US Office of the Historian, 2013b, p. 474.
101. JCPL, Solomon Collection, Speech File, b. 9, fold. Discussion with Morgan Guaranty July 6, 1977, A. Solomon, "Suggested Questions for Discussion with Morgan Guaranty," July 6, 1977.
102. NARA, RG56, OASIA, Office of the Deputy to the Assistant Secretary for International Affairs, Records Relating to International Financial Institutions 1962–1981, b. 8, fold. IM-ID International Monetary: International Capital Flows 1979, "Remarks by Assistant Secretary of the Treasury for International Affairs Fred Bergsten before the Annual Conference of the National Association of Accountants," June 16, 1980.
103. JCPL, NLC-16-42-5-39-1, The Secretary of State to the White House, "Secretary Schlesinger call on Minister of Petroleum Yamani on January 14, 1978."
104. JCPL, NLC-21-53-8-2-0, James Scheuer (US Congress) to Cyrus Vance (US Secretary of State), May 25, 1978.
105. JCPL, NLC-16-42-539-1, The Secretary of State to the White House, "Secretary Schlesinger's call on Minister of Petroleum Yamani January 14, 1978," February 12, 1978.
106. NARA, RG56, Office of the General Counsel. Assistant General Counsel. Records Related to OPEC Financial Affairs 1974–1979, b. 2, fold. J Part 1 of 2 1976–1977, Memorandum of Conversation Ahmad Abdellatif (SAMA)-Gordon Brown-Richard Calder (US Embassy Jidda), "Saudi Investment Policy. Blumenthal Visit," November 8, 1977.
107. JCPL, NLC-1-5-2-45-4, The Situation Room, Memorandum for Mr. Brzezinski "Additional Information Items," January 27, 1978.
108. JCPL, NLC-1-7-5-43-1, The Situation Room, Memorandum for Z. Brzezinski, "Additional Information Items," August 18, 1978.
109. JCPL, NLC-20-19-2-4-3, PRC Meeting on Secretary Blumenthal's Trip to the Middle East, November 9, 1978.

110. NARA, RG56, Office of the Under Secretary for Monetary Affairs, Subject Files of Anthony M. Solomon Under Secretary for Monetary Affairs 1977–1980, b. 2, fold. Gold, EMB LTD Research Economists Report n. 79/12 "The Price of Gold and the Behavior of Exchange Rates," June 26, 1979.
111. On these two trips to UAE, Saudi Arabia and Kuwait see reports, cable and memoranda of conversations held in NARA, RG56, OASIA, Office of Regional and Resources Policy, Briefing Books 1975–1982, b. 2. See also JCPL, NLC-SAFE 17 D-23-10-10-5, Z. Brzezinski to J. Carter, Daily Report, November 20, 1979.
112. JCPL, NLC-15-46-7-31-4, John West (Ambassador), "Saudi Arabia: the Lesson of Iran. After Six Months," July 15, 1979.
113. Evans, John. 1979. Iran declared on default on $500 million loan. *The Financial Times.* November 22.
114. On the Kuwaiti position see JCPL, NLC-16-76-6-5-0, The Am Embassy in Kuwait to the Secretary of State, cable "Kuwaiti Finance Minister Ateeqi blasts US freeze of Iranian Assets," December 14, 1979. See also JCPL, NLC-128-10-5-4-0, Special Coordinating Committee Deputies Meeting, "Iran," November 23, 1979.
115. IMFA, Executive Board Documents, Departmental Memoranda, 1979-Departmental Memoranda, IMF Research Department, "Persistent Surpluses and Deficit on Current Account Among Major Industrial Countries," May 24, 1979.
116. US Government, 1980, pp. 14 ff.
117. JCPL, Anthony Solomon Collection, Speech File, b. 12, fold. NYC Chase Manhattan Luncheon 16 January 1980, "Suggested Talking Points for Chase Luncheon World Economic and International Monetary Outlook," January 14, 1980.
118. NARA, RG56, OASIA, Chronological Files of Deputy Assistant Secretary for International Monetary Affairs F. Lisle Widman 1967–1979, b. 1, fold. F.L. Widman Chron. July 1979, "Recent Economic Developments and the Economic Outlook," July 16, 1979.
119. Council of Economic Advisers, 1979, pp. 36–37.
120. NARA, RG56, Office of the Under Secretary for Monetary Affairs, Subject Files of Anthony Solomon, Under Secretary for Monetary Affairs 1977–1979, b. 2, fold. Gold, Lisle Widman to the Executive Secretary, Memorandum for Volcker-Miller breakfast, annexes, January 17, 1980.

121. NARA, RG56, OASIA, Chronological Files of Deputy Assistant Secretary for International Monetary Affairs F. Lisle Widman 1967–1979, b. 1, fold. WidmanChron Feb 1979, Robert Pelikan (Treasury) to Under Secretary Solomon, Memorandum "Iranian Finances," February 1, 1979.
122. NARA, RG56, Office of the General Counsel. Assistant General Counsel, Records Related to OPEC Financial Affairs 1974–1979, b. 2, Am Embassy Kuwait to the Secretary of State, telegram, "Visit of Under Secretary Cooper to Kuwait," November 2, 1976.
123. JCPL, NLC, 25-97-23-4-9, SCC Deputies Meeting, "Summary of Conclusions." November 23, 1979.
124. NARA, RG56, OASIA, Chronological Files of the Office of Financial Resources and Energy Finance 1974–1977, b. 1, fold. TEFRP: Office of Financial Resources Policy Coordination. Permanent Chron. File August 1975, Michael O'Connor (TESFRP Financial Resources Office), "US attitude toward Kuwaiti investment," undated.
125. NARA, RG56, Office of the General Counsel. Assistant General Counsel, Records Related to OPEC Financial Affairs 1974–1979, b. 3, fold. L 1978, Am Embassy in Kuwait to the Secretary of State, telegram "GOK concern over Proposed Tax IRS Regulation change Re Section 892 Internal Revenue Code Exemption," September 16, 1978; Am Embassy in Kuwait to the Secretary of State, telegram "Proposed Regulation under IRS Code Section 892," October 24, 1978; the Secretary of State to the Am Embassy in Teheran, telegram "Cooper Visit to Kuwait: US Tax Treatment of Kuwait Direct Investment," October 27, 1978.
126. NARA, RG56, Office of the General Counsel. Assistant General Counsel, Records Related to OPEC Financial Affairs 1974–1979, b. 2, fold. I 1977–1979, The American Embassy in Kuwait to the Secretary of State, telegram, January 1979.
127. NARA, RG56, Office of the General Counsel. Assistant General Counsel, Records Related to OPEC Financial Affairs 1974–79, b. 1, fold. F Part 1 of 4 1978–1979, Assistant Secretary Bergsten to Under Secretary Solomon, "Briefing for your meeting with Abdul Aziz al-Quraishi, Governor, Saudi Arabian Monetary Agency," June 12, 1978.
128. Yergin and Stanislaw, 2002; Silber, 2013.
129. Veiger, 2009.
130. NARA, RG56, OASIA, Chronological Files of Deputy Assistant Secretary for International Monetary Affairs F. Lisle Widman

1967–1979, b. 1, Solomon Testimony for Mitchell-Neal Hearings, July 9, 1979.

131. NARA, RG56, Office of the Under Secretary for Monetary Affairs, Subject Files of Anthony M. Solomon Under Secretary for Monetary Affairs 1977–1980, b. 2, fold. G5, "Big Five Finance Ministers Central Bankers," September 4, 1979.

References

Basosi, Duccio. 2012. *Gli Stati Uniti, l'Oro Nero, e l'Economia Politica Internazionale*. Venezia: Edizioni Studio LT2 Edizioni.

Becker, Randy, Wayne Gray, and Jordan Marvakov. 2016. *NBER-CES Manufacturing Industry Database*. Cambridge: National Bureau of Economic Research and US Census Bureau's Center for Economic Studies (NBER-CES). www.nber.org/nberces. Accessed 3 Feb 2015.

Bell, Geoffrey. 1976. The OPEC Recycling Problem in Perspective. *Columbia Journal of World Business* 11 (3): 28–33.

Carter, Jimmy. 2010. *White House Diary*. New York: Farrar, Straus and Giroux.

Coffey, Peter, ed. 1979. *Economic Policies of the Common Market*. London/Basingstoke: Macmillan Press.

Conference on International Economic Cooperation, Final Communiqué on Energy, Raw Materials and Trade, Development, and Finance. 1977. *International Legal Materials* 16 (4): 970–976.

Coombs, Charles. 1974. *Treasury and Federal Reserve Foreign Exchange Operations, February–July 1974*. New York: Federal Reserve Bank of New York.

Cooper, Andrew Scott. 2008. Showdown at Doha: The Secret Oil Deal That Helped Sink the Shah of Iran. *The Middle East Journal* 62 (4): 567–591.

———. 2016. *The Fall of Heaven: The Pahlavis and the Final Days of Imperial Iran*. New York: Henry Holt and Co.

Council of Economic Advisers. 1979. *Economic Indicators, July 1979, Prepared for the Joint Economic Committee by the Council of Economic Advisers*. Washington, DC: GPO.

Declaration of Mr. Khalid Abu al-Sa'ud. 1975. Director of Investment at Kuwait Ministry of Finance, Financial and Banking News. *Middle East Economic Survey*, May.

Department of Commerce. 1975a. *Survey of Current Business* 55 (1).

———. 1975b. *Survey of Current Business* 55 (6).

———. 1975c. *Survey of Current Business* 55 (8).

———. 1975d. *Survey of Current Business* 55 (9).

Department of State. 1977. *Department of State Bulletin,* 650–652, June 20.

Department of the Treasury. 1975. *Annual Report of the Secretary of the Treasury on the State of the Finances for the Fiscal Year Ended June 30, 1975.* Washington, DC: GPO.

———. 1978. *Annual Report of the Secretary of the Treasury on the State of the Finances for the Fiscal Year Ended September 30, 1977.* Washington, DC: GPO.

Fed Shows Scope of US Deposits from Oil Lands. 1976. *The Wall Street Journal,* March 12.

Federal Reserve System. 1977. *Annual Report of the Board of Governors of the Federal Reserve System for the Year 1976.* Washington, DC: GPO.

———. 1978. *Annual Report of the Board of Governors of the Federal Reserve System for the Year 1977.* Washington, DC: GPO.

Financial Times. 1974. July 23.

Frieden, Jeffry A. 2016. *Currency Politics: The Political Economy of Exchange Rate Policy.* Princeton: Princeton University Press.

Macavoy, Paul W. 2003. "Don't Just Stand There..." Treasury Secretary William E. Simon and Fiscal Policy During Stagflation 1975–1976. *Atlantic Economic Journal* 31 (3): 213–218.

Morgan Guaranty Trust Company of New York. 1977. *World Financial Markets,* November.

Office of the Historian. 2013. In *Foreign Relations of the United States (FRUS), 1977–1980, Volume III, Foreign Economic Policy,* ed. Kathleen B. Rasmussen. Washington, DC: GPO.

Peden, Edgar. 1991. Productivity in the United States and Its Relationship to Government Activity: An Analysis of 57 Years 1929–1986. *Public Choice* 69 (2): 153–173.

Rustow, Dankwart A. 1977. US-Saudi Relations and the Oil Crises of the 1980s. *Foreign Affairs* 55 (3): 494–516.

Schmidt, Helmut. 1978. The 1977 Alastair Buchan Memorial Lecture. *Survival* 20 (1): 2–10.

Silber, William L. 2013. *Volcker: The Triumph of Persistence.* New York: Bloomsbury Press.

Spohr, Kristina. 2016. *The Global Chancellor: Helmut Schmidt and the Reshaping of the International Order.* Oxford: Oxford University Press.

Street, James H. 1978. Latin American Adjustments to the OPEC Crisis and the World Recession. *Social Science Quarterly* 59 (1): 61–62.

The New York Times. 1974. August 28.

The Wall Street Journal. 1974. August 28.

US Government. 1980. *Economic Report of the President Transmitted to the Congress January 1980 Together with the Annual Report of the Council of Economic Advisers.* Washington, DC: GPO.

Veiger, Klaus. 2009. *Dictatorship, Democracy and Globalization: Argentina and the Cost of Paralysis 1973–2001.* University Park: The Pennsylvania State University Press.

Yergin, Daniel, and Joseph Stanislaw. 2002. *The Commanding Heights: The Battle for the World Economy.* New York: Simon & Schuster.

6

Conclusion: Dissecting the Interrelationship Between Transnational Capital Markets, Energy Finance, and Development Policies

From the late 1950s, when the US balance of payments began wobbling and the international community lost confidence in the dollar with its depreciating effects, through to the end of anti-inflationary demand management policies set out in the second half of the 1970s to restore balance of payments equilibrium and the dollar's strength, the US elites consistently placed their strategies to resurrect the US hegemony on the international trade and payments system in a seamless strategic framework shared by all US governments. The core concept that united foreign economic policies as different from each other as those under the Kennedy and the Carter administrations, was the linkage they all established between resurrecting the dollar's strength and the US external balance from their plummeting since the late 1950s, and a much needed stabilization of the international trade and payments system. Such linkage was always more topical insofar as over the course of the two decades analyzed in this study the functioning of the international trade and payments system came increasingly under strain as a result of multiple and overlapping factors as varying as the increases in oil and commodities prices, the progressive melting down of fixed but adjustable exchange rates, and the run on US gold stocks that featured international monetary relations over

S. Selva, *Before the Neoliberal Turn*, Palgrave Studies in Economic History,
DOI 10.1057/978-1-137-57443-5_6

the course of the 1960s. Within this framework each US administration undertook strikingly differing strategies in order to simultaneously resurrect the dollar and preserve market openness and monetary integration among the advanced industrial nations, the oil producing developing countries, and the non-oil rich Least Developed Countries (LDCs). A thorough analysis of the policies undertaken in Washington over the time frame considered in this study unfolds both a number of similarities, such as the ones between the Kennedy and Johnson administrations, and some striking differences. An example of the latter is the case of different approaches to the use of the OPEC countries' oil revenues by the Ford and Carter administrations described in Chaps. 4 and 5. In order to pinpoint such continuities and changes in the history of US foreign financial policy this study has considered a number of variables that deeply influenced the ways in which monetary authorities in New York and federal agencies in Washington acted out in the aim of both resurrecting the dollar and the US balance of payments, and reshuffling the international payments system under US leadership. To summarize these, it is worth mentioning what US economic diplomats and policymakers called "energy finance," that to say, the progressive ascendancy of the oil producing nations united either in the Organization of Arab Petroleum Exporting Countries (OAPEC), or in the Organization of Petroleum Exporting Countries (OPEC), on the world financial stage; the meteoric rise of highly liquid short-term capital markets as the specific trajectory in which private capital markets took shape from the mid-1960s throughout the 1970s; and, yet again, the involvement of the largest American commercial and investment banks in implementing the US financial assistance programs to the LDCs and in shaping Washington's commercial bonds with the largest OPEC oil producing countries. All of these factors grew in scale and influence over the time frame considered in this book and came to influence the remaking of US foreign financial policy. This influence can be measured either by analyzing the macroeconomic effects—inflation and competitiveness in foreign markets among others—triggered by these variables, or by pinpointing the impact they exerted on the players involved in shaping US foreign economic policies. Based on this reconstruction, on the one side continued outflow of capital from the United States over the course of the 1960s and the growth of short-term inflation-sensitive Euro-money markets triggered a decline in the supply of capital for long-term investments and an increase in the loan rate for productive and industrial investments. Such an increase in the cost of money came about well in advance of the end of cheap oil prices, specifically from the last few years of the 1960s to the outbreak of the first oil shock. Therefore, a core argument held in Chap. 3 is that such expansion of short-term unregulated capital markets and the unchecked outflows of capital from the United States not only hit hard the US external balance and contributed to undermine confidence in the US currency. Indeed, it also laid the groundwork for the increase in the cost of money for productive investments and international trade financing on which the inflation of the 1970s was grounded. The ascendancy of OPEC in the international economic arena from the turn of the decade to the second half of the 1970s added to these dynamics. In so doing, the increasing growth of transnational capital flows and the rising role of the oil producing countries paired in shaking the macroeconomic conditions on which the system of trade and payments was grounded both under the system of fixed exchange rates and in the framework of floating currencies in the 1970s. As regards the impact of such aforementioned factors on the US policies, during the 1960s mounting cross-national capital flows induced the United States to put a curb on this and to focus their attention on the capital account position, while the ascendancy of oil producers on the world economic stage led Washington to reshape and strengthen its bonds with some of them. Later on, during the 1970s, the involvement of leading American banks in recycling the OPEC's oil revenues had an impact on the functioning of American foreign economic policy objectives insofar as they clashed with the OPEC countries on the terms of international lending, and showed their reluctance to relend the financial assets of oil producers to non-oil LDCs featuring a poor creditworthiness.

Considering these factors, that overtime influenced and intersected the US efforts to restore American external equilibrium in an orderly international system of exchange and payments, it is worth drawing some conclusions and remarks on the changing policies jointly conducted by the US governments, the Federal Reserve System and the international economic institutions of Bretton Woods from the teetering of the US international payments position in the late 1950s through to the eve of watershed monetary tightening inaugurated by the new Chairman of the Board of Governors of the Federal Reserve System Paul A. Volcker shortly after his appointment.

The US governments and monetary authorities formulated different interpretations about the origins, nature and cure for the US external imbalances. From the early 1960s through the Nixon administration they mostly focused on the outflow of capital from the US and the meteoric rise of short-term Eurocurrency markets. However, at the same time they consistently paid great attention to the interrelationship between external equilibrium and domestic growth, a line of action continuously pursued all through the decades covered in this study.

The departing point for this policy focused on capital flight was certainly the ways in which the US monetary authorities reacted to the two economic downturns chronicled in the late 1950s in the United States. Against this backdrop, Chap. 2 demonstrated that even at that time the US made a bet on alternating measures on the capital account to restrict capital outflows with policies focused on the current account position, like foreign trade and military assistance policies designed to better the terms of trade and restrict the volume of dollar-denominated assets held in the international financial system in order to counter the depreciation of the US currency in international exchange markets.

Therefore, the brief overview on this early period, covered in Chap. 2, is worthwhile. In the first instance, the American economy showed unmistakable signs of economic slowdown since the period from 1953 to 1957, when it muddled through two recessions: the first recession occurred in 1957, the second broke out at the end of the decade. At this very dawn of the post-World War II history of American economic slowdown, two distinctive features that marked the US macroeconomic history over the following decades were well under way. On one side, any time the US economy slowed down, the balance of payments worsened: this interconnection sheds light on the long-standing nexus between domestic economic growth and external equilibrium. From the viewpoint of this study this linkage is of utmost interest in that it highlights the interlocking relation between trends in international payments of the advanced industrial economies and the ways in which the competitive position of their manufacturing systems developed over time. According to the reconstruction presented in this research, in shaping American international financial and monetary policies the US foreign economic policymakers repeatedly focused on this correlation. Quite consistently, and particularly under the Carter administration, Washington linked the search for strengthening the value of the dollar and the competitive position of the American economy in foreign markets to recasting a sound equilibrium between capital supply and domestic aggregate demand.

Secondly, if one briefly turns attention back to the second half of the 1950s and the period that preceded the appointment of Kennedy to the White House, it is easy to identify a clear-cut monetary policy aimed at upholding confidence in the US dollar and at countering economic downturns and recessions based on tight monetary stringency.

As a matter of fact, confronted with the sluggish economic junctures of the late 1950s the Federal Reserve Board approved slight and modest reductions in the discount rate. Such reaction to domestic downward sloping growth is vital to better understand Washington's reaction to the early internationalization of private capital markets from the turn of the decade through the 1960s. From the mid to the end of the 1950s the US monetary authorities and the government pushed forward this stance not so much by opposing any reduction in the discount rate, as by a string of other monetary, banking and fiscal policies. They repeatedly countered any decrease in reserve requirements of banks on foreign loans and banking operations, raised taxation of foreign portfolio investments of US banks and pursued a continued, although unsuccessful, attempt to curb the flow of private capital to the European financial centers through a high interest rate policy on long-term financial assets. Finally, they urged US corporations to repatriate capitals. This array of policies implemented prior to the Kennedy administration laid the groundwork on which, during the 1960s, Washington consistently reacted to the development of transnational capital flows and its painful impact on the dollar's stability and on the international exchanges in goods and capital at large. Therefore, prior to the 1960s, the crisis of the US balance of payments was confronted through a combined monetary stringency and enhanced control over capital flight. Unlike the actions of the democratic administrations of the 1960s, such approach to the US balance of payments deficit revolved around a concept of monetary stringency as a means of breaking down the interconnectedness between domestic slowdown and the decline of the US dollar in international exchange markets. The inefficacy of this perspective explains why all through the 1960s the Kennedy and Johnson administrations acted to combine interventions in foreign exchange markets and on the capital account to promote the inflow of private capital and to deter its outflow, and a continued commitment to improve the US balance of payments on current account.

To put it another way, Chap. 2 has demonstrated to what extent by the late 1950s the US economic and monetary policymakers were aware of the interconnectedness between developments in international capital markets and deteriorating stability in foreign exchange markets. However, based on a comparison between the balance of payments deficit financing policies enacted in light of the late 1950s sloping down external equilibrium, and Washington's actions since Kennedy came to power, the striking turn on the part of the government can be analyzed. Since Kennedy thereafter, US policymakers tore aside monetary stringency and focused their attention on measures to enhance capital inflow, and on initiatives designed to implement overseas public expenditures cuts and to draw an increase in US export of civilian and military goods aimed at propping up the current account position. Notwithstanding this different approach to the US balance of payments crisis that divided the Kennedy administration from its predecessors, a long-standing effort to make domestic growth and external equilibrium converge was pushed forward. President Kennedy and Secretary of the Treasury Douglas Dillon worked on devising foreign monetary and economic policy measures capable of both stimulating domestic investment and economic activity, and to restore balance of payments equilibrium on the capital and current accounts. The efforts to stimulate capital inflow should be linked to Washington's commitment not only to ameliorate the capital account position, but also, just as importantly as it was during the 1970s, to finance the supply side through easier money. This effort was pushed forward with the aim of stimulating fixed capital formation and productive investments, as well as the competitive position of US manufacturing in foreign markets. On the other hand, Chap. 2 has demonstrated US commitment in the 1960s to bolster US domestic business activity through a clear turn to abandon high interest rates and to ease tight monetary policy that had dominated the US approach throughout the economic crises of the 1950s. Against this backdrop, it turned out that there was an interrelationship between this policy on the capital account and the US administrations' struggle to expand foreign trade and to reduce foreign spending with the aim of improving the current account position of the United States.

The second issue pinpointed in Chap. 2 pertains to the economic and historical interpretations about the historical origins and developments of unfettered transnational capital flows that over the decade of the 1960s always further undermined the dollar's stability and Washington's capital account position. Reckoning the importance of existing literature in accounting for the stunning growth of unregulated short-term capital markets, it points to one more factor that fundamentally contributed to make the US balance of payments deficit financing policies fail as late as the end of the 1960s.

So far, scholarship in economic history and international economics has explained the increasing cross-border capital flows that featured throughout the 1960s, by calling attention to a string of developments that ranged from the increase in foreign investments of US corporations and banks to the attainment of full convertibility among Western currencies areas united since the Bretton Woods years in the Organization for Economic Cooperation and Development (OECD). Without underestimating these developments, Chap. 2 has drawn attention to the losses in US gold reserves, to US overseas public expenditures—first and foremost US foreign military spending—and to development assistance programs. In the aim of detecting the worsening US balance of payments and the declining confidence in the US dollar, calling attention to these last three issues is noteworthy in that they were the subject of scrutiny, attention and initiatives since shortly after the Kennedy administration came to office throughout the decade.

Since the beginning of the new decade a combined series of dollar-denominated capital outflows and the stunning deterioration in US gold reserves were two developments clearly on track. The run on US gold stocks, mounting capital flights, and the burden of foreign military commitment and development assistance on US foreign spending put the dollar under pressure throughout the decade. All of these factors contributed to weaken the US dollar in foreign exchange markets, while the growth of dollar selling and buying orders undermined both monetary conditions for existing international trade and payments, and the competitive position of US and British economies, the two leading units of accounts for international exchanges in capital and goods, on world trade markets. This process came about—more importantly from the research perspective of this book—well in advance of the events that set off the dismantling of the fixed exchange rate system of Bretton Woods since around 1967 through Nixon's decision to suspend the dollar convertibility into gold. Therefore, it is worth pointing to the US monetary and credit policies over time to trace the continuities and pitfalls that marked the way in which US foreign monetary and financial policymakers approached a range of the most heated economic issues as wide as the US payments imbalances, the weakening of the US dollar, and domestic economic doldrums.

Furthermore, such continued strains account for a much-heralded need to phase out the long-standing approach to the international payments imbalance of the country based on restoring equilibrium on the capital account by means of monetary tightening and high interest rates.

Certainly, among all the reasons that could account for such weakening of the US international payments position and the dollar since as early as the late 1950s onwards, and in order to dissect the policies accordingly implemented in Washington to deal with these issues, it is worth mentioning in the first instance that the attainment of full currency convertibility in 1958 had laid the groundwork for the growth in flows of private capital across nations and, more remarkably from the viewpoint of this study, for the weakening of the dollar. As soon as currency convertibility went fully into effect and most exchange controls were lifted, most European countries moved to let foreign holders of financial assets denominated in the legal tender freely convert them into dollars or other currencies. The aim was to stimulate trade in goods and merchandise in international markets; however, this decision triggered a steady and meteoric expansion of dollar-denominated financial assets held by foreign residents outside the United States. As remarked in Chap. 2, such development explains why, from the end of the 1950s to the beginning of the following decade, some Western European countries increased their dollar holdings substantially.

In confronting the situation, the Federal Reserve System strove to resurrect the dollar and the US international payments position through buying long-term financial instruments and selling short-term assets in order at the same time to stimulate domestic output and to contrast short-term capital outflows.

Secondly, US foreign military spending and the federal government's overseas expenditures had become a cumbersome load on the current account deficit. As the first part of this book has suggested, the Department of State stressed that overseas US military expenditures financed dollar holdings by foreigners. US diplomats stressed that over the first half of the decade these dollar holdings were increasingly used to purchase gold in the US gold markets. Therefore, according to this study it is possible to establish a clear correlation between the policies conducted by the US administrations during the 1960s to reduce military spending and increase export, and the pressing need to lessen the international run on US gold stocks. In either case, the very aim of US policies was to constrain the share of dollar-denominated financial assets in world money supply as a means of preserving the dollar convertibility into gold.

Therefore, if one glosses over the interrelationship between reducing overseas military spending and preserving the US gold stocks, in the field of foreign trade the policies conducted in the 1960s to restore balance of payments equilibrium and world payments prompted Washington to straddle to increase foreign military sales to friendly nations, while at the same time setting plans to reduce its overseas permanent military presence and spending. These trajectories in US foreign economic policy shed light on the interconnectedness between foreign trade and foreign exchange operations. Not coincidentally the advocates of trade liberalization, the most outspoken of whom was probably Under Secretary of State for Economic Affairs George Ball, went for reducing trade barriers and rising US foreign purchases and sales to stimulate dollar-holding European trading partners to import American products in order to finance the US dollar deficit. The objective of high-ranking US economic policymakers and diplomats was to trigger an increase in US dollar earnings or convertible foreign currencies, as well as to prevent the European common market from turning out to be a discriminatory trade area harmful to US exporters. More importantly, the aim was to provide support to the exporters of Latin American agricultural products and merchandise. This two-pronged policy, based on continued attention to trade policy and concern for the future of non-oil producing LDCs, their terms of trade and buying power, marked the US foreign financial policy from the early 1960s to the malaise of the 1970s. The issue of US development assistance and its bearing on the US balance of payments proper to the 1960s, turned out in the 1970s to be not just a means of reducing the liabilities in the US capital account position. In the 1970s, the US straddled to provide multilateral support for the terms of trade and buying power in foreign markets of the non-oil LDCs also, as a vital way to prop up international trade and to keep the non-oil LDCs within it through a smooth rechanneling of the OPEC oil producers' financial assets.

This two-pronged policy, concentrated on propping up the US balance of trade and bolstering the buying power of the non-oil LDCs, was distinctive of US foreign financial policy from the early 1960s to the international economic crisis of the 1970s. Chapters 3 and 4 explored the importance that US foreign economic policymakers placed on making dollar-rich OPEC countries, the American banking system through which the oil producing countries invested the largest portion of oil revenues, as well some newly established international financial arrangements and long-established economic assistance agencies such as the IBRD and regional development banks, finance foreign exchange operations and imports of the non-oil producing Latin American LDCs. Therefore, this attention to the interconnectedness between trade liberalizations and US policy to resurrect its current account position, and the LDCs' buying power in foreign markets is a clear line of continuity from the 1960s to the following decade. In the 1960s, many high-ranking US economic policymakers established a linkage between US trade and financial bonds with the economies of the European Economic Community (EEC), and the destiny of the non-commodity producing LDCs, their terms of trade and purchasing power. For instance, the pursuit of a liberal trade policy was considered essential to foster the export of Latin American agricultural products to Western Europe and to deter any Soviet trading influence on the continent. Against this backdrop, since the early 1960s the Department of State had made a strong case for getting the European partners involved in the development assistance programs carried out under the aegis either of the federal government, or the UN organizations and the IBRD. In turn, as referred to in this study, such commitment—particularly by the Kennedy administration—to get trade arrangements with its European partners was considered a means of laying the groundwork for a foreign financial policy aimed at sustaining the value of the dollar through earning convertible foreign currencies to finance US foreign markets operations for monetary purposes.

Later on, and quite consistently, as early as 1971 the Nixon administration focused on reaching agreements with the Common Market European partners on a set of measures to liberalize trade and capital investments on a bilateral US-EEC basis before approaching any negotiations taking place in the General Agreement on Tariffs and Trade (GATT) to best navigate the US balance of payments deficit and to repair Washington's dollar shortage.

Therefore, as early as the 1960s a substantial cohort of leading US foreign diplomatic and economic policymakers paid much attention to the interconnectedness between restoring the US international payments position and the buying powers of the LDCs in foreign markets. As Chap. 4 highlights, during the decade of the 1970s restoring the buying power and the international payments position of the non-oil producing LDCs was a decisive factor in the decision taken by the US governments and American foreign financial policy policymakers to intensify diplomatic relations with some OPEC member countries and to draw on their booming financial assets in order to resurrect the international trade and payments system. Therefore, in the framework of the economic slowdowns of the time, during both decades the Unites States strove to combine a much-heralded commitment to restore the US balance of payments with continued support for the buying power and terms of trade of the non-oil supplying LDCs, viewed as vital to keep up the international trade and payments system.

In striking contrast with this continuity from the early 1960s to the US foreign economic policies of the 1970s, some remarkable differences between the two decades emerged. The field of Washington's approach to capital market developments comes first on the list. Chapter 2 pointed to the efforts by the Kennedy and Johnson administrations to combine measures to restore the balance of payments on current account and continued attention to stem private capital outflows and the development of short-term Eurocurrency markets. The Kennedy administration focused its attention on the current account, while the Johnson administration reconsidered the importance of curbing capital outflows. In so doing, the Johnson presidency showed the strikingly contrasting approach to such developments in private capital markets of American financial and diplomatic authorities from the 1960s to the 1970s. In contrast to the following decade, investigated in Chap. 4, the US administrations of the 1960s, and in particular the Johnson administration, considered the outflow of capital a threat to the US balance of payments and a hindrance to the scramble for stabilizing the US currency and Washington's foreign economic relations. During his tenure in office Johnson curbed the outflow of capital, while after the first oil crisis of the 1970s the US monetary authorities entailed a positive correlation between the growth of dollar-denominated assets in world capital markets and the struggle to stabilize Washington's international payments position. This has been the subject of specific investigation in Chap. 4. At that time the US authorities worked hard on reshuffling short-term capital markets and on making a shift in the investment policies of oil producers and US banks charged with recycling the oil revenues in the most serviceable way to restore the US balance of payments.

In second instance, the shaping of US foreign financial policies changed at the turn of the decade as structural macroeconomic conditions changed. Over the course of the 1960s, during Nixon's tenure, American monetary and political authorities combined current account measures with actions on the capital account to forestall the decline of the dollar in foreign exchange markets. However, unlike a few years earlier when cheapness and stability on the international commodity markets made the inflationary effects of a weakened dollar not a crash-provoking issue to international payments, the Nixon administration failed in catching the inflationary strains on international oil and commodity markets of a dollar getting continually weaker. Therefore, this set of multiple actions taken under Nixon was merely aimed at counteracting the centrifugal effects of the balance of payments deficit, loss of confidence in the dollar, and enduring capital outflows. The US foreign financial and monetary policies conducted under that administration did not target the inflationary effects of growing capital outflows and the weakening of the dollar on both capital markets and commodity markets. While earlier studies pointed to the inflationary effects of peaking oil prices, Chap. 3 investigated the multiple effects of capital outflows from the United States and the development of short-term highly liquid capital markets, both on the cost of oil import for oil importing countries used to trade in dollar-denominated markets, and on the cost of international lending for debt financing, balance of payments deficit financing and for the purpose of stabilizing the dollar. The chapter pointed to the inefficacy of current account policies conducted under the Nixon administration through tariff and trade policies, as well as through the involvement of US banking, aimed either at favoring non-dollar and non-hard currency-denominated oil transactions, or at lessening the run on US gold stocks.

Based on the reconstruction offered in Chap. 3, it is plausible to establish a linkage between the decade-long US policies to restore US balance of payments equilibrium and dollar stability in international exchange markets, limited in this study to the events that marked the turn of the decade history of US attempts to stabilize the system: from the military and financial implications of changing diplomatic relations in the Middle East and the Mediterranean basin to developments in international monetary relations, through to the unfettered tendency of private financial investors and intermediaries to shift their investment attitudes from long-term investments to short-term highly liquid placements, particularly in the Eurocurrency markets. As the reconstruction offered in the chapter unfolds, from 1969 to 1973 the bust of American foreign economic policies enacted since the dawn of the decade through to 1968 interacted with this tangle of events in a challenging fashion that laid the groundwork for the ensuing ascendancy of new financial powers on the world economic stage at a time when the international monetary and trade system based on the dollar was mostly torn apart. The failure of US foreign economic and financial policies to restore equilibrium in the system of international trade and payments turned into a structural depreciation of the dollar in exchange markets and triggered massive capital flows from New York to Western Europe, from regulated long-term assets to unofficial and highly unregulated short-term financial instruments. Such developments lay at the origins of the increase in both post prices of oil and world commodity markets, and in the loan rates of short-term borrowings. This process, combined with the impact on oil prices and oil supply shortages of the instability that shaped the history of the Middle East since 1967 onward, laid the groundwork both for the final crumbling of the fixed exchange rate system and, more importantly, for the inflationary strains of the following decade. Reasoning along these lines, prior to moving on to analyze the decade of the 1970s in the Chaps. 4 and 5, an examination of the importance of the Eurocurrency and Eurodollar markets in the process was offered in Chap. 3. According to that analysis, while the decade-long crisis of gold, dollar and the fixed exchange rates system triggered these fundamental developments in international capital markets, the meteoric rise of the Eurodollar and Eurocurrency markets caused the depreciation of the currency in which private capital assets and merchandise were traded in the international economy. This process overheated the advanced industrial economies, caused the crumbling of the international trade and payments system born out of the Bretton Woods Conference and lay at the origins of the oil prices hikes of the decade. After detailing the last few attempts on which the United States embarked to recast the dollar in foreign exchange markets through balance of payments deficit financing policies, focused on resurrecting the US current account position in the context of a rising financial might of the OPEC economies to reduce the scale of dollar denominated capital assets, details were provided about the importance of the Eurodollar market in relation to the outbreak of the oil crisis. The development of short-term, inflation-sensitive capital markets both set conditions for the oil price hikes and interacted with the ensuing further depreciation of the dollar in the floating currency system of the 1970s.

Unlike the Nixon administration, the US monetary authorities caught this development as early as the first oil price hikes began reshuffling international investments and stimulated a massive investment shift from long- to short-term financial instruments. One of the main arguments of Chap. 4 is that as early as the first oil shock triggered such capital markets developments, Washington's and New York's authorities began straddling to make the absorption of the oil producers' dollar-denominated investible financial assets the linchpin in the twofold search for improving the value of the dollar in exchange markets and striking the balance between capital supply and aggregate demand in the advanced industrial economies. In the pursuit of this objective, the US scrambled to induce the OPEC members to engage in long-term investments. The very idea, laid down shortly after the first oil price hike in 1974, of drawing upon the OPEC oil producers to trigger an upswing in fixed capital formation, and to prevent a falloff in the supply side of the production chain in light of sustained consumer demand—a process potentially conducive to inflationary strains that would add to the oil price hikes—highlights a very definite target that underlined the US foreign economic policy from 1974 to the end of 1976. The ways in which the Ford administration and the Federal Reserve System managed the recycling of OPEC capital surplus sheds light on Washington's struggle to combine the resurrection of the US dollar and balance of payments with the stabilization of the international economy. Weighing the balance between stable exchange rates in a floating currency system and smooth transnational flows in goods and capital was viewed in Washington as a prerequisite to recasting the system of international trade and payments that encompassed the industrial nations, the oil producers and the non-oil LDCs. As charted in Chap. 4, such ambitious plan met a tangle of hindrances that ranged, among others, from the persistency of short-term highly liquid placements by the oil producers, which was the subject of sticky conflicts with American commercial banks involved in the recycling process, to OPEC's relentless opposition to charge multilateral financial arrangements set up under US leadership, like the International Bank for Reconstruction and Development (IBRD) or the International Monetary Fund (IMF),with channeling its member states capital surplus. Confronted with these limits to its foreign financial policy, from shortly after the first oil shock to the eve of Carter's election to the White House, Washington struggled to make the meteoric expansion in the OPEC financial assets a serviceable instrument to finance US export to the oil producers and American corporations' investments in the largest consumer economies of the Middle East, most remarkably Iran and Saudi Arabia. From the standpoint of US diplomacy, such policy was aimed at establishing a tradeoff between full American support for industrialization and modernization in the Middle East, and Iranian, and more importantly, Saudi support for an oil price moderation policy within

OPEC. This path-breaking attempt to strengthen commercial bonds with Middle Eastern oil producers hails back to a long-standing involvement of some leading American commercial banks and corporations in the region, explored in the previous chapters. Along these lines, since the establishment of bilateral cooperation commissions between the US and the three leading OPEC members analyzed in this study, a research field so far largely neglected in the literature, which deserves further inquiry, Washington decisively turned to put the oil revenues of OPEC members in excess of their outpayments for import of goods and services to finance US export to and investments in the OPEC countries themselves. This action, aimed at fixing up both the issue of mismatches between OPEC and the leading American banks charged with relending petrodollars to oil consumers and poorly performing debt-repayments LDCs, and the seemingly unmanageable effect of dollar-denominated investments in world capital markets on the value of the dollar in a floating exchange system, proved to be short-lived. The role of American banking and their attitude to investing in the Eurocurrency markets did not fade away, while after a mild recovery in the value of the dollar owing to the Western recession of 1975 and its effect on international demand for oil and the volume of oil revenues accrued to the oil producers and reinvested in the international money markets, over the course of 1976 the dollar plummeted once again. Against this backdrop, the implementation of commercial bonds between the largest capital-absorbing OPEC members and the US in order to reduce the dollar component in world money supply and as a means of improving the US balance of payments on both the current and capital accounts through an increase in export to the Middle East and a surge in the repatriation of foreign profits of US corporations respectively, proved to be mostly unsuccessful. From 1976 to the first part of 1977 this dynamic quickly undermined the purchasing power of oil prices and oil producers in foreign markets, as well as the market value of their foreign real estate and financial investments. This development began jeopardizing—Chap. 5 recounts—the stability of US financial relations with Iran and Saudi Arabia. In this framework, it is worth placing the Carter administration's path-breaking turn to link the reorganization of aggregate demand in the advanced industrial economies through demand management and stimulus policies to the reorganization of a stable and sustained international system of trade and payments. As pointed out in this study, rising production costs and declining competitiveness was viewed as a cause for a reduced level of market integration and a worsening US international payments position. Confronted with this perspective, the new administration focused attention on strengthening the linkage between resurrecting the balance of payments and recovering the US and Western economies and their competitive edge in foreign markets. The very argument of Chap. 5 is that under the Carter administration Washington scrambled to link the recycling of OPEC's financial assets to the implementation of demand management policies: drawing upon their oil revenues was a means of financing the supply side alternative to the propelling of private long-term investments. In this respect, it is worth noting that by the second half of the decade the US monetary and federal authorities viewed the recycling of OPEC's "energy finance" not only as a way to finance the permanence of the LDCs in the international trade and payments system, but also as a means of recasting the business cycle in the US and other leading advanced industrial economies. By allocating a portion of Western industrial economies' national GDP and a fraction of petrodollars deposited with Western banking or invested in Western states to fuel fixed capital formation and productive investments, the Carter administration intended to recast the competitive edge of the US economy as a prerequisite to enhance market openness and increased exchanges in goods and capital with its Western partners, as well as the trade bonds in commodities and consumer goods between consumer goods producing industrial nations and the commodity-producing LDCs, most notably the Middle Eastern oil producers. The unreciprocated cooperation from key western partners as West Germany and Japan, which Washington from the London to the Bonn summits and on major bilateral meetings repeatedly put under pressure in order to get them to initiate a policy shift from an export-led growth model to stimulus policies, undermined Carter's strategy to sort out the malaise of the 1970s and his approach to oil revenues recycling. Since 1977 this development, coupled with the unfettered depreciation of the dollar in international exchange markets caused by the failure of past recycling policies, and the ensuing deterioration of bilateral financial relations between Washington and the three leading OPEC members focused on in this study, caused the Carter demand side policy to fail. Chapter 5 details this development from 1978 to 1979, when not only Iran, but also Saudi Arabia and Kuwait, the most remarkable case of a capital-surplus oil producer, complained much with Washington about such developments and increased their leverage power toward the United States. Over the course of the preceding few years, these three countries, and particularly the Saudis, had actively supported a price moderation policy within OPEC in return for either a US commitment to resurrect the US dollar in foreign exchange markets, or a substantial industrial and military presence of Washington in the Gulf to deter any possible Soviet aggression, and facilitated access to OPEC investments in the United States' equity markets. Since 1974 through the Carter years US commitment to defend the dollar had constantly been on the table of bilateral financial relations and negotiations between Washington and these three countries, which used it to increase their leverage power toward the United States. The collapse of the dollar in exchange markets from 1977 to 1978 certainly broke down this pattern of financial and monetary relations. However, at that time this was not the only linchpin, around which the United States' relations with these three countries had been revolving, to fall apart. In fact, in addition to this, the removal or limitation of tax exemption on the Middle Eastern real estate and other investments on the US stock markets stormed relations between Kuwait, Saudi Arabia itself and Washington, while as a result of the Iranian revolution the decision of the United States to declare Iran on default on a number of syndicated dollar loans raised by Teheran with the American banks all contributed to jeopardize Washington's relations with Middle Eastern oil producers and the US stimulus policies based in part on borrowing from oil producers in the region. On the other hand, the decision of the Federal Reserve System in August 1979 to commence a stunning monetary tightening, not only made the tottering of the US currency contribute to continually jeopardizing the Saudis' and Iranian commitment to lessen the oil price hiking policies of OPEC. Indeed, it paved the way for the meteoric ascendancy on the world monetary stage of the striking upswing in interest rates inaugurated since the fall of 1979 by the new chairmanship of the Federal Reserve System, the so called "Volcker revolution."

Neither a policy focused on the scale, size and volume of dollar-denominated capital markets identified as the main cause of the US currency weakening position and Washington's reduced international might, typical of the Nixon and Ford administration, and mustered by the Fed-orchestrated attempt to trigger a shift in the oil producing countries from short- to long-term investments, nor the turn to strike the balance between capital supply and aggregate demand as a prerequisite to increase the competitive edge and to improve the current account position through closer bonds with oil producing and non-oil LDCs, proved to be successful in reverting an almost two-decade-long deterioration in both the US balance of payments and the dollar. It is worth situating against this backdrop the watershed promoted under the new chairmanship of the Federal Reserve System from 1979 to 1980, when a shift from fiscal tightness to monetary tightness as a policy guideline to reshape the competitive position of the American economy as a first step in the restructuring of US external equilibrium and in the remaking of global market integration was laid down. In this turn of the decade new context the IMF itself rethought the concept of conditionality. As correctly pointed out in the literature on the Washington-based institution, since as early as its foundation the Fund's principle of conditionality posed the adoption of orderly domestic economic policies by its member countries as a condition to grant balance of payments assistance programs. Within this framework, the implementation of orderly fiscal and budgetary measures was viewed as a means of increasing market attractiveness to foreign lenders in order to bolster domestic growth and competitiveness. In contrast to this approach, quite consistently with the new monetary tightening course that led the US foreign financial and monetary policy, since the very dawn of the 1980s the Fund itself turned to pose the recasting of international market integration and a sustained degree of exchange in capital and goods as the definitive target of its policy of conditionality. As charted by the unchecked meteoric rise of the non-oil LDCs' external debt and the path-breaking stabilization of inflation in the advanced industrial economies, as well as the improvements in the dollar's strength in exchange markets, the combining of this approach with the monetary and inflationary effects of a tight monetary and interest rates policy by the Federal Reserve System reverted an almost two-decade-long meltdown in the US external balance. Certainly, such measures in international monetary policy ended a two-decade period in the history of US foreign economic policy that—as the reconstruction offered in this study demonstrates—proved to be largely unsuccessful in reversing the parallel worsening of the US balance of payments equilibrium and the decline of the dollar as the linchpin in international trade and payments, that had begun as early as the second half of the 1950s, and continued both in the framework of fixed exchange rates and full dollar convertibility into gold during the 1960s, and amid the floating system of the 1970s. The worsening US international payments position had been accompanied by either a decline in the growth rates such as the economic recessions of the late 1950s, or a staggering falloff in the competitive edge and supranational integration of the advanced industrial economies in general, and the US economy in particular. From the viewpoint of theories in international political economy on the category of economic interdependence, this work permits to establish a linkage between the stability of exchange rates and international payments, and the scope of domestic growth and integration of industrial economies in world markets. In fact, over the two decades examined in this book the US economic and financial policymakers struggled to shape foreign economic policies aimed at the same time at resurrecting the US balance of payments deficit and the dollar, and at shaping stimulus policies to enhance domestic growth and competitiveness in foreign markets. This occurred when the Kennedy and Johnson administrations combined their policies on foreign trade and full support for US military and civilian export; likewise, it was the case in the late 1960s when the Nixon administration's policies aimed to curb capital outflows and to stimulate foreign investments in the US in order to finance the supply side of the American business cycle. Similarly, it is worth placing within this framework the Ford administration's initiatives to expand and tighten commercial and financial bonds between the US and the OPEC oil producers considered in this study, which were aimed at supporting the US business cycle to fuel export. Reasoning along these lines and based on this study, it is possible to establish a linkage between the varying means to better the US balance of payments on capital and current accounts and the dollar's value conducted during these two decades, and the restructuring of US manufacturing and exporters' purchasing power and competitive edge in foreign markets. Finally, such US ambition to link the recasting of US international payments position to the reorganization of domestic growth and competitiveness is even more apparent from the Carter administration's effort to link the recycling of OPEC's foreign investments to the fuelling and implementation of stimulus policies in the United States and across major Western economies. This study has argued that Washington placed this, almost quarter-century, foreign economic policy against the backdrop of the attempt to reorganize the global trade and payments system and to prevent the non-oil LDCs from suffering the most from the international economic crises that afflicted the West, and from slipping away from the western jumble of trade and payments. In this respect, this study suggests, the failure of US policies to stabilize the dollar in foreign exchange markets and to resurrect Washington's international payments position triggered consequences and implications much broader than the incapability to reorganize a smoothly functioning balance between international payments stability and transnational capital flows on the one side, and sound domestic growth and supranational integration of US and other industrial economies on the other. In fact, it prevented the preserving and reshaping of a stable and open international trade and payments system based on closer commercial partnership between industrial nations and the LDCs, and continued transnational capital flows.

Against this backdrop, it is possible to better understand, because the decision of Paul A. Volcker to undertake a stunning monetary tightening policy triggered consequences much larger than the halting of inflationary strains and economic malaise that had ravaged the US and Western economies over the previous decade, and the reverting of a collapsing dollar in foreign exchange markets and the system of international trade and payments pegged to it. As much as the US foreign financial policy conducted over the decades covered in this study, constantly focused on the non-oil LDCs through its development assistance policy in the early 1960s and the recycling of OPEC's oil revenues prior to and since the outbreak of the first oil shock, the Volcker shock lays at the origins of the international debt crises that afflicted the oil and non-oil LDCs since the very beginning of the following decade. In this respect, this study demonstrates that in order to understand this story—largely uncovered in the historical and economic literature—that marked the beginning of the new decade, it is essential to look back at the shaping and failure of international monetary and financial policies that were the linchpin of the waning postwar international economic order and that the United States with its cohort of international economic and financial institutions, set out from the early 1960s through the Carter administration. Likewise, in order to understand and research the changing nature of the national economic and monetary policies of the advanced industrial economies that since the early 1980s turned to monetary stringency and halted domestic expansionary policies, it is vital to better understand that not only the decade of the 1960s, but also the shattered 1970s, were constantly marked by the effort of the United States to combine international trade and payments integration with sustained aggregate demand through demand management policies financed by borrowing in foreign capital markets. The trajectories of such a path of borrowing were either the short-term markets that boomed from the 1960s to the early 1970s, or the capital markets, vastly propelled by the oil producers over the course of the 1970s and up to the end of the Carter administration. In this respect, this work offers a different perspective on the nature and place of the 1970s in the international economic history of the twentieth century, at least from the vantage point of the United States. Unlike most prominent studies in international political economy, economic sociology and international economics on the decade, according to this scholarship the 1970s can be considered the last decade of a half century era in the history of domestic and international economic policies that revolved around the linchpin of demand management policies, which over time alternated or mixed up—according to which economic regime is considered—supply side policies based on the propelling of fixed capital formation and technological upgrade, and support for aggregate demand. The last policy was based on either fiscal policies or international monetary policies and exchange rate measures designed to nurture at the same time industrial competitiveness and the purchasing power of domestic markets.

To put it another way, the strategies pursued on the capital and current account position by the US governments from the Kennedy to the Carter administrations failed, but the slipping away of the LDCs from the multilateral system of payments since the beginning of the 1980s, still largely overlooked in the historical literature, demonstrates that the run up to anti-inflationary monetary stringency failed in remaking the US currency the pivot of a genuinely global system of exchange in commodities and consumer goods, and flows in capitals.

Glossary of Events

1967	International gold crisis of -
1968	US Foreign Military Sales Act of -
1971	Domestic and international inflation
	International realignments of currencies of December -
	Smithsonian meeting in December -
	Smithsonian agreements (Washington, 18 December 1971)
1972	British sterling crisis of June -
1973	(Nixon) Foreign Policy Report
	Oil embargo
	Oil price hikes of the fall of -
	Oil price increases
	Round of trade negotiations
	Second devaluation of the dollar on 12 February -
	Suspension of dollar's convertibility in the fall of -
	Teheran OPEC meeting held in December -
	Trade Reform Act
1974	Bilateral US-UK meetings, July
	OPEC meeting, September
	Proposal by Kissinger to establish a Special Trust Fund managed by the IMF, Chicago, November
	US-Saudi Arabian Joint Commission on Economic Cooperation (established in the late Spring)

S. Selva, *Before the Neoliberal Turn*, Palgrave Studies in Economic History,
DOI 10.1057/978-1-137-57443-5

	Witteveen trip to the Middle East, April 1974
	29th session of the United Nations General Assembly in the early fall of -
1975	IMF second Oil facility, set up in -
	International recession of -
1977	International Monetary Conference, Tokyo, May 1977
	London Economic Summit, May
	Seven Nation Summit, late Spring
1978	Blumenthal visit to the Middle East, November
	Saudi-Iranian agreement to maintain a crude oil price freeze for the entire year
1979	Miller visit to the Middle East
1970s	First oil crisis of the -
	Floating currency system of the -
	International inflation of the -
	International economic system of the -
	Two energy crises of the -
	Two oil crises of the -

Author Index[1]

[1] Note: Page numbers followed by "n" denote endnotes.

S. Selva, *Before the Neoliberal Turn*, Palgrave Studies in Economic History,
DOI 10.1057/978-1-137-57443-5

Y

Z

Subject Index[1]

[1] Note: Page numbers followed by "n" denote endnotes

S. Selva, *Before the Neoliberal Turn*, Palgrave Studies in Economic History,
DOI 10.1057/978-1-137-57443-5

J

K

L

CPSIA information can be obtained
at www.ICGtesting.com
Printed in the USA
BVHW022029290119
538999BV00017B/283/P

VPT000005155 1